CULTURAL CRIMINOLOGY
UNLEASHED

Edited by
Jeff Ferrell, Keith Hayward,
Wayne Morrison and Mike Presdee

glasshouse
press

London • Sydney • Portland, Oregon

First published in Great Britain 2004 by
The GlassHouse Press, The Glass House,
Wharton Street, London WC1X 9PX, United Kingdom
Telephone: + 44 (0)20 7278 8000   Facsimile: + 44 (0)20 7278 8080
Email: info@cavendishpublishing.com
Website: www.cavendishpublishing.com

Published in the United States by Cavendish Publishing
c/o International Specialized Book Services,
5824 NE Hassalo Street, Portland,
Oregon 97213-3644, USA

Published in Australia by The GlassHouse Press,
45 Beach Street, Coogee, NSW 2034, Australia
Telephone: + 61 (2)9664 0909   Facsimile: +61 (2)9664 5420
Email: info@cavendishpublishing.com.au
Website: www.cavendishpublishing.com.au

British Library Cataloguing in Publication Data
A record is available from the British Library

Library of Congress Cataloguing in Publication Data
Data available

ISBN 1-90438-537-0
ISBN 978-1-904-38537-0

1 3 5 7 9 10 8 6 4 2

Printed and bound in Great Britain

Cover image supplied by Cécile Van de Voorde

"pourin' off of every page"

Acknowledgments

The seeds of *Cultural Criminology Unleashed* were first sown at a small conference held at the University of London's Chancellor's Hall in the late Spring of 2003. Organised by two of the book's editors – Keith Hayward and Wayne Morrison – and generously supported by a financial bursary from the University of London's External Law Programme, the *First International Conference on Cultural Criminology* drew together a host of scholars from a range of disciplines and theoretical orientations. From the outset it was clear that there was much heat and light around the theories and political positions that animate cultural criminology, and the conference proved a stimulating forum for presenting current thinking and research in this area. Importantly, the conference also contributed to a shared sense of urgency among many of its participants, a sense that the time for a fully developed cultural criminology had now arrived.

This collective urgency to push forward a culturally inspired criminology was further evidenced by the dynamic group of international scholars that subsequently came forward to be a part of this collection. Consequently, it is the contributors to *Cultural Criminology Unleashed* that the editors would most like to thank. Their enthusiasm for the project and above all their good grace in the face of fast-closing deadlines set by editors determined to drive the book through on time was tremendously appreciated. We hope they like the results.

We must, of course, thank our friend and Commissioning Editor at GlassHouse Press, Beverley Brown, whose support and enthusiasm has never once wavered since we first approached her with the idea for this collection. Likewise, our editor, Ruth Massey, has also been a model of patience, efficiency and professionalism. Ruth was also instrumental in ensuring that the book was published in good time. Thanks more generally to all the good people at GlassHouse/Cavendish.

Nearly 10 years ago now, Ferrell and Sanders' *Cultural Criminology* (Northeastern University Press, 1995) began the process of weaving the many intellectual and political threads of cultural criminology into a coherent model of analysis and critique; with *Cultural Criminology Unleashed*, and the many new lines of intellectual inquiry its contributors bring to it, that process continues. The editors dedicate this book to all those many scholars and researchers around the world who continue to support and participate in the ongoing project of cultural criminology. We hope that *Cultural Criminology Unleashed* can contribute in some way to our shared purpose and passion.

From Jeff, Mike and Wayne, many thanks to Keith for taking on the lion's share of the burden of organising the authors and turning around the text. We would not have been able to meet our deadlines without his energy and dedication.

Jeff Ferrell, Keith Hayward,
Mike Presdee and Wayne Morrison
October 2004

About the Contributors

Heitor Alvelos, PhD (RCA), MFA (SAIC) is Senior Lecturer in Communication Design at the University of Oporto – School of Fine Arts, and a Visiting Tutor at the Drawing Studio of the Royal College of Art. He researches contemporary audiovisual culture, and is also a multimedia artist designer whose work has been exhibited/published/presented since 1983.

Frank Bovenkerk is a cultural anthropologist and Professor of Criminology at the Willem Pompe Institute for Criminal Law and Criminology, University of Utrecht in the Netherlands. He has published extensively on migration, discrimination and organised crime.

David C Brotherton grew up in the East End of London, where he worked in various blue-collar jobs while organising labour and youth. He came to the US in the early 1980s where he gained his doctorate in Sociology from UC Santa Barbara. In 1994, David moved to New York, where he continued his research on youth resistance and marginalisation, co-founding the Street Organization Project at John Jay College in 1997. In 1998 and 2001, he co-organised the first academic/practitioner/community conferences on street youth to be held in New York since the 1960s and is currently preparing for a third conference to be held in Brazil. During 2002–03, David was a Visiting Professor of Law and Sociology at the Autonomous University of Santo Domingo (Dominican Republic) and organised the first ever conference on deportees from the US. He has published two books with Columbia University Press: *The Almighty Latin King and Queen Nation: Street Politics and the Transformation of a New York City Gang* (co-authored with Luis Barrios, 2004) and *Gangs and Society: Alternative Perspectives* (co-edited with Louis Kontos and Luis Barrios, 2003). A third book entitled *Cross-Cultural Perspectives on Youth, Marginalization and Empowerment*, co-edited with Michael Flynn, is forthcoming.

Chris Cunneen teaches criminology at the University of Sydney Law School. He is also Director of the Institute of Criminology, University of Sydney, and Chairperson of the New South Wales Juvenile Justice Advisory Council. He has published a number of books, including *Conflict, Politics and Crime* (Allen & Unwin, 2001), *Indigenous People and the Law in Australia* (co-authored with Terry Libesman, Butterworths, 1995), *Juvenile Justice. Youth and Crime in Australia* (co-authored with Rob White, Oxford University Press, 2002), and co-edited *Faces of Hate: Hate Crime in Australia* (Federation Press, 1997).

Mark Fenwick is currently an Associate Professor at the Faculty of Law, Kyushu University, Japan.

Jeff Ferrell earned his PhD in Sociology from the University of Texas at Austin, and is currently Associate Professor of Criminal Justice at Texas Christian University. He is the author of *Crimes of Style* (Northeastern University Press, 1996), *Tearing Down the Streets* (Palgrave/Macmillan/St Martin's, 2001/2002), and *Empire of Scrounge* (New York University Press, forthcoming 2005), and is lead co-editor of three books: *Cultural Criminology* (Northeastern University Press, 1995), *Ethnography at the Edge* (Northeastern University Press, 1998), and *Making Trouble* (Aldine de Gruyter, 1999). He is the founding and current editor of the New York University Press book series Alternative Criminology, and one of the founding editors of the journal *Crime, Media, Culture: An International Journal* (Sage). In 1998 he received the Critical Criminologist of the Year Award from the American Society of Criminology.

Chris Greer is Senior Lecturer in Criminology at the University of Northumbria in Newcastle, UK. His research focuses on criminological theory, media representations of crime, deviance and control, the construction of victimhood, and the intersections between crime and culture. Chris' first book, *Sex Crime and the Media: Sex Offending and the Press in a Divided Society* (Willan, 2003), was shortlisted for the Philip Abrams Memorial Prize 2004. Chris is also founding editor, with Yvonne Jewkes and Jeff Ferrell, of *Crime, Media, Culture: An International Journal*, to be launched with Sage Publications in 2005.

Steve Hall is Senior Lecturer in Criminology at the University of Northumbria in Newcastle, UK. His recent published work includes critical analyses of a range of contemporary criminological issues, including youth violence, governance and control, social exclusion and social order. Steve is also a successful musician.

Mark S Hamm is Professor of Criminology at Indiana State University, USA. He is the author of numerous books and articles on terrorism and human rights, including *In Bad Company: America's Terrorist Underground* (Northeastern University Press, 2002), *American Skinheads: The Criminology of Hate Crimes* (Praeger, 1993), and *The Abandoned Ones: The Imprisonment and Uprising of the Mariel Boat People* (Northeastern University Press, 1995).

Keith Hayward is Lecturer in Criminology at the School of Social Policy, Sociology and Social Research, University of Kent, Canterbury, UK. Whilst his primary research interest is criminological theory (in particular the relationships between consumer culture and crime) he has also published in the areas of youth crime, social theory, popular culture and terrorism. He is the author of *City Limits: Crime, Consumer Culture and the Urban Experience* (GlassHouse Press, 2004), and co-editor of *Criminology* (Oxford University Press, forthcoming 2005). He is a regular contributor to media discussions about crime and culture and acts as Vice Chair of the British Society of Criminology's *Theory Network*.

Curtis Jackson-Jacobs is a doctoral student in Sociology at UCLA. He has written about American gang research, college-student crack users, and youth fighting.

Tony Jefferson is Professor of Criminology at Keele University, UK. After a short spell as a secondary school teacher, he spent five years at the Birmingham Centre for Contemporary Cultural Studies (1972–77), since when he has researched and taught criminology, principally at the University of Sheffield (1977–96), more recently at Keele University (1997–present). His research interests have spanned youth subcultures, the media, the state, policework, race and crime, masculinities, fear of crime and, most recently, racially motivated violence. His most recent book, with Wendy Hollway, is called *Doing Qualitative Research Differently* (Sage, 2000).

Fiona Measham is Lecturer in Criminology at Lancaster University, UK. She has conducted research in the field of legal and illicit drugs, gender, licensed leisure and cultural criminology for over 15 years. She is co-author of *Illegal Leisure* (Routledge, 1998) and *Dancing on Drugs* (Free Association Books, 2001), based on two large scale studies of young people's drug and alcohol use. Current research projects include a study of 'binge drinking' and bounded consumption; and an analysis of young people, gambling and the state regulation of leisure. Recent publications include an historical analysis of the attempted criminalisation of English barmaids and a consideration of the relationship between drugs, spatiality and control.

Wayne Morrison is Reader in Law at Queen Mary, University of London, and Director of the External Laws Programme of the University of London. His research and publications span criminological and legal theory. Recently he has worked towards a more global criminology that includes topics traditionally excluded from the canon, such as genocide.

Stephen L Muzzatti received his PhD in Sociology from York University in Toronto, Canada. After several years of teaching in the US, Stephen recently returned to Toronto where he is currently an Assistant Professor of Sociology at Ryerson University. He has written on such diverse topics as critical pedagogy, deviance theory, state crime, Marilyn Manson and motorcycle culture. He is a member of the American Society of Criminology's Division on Critical Criminology and co-editor of *The Critical Criminologist* newsletter.

Maggie O'Neill is Reader in Sociology at Staffordshire University, UK, and has written widely on sex work, refugees, asylum seekers, renewed methodologies for social research, community cohesion, feminisms and critical theory. Her books include *Adorno, Culture and Feminism* (Sage, 1999), *Prostitution and Feminism* (Polity, 2001), *Prostitution: A Reader* (Sage, 2004) with Roger Matthews, and *Gender and the Public Sector* (Routledge, 2004) with Jim Barry and Mike Dent.

Mike Presdee is a member of the School of Social Policy, Sociology and Social Research, University of Kent, Canterbury, UK. He is the author of *Cultural Criminology and the Carnival of Crime* (Routledge, 2000).

Karin Schofield works as a Senior Consultant for Matrix Research & Consultancy, an independent organisation that provides research and consultancy services to public sector clients. Karin undertook the research which informed her chapter whilst a research student at the University of Glamorgan. She submitted her MPhil thesis, which looked at the cultural construction of paedophilia and child sexual abuse, in 2002.

Julie Stubbs is Associate Professor and Deputy Director of the Institute of Criminology in the Faculty of Law, University of Sydney. Her main research interest concerns violence against women, with particular reference to the intersection of race/ethnicity and gender, restorative justice, domestic violence law reforms, defences to homicide and battered woman syndrome. Her publications include *Negotiating Child Residence and Contact against a Background of Domestic Violence* (a report with Miranda Kaye and Julia Tolmie), *Gender, Race and International Relations: Violence against Filipino Women in Australia* (with Chris Cunneen, Federation Press, 1997) and *Women, Male Violence and the Law* (Federation Press, 1994).

Kenneth D Tunnell is Professor at Eastern Kentucky University. His publications include numerous articles in sociology and criminology journals and four books: *Choosing Crime* (Nelson Hall, 1992); *Political Crime in Contemporary America* (Garland, 1993); *Living Off Crime* (Rowman & Littlefield, 2000); and the recent monograph with New York University Press, *Pissing on Demand: Workplace Drug Testing and the Rise of the Detox Industry* (2004).

Heli Vaaranen, PhD, is a research fellow in the Department of Sociology, University of Helsinki, Finland. Her research interests include urban life, 'edgework', young relationships and the method of ethnography.

Cécile Van de Voorde is a PhD Candidate in Criminology and Presidential Fellow at the University of South Florida (Tampa, Florida). She has a law degree from the Grenoble School of Law (France), and a MA in Criminology from Indiana State University. Ms Van de Voorde specialises in the study of suicide terrorism. Her other areas of interest include hate and bias crimes, sex crimes, behavioural analysis, crime and popular culture, and ethnography. Her passion for documentary photography and photojournalism enables her to both complement her field research and escape from her work.

Jonathan Wender recently completed his doctorate in criminology at Simon Fraser University in British Columbia. The title of his dissertation is *Policing as Poetry: Phenomenological and Aesthetic Reflections Upon the Bureaucratic Approach to Human Predicaments*. He has served as a police officer in Washington State (US) since 1990, and is currently assigned as a patrol sergeant.

Simon Winlow is Lecturer in Sociology at the University of York, UK. His previous work includes *Badfellas: Crime, Tradition and New Masculinities* (Berg, 2001) and *Bouncers: Violence and Governance in the Night-time Economy* (with Dick Hobbs, Philip Hadfield and Stuart Lister) (Oxford University Press, 2002).

Yucel Yesilgöz is a Turkey-trained lawyer who defended his PhD dissertation on *Allah, Satan and the Law* (in Dutch). Together with Frank Bovenkerk he directs a large research program on multiculturality in the administration of criminal law.

Jock Young is Distinguished Professor of Sociology at the John Jay College, City University of New York. He is also a visiting professor at the University of Kent, UK. His most recent book is *The Exclusive Society* (Sage, 1999). He is at present finishing its sequel, *Crossing the Borderline*, and a book on criminological theory, *Merton's Dream and Quételet's Warning*.

Contents

Part 3
Marginal Images

Part 4
Breaking Open the City

Part 5
Terms of Engagement

Part 6
Questions of Agency and Control

Fragments of a Manifesto:
Introducing *Cultural Criminology Unleashed*

Jeff Ferrell, Keith Hayward, Wayne Morrison and Mike Presdee

The title of this book, *Cultural Criminology Unleashed*, is meant to be suggestive, even audacious. Talk of the leashed and the unleashed suggests struggling against confinement, a pent-up energy pulling against its limits. Then, at the moment of unleashing – depending on how one frames the metaphor – a couple of possibilities: an outbreak of resistance against all that is conventional and constraining or, more prosaically, some great mad dog charging off into the distance.

This book embodies something of all these metaphoric possibilities. Certainly its editors, and many of its contributors, have over the years felt themselves tethered, if not choked, by conventional criminology. Just as clearly, many of us have begun to see over the past decade or so that an emerging cultural criminology could loosen the methodological, theoretical and substantive constraints of those conventions, prying free from criminology's stranglehold on meaning, style and interpretation. With this book it is certainly our intention to continue to expand this project – to let loose more of the imaginative case studies and analytic innovations that have come to define cultural criminology. As for that unfettered mad dog, we'll leave that metaphor to our critics – for they will surely find a bit of that here as well.

In the same way, *Cultural Criminology Unleashed* is meant to be provocative, irreverent, even confrontational, both in title and in content. This sharp-edged stylistic and epistemic ethos has been a defining feature of cultural criminology as a significant alternative to the stultifications of conventional criminology from the first – whether one marks the first moments of cultural criminology as the Birmingham School and the New Criminology of the 1960s and 1970s or the publication of *Cultural Criminology* (Ferrell and Sanders 1995) and similar books in the 1990s. Given this, we offer the following introduction to *Cultural Criminology Unleashed* in the form of a manifesto, or, perhaps more accurately, as fragments of a manifesto.

It's not just that a manifesto seems appropriate to an emerging movement within and against criminology. There's also the fact that a manifesto is by its nature a cultural construction. As such, it is meant to be suggestive, injunctive and, in the context of received wisdom, absurd. At the same time, no manifesto should be mistaken for a claim to truth, as with the manifestos of modernity, most of which now stand as ironic and redundant monuments to the failure of grand narratives. What follows, then, is a provocation, not a prescription – an absurdity structured around loose themes that don't have to add up to a monolithic unity but open up a series of enticing vistas. They should be seen as pieces of the same puzzle, each explaining and intertwining with the other to unleash the potential of a cultural criminology.

Theorising crime, culture, and criminology

Theories of crime and crime control are too important to leave to statisticians or theoreticians floating adrift from the immediacy of transgression. The criminological production of numeric summaries, cross-correlations, statistical residues and second-hand data sets may serve the needs of the crime control industry, the campaigns of politicians, or the careers of academic criminologists – but let's no longer fool ourselves that they serve to make sense of crime and crime control, or move us toward social arrangements less poisoned by fear, violence and exploitation. If theoretical models are to serve as an antidote to the machinery of administrative criminology, it is essential that they emerge from the lives of criminologists and criminals alike. While a theory's analytical elegance is one measure of its value, by equal measure it should take shape as an elegant story that captures the gritty particularities of everyday experience. Told well, theoretical stories of crime and crime control are by turns mundane, extraordinary, damaging and astonishing.

Of course, there is nothing intrinsically new about these claims. Such notions have circulated as an evocative counterpoint to the narrow abstractions of administrative criminology for many decades (for example Becker 1963; Matza 1969; Polsky 1998), a seductive undercurrent that has swept along many of the contributors to this volume. This book's opening section sets itself the task of making this undercurrent manifest. As the first chapters illustrate, the theories that animate cultural criminology – from subcultural analyses to critiques of oppressive structures, from social theory to phenomenological exegeses – manifestly engage with the lived politics of crime, culture and criminology as an integrated whole. Moreover, they do so in ways that reflect the peculiarities and particularities of the late modern socio-cultural milieu.

Tony Jefferson and Mike Presdee, for example, both highlight the inseparable intertwining of theoretical development and biographical narrative, Jefferson by tracing this inseparability within his own intellectual evolution, Presdee by stressing the centrality of autobiographical storytelling in theoretical constructions of criminality and crime control. The existential dynamics suggested in these two accounts gather theoretical traction in Jonathan Wender's call for the integration of a structural phenomenology with the practice of cultural criminology. For Wender especially, this phenomenological orientation is no abstract exercise. It emerges instead out of the experiences of situated violence that constitute his day-to-day round as a police officer on the streets of Seattle, Washington. Likewise, Jeff Ferrell outlines the everyday phenomenology of style and subculture that animates the interplay between criminality and social control; as he shows in this seminal piece, style operates as a grounded dynamic, a central symbolic practice, for agents of legal control as much as for those caught up in criminal subcultures. These and other themes come together in Jock Young's stellar critique of the mainstream criminological enterprise and its complicity in the expansion of criminal justice. As Young demonstrates, this coupling of social control criminology with the bureaucratic apparatus of criminal justice spawns a machinery of atheoretical statistical calculation, a machinery stripped of cultural nuance and situational meaning.

This first constellation of chapters, then, sets the theoretical pitch for a cultural criminology of late modernity but without in any way exhausting cultural criminology's theoretical potential. In fact, the theoretical orientations outlined in these first chapters continually resurface throughout the remainder of *Cultural Criminology Unleashed*, sometimes as explicit analytic models, at other times as expressions of discovery and documentation, but always in violation of disciplinary and geopolitical borders.

Across the borders of crime and culture

In the same way that we cannot allow the late modern nation state to set the terms of our engagement with crime and justice, we cannot allow the late modern state to confine criminology within its established boundaries, whether geographical or political. In globalised times – whatever the variants of that term – we need an international criminology capable both of meeting the many challenges of 'fluid modernity' (Bauman 1995) and of following the flow of crime and transgression as it seeps across traditional categories and borders. Given such nebulous conditions, when crime itself violates national, juridical, cultural and even ecological barriers, criminologists can ill afford to work only within traditional legal frameworks and conventional criminological definitions of crime. Under such slippery social conditions, traditional categories of crime and culture readily collapse into each other, further confounding our ability to confront crime as a timeless or abstract category of human behaviour. Whilst this conflation of crime and culture has always occurred – indeed cultural criminology was all but founded on this central premise – the speed with which these two now collide and interweave makes our task as cultural criminologists ever more urgent. In the same way that crime today escapes the abstract legal categories meant to confine it, it increasingly slips across borderlines of nation and culture. Dealing head-on with this cultural fluidity and global porosity must be one of the central tasks of a truly international cultural criminology.

In its own small way, *Cultural Criminology Unleashed* reflects and embodies this ethos of internationality. From its inception at the First International Conference on Cultural Criminology[1] through its transatlantic editing process, to the subsequent inclusion of a wide range of contributions by international scholars, *Cultural Criminology Unleashed* has been designed to establish homology between culturally eclectic subjects and a diversity of criminological perspectives and epistemologies. Setting the pitch for the section of the book that engages with these themes most directly, the New Zealand criminologist, Wayne Morrison, sets out to debunk the very foundations of theoretical criminology as an exercise in scientific and pedagogic objectivity. Tracing a story that takes the reader from Lombroso's Museo di Antropologia, Turino, Italy, to the Aboriginal Australian outback, and on to the complications of essentialising Maori culture of New Zealand, Morrison offers a compelling account that skews standard, cookie-cutter, textbook criminology.

In a groundbreaking piece from the Netherlands, Frank Bovenkerk and Yucel Yesilgöz emphasise the essential importance of ethnicity and immigration for the contemporary practice of modern criminal justice systems. Bovenkerk and Yesilgöz powerfully document the need for a multiculturalism that goes beyond the lip service of liberal commentators and truly engages with the complex intersections of culture, crime and criminal justice. Australian criminologists Chris Cunneen and Julie Stubbs brilliantly reaffirm and amplify these themes in examining the dangerous gender politics of 'mail-order brides' and the everyday violence they face as they attempt to negotiate boundaries of culture and false expectation. In what serves as an exemplar of transnational cultural criminology, this chapter crosses national borders with the same fluidity that it transcends theoretical constraints. Shifting patterns of understanding likewise emerge as a key theme in the work of the

---

1   9–10 May 2004, University of London. For a review of the key papers presented at this conference, see the Cultural Criminology Special Edition of *Theoretical Criminology* (Vol 8 No 3, August 2004).

Irish criminologist Chris Greer – only this time the borders to be traversed are those of the 'real' and the 'virtual'. Taking notions of 'community' as his foci, Greer looks at the way communities might be re-imagined amidst the circulating semiology of crime under conditions of late modernity.

Marginal images

Like all dimensions of social life, crime and crime control operate as cultural enterprises. Both are constructed out of ongoing symbolic interactions that themselves emerge across a range of intertwined social and political processes. The meaning of both crime and crime control resides not in the essential (and essentially false) factuality of crime rates or arrest records; it emerges instead from a contested process of symbolic display, cultural interpretation and representational negotiation. Mediated anti-crime campaigns, imagined crime waves and constructed crime panics, illicit subcultures appropriating mass media fabrications of counter-cultural imagery – all of these circulate within an endless spiral of meaning, a Möbius strip of culture and everyday life.

In cultural criminology the anti-essentialist insights of labelling theory are writ large and so reinvented; the meaning, the reality of 'the thing itself' forms and re-forms as a process negotiated through display and interpretation. This process emerges in the midst of face-to-face interaction and, increasingly, out of the endless recirculation of signs and symbols. Put differently, the 'symbolic' of symbolic interaction expands, explodes, engulfing as it does so nuances of subcultural style, efflorescences of mass-produced imagery, and public displays of crime and control.

For cultural criminologists the task is to study and critically intervene in this process – not to perpetuate the fallacy of essentialist factuality. We cannot afford to abandon the politics of crime and crime control to intellectual reactionaries and neo-conservative demagogues – that is, to those who would claim to offer definitive explanations of, and hermetic protections from, the threat of crime, whether perpetrated by street thugs or 'rogue states'.

In fact, under contemporary conditions a remarkable inversion is all but complete. Images of crime and crime control have now become as 'real' as crime and criminal justice itself – if by 'real' we denote those dimensions of social life that produce consequences; shape attitudes and policy; define the effects of crime and criminal justice; generate fear, avoidance and pleasure; and alter the lives of those involved. In this light Karin Schofield confronts the politically dangerous issue of paedophilia. As she documents, mediated constructions of paedophilia carry real consequences; they often reproduce the very phenomenon they claim to condemn and, along the way, increase the experiential dangers associated with it. Kenneth Tunnell's chapter rotates the consequential kaleidoscope of mediated crime representation in another direction. Tunnell analyses the ways in which ill-informed crime reporting serves not only to reproduce dangerous mythologies about drugs – in this case so-called 'hillbilly' heroin – but to reinforce stereotypical portrayals of marginalised groups. Ratcheting up this critique of media complicity in constructing cultural intolerance, Stephen Muzzatti pulls no punches in his analytic counter-attack on those media and political agents who seek to contain the righteous anger of Marilyn Manson, 'Goth' youth, and other inhabitants of the teenage wasteland.

Breaking open the city

As numerous theorists of the city have argued (Raban 1974; de Certeau 1984; Hayward 2004), a city can only really be understood, and thus theorised, when viewed as a 'duality'. One dimension defines the city as mapped by mass planning, rationalistic discourse, quantitative data and demographics; the other opposing dimension defines the city as a more experiential place – an alternative reading of urban space in terms of possibility and dream, subculture and style. Most memorably, de Certeau (1984: 92) frames this dualism by contrasting two views of the city. The first is the 'Concept-city': a bird's-eye (or mass planner's) view of the city from atop the World Trade Center, an abstraction of grids, paths and patterned regularity. The second is the perspective from ground level, the view one has when walking or cycling through the city, a view cluttered by the sorts of street level interaction and intersubjectivity that never feature in the plans and maps of the 'official' city.

This 'dual' analysis of urban space – this tension between the sanitised official life of the city and the gritty realities of its 'underlife' (to paraphrase Goffman 1961) – runs throughout cultural criminology. Within this rubric, crime and criminality emerge not as abstractions but rather as a complex nether world bubbling up from under the surface of the city's manicured and manipulated appearance (a nether world better glimpsed by ethnographers than by survey researchers and city planners). As Presdee puts it, this nether world 'is lived in the cracks and holes of the structures of official society. It searches for and finds the unpunishable whilst official society seeks to dam up the holes, and fill the cracks, criminalizing as it does and making punishable the previously unpunishable' (2000: 9). This struggle between the forces of rationalisation and those of existential possibility and lived experience is essential to a cultural criminology of the city.

Such themes are central to Keith Hayward's chapter, in which he confronts mainstream criminology's failure to engage with the experiential, street level dimensions of city life. Hayward shows how administrative 'crime mappers' have today attained a level of abstraction that de Certeau could never have imagined: not content to perch atop the city's tallest skyscraper, today they ascend to the celestial heavens via the use of Global Information Satellites. This, quite literally, is criminology's 'out of this world' future; here the space satellite functions as an all-seeing eye, its panoptic gaze mapping the city as a totalising abstraction. Yet, lost in this reading of the city are the complex spatial dynamics of make-or-break street life; ignored are worlds where the experience of criminality and victimisation emerge from lives lived and rules bent within micro spatial urban settings. Reporting from inside one of these urban worlds – the nether world of urban scroungers and illicit trash pickers – Jeff Ferrell similarly exposes the city's lost humanscapes of culture and crime. Ferrell documents a hidden world that remains marginal in both its spatial and legal dynamics, a world of porous and ambiguous interconnections between private property and public need, scrounging and theft – and a world, he argues, that must remain so if it is to serve the needs of the city.

Heitor Alvelos documents a symbolic city of porous margins in another register, and with another set of consequences. Alvelos traces the increasingly ambiguous boundaries between illegal urban graffiti and approved corporate advertising strategies in the flux of the late modern city. In doing so, he reveals a city of orchestrated semiotic confusion – a city where corporate advertisers appropriate the edgy iconography and streetwise sensibility of urban graffiti in a bid to flood everyday urban life with wave after wave of disposable consumer products. For Alvelos, though, this semiotic ambiguity signals something more than new forms of corporate branding: it suggests the death of the city's subcultures of resistance. Changing tack, yet continuing to document social patterns and urban experiences inside the city – this time the sprawling Japanese 'mega-city' – Mark Fenwick highlights the complicity of Japanese politicians and the media in the creation of so-called 'crime talk'; a destructive communicative mode that ignores the specific realities of local crime problems and instead promotes an image of a growing threat of crime based on the demonisation and vilification of socially marginalised 'others'.

Terms of engagement

While, in contrast to conventional criminology, cultural criminology opens up the study of crime and deviance to a broader range of subjects – the city, the media, globalisation, and other discourses of late modernity – it also offers new terms of engagement with these spheres. In this sense the 'cultural' in cultural criminology denotes not only new *objects* of analysis but also new *modes* of analysis and methodology more attuned to situated meaning and symbolic significance. Essential to the enterprise of cultural criminology, then, is an emphasis on stylised representation as both 'object' and 'method' of study. Consequently, cultural criminological writing and research tends to look and feel different from the 'normal science' of positivist criminology. This difference is significant. It is not that cultural criminology excludes the possibility of numerical summaries, or inevitably prioritises aesthetic considerations over and above the hard practicalities of crime and crime control. It is just that, in choosing any mode of analysis or representation, cultural criminologists remain conscious of pluralities of meaning and possibilities of alternative perception. The chapters that comprise this section reveal something of these possibilities; they exemplify the multifarious terms of engagement through which cultural criminology approaches issues of crime and transgression.

Fiona Measham's chapter, for example, explores the potential value of cultural criminology to the field of drug research. Challenging established methodological and statistical approaches to drug and gender research, she calls for a 'criminology of transgression' capable of locating contemporary recreational drug use within broader contexts of hyper-consumption, shifting patterns of leisure and gender, and emerging rubrics of social control. Likewise, Maggie O'Neill draws on her long history of innovative culture work to imagine new ways of understanding and articulating the corrosive experiences of crime and victimisation. Breaching the boundaries of conventional criminological method and knowledge, O'Neill presents a provocative mélange of art, storytelling and performance in an effort to expand and enliven the methodological horizons of cultural criminology.

While Measham and O'Neill offer insights into new methodological possibilities, the next two chapters in the section situate these possibilities within the rhythmic specificities of street life. Emerging as they do out of two very different temporal moments in the research process, both chapters capture something of what it means to undertake ethnography enlivened by the sensibilities of cultural criminology. Deeply immersed for some time in the urgent danger of the street brawler's underworld, Curtis Jackson-Jacobs presents a gripping account of the 'attractions of fighting as an underdog'. Constructing a dramaturgical phenomenology of street brawling as collective action, he situates a sophisticated theoretical analysis within the chaotic lifeworlds of his 'shit-talking', street-fighting protagonists. Writing from within a much earlier moment in the process of field research and theoretical analysis, Heli Vaaranen suggests a nascent cultural criminology of Helsinki's illegal street racers. Offered in the form of evocative 'notes from the field' – as a way of illustrating the method and style of cultural criminology's emergence in the research setting – Vaaranen's work takes us inside a hyper-masculine world of supercharged emotions and sexually charged seductions. Through it, she reveals not only the dynamics of illegal street racing but the process of documenting the moment-to-moment interplay of culture and criminality.

Questions of agency and control

A line of critique sometimes aimed at cultural criminology suggests that, in prioritising image and style, cultural criminology devolves into a decorative criminology, a fanciful exercise lacking in political action or transformative potential. This critique, though, mistakes method for meaning. In utilising dynamic methods and alternative aesthetic tools, cultural criminology seeks to confront emerging modes of power and control in the late modern world, and looks to unearth otherwise unnoticed possibilities of everyday agency and resistance. After all, in a world where power is increasingly exercised through mediated representation and symbolic construction, struggles over power and control become cultural in nature. Given this, battles over image, style and representation emerge not as decorative abstractions but as essential moments in the contested negotiation of late modern reality. Cultural criminology seeks to create a criminology that is more critical, not less – a criminology capable of confronting agencies of control and relations of power with analytic practices capable of penetrating the very representations through which power and control are exercised.

Some three decades ago, theorists associated with the Birmingham School and the National Deviance Conference (for example Hall and Jefferson 1976; McRobbie and Garber 1976; Hall *et al* 1978; Taylor *et al* 1973) began to highlight how new forms of political power, class control and experiential resistance played out within the everyday politics of late capitalism. As the Birmingham School memorably showed, and as the following chapters suggest, sharply drawn analytic distinctions between 'culture' and 'economy', exclusive conceptualisations of 'politics' versus 'ideology', discrete categories of 'form' and 'content' can no longer capture the complex linkages between power, control and criminality. As a locus of criminality, surveillance and control, social class exists not as an abstract economic category but as a rich cultural milieu saturated with diverse experiences, from pain, loss and isolation on the one hand to fun, pleasure and transgression on the other. Under conditions of late capitalism, global economies run on the endless creation of hyper-consumptive panic, on the symbolic construction of new needs and new wants, on a spinning web of (dis)information and desire. In the contemporary world, culture, economy and politics intertwine to the point that one is always implicated in the practice of the other – and from this world emerge new forms of criminality and control, deformities of day-to-day survival, that hopelessly confound culture and economy with human agency and human transgression.

The chapters gathered in this final section collectively suggest a cultural criminology that can account for this confounding of crime, agency and control within the cultural dynamics of late modernity. Focused as they are on distinct cases of crime, victimisation and law, though, the chapters quite appropriately document distinctly different cultural constellations within this broader dynamic, and in fact offer a variety of perspectives on the contested relationship between agency and control. Jeff Ferrell, for example, contrasts the ideologically overblown 'war on drugs' in the United States with the inattention paid to the tens of thousands of deaths brought about each year by the automobile. In this context, he explores the roadside shrines constructed by the friends and families of those killed in automobile accidents, and finds in these remarkable manifestations of human agency a critical perspective on the corporate crimes of the automobile. Likewise, David Brotherton documents the broad symbolic construction of the United States 'street gang problem' in the media, criminology and criminal justice, critically contrasting this ideological construction with the particular practices of a well-known street gang, the Almighty Latin King and Queen Nation. As Brotherton shows, the members of the ALKQN have actively resisted the 'definitional privilege' of those who would conceptualise and control them, and in fact have consciously engaged in transforming themselves into what might more accurately be conceptualised as a street organisation or social movement.

Exploring lost industrial communities and shattered local economies left in the wake of globalised capitalism's outward expansion, Steve Hall and Simon Winlow document a darker dynamic: the dangerous intertwining of predatory urban barbarism with hyper-consumptive individualism. Unlike Ferrell and Brotherton, Hall and Winlow find among their British subjects of study little in the way of cultural agency or active resistance. Instead, they discover forms of criminality that reflect an erosion of social bonds; a rise in competitive instrumentalism; and a breakdown in the 'pseudo-pacification process'. Returning to the United States, Mark Hamm documents a different sort of danger as he exposes the carefully orchestrated politics of fear that provides the ideological underpinnings for the post-9/11 USA Patriot Act. Hamm further demonstrates that the Patriot Act offers little but obfuscation to the public and the criminologist – but he also documents the widespread emergence of cultural resistance to the Act and to its undermining of civil liberties.

In sum, then, the chapters collected in this final section – and indeed the chapters that make up the whole of *Cultural Criminology Unleashed* – are intended to confront both the conventional practice of academic criminology and the conventional understandings of crime and crime control that circulate amidst the overlapping domains of criminal justice, mass media and popular culture. In this way *Cultural Criminology Unleashed* is meant to unleash equal parts epistemic disruption and, we might hope, intellectual enlightenment. But in case the unleashing of enlightenment is perhaps a bit grandiose, we close this introductory essay with a more modest metaphor drawn from the world of professional cycling. In pro bike racing, there are many roles for cyclists to play: the *grimpeur*, the mountain ascent specialist; the *rouleur*, the hard-driving cyclist who thrives in time trial stages or on rolling, flatland courses; the *domestique* or *gregario*, the reliable, durable team player, who, in the midst of the race, protects his/her team leader, and fetches and carries for team mates. And then there is the *casinista* – an Italian slang term for the cyclist who brings, if nothing else, a bit of creative chaos to the race.

Lest the course of conventional criminology become too certain, lest its progress be too well orchestrated and controlled by the *domestiques* of social science and statistical analysis, we offer *Cultural Criminology Unleashed* as a fast-closing *casinista*. Let the chaos begin.

References

Bauman, Z (1995) *Life in Fragments: Essays on Postmodern Morality*, London: Sage

Becker, HS (1963) *Outsiders: Studies in the Sociology of Deviance*, New York: Free Press

de Certeau, M (1984) *The Practice of Everyday Life*, Berkeley, CA: University of California Press

Ferrell, J and Sanders, CR (eds) (1995) *Cultural Criminology*, Boston: Northeastern University Press

Goffman, E (1961) *Asylums*, London: Penguin

Hall, S and Jefferson, A (eds) (1976) *Resistance through Rituals: Youth Subcultures in Postwar Britain*, London: Hutchinson

Hall, S, Critcher, C, Jefferson, T, Clarke, J and Roberts, B (eds) (1978) *Policing the Crisis: Mugging, the State and Law 'n' Order*, London: Macmillan

Hayward, KJ (2004) *City Limits: Crime, Consumer Culture and the Urban Experience*, London: GlassHouse Press

McRobbie, A and Garber, J (1976) 'Girls and subcultures: an exploration', in Hall, S and Jefferson, T (eds), *Resistance through Rituals: Youth Subcultures in Postwar Britain*, London: Hutchinson, pp 209–22

Matza, D (1969) *Becoming Deviant*, Englewood Cliffs, NJ: Prentice Hall

Polsky, N (1998) [1967] *Hustlers, Beats, and Others*, New York: Lyons (expanded edition)

Presdee, M (2000) *Cultural Criminology and the Carnival of Crime*, London: Routledge

Raban, J (1974) *Soft City*, London: Hamilton

Taylor, I, Walton, P and Young, J (1973) *The New Criminology*, New York: Harper & Row

Part I

Theorising Crime, Culture, and Criminology

Chapter 1
Voodoo Criminology and the Numbers Game

Jock Young

Cultural criminology is of importance because it captures the phenomenology of crime – its adrenaline, its pleasure and panic, its excitement, and its anger, rage and humiliation, its desperation and its edgework. I wish to argue that cultural criminology not only grasps the phenomenology of crime but, for that matter, is much more attuned to phenomenology of everyday life in general in this era of late modernity. We are confronted at this moment with an orthodox criminology which is denatured and desiccated. Its actors inhabit an arid planet where they are either driven to crime by social and psychological deficits or make opportunistic choices in the criminal marketplace. They are either miserable or mundane (see Hayward and Young 2004). They are, furthermore, digital creatures of quantity, they obey probabilistic laws of deviancy – they can be represented by the statistical symbolism of lamda, chi and sigma, their behaviour can be captured in the intricacies of regression analysis and equation.

The structure of my argument is that, given that human beings are culture-creating beings and are endowed with free will, albeit in circumstances not of their own making, the *verstehen* of human meaning is, by definition, a necessity in any explanation of human activity, criminal or otherwise (see Ferrell 1997 for more on the notion of 'criminological *verstehen*'). It is in late modernity that such creativity and reflexivity becomes all the more apparent, and yet – here is the irony – it is at precisely such a time of the cultural turn that a fundamentalist positivism occurs within the social 'sciences' with increasing strength and attempts at hegemony.

Let us first of all examine the intimate links between late modernity and cultural criminology. The late modern period is characterised by disruption of employment and of marital stability, by greater spatial mobility, by a pluralism of contested values, by the emergence of mediated virtual realities and reference points, and by the rise of consumerism. It embodies two fundamental contradictions: firstly a heightened emphasis on identity in a time when lack of social embeddedness serves to undermine ontological security, and secondly a stress on expressivity, excitement and immediacy at a time when the commodification of leisure and the rationalisation of work mitigates against this. This is a world where narratives are constantly broken and re-written, where values are contested, and where reflexivity is the order of the day (see Young 1999). For all of these reasons a criminology which stresses the existential, which is focused upon subcultures of creativity and style, which emphasises the adrenalised excitement of human action on the one hand, and tedium and commodification on the other, goes with the grain of everyday life. Moreover, and counter to claims to the contrary (see Garland 2000), rational choice/routine activities theory does not fully mirror the texture of the time, but only one part of it. Let us start by looking at the situation of late modernity.

The loosening of the moorings

In late modernity there comes an increasing awareness of the social construction of boundaries and their contested nature. That is, any sense of the absolute, the reified, the natural, becomes exceedingly precarious. In this process people become more aware of their own role as actors in society. For, although the existential condition and the creation of human meaning has always been part of what we mean by social, this certainty becomes all the more apparent in late modernity. Why is this?

(a) **Voluntarism**: on the back of the movement towards flexible labour and the modern consumer society, with a myriad of choices, an individualistic society arises where chance, expressivity, meaningful work and leisure becomes an ideal. The American Dream of the post-war period, with its stress on taken-for-granted ends of material comfort, is overtaken by a new First World Dream, where meaning and expression are paramount and where lifestyles are to be created. Finding yourself becomes more important than arriving.

(b) **Disembeddedness**: the flexibility and mobility of labour and the increased instability of the family result in people's lives becoming disembedded from work, family and community. This identity does not immediately and consistently present itself. The irony, then, is that just as there is a greater stress on creating one's identity, the building blocks of identity become less substantial. Furthermore, in a lifetime of broken narratives, constant re-invention becomes a central life task.

(c) **Pluralism and contest**: increased emigration creates a pluralism of value and this is augmented by the plurality of lifestyles that are created in more individualistic societies. People are, therefore, presented with a social world where values are contested and where there are alternatives of appropriate behaviour and aspiration.

(d) **Mass media and virtual realities**: in late modernity the mass media expands in terms of the percentage of time of a person's life that it takes up – in England and Wales, for example, television and radio alone take up an extraordinary 40% of the average person's waking life, or 60% of the free time of those in work. The media overall becomes more multi-mediated, diversifying and relating to wider audiences (see McRobbie 1994). As the physical community declines, the virtual community arises, carrying with it virtual realities with new and emerging role models, subcultures of value, vocabularies of motive and narratives both fictional and 'factional'.

Thus, Zygmunt Bauman contrasts the post-war modern world with the late modern world of liquid modernity. In the former there were

> patterns, codes and rules to which one could conform which one could select as stable orientation points and by which one could subsequently let oneself be guided, that are nowadays in increasingly short supply. It does not mean our contemporaries are guided solely by their imagination and resolve and are free to construct their mode of life from scratch and at will, or that they are no longer dependent on society for the building materials and design blueprints. But it does mean that we are presently moving from an era of pre-allocated 'reference groups' into an epoch of 'universal comparison', in which the destination of individual self-constructing labours is endemically and incurably underdetermined, is not given in advance, and tends to undergo numerous and profound changes before such labours reach their only genuine end: that is, the end of the individual's life.
>
> These days patterns and configurations are no longer 'given', let alone 'self-evident'; there are just too many of them, clashing with each other and contradicting one another's

commandments, so that each one is stripped of a good deal of compelling, constraining powers. (Bauman 2000: 7)

Such changes accompanying the cultural turn have extraordinary implications for sociology, particularly for explanation, but also for measurement and research practice. Let us note at this juncture the significant changes in identity formation and with it the vocabulary of motives associated with given roles and structural positions. For the combination of the ideal of choice, disembeddedness and pluralism engenders a situation where vocabularies of motives begin to lose their fixed moorings in particular parts of the social structure and in specific social circumstances. That is, the old rigid moorings of Fordism, the demarcations of class, age and gender, the concentric demarcations of the Chicago model of space in the city begin to dissolve. Vocabularies of motive become loose and cast adrift from their structural sites; they can shift and be fixed elsewhere. This is not willy-nilly: there obviously has to be some fit between structural predicament and subcultural solution, but the level of determination and predictability diminishes. Furthermore, they can be bricollaged elsewhere in the system: they can be reinterpreted, transposed and hybridised. And, finally, and most crucially of course, they can be changed and innovated, sometimes dramatically.

Let us, for a moment, look at the relationship between material and social predicaments, identity, vocabularies of motive and social action, taking crime as an example (although we could as well focus on, say, educational achievement or sexual behaviour). There is an extraordinary tendency to suggest that the motive to commit crime springs fully fledged out of certain material predicaments (eg poverty, unemployment) or social circumstances (eg lack of control) or biological characteristics (eg youth and masculinity), almost as if no connecting narrative or human subjectivity were necessary (see Katz 2002). In reality, a situation like poverty will result in totally different assessments and responses dependent on the narratives which the subjects use to interpret their predicament – indeed, the very assessment of whether one is poor or not will depend on social interpretation. There can be no causality in society without reference to meaning, and even high correlations – as all the methods textbooks tell us – do not necessitate causality (see Sayer 1992). What is necessary is to understand that we live in a situation where such meanings change rapidly and do not adhere fixedly to particular social roles, or material predicaments. Concepts of what it is to be young, what it is to be female, what pleasures we should expect, our attitudes to work, sexuality and leisure have all been dramatically recast. None of these changes was predictable from the social and cultural 'variables' present before these fundamental roles and values were reinvented. They are understandable, in retrospect, in terms of responses to material and social change, but they were re-fashioned by human actors who simply rewrote their narratives. Let me give an example: the teenage 'revolution' was one of the great changes of the late 20th century – something so dramatic that, as so often with such sweeping changes, we can scarcely see it now. No one knew what the youth were going to do with their new position and status. If you were attempting to predict crime rates from the 'variables' which seemed to explain crime rates in the 1950s, you would have talked about inequalities, employment levels, educational achievement, percentage of adolescent males in the population, divorce rates, etc. But even the most sophisticated statistical analysis (very unlikely at that time) could not have predicted the extent of youth crime, and the reason for this is palpably simple: you could not have anticipated what was to happen to 'youth'.

Let me turn now to the problem of measurement, and here I will repeat the structure of my argument. First I will note how the social and meaningful nature of human action makes positivistic methods inappropriate; secondly I will indicate how the situation of late modernity heightens this situation. To do this I will turn first of all to a debate within the sociology of sex.

Measurement and the sexologists

In April and May 1995 the columns of the *New York Review of Books* were subject to a remarkable and, some would say, acrimonious debate. It was an argument which was, to my mind, one of the most significant examples of academic whistle-blowing, wide ranging in its critique, apposite in its targeting and reasoning, timely and badly needed, yet falling, as we shall see, on stony ground.

On one side of this skirmish was Richard Lewontin, Professor of Zoology at Harvard, a distinguished geneticist and epidemiologist; on the other was a team of sociologists led by Edward Laumann and John Gagnon from the University of Chicago, who had recently published *The Social Organisation of Sexuality* (1995a) and its popular companion volume *Sex in America: A Definitive Survey* (Michael *et al* 1995). On the sidelines, chipping in with gusto, was Richard Sennett, joint Professor of Sociology at the LSE and NYU.

This debate is of interest because it represents a direct confrontation of natural science with sociology or social science, as it is often hopefully and optimistically called. Such encounters are relatively rare and tend to occur when particularly politically distasteful findings are presented to the public as cast iron and embellished with the imprimatur of science. A recent example of this was the publication of Richard Herrnstein and Charles Murray's *The Bell Curve* (1994), accompanied by pages of statistical tables which purported to present the scientific evidence for the link between race, IQ and, indeed, crime. At that time many prominent scientists, including Steven Rose and Stephen Gould, were moved to intervene, but normally the walls between disciplines remain intact: indeed a collegial atmosphere of mutual respect coupled with lack of interest ensures that parallel and contradictory literatures about the same subject can occur in departments separated sometimes by a corridor or, more frequently, a faculty block. In the case of the natural and social sciences this is complicated by a unidirectional admiration – a one-sided love affair, one might say – or at least a state of acute physics envy – between the aspiring social scientist and the natural sciences. Be that as it may, a considerable proportion of sociologists, the vast majority of psychologists and an increasing number of criminologists embrace, without thought or reservation, a positivistic path. Namely, natural scientific methods can be applied to human action, behaviour is causally determined, incontestable objectivity is attainable, and precise quantitative measurement is possible, indeed preferable. In the case of criminology, this entails the belief that the crimes of individuals can be predicted from risk factors and that rates of crime can be explained by changes in the proportion of causal factors in the population.

Richard Lewontin sets out to review the two books. They arose on the back of the AIDS crisis and the need to understand the epidemiology of its spread. The survey was eventually well funded by research foundations, and was conducted by NORC, the premier social survey research organisation in North America. The project involved a sample of 3,432 people representing 200 million post-pubertal Americans.

Just for a minute let us think of the audacity of the sample survey – and this one was more thoroughgoing than most – to claim to generalise from such a small number to such a large population of individuals. Lewontin's critique is on two levels, one the problem of representativeness and two – and more substantially – the problem of truth.

Let us first of all examine the problem of representation. An initial criticism is that the random sample was not actually from the total population. It was based on a sample of addresses drawn from the census, but it excluded households where there were no English-speakers, and no one between the ages of 15 and 59. Most crucially it excluded the 3% of Americans (some 7.5 million) who do not live in households because they are institutionalised or homeless. This latter point is, as Lewontin indicates, scarcely trivial in understanding the epidemiology of AIDS as it excludes the most vulnerable group in the population, including those likely to be victims of homosexual rape in prison, prostitution, reckless drug use, and sexually 'free' college aged adolescents, etc. The random sample is not, therefore, drawn from the population as a whole: a *very* atypical population is omitted. Such a restriction in population sampled is a usual preliminary in survey research.

However, once this somewhat restricted sample was made, the research team did not stint in their efforts to get as large a response rate as possible. After repeated visits, telephone calls and financial inducements ranging from $10 to $100, the result was a response rate of 79% – of which they were duly pleased. But, as Lewontin points out: 'It is almost always the case that those who do not respond are a non-random sample of those who are asked' (1995a, p 28). In this case it could well be prudishness, but in the case of other surveys equally non-random causes of non-responses. For example, in our own experience of over 15 large-scale crime and victimisation studies that were run at the Centre for Criminology, Middlesex University (see for example Jones *et al* 1986; Crawford *et al* 1990) we made every effort to reduce non-response but never managed better than 83%. Indeed, criminal victimisation surveys as a whole have between one fifth to a quarter of respondents whose victimisation is unknown. As I remarked at the time, in the thick of quantitative research:

> It goes without saying that such a large unknown population could easily skew every finding we victimologists present. At the most obvious level, it probably includes a disproportionate number of transients, of lower working class people hostile to officials with clipboards attempting to ask them about their lives, and of those who are most frightened to answer the door because of fear of crime. (Young 1988: 169)[1]

Lewontin's first point ('the problem of representativeness') is, therefore, clear and is as applicable to criminology as it is to sociology. Let me at this point remind the reader of Quételet's warning. Adolphe Quételet, the founder of scientific statistics, and a pioneer in analysing the social and physical determinants of crime, introduced

---

1 Even panel studies which follow a given population over time suffer from this problem. Take the famous Seattle Social Development Project as an example (see Farrington *et al* 2003). This is a prospective longitudinal survey of 808 children. To start with, these are the children/parents who consented to be included out of the population of 1,053 fifth-grade students targeted – that is, it has a 70% response rate from the outset – with 30% refusing consent. Secondly, youths dropped out over time so, for example, by the age of 12 the sample fell to 52%. There is, of course, every reason to suspect that those who initially did not consent and those who fell out of the panel might have different delinquency patterns from those who consented and remained within the panel.

into academic discussion in the 1830s the problem of the unknown figure of crime, that is, crime not revealed in the official statistics:

> This is also the place to examine a difficulty ... it is that our observations can only refer to *a certain number of known and tried offenders out of the unknown sum total of crimes committed*. Since this sum total of crimes committed will probably ever continue unknown, all the reasoning of which it is the basis will be more or less defective. I do not hesitate to say, that all the knowledge which we possess on the statistics of crimes and offences will be of no utility whatsoever, unless we admit without question *that there is a ratio, nearly invariably the same, between known and tried offences and the unknown sum total of crimes committed*. This ratio is necessary, and if it did not really exist, everything which, until the present time, has been said on the statistical documents of crime, would be false and absurd. (Quételet 1842: 82)

Quételet's fixed ratios are, of course, a pipe dream, as unlikely as they would be convenient. His warning, written in 1835 (English translation 1842) has echoed throughout the criminology academy for the last 170 years. If we do not know the true rate of crime, all our theories are built on quicksand. They will be of 'no utility', 'false', and indeed 'absurd'. Legions of theorists from Robert K Merton through to James Q Wilson have committed Giffen's paradox: expressing their doubts about the accuracy of the data and then proceeding to use the crime figures with seeming abandon. This is particularly true in recent years when the advent of sophisticated statistical analysis is, somehow, seen to grant permission to skate over the thin ice of insubstantiality (Giffen 1965; Oosthoek 1978). Others have put their faith in statistics generated by the social scientist, whether self-report studies or victimisation surveys, as if Quételet's warning no longer concerned them and the era of 'pre-scientific' data was over.

Indeed, Richard Sparks and his associates, in the introduction to their groundbreaking British victimisation study, summarised the decade of American research prior to their own with a note of jubilation: 'Within a decade ... some of the oldest problems of criminology have come at least within reach of a solution' (Sparks *et al* 1977: 1). As we have seen, the problem of non-response means that such a resolution of the age-old problem of measurement is not resolved. It would be so, of course, if the non-respondents were just – or almost – like the respondents, and indeed such an excuse is often invoked with as much likelihood of validity as Quételet's ratios. As it is, the atypicality of non-respondents is likely to overturn the significance levels of any probabilistic sampling. Richard Sparks was quite clear about this in his assessment of the potential of victimisation studies. His initial excitement became tempered by considerable caution. Thus he writes, 10 years later:

> Much too much fuss is made, in practically all official NCS publications, about statistical significance (ie allowance for sampling variability). A variety of standard errors and confidence intervals for NCS data are now routinely quoted in those publications. Yet it is clear that *non*sampling error is of far greater magnitude in the NCS; adjustments ... may offset some of this nonsampling error, though only in a ballpark way, which makes questions of sampling variability virtually irrelevant. My own view (not shared by all) is that if after commonsensical adjustment a trend or pattern appears which makes some sense, then it ought not to be disregarded even if it does not attain some magical level of statistical significance. (1981: 44 n 42)

Telling the truth?

But let us go on to Lewontin's next criticism: the problem of truth. And here the problem is even more important and substantial than that of non-response and the dark figure. This revolves around the key question of whether those who responded to the questionnaire were in fact telling the truth. That is, social surveys may not only have dark figures of non-respondents, but a dark figure of non-response – and indeed 'over-response' – amongst the respondents themselves.

It is rare for surveys of attitude or self-reported behaviour to have any internal check as to validity. After all, if people say they would rather live by work than on welfare, if they profess liberal attitudes on racial matters, or if they tell you that they were assaulted twice last year, how is one to know that this is not true? One may have one's suspicions, of course, but there are few cast iron checks. Every now and then, however, anomalies stare you in the face. In the case of the sexual behaviour survey there is a particularly blatant example. The average number of heterosexual partners reported by men over the last five years is 75% greater than the average number reported by women. This is an obvious anomaly. It is, as Lewontin points out, like a violation of the only law in economics that the number of sales must be equal to the number of purchases. What is startling is that the researchers are well aware of this. Indeed, they devote considerable time to debating the reasons why this 'discrepancy' might have occurred and conclude that the most likely explanation is that 'either men may exaggerate or women may underestimate'. As Lewontin remarks:

> So in the single case where one can actually test the truth, the investigators themselves think it most likely that people are telling themselves and others enormous lies. If one takes the authors at their word, it would seem futile to take seriously the other results of the study. The report that 5.3 percent of conventional Protestants, 3.3 percent of fundamentalists, 2.8 percent of Catholics, and 10.7 percent of the non-religious have ever had a same-sex partner may show the effect of religion on practice or it may be nothing but hypocrisy. What is billed as a study of 'Sexual Practices in the United States' is, after all, a study of an indissoluble jumble of practices, attitudes, personal myths, and posturing. (1995a: 29)

What is of interest here is the awareness of thin ice, yet the ineluctable desire to keep on skating. Just as with Giffen's paradox, where the weakness of the statistics is plain to the researchers yet they continue to force-feed inadequate data into their personal computers, here the problem of lying, whether by exaggeration or concealment, does not stop the researchers, for more than a moment, in their scientific task. Of course, as a sociologist, such findings are not irrelevant: they inform you much about differences in male and female attitudes to sex – what they *don't* tell you is about differences in sexual behaviour. Yet what Richard Lewontin is telling us is that interview situations are social relationships – that results are a product of a social interaction and will vary with the gender, class and age of the interviewer and interviewee. But here we have it: it needs a Professor of Biology to tell sociologists to be sociologists. Thus, he concludes:

> The answer, surely, is to be less ambitious and stop trying to make sociology into a natural science although it is, indeed, the study of natural objects. There are some things in the world that we will never know and many that we will never know exactly. Each domain of phenomena has its characteristic grain of knowability. Biology is not physics, because organisms are such complex physical objects, and sociology is not biology because human societies are made by self-conscious organisms. By pretending to a kind of knowledge that it cannot achieve, social science can only engender the scorn of natural scientists and the cynicism of humanists. (1995a: 29)

Of course this is not the end of it. Edward Laumann and his colleagues are outraged. They do not think it 'appropriate for a biologist' to be reviewing their work, he does not have the right 'professional qualifications' – 'his review is a pastiche of ill-informed personal opinion that makes unfounded claims of relevant scientific authority and expertise' (Laumann *et al* 1995b: 43). Lewontin, in reply, notes caustically that it is understandable that the team

> would have preferred to have their own work reviewed by a member of their own school of sociology, someone sharing the same unexamined methodological assumptions. They could avoid the always unpleasant necessity of justifying the epistemic basis on which the entire structure of their work depends. (Lewontin 1995b: 43)

As to his incompetence with regard to statistical analysis, he admits to being a bit disturbed at having to reveal his CV, but points out that he has a graduate degree in mathematical statistics which he has taught for 40 years and this is the subject of about one-tenth of his publications, including a textbook of statistics!

And, of course, such a process of believing in the objectivity of data is fostered by the habit of researchers of *not* conducting their own interviews, of employing agencies such as NORC, or using second-hand data, in terms of using older datasets or even a meta-analysis of past datasets. So the data arrives at their computers already punched, sanitised: it is a series of numbers with scientific-looking decimal points. Human contact is minimised and a barrier of printout and digits is raised between them and human life.

But let us leave the last remarks of this section to Richard Sennett. He congratulates Lewontin on the brilliance of his analysis, he laments the current fashion of scientific sociology, and concurs with Lewontin's remark that, if work such as this is typical, then the discipline must be in 'deep trouble'. That's putting it mildly, suggests Sennett: 'American sociology has become a refuge for the academically challenged' (1995: 43). But he adds that mere stupidity cannot alone explain the analytic weakness of such studies, for 'sociology in its dumbed-down condition is emblematic of a society that doesn't want to know much about itself' (*ibid*).

Lessons for criminology

But what has all of this to do with criminology? A great deal and more, for it is probably criminology, of all the branches of sociology and psychology, where the problem of unchecked positivism is greatest. The expansion of academic criminology was a consequence of the exponential increase in the size of the criminal justice system just as the shift from students studying social policy/administration to studying criminology parallels the shift from governmental interventions through the welfare state to those utilising criminal justice. The war on crime followed by the war on drugs and then the war on terror. This has been accompanied by an expansion in funding designed to evaluate and assess governmental interventions and programmes. The material basis for the revitalisation of positivist criminology is considerable and, certainly within the United States, approaching hegemonic (see Hayward and Young 2004).

Embarrassing findings

Criminological research is replete with findings that range from the very unlikely to the ridiculous. I will give just a few examples.

Rarity of serious crimes

Victimisation studies consistently report levels of serious crime that are gross underestimations and are *freely admitted* as such. For example, the first *British Crime Survey of England & Wales* in 1982 found only one rape and that attempted.

Variability of findings with different instruments

If we take sensitive topics such as incidence of domestic violence, the range of figures is extraordinarily wide – and, in no doubt, underestimates. Thus in 1998 the percentage of women experiencing domestic violence, defined as physical assault with injury, was 0.5% in the police figures, 1% in the *British Crime Survey*, and 2.2% when Computer Assisted Self-Interviewing was used. An independent survey found a rate in the region of 8% (Mooney 1999). Which figure in this range is one going to feed into one's PC? What sort of science is it where estimations of a variable vary sixteenfold?

Self-report studies

Self-report studies consistently come up with results showing that there is little variation in levels of juvenile delinquency between the working class and the middle class and between black and white, and produce a considerably reduced gap between males and females. Hence Tittle and his colleagues' extraordinary claim that there is no relationship between class and crime, which has been taken at face value by many theorists. All one can record about this surmise is John Braithwaite's pithy remark:

> It is hardly plausible that one can totally explain away the higher risks of being mugged and raped in lower class areas as the consequence of the activities of middle class people who come into the area to perpetrate such acts. (1981: 37)

The assault rate on white men

The United States NCVS regularly comes up with results which show that the assault rate reported by white men is higher than or just about equal to that of black men. For example, in 1999 the rate was 32.3 per 1,000 for whites compared to 31.0 per 1,000 for blacks. This runs totally against evidence from homicide rates or other indices of violence, which would suggest a much higher rate for blacks (see commentary in Sparks 1981).

Findings of International Crime and Victimisation Studies

The International Crime and Victimisation Study (van Kesteren *et al* 2000) frequently finds rates of reported violence between nations which are almost the inverse of the homicide rates (see Young 2004).

The pluralism of the dark figure

Up to now we have discussed either technical problems of non-response or the more substantive problem of exaggeration or lying. I want now to turn to a third problem which generates even greater and more impenetrable barriers for scientific quantification. The first two problems – which Lewontin addresses – presume that there is an objective data out there which can be registered. However, there is a profound difference between measurement in the natural world and measurement in society, namely that the definitions of social phenomena are constructed by individuals and in this they will vary with the social constructs of the actors involved. If one hands out a dozen metre rules to students and asks them to measure the length of the seminar room, they will come to a common agreement with a little variation for accuracy. If one asks the room full of students to measure levels of violence they are, so to speak, already equipped with a dozen rules of different gauge and length. They will come out of the exercise with different amounts of violence because their definitions of violence will vary. And the same will be true of the respondents to a victimisation study. All of us may agree that a stab wound is violence, but where along the continuum does violence begin: is it a shove (if so, how hard?), is it a tap (if so, how weighty?), or perhaps it is a harsh word, an obscenity, a threat? People vary in their definitions and tolerance of violence: there is a pluralism of measures.

Let us look at two 'anomalies' in this light. The peculiar results of the International Crime and Victimisation Studies, where the rates of violence reported are approximately the inverse of the rates of violence occurring if we are to trust the homicide figures, may not only be due to the fact that reporting to strangers distorts the level of violence. It may be that countries with low levels of violence have low levels of tolerance of violence and thus report acts which other, more tolerant/ violent nations might ignore. Similarly the comparatively higher rate of violence against white compared to black men may reflect differences in definition as to what constitutes 'real' violence. Once we have acknowledged the pluralism of human definition, we can then return to the dark figure with even greater doubts and trepidations. For the dark figure will expand and contract not merely with the technical means we bring to it, but with the values of the respondents and indeed the categories of the interviewers. And the social rather than the merely technical permeates our measurement on all three levels: from the respondents who refuse to talk to us, to those that in their relationship with a stranger (of class, gender, age, and perhaps ethnicity) will attempt to convey an impression of themselves (a product of their own personal narrative which they have woven around the 'facts' of their lives), to the values and meanings which the interviewer brings to the table.

Eysenck's dilemma

It is important to stress how damaging such findings are for the positivist, for the scientific project of studying humanity. For positivism needs fixed categories, agreed measurements, objective and uncontested figures. The late Hans Eysenck, the doyen of psychological behaviourism, recognised this quite clearly in the last book he wrote on criminology with his colleague Gisli Gudjonsson. In *The Causes and Cures of Criminality* (1989) they began by taking issue with the authors of *The New Criminology* (Taylor *et al* 1973) in their assertion that crime is not an objective category but a product of varying legal fiat – Eysenck and Gudjonsson quite clearly recognise this as an obstacle to science and get round the argument by differentiating two types of crime: victimless and victimful crime. Victimless crimes – and they give examples from prostitution to anal sex – they concede, are subjectively and pluralistically defined. These are eliminated from the realm of objectivity – but victimful crimes, and here they list such phenomena as theft, assault, murder and rape, are, they argue, universally condemned and, therefore, clearly objective. This is obviously untrue: all of these crimes are subject to varying definitions – to talk of them having a fixed nature is to teeter on the brink of tautology. Rape is, of course, universally condemned because it is an illegal sexual attack, but what constitutes rape varies and, indeed, expands with time, witness the acknowledgment of marital rape *as* rape. And assault, as we have seen, is greatly dependent on our tolerance of violence.

The impact of late modernity on measurement

In the introduction to this chapter I noted how in late modernity the causes of crime become loosened from their fixed structural moorings, that the 'same' circumstances become imbued with different meanings. The causes of crime, in the sense of a narrative leading from personal circumstances to crime committed, are more varied; they are in a less fixed relationship. We have seen in our discussion of measurement how the effects – the outcome of such a narrative – are subject also to differential interpretations. They are part of this constructed narrative of meaning both of the actor and in the actor's relationship to the interviewer in the act of measurement. But here once again such a social construction is also subject in late modernity to greater contest and pluralism of definition. So the hidden figure expands and contracts with the values we bring to it. In a pluralist society it is no longer possible to talk of a hidden figure x with which we can attempt to measure; there are a whole series of hidden figures x, y, z etc.

The bogus of positivism

The positivist dream of a scientific sociology of crime, which attempts to objectively relate cause and effect, becomes all the more impossible in late modernity. As we have seen, both the causes of crime and the definitions of crime, that is, the outcome or effects, become problematised. To move from, say, unemployment to crime, or deprivation to crime, you need narratives; correlation alone cannot assure causality, it is only the narratives which link factors to outcomes that can do this. People turn 'factors' into narratives – they are even capable of turning such factors on their heads. Furthermore, what is crime itself is part of this narrative. It is a variable dependent on subcultural definition and assessment.

The bogus of positivism is that it only *seemed* to work when the world was reasonably static, where vocabularies of motive seemed organically linked to points in the social structure and where definitions of crime were consensual and unproblematised. The loosening of moorings in late modernity, and the multiple problematisation consequent on pluralism destroys this illusion. As Martin Nicolaus exclaimed in his famous article in *Antioch Review* so many years ago, 'What kind of science is this, which holds true only when men hold still?' (1969: 387).

We live in a time of rapid change. In these times, rather than the variables determining the change, it is almost as if the change occurs and the factors seem to scuttle after them. Prediction of real life events of any consequence has always been a lamentable failure in the 'social sciences' – just think of the collapse of communism and look at the writings of political scientists prior to the days of *glasnost*. In criminology we have witnessed in our lifetime two dramatic changes which run completely contrary to our scientific predictions. First of all, in the period from the 1960s, the crime rate increased remorselessly in the majority of industrial countries despite the fact that all the factors which previously had been identified as reducing crime were on the increase (eg wealth, education, employment, housing). I have termed this elsewhere the 'aetiological crisis' in criminological theory (1994). This crisis set in motion an intense debate amongst criminologists and formed the basis for the extraordinary creativity and plethora of theories that occurred in the last 30 years. But having spent the whole of our professional lives researching why crime should almost inexorably go up (whether due to relative deprivation, broken homes, social disorganisation, breakdown of controls, labelling, etc), we find ourselves in the infuriating position of the crime rate in very many industrial countries (including the US and the UK) beginning to go down, against all predictions that I know of. Here we have a double trauma, or whammy, if you want!

The crime drop in America and the crisis of positivism

On 16 November 2000, in San Francisco, the American Society of Criminology gathered to discuss a most extraordinary happening in the world of crime. From 1991 onwards, violent crime in the United States, which had led the advanced world by far in rates of murder and robbery, had begun to fall. Homicide dropped by 35.7% from 1991 to 1998 (from 9.8 to 6.3 per 100,000) (Blumstein and Wallman 2000). Al Blumstein, of the National Consortium on Violence Research, had brought together a dazzling array of experts: demographers, economists, sociologists and criminologists, all contributing their views on the change with graphic charts and probing statistical analysis. I listened with fascination to how they factored each of the developments over the period to explain the phenomenon, from changes in the distribution of handguns, the extraordinary prison expansion, zero-tolerance policing, down to changes in crack-culture and technology. At the end of the session they asked for comments from the audience, no doubt expecting some detailed remark about policing levels or the influence of handgun availability, or such like; but the first question, from a Canadian woman, was something of a revelation. She pointed out, ironically, how Canadians were supposed to be condemned to culturally lag behind their American cousins, but that they too had had a drop in violence, despite the fact that they had not experienced such a period of rapid prison expansion, that zero-tolerance policing was not *de rigueur* and that Canada had only a small problem of crack-cocaine (see commentary in Ouimet 2002). A Spanish woman, who said something very similar about her own country, followed the Canadian. In fact there had been a crime drop in 13 out of 21 industrial countries during 1997–98 (Barclay *et al* 2001; Young 2004).

Blumstein's team focused on the relationship between variable changes and the drop in violence. Once international data is examined one must seriously question whether they were looking at the correct variables. Furthermore, to cap it all, they traced their line of correlation between these variables and the level of violence when, in fact, property crimes were also declining. The most immediate explanation of this is that we are encountering 'spurious causality' (see Sayer 1992: 193). But the enigma of the crime drop takes us far beyond the world of technical mistakes. The usual procedure in such analysis is to take the demographics and other factors which correlate with crime in the past and attempt to explain the present or predict the future levels of crime in terms of changes in these variables. The problem here is that people (and young people in particular) might well change independently of these variables. For in the last analysis the factors do not add up and the social scientists begin to have to admit the ghost in the machine. Thus, Richard Rosenfeld of Blumstein's team writes ruefully:

> If the church is the last refuge of scoundrels, 'culture' is the final recourse of social
> scientists in search of explanations when existing economic, social and political theories
> have been exhausted. (2000: 157)

So there we have it, subculture becomes the final refuge of scoundrels! And
Rosenfeld comments, 'It is possible that American adults are becoming, in a word,
civilised' (*ibid*: 156).

From a more sympathetic perspective, Andrew Karmen in his meticulous
analysis of the New York crime drop – *New York Murder Mystery* (2000) – casts his eye
across all the various explanations, judiciously giving them various explanatory
weightings, but at the end of the book talks of 'the final demographic factor which
might be the most important of all' (2000: 249). But then, he reflects, 'the shift is not
even strictly demographic in nature: it is attitudinal and behavioural as well as
generational' (*ibid*). And, he adds, 'Unfortunately the existence of this suspected
evolution in subcultural values defies precise statistical measurement. It is not clear
what kind of evidence and statistics could prove or disprove it'. Karmen points to the
possibility of profound changes in the norms of urban youth culture. And here he
refers to the pioneering work of Ric Curtis, the New York urban anthropologist who
talks of the 'little brother syndrome'. That is, where younger children, having
witnessed the devastating effects of hard drugs, gun culture, intensive crime on their
older brothers, decide that these things are not for them – they are no longer hip and
cool – the culture evolves and turns its face against the past. This observation has
ready resonance with, for example, any attempt to understand changes in drug use.
These do not seem to relate to changes in social factors or the impact of the war
against drugs. They seem to relate to changes in fashion, although this is perhaps too
light a word for it – changes in subcultural project would probably be more fitting.

Curtis relates these changes closely to the development of late modernity and to
the loosening of the moorings which I referred to at the beginning of this chapter.
Thus he writes: 'The postmodern global economy is one in which identity formation
is less dependent upon the influence of family, neighborhoods, race/ethnicity,
nationality and history, and more than anywhere else the inner city is an empty
canvas, an open frontier where new structures, institutions and conventions are
waiting to be built' (1998: 1276).

An open season on numbers?

Am I suggesting an open season on numbers? Not quite: there are obviously (as
Sennett points out in the *Sex in America* debate) numbers which are indispensable to
sociological analysis. Figures of infant mortality, age, marriage and common
economic indicators are cases in point, as are, for example, numbers of police,
imprisonment rates and homicide incidences in criminology. Others such as income
or ethnicity are of great utility but must be used with caution. There are things in the
social landscape which are distinct, definite and measurable; there are many others
that are blurred because we do not know them – some because we are unlikely ever
to know them, others, more importantly, because it is their nature to be blurred.
Precision must constantly be eyed with suspicion, decimal points with raised
eyebrows. There are very many cases where statistical testing is inappropriate
because the data is technically weak – it will simply not bear the weight of such
analysis. There are many other instances where the data is blurred and contested and
where such testing is simply wrong. Over the last decade there has grown up a

peculiar formula for writing journal articles. The introduction usually presents two theories in competition but they are strange one-dimensional creatures almost unrecognisable compared to the real thing by virtue of being rendered simple and decontextualised for the purposes of operationalisation. This acephalous introduction, this headless chicken of an argument, is followed by an extensive discussion of measures, whilst the data itself is usually outsourced from some past study or bought in from a survey firm. An obligatory recession analysis follows, an erudite statistical equation is a definite plus, and then the usually inconclusive results are paraded before us. The criminologists themselves are far distant from crime out there, hidden behind a wall of verbiage and computer printout, the barrier graphited with the Greek letters of statistical manipulation.

What can we do to get out of this sanitised redoubt? What is needed is a theoretical position which can enter in to the real world of existential joy, fear, false certainty and doubt; which can seek to understand the subcultural projects of people in a world riven with inequalities of wealth and uncertainties of identity. What we need is an ethnographic method that can deal with reflexivity, contradiction, tentativeness, change of opinion, posturing and concealment. A method which is sensitive to the way people write and rewrite their personal narratives. Our problems will not be solved by a fake scientificity but by a critical ethnography honed to the potentialities of human creativity and meaning.

References

Barclay, G, Tavares, C and Siddique, A (2001) *International Comparisons of Criminal Justice Statistics, 1999*, London: Home Office

Bauman, Z (2000) *Liquid Modernity*, Cambridge: Polity

Blumstein, A and Wallman, J (eds) (2000) *The Crime Drop in America*, Cambridge: CUP

Braithwaite, J (1981) 'The myth of social class and criminality reconsidered' 46 *American Sociological Review* 36–57

Crawford, A, Jones, T, Woodhouse, T and Young, J (1990) *The Second Islington Crime Survey*, Centre for Criminology, Middlesex University

Curtis, R (1998) 'The improbable transformation of inner city neighborhoods: crime, violence and drugs in the 1990s' 88(4) *Journal of Criminal Law and Criminology* 1233–66

Eysenck, H and Gudjonsson, G (1989) *The Causes and Cures of Criminality*, New York: Plenum

Farrington, D, Joliffe, D, Hawkes, D, Catalano, R, Hull, R and Kosterman, R (2003) 'Comparing delinquency careers in court records and self-reports' 41(3) *Criminology* 933–58

Ferrell, J (1997) 'Criminological *verstehen*: inside the immediacy of crime' 14 *Justice Quarterly* 3–23

Garland, D (2000) 'The new criminologies of everyday life: routine activity theory in historical and social context', in Van Hirsch, A, Garland, D and Wakefield, A (eds), *Ethical and Social Perspectives on Situational Crime Prevention*, Oxford: Hart

Giffen, P (1965) 'Rates of crime and delinquency', in McGrath, W (ed), *Crime Treatment in Canada*, Toronto: Macmillan

Hayward, K and Young, J (2004), 'Cultural criminology: some notes on the script' 8(3) *Theoretical Criminology* 259–73

Herrnstein, R and Murray, C (1994) *The Bell Curve*, New York: Free Press

Jones, T, McClean, B and Young, J (1986) *The Islington Crime Survey*, Aldershot: Gower

Karmen, A (2000) *New York Murder Mystery*, New York: New York UP

Katz, J (2002) 'Start here: social ontology & research strategy' 6(3) *Theoretical Criminology* 255–78

Laumann, E, Gagnon, J, Michael, R and Michaels, S (1995a) *The Social Organisation of Sexuality: Sexual Practices in the United States*, Chicago: University of Chicago Press

Laumann, E, Gagnon, J, Michael, R and Michaels, S (1995b) 'Letter to Editor' 42(9) *New York Review of Books* (May), p 43

Lewontin, R (1995a) 'Sex in America' 42(7) *New York Review of Books* (April), pp 24–29

Lewontin, R (1995b) 'Letter to Editor' 42(9) *New York Review of Books* (May), pp 43–44

McRobbie, A (1994) *Postmodernism & Modern Culture,* London: Routledge

Michael, R, Gagnon, J, Laumann, E and Kolata, G (1995) *Sex in America: A Definitive Survey,* Boston: Little Brown

Mooney, J (1999) *Gender, Violence and the Social Order,* London: Macmillan

Nicolaus, M (1969) 'The professional organization of sociology: a view from below', *Antioch Review* (Fall), pp 375–87

Oosthoek, A (1978) *The Utilization of Official Crime Data,* Ottawa: Supply and Services

Ouimet, M (2002) 'Explaining the American and Canadian crime "drop" in the 1990s' 44 *Canadian Journal of Criminology* 33–50

Quételet, A (1842) *Treatise on Man,* Paris: Bachelier (first published 1835 as *Sur l'homme et sur les développements de ses facultés, ou Essai de physique sociale,* 2 volumes)

Rosenfeld, R (2000) 'Patterns in adult homicide: 1980–1995', in Blumstein, A and Wallman, J (eds), *The Crime Drop in America,* Cambridge: CUP

Sayer, A (1992) *Method in Social Science,* 2nd edn, London: Routledge

Schwendinger, H and Schwendinger, J (1985) *Adolescent Subcultures and Delinquency,* New York: Praeger

Sennett, R (1995) 'Letter to Editor' 42(9) *New York Review of Books* (May), p 43

Sparks, RF (1981) 'Surveys of victimization – an optimistic assessment', in Tonry, M and Morris, N (eds), *Criminal Justice Vol 3,* Chicago: University of Chicago Press

Sparks, RF, Genn, H and Dodd, K (1977) *Surveying Victims,* Chichester: Wiley

Taylor, I, Walton, P and Young, J (1973) *The New Criminology,* London: Routledge and Kegan Paul

Tittle, C, Villemmez, W and Smith, D (1978) 'The myth of social class and criminality' 43 *American Sociological Review* 643–56

van Kesteren, J, Mayhew, P and Nieuwbeerta, P (2000) *Criminal Victimization in 17 Industrialized Countries: Key Findings from the 2000 International Crime Survey,* The Hague: Ministry of Justice, WODC

Young, J (1988) 'Risk of crime and fear of crime: a realist critique of survey-based assumptions', in Maguire, M and Pointing, J (eds), *Victims of Crime: A New Deal,* Milton Keynes: Open UP

Young, J (1994) 'Incessant chatter: recent paradigms in criminology', in Maguire, M, Morgan, R and Reiner, R (eds), *The Oxford Handbook of Criminology,* 1st edn, Oxford: OUP

Young, J (1999) *The Exclusive Society,* London: Sage

Young, J (2004) 'Winning the fight against crime', in Matthews, R and Young, J (eds), *The New Politics of Crime and Punishment,* Devon: Willan

Chapter 2
From Cultural Studies to Psychosocial Criminology: An Intellectual Journey

Tony Jefferson

Introduction

In the small space available to me, I want to take the reader on an intellectual journey that covers the key theoretical shifts in my transformation, over a 30-year period, from postgraduate student at the (now closed) Birmingham Centre for Contemporary Cultural Studies (CCCS) in the early 1970s to Professor of Criminology at Keele University writing about psychosocial criminology. My hope is that this will act both as a reminder to students of cultural criminology of some of the intellectual roots of contemporary thinking about culture, and as an argument justifying the taking of my particular psychosocial route. In broad terms, my journey started out focused on the relations between culture and structure and has ended up exploring the connections between the psyche and discourse. Initially, the complexities of the social world dominated; latterly, the complexities of the psyche. Interest in the determinacy of structural relations has been replaced by an engagement with the historical contingencies of changing discursive formations, the logic of correspondence replaced by the disjunctive logic of psychoanalysis. Power, now seen as dislodged from structure, has become an omnipresent and relational phenomenon (which does not mean simply an interactional phenomenon); and class as the key focus has been eclipsed by an interest in gender. The transitional hinge coupling these shifts has been an approach to mediations, originally influenced by structural linguistics, which breaks with the transparency of 'mediation as representation' in favour of a constitutive model where mediations produce their own effects.

Structure, cultures, biographies and expressive relations: the 1970s, *Resistance through Rituals* and *Policing the Crisis*

A key theoretical focus for members of CCCS in the early 1970s was how to understand the relationship between culture and structure. For those of us in the youth subcultures group, this was to be explored empirically through the succession of post-war youth subcultures in the UK. This work built on that of Phil Cohen (1972) who, in an influential article called 'Sub-cultural conflict and working class community', argued:

> [T]he latent function of sub-culture is this – to express and resolve, albeit 'magically', the contradictions which remain hidden or unresolved in the parent culture. (Cohen 1972: 23)

In other words, the succession of exotic youth sub-cultural styles in the UK from the Teds to Mods and Rockers and Skinheads (and all the hybrid styles in between) were symbolic cultural expressions of structural contradictions. Cohen also read these subcultures within a Freudian frame of reference, arguing that they were a compromise solution between the needs of adolescence to be autonomous of and different from their parents as well as to be able to hang onto the security of existing parental identifications. This meant that sub-cultural conflict 'serves as a displacement of generational conflict, both at a cultural level, and at an interpersonal level within the family' (*ibid* 1972: 26).

Our marxism blinded us to this Freudian interpretation and we focused on the notion of reading subcultural styles as symbolic (or ritualised) evidence of 'resistance' to the particular class-based oppressions to which working-class youth were then subject. The novelty of each style was a function of it being 'doubly' constructed: in relation to youth's own generationally-specific version of their subordinate class culture as well as to the dominant culture. The logic of the argument linking structure and culture was expressive: youth subcultures were expressions of structurally-based class domination. Biography appears, if only fleetingly, at the point in the argument where we distinguish between three levels: 'structures', which we defined as 'the set of socially organised positions and experiences of the class in relation to the major institutions and structures' (Clarke *et al* 1976: 57); 'cultures', which we defined as 'the range of socially-organised and patterned response to these basic material and social conditions' (*ibid*); and 'biographies', which we defined as 'the "careers" of particular individuals through those structures and cultures – the means by which individual identities and life-histories are constructed out of collective experiences' (*ibid*). Despite the addition of a new level, the logic remained the same: the level of biography could only be made sense of in terms of structures and cultures; and these, as we had already argued, were 'expressively' related.

Policing the Crisis (Hall *et al* 1978), a book written at much the same time as *Resistance through Rituals* (Hall and Jefferson 1976), states in the Introduction that it is '*not* a book about why certain individuals, as individuals, turn to mugging' (p vii) but is a book about 'the social causes of "mugging"' and 'why British society *reacts to mugging*, in the extreme way it does, at that precise historical conjuncture – the early 1970s' (emphasis in original). However, it, too, adopts the 'structures-cultures-biographies' framework when, in the final chapter, it returns to 'The politics of mugging' (as opposed to the reaction to it).[1] There, in addition to talking about 'the structures of "secondariness"' (pp 339–48) and the culture of 'resistance' (pp 348–61) these bred, we offer a 'typical biography' (p 361) for a young black male youth of the kind that could lead him to become a 'mugger'. This imagined account, which includes racial fights at school, unemployment or a series of 'dead-end' jobs, rows at home, homelessness, and run-ins with the police, is a sort of processual amalgam of

---

1 Although *Policing the Crisis* was not written as a contribution to criminology, its 'structures-cultures-biographies' framework resembled that proposed in the final chapter of the best-known text within the tradition of radical or critical criminology, namely *The New Criminology* (Taylor, Walton and Young 1973). Here, they called for a criminology that was attentive to both the activity of crime and the reaction to it (the latter signalling a strong nod to their debt to symbolic interactionism and 'labelling' theory) at three levels:

(a) the wider origins of the action/reaction or the level of political economy (our structures);

(b) the immediate origins of the action/reaction or the level of social psychology (our cultures);

(c) the actual act or the level of social dynamics (our biographies).

(They were also concerned with the outcome of the reaction on the deviant's further action – in recognition of the importance to labelling theory of the deviancy amplification spiral.)

all that we knew about black youth in the 1970s – their alienation, anger and desperation – rendered biographical. In terms talked about earlier, it is an account in which the structures of secondariness and cultures of resistance are expressed biographically. In a recent article, Jo Goodey (2000) talked approvingly of our 'typical biography', as if the point of biographical work was to produce such typical portraits. For reasons I shall come to, I think that the typical biography offers too social an account of biography, with no weight at all given to psychic life.

To put all this in broader terms, this work was part of an ongoing critique of other pioneers within cultural studies, namely Raymond Williams and the historian EP Thompson, for whom lived experience was crucial. Theoretically, this became defined as a struggle between 'culturalism', which prioritised the role of consciousness, and structuralism, where consciousness was an 'effect' of structure. As Stuart Hall (1980: 66) summarised the debate:

> Whereas in 'culturalism', experience was the ground – the terrain of 'the lived' – where consciousness and conditions intersected, structuralism insisted that 'experience' could not, by definition, be the ground of anything, since one could only 'live' and experience one's conditions in and through the categories, classifications and frameworks of the culture. These categories, however, did not arise from or in experience: rather, experience was their 'effect'.

This, of course, had profound implications for the study of human agency. At the time, as the notion of cultures being symbolic expressions of structural contradictions suggests, we came down on the structuralist side of the argument; but, as the idea of 'resistance' and our intellectual debt to Gramsci's insistence on the importance of political struggle within historical conjunctures also suggests, our Althusserian structuralism was always in tension with our Gramscian historicism. For some of our Centre critics (eg Coward (1977) and Sparks (1996)), this made for an incoherent mixture of expressive marxism (our structuralism) and an 'ideological' reading of signification (our culturalism). Perhaps. But perhaps, paradoxically, the work's strength lay precisely in its ability to straddle both traditions: by reading Gramsci through Althusser we could use Althusser's structuralism to negate Gramsci's incipient culturalism, and vice versa. Be all that as it may, the conception of agency, within either a structuralist or a culturalist tradition, was one with which I was to become increasingly unhappy. But that was still some way off.

Relative autonomy and the problem of mediations: the 1980s and understanding policework

One could argue that the relation between the levels – structural/cultural; economic/political/ideological – was *the* problem for 20th century marxism. Althusser's insistence on the political and the ideological levels being relatively autonomous from the economic level that was, nonetheless, determinant '*in the last instance*' (Althusser 1969: 112; emphasis in original) – even though, in real historical time 'from the first moment to the last, the lonely hour of the "last instance" never comes' (*ibid*: 113) – defined the problem that proved insoluble within the terms of its structuralist straitjacket. Insolubility notwithstanding, the general questions for many of us became:

(1) How were economic conditions/structural contradictions *mediated* (at the other levels)?

(2) How did such mediations impact at the level of *consciousness*?

The first of these questions preoccupied me for the decade of the 1980s when I researched and wrote on policing in an attempt to understand the 'relative autonomy' of the police, a major institution of the capitalist state (in Althusser's terms part of both the Repressive State Apparatus as well as the Ideological State Apparatuses), which was itself crucial to an understanding of the political and ideological levels. Through a participant observation study assisted by a lot of grounded theorising, we (Roger Grimshaw and I) identified and explored the relations among four key structural mediations – that we identified as the law, the organisation, the occupational culture and the public (and reconceptualised as three structures, namely, law, work and democracy). In turn we were able, I think consistently, to explain how and why different kinds of policework – beat patrol policing, community policing, specialist public order policing and detectives – operate in rather different ways; how the structure of law determined which of the structures was dominant in any given instance of policework (Grimshaw and Jefferson 1987; see also Jefferson and Grimshaw 1984 and Jefferson 1990). Certainly, we were able to show that a purely symbolic interactionist approach with its myopic attentiveness to the detail of the immediate, cultural life-world of police officers (and its scandalous inattention to the structural conditions that made 'cop culture' possible) was misleading. Although we enlarged the conception of what constituted a structural understanding of policework to encompass new mediations, overall we still failed to transcend our structuralist starting point (despite our efforts to invoke Gramsci and Foucault). In a field that was hostile to marxism in both its structuralist and culturalist variants, perhaps we should not have been surprised that this work found few supporters.

Post-structuralism, discourse and the unconscious: the 1990s, masculinity, fear of crime and the psychosocial

The question of how mediations impacted at the level of consciousness, the second of the two questions mentioned earlier, was one that also preoccupied Althusser. In the second part of his classic essay 'Ideology and ideological state apparatuses' (1971), he reworks ideas of the psychoanalyst Lacan to argue that ideology works essentially through misrecognition since it 'represents the imaginary relationship of individuals to their real conditions of existence' (p 153). Crucially, the experiencing subject is an effect of ideology since *'all ideology has the function ... of "constituting" concrete individuals as subjects'* (p 160; emphasis in original). In other words, ideology works because we, as ideological subjects, live these imaginary relations as if they were true: as if they were the real relations in which we live (cf Hirst 1976: 12). For a while this understanding of ideology seemed promising. It was certainly seen to offer a way of transcending the reductive idea within traditional marxism of ideology as a set of false ideas producing, in turn, the false consciousness of the pre-revolutionary proletariat. In its use of the psychoanalytic ideas of Lacan, it appeared to offer a route to a more complex understanding of the psyche. But, as we shall see, Lacan too was trapped within a structuralist straitjacket. This certainly constituted part of his appeal to Althusser (see Althusser 1993: 186); however, something else was needed to advance our understanding of consciousness, false or otherwise.

In biographical terms this conjuncture coincided with the development of my interest in masculinity, the origins of which were political (the emergence of feminism), professional (inheriting a course entitled 'Women, feminism and the law'), and personal (needing a better understanding of difficulties in my personal life). Inspired by the notion 'the personal is political' and especially by the increasing awareness of disjunctions between the two – the professionally successful who were personally unhappy; the rationally coherent who were emotionally a mess – the issue of subjectivity (or how mediations impacted at the level of consciousness, to use the terms of the inherited marxist problematic) seemed unavoidable. However, despite feminism's concern with the personal, men did not seem to warrant the same sensitive attention being visited upon the erstwhile 'invisible' lives of ordinary women. For radical feminists, busily revamping our understanding of sexual offences and domestic violence, the male subject disappeared into everyman to become the bearer of all patriarchy's woes: dominant, powerful, controlling – and always potentially violent. The emergent pro-feminist men's movement, of which I was briefly a part, was too apologetic for the millennia of ills 'we' had visited on our mothers, sisters and wives to challenge such a uni-dimensional portrait. Politically, I thought this was disastrous, arguing that unless men recognised themselves in the portraits offered up in their name, they were unlikely to be moved to want to change (Jefferson 1994: 11).

Unfortunately, other feminist accounts of gender, even those that took psychoanalysis (and hence subjectivity) seriously, remained, ultimately, overly social. In Connell's *Gender and Power* (1987) – the first and best of his many books on gender – he has a chapter on 'Gender formation and psychoanalysis'. There he looks at a range of psychosocial approaches to gender formation, many of which – from Karl Mannheim, Wilhelm Reich and the Frankfurt School to more contemporary feminists like Nancy Chodorow in the object relations tradition and Juliet Mitchell and Luce Irigaray in the Lacanian tradition – adopt a position he calls 'embedding'. By this he understands the process by which social movements (like fascism) or social systems (like capitalism or patriarchy) 'can establish links with unconscious mental processes and thus gain mass support regardless of [their] irrationality and destructiveness' (Connell 1987: 201).

In the case of Nancy Chodorow in *The Reproduction of Mothering* (1978), the irrationality of patriarchy and the sexual division of labour is reproduced because, psychodynamically, boys and girls establish 'different patterns of attachment to the mother' (Connell 1987: 202). These result in the 'typical' girl having a greater need for relatedness (and thus in her being better equipped psychologically for mothering than men) and the typical boy's greater need for autonomy. Despite Chodorow's (1989: 7) later disavowal of this thesis for 'giving determinist primacy to social relations', it has been a massively influential neo-Freudian account of gender development. Although it offers a theorisation of the links between unconscious mental processes and society (unlike our exclusively social attempt in *Policing the Crisis*), it remains a typical, somewhat normative, biography. Put another way, 'embedding' theories, whatever their other particular merits (for which I have no time here) ignore the difficulties many experience in becoming socialised and hence the complexities involved in theorising the relation between subjectivity and the social; what we might call the disjunctive logic of psychoanalysis.

At this point, fortuitously, I discovered *Changing the Subject* (Henriques et al 1984/1998). First published in 1984, its goal was to revamp traditional psychology's crude, 'rational-unitary' notion of the subject, in the light of feminism and post-structuralist theorising, especially the work of Saussure on linguistics, Foucault on discourse, and the neo-Freudian writings of the analysts Jacques Lacan and Melanie

Klein. This was a sophisticated, multi-faceted and developing set of arguments (cf Hollway 1989). For present purposes, however, suffice to say that, over time, the structural linguistics of Saussure gets abandoned in favour of a thoroughly historicised, post-structuralist view of language. Lacan's rereading of Freud through the lens of structural linguistics (with its resulting universal subject who is forever condemned to misrecognise him- or herself in language and to desire the impossible return to the pre-oedipal moment of narcissistic union with the mother) is replaced by a relational version of the psychoanalytic subject. The first of these moves entailed a shift from language to discourse; the latter, the move to Klein.

Where structural linguistics rendered the sign arbitrary but went on to fix its meaning, thereby undercutting its radical potential, Foucault permanently unfixed meaning. He did this by thoroughly historicising it through his fundamental idea of 'discourse': 'a group of statements which provide a language for talking about a particular topic at a particular historical moment' (Hall 1992: 291), but also anything that produces meaning. Since 'things' only acquire meaning within discourse, we can only know anything about the world – the structures and cultures of class, race and gender, for example – through the discourses historically available to do so: 'nothing has any meaning outside of discourse' (Foucault 1972). Since relations of power construct everything, including all fields of knowledge, truth becomes relativised: historical 'regimes of truth' emerge from the successful application of power/knowledge within particular discursive formations.

But, if Foucault offers an important new and historicised way of thinking about the social, which as we shall see was to prove indispensable for the authors of *Changing the Subject*, his account of the subject, despite his increasing interest in the topic and later changes in conceptualisation, remains, like Lacan's linguistic subject, too social because, in Foucault's case, too discursive. The idea that nothing has any meaning outside of discourse tells us nothing about how we come to locate ourselves within a discourse, and hence make sense of it. As Stuart Hall (2001: 80) puts it, we 'must locate ... ourselves in the position from which the discourse makes most sense, and thus become its "subjects" by "subjecting" ourselves to its meanings, power and regulation. All discourses, then, construct *subject positions*, from which alone they make sense' (emphasis in original).

The important question this poses is how particular subject positions come to make 'most sense' to particular subjects. Clearly structural location (in terms of class, race, gender and the like) can provide no guarantee of consciousness, as the endemic and insoluble problem of 'false consciousness' was to prove for marxists and later for feminists, most distressingly in the phenomenon of women who continued to 'love' their abusive husbands. It was this particular 'gap' in Foucault's theorising that forced the authors of *Changing the Subject* back to psychoanalytic theory, specifically to the work of Melanie Klein.

Like Freud, Klein's theory is rooted in biological premises, such as the centrality of the instincts of Life and Death and their role in unconscious phantasies. However, it is her radical notion that 'instincts are *always directed towards objects*' (Frosh 1999: 122; emphasis in original) that 'holds out a perspective for the construction of a psychoanalysis that takes account of social relations' (*ibid*: 127). Moreover, in spelling out processes by which an initially split psyche can achieve some integration, it does enable observable differences in the levels of integration of actual subjects to be explained (as well as having a rather more progressive political potential than the unchangeable and illusory world founded on 'lack' of the Lacanian subject).

Crucial to Klein's 'object relational' approach are the earliest, relational defence mechanisms of 'splitting' (the holding apart of good and bad impulses), 'projection' ('the phantasised insertion into the external world of impulses that originate within oneself': Frosh 1999: 128), 'introjection' ('the phantasised taking into the self of material that lies outside': p 128) and 'projective identification' (when 'parts of the self are projected on to external objects and then identified with': p 130). By separating the good from the bad, these defence mechanisms protect the fragile, emergent ego from the earliest anxieties and thus play a crucial developmental role. Although things can go wrong with splitting, gradually:

> if all goes well and is not disrupted either by excessively strong constitutional destructiveness or by a harmful environment, the child forms the belief that the ideal object is stronger than the bad object and, commensurately, that her or his own libidinal impulses are stronger than her or his destructive ones. This makes it easier for the ego to identify with the ideal object, in turn making the use of extreme mechanisms of defence less necessary. (Frosh 1999: 132–33)

When the child is able to perceive the mother as a whole object, as the source both of nurture (good) and frustration (bad), the child's attitude towards her is characterised by ambivalence. Klein referred to this as the depressive position. It is important to stress two things about this: the paranoid-schizoid position is never simply outgrown but can characterise adult relations as well; its transcendence does depend on the quality of the child's experiences with the environment: 'the necessary condition is that there should be a predominance of good over bad experiences. To this predominance, both internal and external factors contribute' (Segal 1973: 37, quoted in Frosh 1999: 132).

Wendy Hollway, both in *Changing the Subject* and in her later, single authored text, *Subjectivity and Method in Psychology* (1989), used these ideas to make sense of her material on adult heterosexual relationships. Broadly, she identified three contemporary discourses of sexuality (male sexual drive, 'have/hold' and permissive) and how gender-differentiated power relations affect the available subject positions: for example, the absence of a subject position for women in the male sexual drive discourse. Here is Foucault in concrete action. The take up of particular subject positions can only be understood, she argues, in terms of 'investment' – some satisfaction these deliver for an individual, some reason that 'is not necessarily conscious or rational' (Hollway 1984: 238). Investments can only be understood in relation to an individual's particular history, or biography, and, since the taking up of subject positions is a relational activity, inter-subjectively. Here Klein is used to show the importance of power and anxiety in relational dynamics:

> Over and again in my material, I found that the positions that people took up in gender-differentiated discourses made sense in terms of their interest in gaining them enough power in relation to the other to protect their vulnerable selves ... It led me to think that it was not so much desire but power which is the motor for positioning in discourses and the explanation of what is suppressed in signification ... (Hollway 1989: 60)

Partly because she often found that the positions that made people feel vulnerable in relationships were projected onto the other, a defensive manoeuvre originating in anxiety, she concluded that 'anxiety ... provides a continuous, more or less driven, motive for the negotiation of power in relations' (Hollway 1989: 85) However, to ward off any charge of biologism, given Klein's primordial view of anxiety, she also suggests a way of reading anxiety as a product of culture not nature: '[T]he way that the infant is positioned by adults, as a result of their anxieties, defence mechanisms and power relations, as well as their access to differentiated positions in discourses, means that anxiety for human infants can be culturally inevitable, rather than naturally so' (p 85). One easily recognisable example used to demonstrate all this is the fear of commitment shown by many of her male respondents. Discursively, commitment is signified by the subject position in the 'have/hold' discourse. Taking up such a position with all the associated significations of closeness and dependency can make men feel vulnerable. This then gets suppressed in the interest of self-protection and may be projected onto a female partner. If she successfully introjects this projection a conventionally gender-differentiated relationship results.

Overall, it is hard to disagree with her endpoint:

> Relationships are always the product of two or more people's unique histories, the contradictions between meanings (suppressed and expressed), differentiated positions in available discourses, the flux of their continuous renegotiated power relations and the effect of their defence mechanisms. Thus they are never simply determined, either by the intentions of those involved, or by language/discourse. (Hollway 1989: 84–85)

It was this broad approach that seemed to offer a way of thinking about masculinity that was attentive to both the inner, psychic realm and the external world of social meanings. Thus, my Tyson project was conceived.

Mike Tyson and the destructive desires of masculinity

I named my Tyson project 'the destructive desires of masculinity' (Jefferson 1996a, 1996b, 1997, 1998) because my starting point was a question implicitly addressed to simplistic versions of sex role theorising underpinning both traditional social psychological and radical feminist accounts of gender formation; namely, if sex role socialisation was a relatively unproblematic achievement, and men appear to get the better deal, how can we explain why so many men apparently self-destruct? In Tyson's case, how was it that a millionaire boxer with the world apparently at his feet managed to 'blow it' so comprehensively? In other words, how might outer world masculine success be thought about in relation to a disastrous personal life which included, among other things, allegations of sexual assault, a rape conviction, domestic violence and a failed marriage? What I did in attempting an answer to this apparent (but common) paradox, over a series of papers, was, first, to deconstruct his life discursively and then analyse the subject positions he appeared to adopt in terms specifically of the gendered nature of the anxieties that seemed to result from the times when he did adopt more vulnerable positions. My data comprised all (which was considerable) that was then published about Tyson – journalistic biographies, books (of the trial), magazine and newspaper articles. Although I did manage to interview some journalists in Indianapolis in connection with the rape trial, and his appellate lawyer, Alan Dershowitz, this was essentially an analysis of his life as mediated by journalists. This creates certain problems, of course, when dealing with a high-profile 'celebrity' figure like Tyson: circulating 'myths' can quickly acquire the status of 'fact'. But, with care and an enquiring scepticism, along with a general willingness to test (or ignore) contentious claims, it is possible, I think, to use such material productively. In theoretical terms, it did not shift the terms of the debate that I outlined in the last section, although it did offer an analysis based on a whole biography rather than the focused interviews of Hollway (1989).

Anxiety, gender difference and the fear of crime

The next big move for me was an Economic and Social Research Council-funded project with Wendy Hollway on Fear of Crime. Fear of crime was, and is, topical within criminology for a host of reasons too numerous to outline here. We saw this as an opportunity to test the psychoanalytically (specifically now, Kleinian) inspired psychosocial theorising that by now informed both our work as individuals. Although 'gender difference' found its way into the title, surprisingly it played little part subsequently. Rather, our concern was to introduce a third theoretical term – anxiety – into a debate that had become hopelessly hung-up on the idea that only two terms – risk and fear – were relevant. But, when risk (routinely) failed to predict fear, as it was assumed it should have done, fearful subjects at low risk of crime were dismissed as 'irrational' and in need of education about their real level of risk (much in the way that racism is seen as a simple function of ignorance to be dealt with by education). Our solution was to theorise the relation between personal anxiety and the position of the fearing subject within the historically specific discourse of fear of crime, and then to demonstrate, through the transcripts of interviews conducted with men and women from both a high-crime and a low-crime housing estate in a northern English city, how anxiety could explain the 'irrational' fearing subject, albeit through singular, biographical routes. In conducting interviews designed to detect anxiety that is always defended against, we developed what we came to call the Free Association Narrative Interview method, where narratives were elicited using open questions and followed up along the tracks of the subject's free associations after the fashion of the psychoanalytic session (see Hollway and Jefferson 2000).

Conclusion: the new millennium

The most recent theoretical move for me has come through the effort to understand more specifically the relationship between anxiety and masculinity, drawing especially on the work of Jessica Benjamin (1998). Space does not permit me to take this further here (see Jefferson 2002), but it is an indication of much still to be done on the psychosocial front. My journey to this point is inevitably somewhat idiosyncratic in that contingent opportunities and unconscious motivations have played their part. However, I hope also to have demonstrated a logic in the journey, one that is broadly traceable to the intellectual problems thrown up by marxism in both its culturalist and structuralist modes of theorising. In doing so, I have tried to stay true to what I take to be the enduring concerns of cultural studies: the products, practices, institutions and meanings of culture, their relation to power and to how they are subjectively experienced and changed over time.

No doubt others who have taken a different route might conclude in similar fashion. So, let me re-emphasise the differences of my psychosocial approach from other dominant approaches in contemporary cultural studies, namely, Lacanian, discursive and identity-based approaches. Although I have found a Kleinian-influenced approach to my data more rewarding, I am aware of the enormous influence of Lacan on contemporary cultural studies. Could it be that Lacan and Klein can be usefully deployed in tandem, depending on the topic in question? Maybe; but, given that Lacan was even more of a structuralist than Althusser (1993: 333), serious misgivings remain, I'm afraid. I have similar doubts about discursive analysis (now so often the methodological tool of choice) when it is conducted without any attention to the question that has long preoccupied me, namely, that of motivational investments in particular subject positions in discourse. Finally, identity-based work, in which everybody expresses an interest these days. However complexly fragmented, the post-modern conception of identity is still invariably cultural or social, devoid of an inner world; which is to say, s/he has no subjectivity. As I see it, a subject-less identity seems no advance on an Althusserian one of subjects as (psychic-less) effects of structures. In the light of what we now know about Althusser's biography (Althusser 1993) – his life-long battle with depression, chronic anxiety, constant suicidal tendencies, strong fear of women and the recurrent bouts of 'madness' during one of which he murdered his wife – to see his identity as a philosopher and communist as unrelated to his tortured psyche is a form of denial. Althusser himself eventually conceded this when, in his longest (and most moving) piece of writing, his autobiographical memoir written in the painful aftermath of facing the fact that he had killed his beloved Helene, he tries to make sense of his life; in my terms, psychosocially.

If the collapse of communism, represented most dramatically by the destruction of the Berlin Wall in 1989, signified an obvious watershed that transformed the theoretical landscape of cultural studies forever (most obviously in the 'death' of marxist cultural studies; see Sparks 1996: 72), it is a pity that the collapse of Althusser's mental health, exemplified most tragically in the killing of his wife in 1980, was not accorded any theoretical significance whatsoever, but dismissed as a moment of 'madness' – and then ignored. Had we been forced to think about it, we could not have avoided the psychosocial connections that are threaded through his memoir. As a psychosocial account of a 'domestic' murder it is exemplary; at which point, fortuitously, we return to criminology.

Conclusions are always somewhat artificial, not least because of the illusory nature of an endpoint. In reality, I continue to grapple with the issues raised here, currently through the writing of a book on psychosocial criminology and participating in a research project on racial violence using FANI-type interviews with people convicted of racially motivated offences. The hope, as always, is that more reading, researching, thinking, discussing and writing will generate new insights and understandings; the fear, never far behind, is that any small gains will be accompanied by the loss of what you thought you knew, be challenged or ignored, or simply be overtaken by events in the world. Writing these words reminds me of Gramsci's much pithier phrase: 'pessimism of the intellect, optimism of the will'. Pinned to Stuart Hall's office door for years, they were virtually the first words I saw at Birmingham. Over the years I have taken great comfort from them. Now, I feel more ambivalent about them: splitting the will from the intellect seems too simple, too idealistic. Perhaps this change best sums up my journey. Or, as Dylan so cryptically put it 40 years ago, 'Ah, but I was so much older then, I'm younger than that now'.

References

Althusser, L (1969) 'Contradiction and overdetermination', in *For Marx*, Harmondsworth: Penguin

Althusser, L (1971) 'Ideology and ideological state apparatuses', in *Lenin and Philosophy and Other Essays*, London: New Left Books

Althusser, L (1993) *The Future Lasts Forever: A Memoir*, New York: New Press

Benjamin, J (1998) *Shadow of the Other*, New York: Routledge

Chodorow, NJ (1978) *The Reproduction of Mothering*, Berkeley: University of California Press

Chodorow, NJ (1989) *Feminism and Psychoanalytic Theory*, London: Yale UP

Clarke, J, Hall, S, Jefferson, T and Roberts, B (1976) 'Subcultures, cultures and class: a theoretical overview', in Hall, S and Jefferson, T (eds), *Resistance through Rituals*, London: Hutchinson

Cohen, P (1972) 'Subcultural conflict and working class community' 2 *Working Papers in Cultural Studies* 5–51

Connell, RW (1987) *Gender and Power*, Cambridge: Polity

Coward, R (1977) 'Class, "culture" and the social formation' 18(1) *Screen* 75–105

Foucault, M (1972) *The Archaeology of Knowledge*, London: Tavistock

Frosh, S (1999) *The Politics of Psychoanalysis*, 2nd edn, Basingstoke: Macmillan

Goodey, J (2000) 'Biographical lessons for criminology' 4(4) *Theoretical Criminology* 473–98

Grimshaw, R and Jefferson, T (1987) *Interpreting Policework*, London: Allen & Unwin

Hall, S (1980) 'Cultural studies: two paradigms' 2(1) *Media, Culture and Society* 57–72

Hall, S (1992) 'The west and the rest', in Hall, S and Gieben, B (eds), *Formations of Modernity*, Cambridge: Polity/Open University

Hall, S (2001) 'Foucault: power, knowledge and discourse', in Wetherell, M, Taylor, S and Yates, S (eds), *Discourse Theory and Practice*, London: Sage

Hall, S and Jefferson, T (eds) (1976) *Resistance through Rituals*, London: Hutchinson

Hall, S, Critcher, C, Jefferson, T, Clarke, J and Roberts, B (1978) *Policing the Crisis*, Basingstoke: Macmillan

Henriques, J, Hollway, W, Urwin, C, Venn, C and Walkerdine, V (1984/1998) *Changing the Subject*, London: Routledge

Hirst, PQ (1976) 'Problems and advances in the theory of ideology', Cambridge: Cambridge University Communist Party

Hollway, W (1984) 'Gender difference and the production of subjectivity', in Henriques, J, Hollway, W, Urwin, C, Venn, C and Walkerdine, V (1984/1998) *Changing the Subject*, London: Routledge

Hollway, W (1989) *Subjectivity and Method in Psychology*, London: Sage

Hollway, W and Jefferson, T (2000) *Doing Qualitative Research Differently*, London: Sage

Jefferson, T (1990) *The Case Against Paramilitary Policing*, Buckingham: Open UP

Jefferson, T (1994) 'Theorising masculine subjectivity', in Newburn, T and Stanko, EA (eds), *Just Boys Doing Business?*, London: Routledge

Jefferson, T (1996a) 'From "little fairy boy" to "the compleat destroyer"', in Mac an Ghaill, M (ed), *Understanding Masculinities*, Buckingham: Open UP

Jefferson, T (1996b) '"Tougher than the rest"' 6 *Arena Journal* 89–105

Jefferson, T (1997) 'The Tyson rape trial' 6(2) *Social and Legal Studies* 281–301

Jefferson, T (1998) 'Muscle, "hard men" and "iron" Mike Tyson' 4(1) *Body & Society* 77–98

Jefferson, T (2002) 'Subordinating hegemonic masculinity' 6(1) *Theoretical Criminology* 63–88

Jefferson, T and Grimshaw, R (1984) *Controlling the Constable*, London: Muller/The Cobden Trust

Segal, H (1973) *Introduction to the Work of Melanie Klein*, London: Hogarth

Sparks, C (1996) 'Stuart Hall, cultural studies and marxism', in Morley, D and Chen, K-H (eds), *Stuart Hall*, London: Routledge

Taylor, I, Walton, P and Young, J (1973) *The New Criminology*, London: Routledge and Kegan Paul

Chapter 3
The Story of Crime: Biography and the Excavation of Transgression

Mike Presdee

Anti-social behaviour: inertia, resistance and silence.

(Baudrillard 1990: 10)

The history and dominant themes of cultural criminology have been discussed and rehearsed elsewhere, especially in the recent cultural criminology edition of *Theoretical Criminology* (Vol 8 No 3, 2004). Here I want to concentrate on one particular recurring theme: the prioritising of biographical accounts of everyday life – with their ability to produce superior descriptions and explanations of crime and transgression – over and against quantitative accounts of crime, criminality and criminalisation that re-produce numerical life rather than everyday life. Since the emergence of academic disciplines structured on 'rational' lines, there has been a seemingly irrevocable disjuncture between scientific knowledge and everyday experience, with the former dominating research into the latter. This quantitative rational scientific approach is epitomised by those government agencies that I have described elsewhere as 'fact factories' (Presdee 2004), their role being the production of 'suitable' facts to support governments and their existing and future political agendas. But too much information is no information. The more facts we have the less we really know. Facts are in reality a form of disinformation, an obesity of the system that distorts rather than informs and gives shape. They become the 'sacred shit' of a rational society (Baudrillard 1990: 43).

But why this aversion to and wariness of institutional/political rational scientific research? Firstly I have a problem with its unquestioning sense of what crime is and is about. For administrative criminology, crime is unproblematic in that it is simply that which is described and measured. There is a certainty contained within this approach. After all, you don't measure a room for a new carpet if you can't know its length, breadth and area. We measure what we know and know of. If we know of crime we can measure it, record it, quantify it. For administrative criminology, crime and disorder constitute taken-for-granted categories, unproblematic in their reality.

My second objection is quite simply the way that political parties have the ability to influence both what is researched and how it is researched through the mobilisation of their own power. The rational research methodology is employed precisely because it masks this process of mobilisation. As Pfeffer (1981: 13) observed: 'The emphasis on rationality and efficiency and the de-emphasis on power and politics assures [the general public] ... that ... power ... is indeed, being effectively and legitimately employed.'

These seemingly 'invisible' practices of power hidden within the seams of science create an ethos of the 'necessity' for and the 'naturalness' of a particular pattern of research – a pattern that reflects no more or less than the power and privilege contained within political processes. The result is a nurtured ignorance of the reality of 'real' life, 'lived' life, 'everyday' life. The aim of 'power driven research' then is to prevent people actually raising issues which politicians do not want raised. It is the power to prevent issues actually reaching the agenda or the decisional arena and hence becoming matters of open dispute. It then becomes obvious to all, for example, that we need research into the 'evilness' of 'youth' rather than the oppression of young people; the evils of drink and drugs rather than why we take substances that might even include enjoyment and the excitement of transgression. As the process of political cleansing takes place so the 'political' is removed from the research process leaving, once again, everyday life problematised and pathologised, where people rather than the political process become the subject of research. Yet, from a political perspective, we are all acutely aware that nothing has really started simply because nothing has really come to an end. The political promises of progress, equality and liberty are woven into the seams of history alongside the threads of failure.

It is Lukes' (1974: 24) 'third dimension of power' that is important here. As criminologists we need to consider 'the many ways in which potential issues are kept out of politics [and research] whether through the operation of social forces or through individuals' decisions. This moreover, can occur in the absence of actual observable conflict, which may have been successfully averted, though there remains here an implied reference to potential conflict'.

Contemporary 'spin' shows how power from time to time seeks to avoid resistance either by presenting 'facts' in certain ways or simply by not creating them.[1] It is the role of administrative criminology to help in this process. But the 'rational' research agenda has intrinsic problems in that the difference between rationality and irrationality is that the rational social world *must* make sense whilst the real world of everyday life rarely does. Quantitative research must in the end 'add up' and show clearly and conclusively what is going on and what is to be done. As Scott Lasch remarks:

> In a society that has reduced reason to mere calculation, reason can impose no limits on the pursuit of pleasure – on the immediate gratification of every desire no matter how perverse, insane, criminal or merely immoral. For the standards that would condemn crime or cruelty derive from religion, compassion, or the kind of reason that rejects purely instrumental applications and none of these outmoded forms of thought or feeling has any logical place in a society based on commodity production. (1979: 69)

In a sense Lasch alludes here to the lack of compassion in calculative research approaches, and how such methods are unable to either grasp or understand crime or the causes of crime. This is a methodology where lived experience becomes 'pathologised' or 'marginalised' by the official accounts of crime. For most state researchers (but by no means all) there exists a 'poverty and marginality of experience to which they have no access, structures of feeling that they have not lived within (and would not like to live within). They are caught then in a terrible exclusion from the experiences of others' (Steedman 1986: 17; Ferrell 1997).

This exclusion of the researcher is a form of revenge by the researched, personal compensation for their exclusion from mainstream society. It is a refusal to 'give up' easily one's life for analysis in order that political cures can be administered. The desires that are part of us all lie buried deep within everyday consciousness not

---

1   For a recent example of this practice at work within British criminological research see Tombs and Whyte 2003.

readily available for measuring and monitoring. Yet these emotions are essential elements in understanding the story of crime, they need to be excavated and explored in a way that does not denigrate the lived experiences, the emotional and social responses of the human beings that make up what we call 'society'. EP Thompson (1976: 110) once pleaded elegantly for politicians to stop 'dispensing the potions of analysis to cure the maladies of desire' when he observed that 'the motions of desire may be legible in the text of necessity and may then become subject to rational explanations and criticism. But such criticism can scarcely touch these motions at their heart'.

Indeed it is the sheer stunning theatre of rationality in such research that in the end seems obscene. An excrescence of facts descends on social science, burying everyday life. As Baudrillard remarked, in typical style:

> the rational systems of morality, value, science, reason, command only the linear evolution of societies, their visible history. But the deeper energy that pushes even these things forward comes from elsewhere. From prestige, challenge, from all the seductive or antagonistic impulses, including suicidal ones, which have nothing to do with a social morality or a morality of history of progress. (1990: 72–73)

How best, then, to 'excavate' what Gramsci called the 'précis of the past,' the narratives of everyday life (Gramsci 1971: 353)? We are all the products of everyday life and as such we all have everyday stories. Our identity expressed in the notion of 'I am' contains, as John Berger (1980: 379) memorably pointed out, all our histories, all our biographies, all that has made us what we are. In this sense we are living histories that can be excavated both by ourselves and by others. Elsewhere he commented that everyday life often contained the 'endless longing of the underprivileged that history and life be different from what it has been and what it still is'. He went on to say that much of life is 'concerned with loneliness' and the 'contemplation of time passing without meaning' (ibid: 90–91). This 'unbearable lightness of meaning' that characterises contemporary life leads politicians to make meaning from administration and order, priests from spiritualism, and the dominated from consumption and hedonism. Contrary to Berger's approach, the everyday is not devoid of meaning making, quite the opposite: indeed it is the very place where a sense of popular history is carved and constructed through everyday experience, something clearly recognised within other cultures where 'wisdom' is seen as more valuable than 'knowledge'. Our 'excavations' of everyday life seek to recognise that experience and wisdom can tell us more than official research understandings of life experiences. These experiences lie not just in language but, as Collins suggests, in the created cultural artefacts of social groups.

> Experience as a criterion of meaning with practical images as its symbolic vehicle is a fundamental epistemological tenet in African-American thought systems. (Collins 1990: 209)

It is here in the hazy ephemeral 'being' of everyday life, where 'all that is solid melts into air', that social excavation must take place as we concern ourselves with social lives already formed. In a sense we have arrived too late to know and are left with attempts to excavate that which has already happened. Now we must be involved in the appropriation of the social where we examine both our own past and the past of others. When we look at ourselves, our own creations, it is with the 'seeing' of 'one stranger on another'. We can examine our own histories through our own biographies, but it is not enough to 'speak' history, we must historicise, analyse, that which we describe. (Auto)biography is the raw material, our raw material; it cannot stand on its own, it needs to be 'worked on'.

Our aim in taking a biographical and auto-biographical approach is to take the defiance, the anger, the resentment, the loneliness, the love, the fun, the warmth of an individual life and attempt not to celebrate it but to recognise it as real, as real history, as lived life that will stand as history longer than all the facts created and concocted by all the contemporary alchemists of numerical life who suck the human from life leaving behind the residual numerical skeleton of humanity.

Biography takes that hidden within more traditional academic discourses and brings it to life. If the self is intrinsically social then writing about the 'self' is a sociological act, an interrogating of the 'truths' of experience. As C Wright Mills (1959: 8) maintained, 'the sociological imagination enables us to grasp history and biography and the relations between the two within society. That is its task and its promise'. And I believe it is ours too.

We need both an honesty in what we write and a sociological imagination. Those who transgress are not 'present' in the official 'vocabularies' of crime which have already been appropriated by ideology. The official languages of crime condemn the criminal before trial and our aim must be to re-insert the subject into the discourses of crime. Crime itself is constructed deep in the cracks that make up everyday life. (Auto)biography transforms lived life into a linguistic form that becomes the object of study and once again the subject and the object are as one.

Those actions that make life bearable, that are oppositional, resistant to the dominant culture and its moralities are now able to be 'put' before us. People – our subjects – are not simply the 'blind' result of economic relations. In negotiating social structures they both interpret their lives and invest meaning in their lives. Yet there are no unlimited options for them, there are only so many possibilities open to them, including crime and transgression. In this way they act both individually yet within a collective, a class.

We can, then, bring into the light the lived process of increasing isolation and deepening poverty with its first forms of lived resistance. Vice and transgression have an energy that perverts reality, creating the spectacle of debauchery (anarchic life) that shatters Platonic life. Here is the anarchic carnival of everyday life where 'joy and the fulfillment of desires prevail over toil' (Lefebvre 1971: 16). After all, the 'fun' of gambling is more powerful than work with its promise of 'release' from poverty and failure.

We need always to remind ourselves that we are not 'pieces of nature' but have 'become' who we are and therefore are subject to change. In allowing the stories of life to include the minutest of details; in investing all stories with the description of truth; in not being judgmental; and finally in not allowing pre-existing prejudice to interfere with the stories we gather, then, and only then, will we begin to fully understand the story of crime. With excavation we begin to understand how crime comes into being, the causes of crime and the creation of the criminal whilst appreciating more that crime can only be created through social relations made within a dominant culture and determined by a dominant morality.

That is, we will see the 'humanness' of the crime story if we let people write and tell their stories without hindrance. In the past this approach was seen as the domain of the 'analyst' using the Freudian notion that every life, every existence, has a story. Now it must become the domain of the criminologist! Empathy can be an obstacle to knowledge, to knowing and understanding the 'social dressage' of life and how we come to behave properly or not within our social position. Yet we need to examine the emotional world of the everyday as a means perhaps of achieving change. It is at times a harrowing experience just listening but listen we must. We need to work out the ways in which we and others construct ourselves in the active creative process of producing our identities, to see how we create our own chains, our own constrictions. Then and only then will we be able to see the 'hidden injuries of class'.

What, then, is the meaning, the 'point' of the crime story? Does it talk of 'things' or 'relationships,' 'success' or 'drama'? We never forget that all sections and segments of society have emotions: they hurt, they hate, they envy, they love, they feel anxious; their stories of transgression are full of the emotions of everyday lives lived within the structures of loss, envy, and the sheer celebration of their place in society.

Once again I mention the continuing conundrum of celebration. What elements of biographical work, if any, should we celebrate? Should we, ought we, celebrate defiance in all its forms, even though it might be violent, racist, sexist? Should we, ought we, celebrate the immoral and the unethical just because it 'resists' overwhelming oppression? Is it the sheer *joie de vivre*, against all odds that we want to applaud, those irrational and irresponsible acts that fly in the face of official rational life? Or is it the sheer sense of survival that we admire because it shows that, yes, there is life in many forms outside of the ordered banality of contemporary capitalism? For the excluded everyday life is characterised by an unarticulated form of social anarchy: yet surely they simply want to be included, to be part of a more equal and just society? Are we then in danger of living our own defiance through them, through those whose ethnographies we explore and use? In the end it is 'they' who celebrate that they feel alive through whatever transgressive acts become part of their everyday lives. We can only contemplate their celebration as being a necessary part of their everyday lives in that there appears to be a need to celebrate transgression, defiance, resistance as an integral part of everyday life. Triumph over authority and authority's imperatives is part and parcel of everyday existence. Indeed crimes of excitement, like conspicuous consumption, need to be seen, to be public, in a sense to be very much 'in your face'.

There is, as Raymond Williams suggested, a connection between past and present that neither we nor those on whom and with whom we work can escape. For example, I cannot conveniently lose my working class upbringing and early adult life. It still structures my way of seeing and interpreting the world. As such my new world is very much influenced, even structured, by my old. The question is what I do with my past and what we do with the stories and insights of the personal lives of others. The point of biographical work is in the interpretation of stories and in how we use them. We need to foreground them, historicise them, make them 'work' for those whose lives we have been privileged to be part of. Our role is not to celebrate but to excavate. Yet the process of excavation necessarily involves critique, and in the writing and publishing of what we find, do we not (once more) betray our subjects for whom I have already suggested we are attempting to work?

Why then do we need to know about the personal intricacies of everyday life? Simply put, because everyday life is essentially about lived loss ... of what we thought we could have, could possess, could be, could experience. When a child is born we look for signs of 'intelligence' that tell us that s/he will be a doctor or lawyer. We cling hopelessly to the idea of a classless meritocracy. Slowly horizons narrow rather than widen as the realities of a powerless life, indeed dare we say a working class life, begin to be realised. From this point the culture of the excluded becomes the culture of exile. In contemporary life we can compare ourselves quickly with others, thereby making the 'loss' clearer, more visible, more acute – felt more deeply than ever before. Previous working class communities provided an enclave that acted as a buffer to the outside world. In a more individualised world the 'loss' is more in focus. We are more 'shamed' than ever before, shamed by failure, by social position, by poverty, by being bad parents, by bad behaviour. Shame produces violence, destruction and social despair. Loss hurts – compensation culture results. Here is where we find the culture of binge drinking, of criminalised fun and enjoyment, a culture that has become defined (in the broadest of terms) as anti-social behaviour.

Loss is the denial of access to a choice of life: the denial of things – that is restrictions on consumption, what we can buy, have, own. It is the denial of emotions such as anger – anger over the very act of denial itself. Here anger must be managed rather than felt and acted upon. What is demanded is a resignation to what 'is' rather than revolt about loss and denial. In this way working class life is deemed (by the dominant culture) to be immature, childlike, rather than, like a mature mind, being able to accept how things are.

But what are the responses of a life lived through denial? If we accept that the everyday experience of exclusion in itself promotes envy and that envy is the 'social and subjective sense of the impossible unfairness of things' (Steedman 1986: 111), then we begin to see that the crime story is a story of unfulfilled lives and desires. The result is an anger, envy and desire for a life denied and for the things we do not possess and furthermore in this society should not have. Envy is an emotion that is no longer 'allowed', not acceptable, thereby transforming itself into the social actions of destruction and crime. Melanie Klein (1975: 306–07) argued that envy had not the sophistication of jealousy and that hatred comes of envy and exclusion, making reparation impossible – which is why social reparation to the oppressed through the work of social policy and social 'work' presents us in the end with no answers.

Now we can begin to see that crimes in everyday life are often about loss and wanting. The media daily remind us of what we don't have, our loss, and in so doing accentuate our wants and desires, something which in turn feeds our state of envy. In the excavation of my own life, *The Muck of Ages*, I describe how crime and 'wanting', for me at least, came together.

> Somewhere, sometime, I started to steal; from my father, the paper shop, the church collection, Woolworth's, Ron next door. Suddenly, it seemed, I was aware of wanting and of being 'without' as advertising and consumerism, driven by the new post war wealth began to be part of my life. When I was very young you either had or you didn't; not really conscious of needing possessions, but simply 'having' or 'not having', yet needing to 'have' to be 'part of', to join in. I wanted to possess, to be a consumer, to own, to escape into the world of the object. Possessing was visual, everyone could see what you were, what you owned: toys, clothes, school uniform, sports gear, food, even haircuts. (Presdee 1988)

Indeed, the excluded even steal in their dreams when, in a Freudian sense, they steal the parents they really want. The parents stolen in our dreams are always parents who have, who own, who live lives devoid of wanting (Steedman 1986: 112). Everyday life in any segment of society is always 24/7; we cannot escape, it never goes away. It is there in our sleep and it is there waiting for us when we wake. Our identities come into being as we seek through culture to soften the chafing of the chains of dominance. In this way our identities reflect either freedom or oppression.

> I had always hoped that Peter Latham would become my friend, but he never did. He was everyone's favourite from the posh side of town and in the privacy of night I created a world where he and I were friends and he invited me to his home where we could have tea together, play together and engage in deep conversations about Latin and cricket and discuss going on holiday together. It was all there in my mind. What his home was like, his parents were like, his life was like. We were friends forever and when I wandered around the green on my own I talked to him and played with him, acting out our life together, oblivious to all outsiders. In reality in the classroom he treated me with indifference, taking my laughter and never repaying it, and try as I might he was never interested, he simply took my jokes and ran. (Presdee 1988)

But 'official' society denies us any response to our loss. Anger and envy, the emotions of loss, are, we are told, to be 'managed' and policed. Above all they must be aimed, as Frank Furedi suggests, at the 'manipulation of people's feelings' which is 'frequently seen as the antidote to anti-social behaviour' (Furedi 2004: 199). Now anger management is the response to a life of exclusion, a form of non-acceptance of and pathologisation of the excluded. It is the ultimate act of rendering justified anger as impotent. What we need is not 'things' but 'therapy'! Politicians promise policies that will deliver a benign feeling of therapeutic happiness they call the 'feel good' factor – or what I often call the 'happy as a pig in shit' approach to life. David Beckham has a personal trainer; the deprived a social worker, probation officer, school non-attendance officer.

> The rules that come with the process of 'acquiring' and 'ownership', seemed more difficult to accept than those of time and place. Stealing time, although an offence, was easier to hide and explain, but stealing 'possessions' was more complex, for whereas stealing 'time' could get you the sack, stealing 'possessions' could get you gaol. But why was it that some people were allowed possessions and others not? Why did some have bikes and others not? Some big homes and others not? Increasingly as I got older, I became more sensitive about displaying myself and my everyday possessions that enabled people to, at a glance, 'place me'; know where I was from and so know when I was 'straying'; when I was out of my place. The accoutrements of class were becoming like a uniform, displaying my rank and position to everyone. I began to feel ashamed of my sewn-up canvas satchel from 'Woolies', that stood out from the shiny leather ones hanging on the backs of other desks. From my shame, slowly developed both defiance and aggression as I excessively and openly consumed, displaying my fragile and dishonest wealth to everyone; a rather disheveled and unkempt young boy growing fat and angry. As I put on weight, so I learned to push it around. I started to learn about violence as an answer to ridicule, and I started to glorify ugliness, learning how to disrupt the sensitivities of those from more sophisticated backgrounds. I learned that the fart and the fist were my only answer, they could take it or leave it. (Presdee 1988)

As criminologists we need to listen to the 'crime stories' of both others and ourselves and begin the long, difficult, but necessary task of 'working it out'. Rather than being judgmental and superior distant beings we need to recognise that we too respond in a human way to the many structures within which we live our lives as academics. We are not special, not separate, not different. We need to be close to all those living the crime story, including ourselves, and work it out together.

References

Baudrillard, J (1990) *Simulations*, London: Pluto

Berger, J (1980) *About Looking*, London: Writers and Readers

Collins, PH (1990) *Black Feminist Thought: Knowledge, Consciousness and the Politics of Empowerment*, London: HarperCollins

Ferrell, J (1997) 'Criminological *verstehen*: inside the immediacy of crime' 14(1) *Justice Quarterly* 3–23

Furedi, F (2004) *Therapy Culture: Cultivating Vulnerability in an Uncertain Age*, London and New York: Routledge

Gramsci, A (1971) *Selections from the Prison Notebooks*, London: Lawrence and Wishart

Klein, M (1975) 'Love, hate, and reparations', in *Love, Hate and Reparations and Other Works, 1921–1948*, London: Hogarth

Lasch, C (1979) *The Culture of Narcissism*, Oxford: Blackwell

Lefebvre, H (1971) *Everyday Life in the Modern World*, London: Harper & Row

Lukes, S (1974) *Power: A Radical View*, London: Macmillan

Pfeffer, J (1981) *Power in Organisations*, Marshfield, MA: Pitman

Presdee, M (1988) *The Muck of Ages*, unpublished

Presdee, M (2004) 'Cultural criminology: the long and winding road' 18(3) *Theoretical Criminology* 275–85

Steedman,C (1986) *Landscape for a Good Woman: A Story of Two Lives*, London: Virago

Thompson, EP (1976) *William Morris: Romantic to Revolutionary*, New York: Pantheon

Tombs, S and Whyte, D (2003) 'Why bad news is no news and crime is big business', *The Times Higher Education Supplement*, 21 November

Wright Mills, C (1959) *The Sociological Imagination*, Oxford: OUP

Chapter 4
Phenomenology, Cultural Criminology and the Return to Astonishment

Jonathan Wender

> A fact is something real, but it is not reality.
>
> *(Heidegger 2001: 54)*

Introduction

An improbable vantage point

The reader will be better able to engage with this chapter if I begin by describing the unusual nature of my interrelated theoretical and practical perspectives. Simply stated, I write as a 'philosopher-cop', who divides his time between academia and street-level policing. Many readers will correctly imagine that a philosopher-cop must be a 'fish out of water' in the realm of policing; however, the reciprocal supposition may not occur to them that I likewise find myself to be no less of an anomalous presence in the world of criminology. In fact, while self-consciously philosophical thinking constitutes a striking incongruity in bureaucratic policing, this is equally so with respect to its place in mainstream criminology. I offer this observation not as biographical trivia, but because I think it represents a telling manifestation of an elective affinity that unites late modernity's predominant bureaucratic and social scientific approaches to crime.

The capacity for astonishment

This elective affinity may be traced to a set of ontological first principles shared by bureaucracy and mainstream social science. After identifying some of these principles, and briefly considering how they form the common foundations of bureaucratic and mainstream social scientific praxis, I shall relate the story of a man who decides to trample on a woman's head. If the preceding sentence has aroused in you even the slightest sense of disconcertment, surprise, or uneasy anticipation, then you have already taken an initial step along the path that I propose to map out and briefly travel in this chapter. The path departs from a point where phenomenology merges with aesthetic reflection, and offers one possible route towards a 'return to astonishment' in late modernity's engagements with crime, transgression, and evil. It is a route that also quite naturally follows the terrain of cultural criminology.

In precise terms, the path to be taken here follows the approach underlying my larger endeavour of a *phenomenological aesthetics of encounter*. The guiding principle of a phenomenological aesthetics of encounter holds that aesthetic forms may be used to reveal aspects of human presence, which are otherwise overlooked in the self-interpretations of everyday action, and their second-order interpretation by mainstream social science (see relatedly Katz 1988 and Ferrell's 'Style Matters', this volume). The aim of this endeavour is to revive a deliberate, mindful attunement to the fullness and mystery of human existence, by approaching human beings other than through their social scientific and bureaucratic reduction to 'subjects' or 'problems'.

The elective affinity between bureaucracy and social science

Critical reflections upon the nature of modernity have long recognised that there is an elective affinity between mainstream social scientific knowledge and bureaucratic praxis, which ultimately derives from their shared ontology. This ontology is enacted through processes of rationalisation, and in the reification of the human being as an abstract 'subject' and calculable 'object'. Well before Foucault developed his genealogical analysis of the disciplinary production of the modern 'individual', Marx, Nietzsche, Weber, the Frankfurt School, and others had all, in varying ways, explored the epistemic nexus linking modern administration, social science, and the self-conception of modernity. My immediate concern is the specific form that this nexus takes in mainstream criminology, through the interweaving of speculative reflections on evil, transgression and human nature with statistical analysis and bureaucratically enacted social control.[1]

The particular elective affinity between modern bureaucracy and mainstream criminology may likewise be traced directly to its ontological roots, which lie in the grounding concepts that inform and orient both kinds of praxis.[2] Once the existence of those roots has been acknowledged, and their profound influence understood, it becomes possible to show how they nourish and support the most mundane kinds of everyday thinking. At the same time – and in a decisively paradoxical fashion – these roots impart to such thinking the illusory notion that it subsists autonomously, apart from its ontological origins.

Human being as a 'problem'

Considered together, the approaches of mainstream social science and bureaucracy rest upon a commanding ontological principle, which I call 'the problematisation of human being'. The problematisation of human being constitutes the guiding notion at the centre of the elective affinity between late modernity's predominant intellectual and practical engagement with 'crime'. Viewed in a historical, social and philosophical context, this form of engagement is extraordinary; for despite the assimilation of the problematisation of human being into the unconsidered, commonsense thinking of mainstream social science and bureaucracy, it is neither natural nor intuitive to look upon another person as 'being a problem'. Quite the contrary, such a perspective manifests the contingent effects of its grounding concepts, from which it is inseparable.

---

1   For further elaboration of the intersection of criminology and modern social administration, see, among many other works, Nelken 1994; Hogg 1998; and Garland and Sparks 2000.
2   The term 'grounding concepts' as I use it here is identical to Martin Heidegger's notion of *Grundbegriffe*, which Stambaugh translates as 'fundamental concepts'. According to Heidegger (1996: 8), '[f]undamental concepts [*Grundbegriffe*] are determinations in which the area of knowledge underlying all the thematic objects of a science attain an understanding that precedes and guides all positive investigation'. For a recent explication of criminology's philosophical underpinnings see Arrigo and Williams (2005).

The preceding characterisation does not merely describe the nature of bureaucratic and social scientific praxis: it expresses the universal conditions intrinsic to all forms of understanding, interpretation, or practical action (see Gadamer 1989 and Heidegger 1996). Any form of praxis, no matter how outwardly 'simple' it might seem, necessarily involves the enactment of ontological notions that define particular beliefs about the nature and meaning of human existence.

A phenomenological critique of the human being as 'problem'

If praxis occurs through the enactment of ontological first principles, it follows that by identifying these principles and suspending their contingent effects, we might realise the full extent of their influence. Likewise, by substituting a contrasting set of ontological first principles for the one we previously accepted without reflection as the unshakable foundation of commonsense, it becomes possible to arrive at an altogether different comportment towards reality. This briefly describes phenomenology's method of the *epoché*, which it uses in attempting to get 'to the things themselves' (see Husserl 1970: 121–47 and 1982, esp pp 51 ff). In the context of thinking critically about late modernity's engagement with 'crime', the *epoché* offers a means of 'suspending' or 'bracketing' the everyday stance of criminological and bureaucratic practitioners, and thereby makes it possible to see what underlies their respective 'natural attitudes' (see Husserl 1982: 53–55). These 'natural attitudes' enable both forms of praxis unquestioningly to engage human being as an abstract problem. In contrast, when differently regarded in the wholeness of its presence, human being reveals itself as utterly mysterious and astonishing.

Attempting such a 'different regard' will occupy the remainder of this chapter. By focusing upon the incident of a man who tramples on a woman's head, and viewing this moment of evil through an aesthetic, rather than a bureaucratic or social scientific eye, we shall glimpse some of what escapes the gaze of problematisation, and thus realise why late modernity's prevailing approaches to crime often leave unconsidered the most crucial aspects of human predicaments.

A moment from the street: Gary and Pamela

At about 1:30 am on a cold, wet winter morning, a colleague and I were dispatched along with an ambulance to a large block of flats after a report of a woman with a head injury. Although the woman told the police operator that she had accidentally slipped and fallen, the operator found the circumstances of the call to be suspicious, and thought it more likely that she had been assaulted.

When my colleague and I arrived at the scene of the call, we found the woman sitting on the kerb in the pouring rain, cradling her head in her hands. She was bleeding from a badly swollen, egg-sized lump on her forehead. The woman, Pamela,[3] was dazed and incoherent. I asked her how she had injured her head. 'It's nothing,' she demurred flatly; 'I just fell down.' I knew immediately from the tone of her voice that she was lying. As my colleague and I persisted in asking Pamela what had really happened, she eventually revealed that her boyfriend, Gary, had assaulted

---

3   All names have been changed.

her. Pamela was clearly terrified of Gary. She would not even divulge her address, apparently out of fear that he would blame her if he were arrested.

Paramedics transported Pamela to the emergency room for further evaluation. An officer followed the ambulance to the hospital to gather evidence, and to see if Pamela was able or willing to give a formal statement. In the meantime, another officer and I went to Pamela's flat to see if we could find Gary. Although the exact circumstances of the incident remained unclear, we knew that there was probable cause to arrest Gary for domestic violence assault.

The lights in the flat were on, but no one responded to our loud knocking. I checked the front door, and discovered that it was unlocked. We suspected that Gary was inside the flat, and proceeded to search it. Our suspicions proved correct: my colleague found Gary hiding beneath a bed. I ordered Gary to crawl out, and to remain prone on the floor. He emerged, but immediately tried to stand up. My partner and I pulled him back down to the floor, and handcuffed him after a brief struggle. Gary reeked strongly of liquor and sweat, and was experiencing wide mood swings. When my partner searched Gary, he found several boxes of handgun ammunition in his coat and trouser pockets. We also retrieved three handguns from the bedroom where he had been hiding.

During an interview at the police station following his arrest, Gary waived his right to silence and legal counsel, and gave one of my colleagues a disturbingly frank account of his assault against Pamela. Gary said that he and Pamela had been drinking together in the flat block's clubhouse, where tenants gather to socialise. Gary explained that when they left, Pamela slipped on the wet concrete, fell down a short flight of stairs, and landed on her hands and knees. When asked what happened next, Gary replied, 'I just decided to kick her in the head'. He confessed that he jumped from the top step, and intentionally landed his heavy work boot right on the back of Pamela's head, driving it into the concrete with the full force of his bodyweight. The interviewing officer found hair from Pamela's head on the sole of Gary's boot. He entered the boot and hair into evidence, along with matching hair samples from Pamela.

Gary began sobbing after he confessed to assaulting Pamela. However, Gary's written statement was emotionless. Unlike many domestic violence suspects, who seek to rationalise their actions, Gary offered no claim that Pamela had provoked the attack, and made no effort to conceal the fact that, on the spur of the moment, he had simply decided to stomp on his girlfriend's head after she had already fallen on the wet steps. Gary was booked into gaol for felony domestic violence assault.

After the attack, Gary returned home, leaving Pamela unconscious on the sidewalk in the pouring rain. Hospital staff said that, under the circumstances, she easily could have been critically injured or killed. As it happens, she escaped with a mild concussion.

Pamela subsequently disclosed a long history of domestic violence in her relationship with Gary, including multiple episodes of attempted strangulation, and an incident in which she said he cocked back the hammer of a pistol, put it to her head, and threatened to kill her. Despite all of this, Pamela made it clear that she would not co-operate with prosecutors and investigators.

Re-thinking method as approach

Gary's attack on Pamela became the subject of a criminal case that began with the patrol response by my colleagues and me, and expanded to include – among others – detectives, a domestic violence investigator and victim advocate, records personnel, and prosecutors. As part of this process, the attack was translated into a statistical datum, deemed officially significant and preserved accordingly using a wide range of bureaucratic instruments: officers' activity logs, counts of dispatched 'calls for service', federal and state criminal records, crime analysis reports, expenditure calculations for domestic violence grant funds, and so forth. The attack could also, in like manner, become the 'object' of criminological research. Indeed, with its discussion here, such a transition from bureaucratic praxis to intellectual reflection seems altogether simple and unproblematic.

It is at this very point that we must pause, and suspend the natural attitude that frames this otherwise unconsidered dynamic. In doing so, we suddenly find ourselves facing an urgent question: how is the utterly astonishing act of one human being intentionally trampling on the head of another made a significant 'matter of fact' by intersecting forms of bureaucratic and social scientific interpretive praxis? To engage this question from a phenomenological perspective, we may rephrase it by asking how it is that bureaucracy and mainstream criminology *approach* an incident such as Gary's assault against Pamela. This reformulation discloses something decisive about the ontological relation between method and proximity, and also suggests why the metaphor of the path that I use above, in the introduction, represents more than stylistic preference.[4] In particular, a phenomenological analysis of the concept of 'method' reveals that before its formal engagement as a scientifically or practically manageable 'problem', method centres upon deciding how to ascribe meaning to the people and things in whose presence we already find ourselves.

A phenomenological comment on 'method'

This is why the question 'what is your method?' may also be stated as 'what is your method for approaching this situation?' or 'how do you approach this subject?'. Both phrases indicate how, prior to any formal reflections upon method and methodology, we have an elemental idea that 'method' involves *coming near* to someone or something. To find the 'best method' for accomplishing a given task is thus understood as determining how one ought to *approach* it. When we speak of the 'best method', we often refer metaphorically to the best or easiest 'way' to arrive at a given end (see Heidegger 2001: 101). Literally understood, to approach something means to draw near to it. However, the idea of approach extends beyond physical proximity: in an abstract or metaphorical sense, to approach something is to be concerned with it or to engage it from a certain intentional stance.

Hence, the technical 'problem of method', which most forms of praxis ordinarily engage strictly in limited operational or epistemological terms, is ontologically contingent upon the irreducible state of existential proximity. With this idea in mind, further phenomenological analysis will allow us to bracket the natural attitudes underlying criminological and bureaucratic 'method' in a manner that begins to reveal their ontological contingencies.

---

4   Readers familiar with the work of Heidegger will also recognise here and in the introduction my debt to his *Holzwege* (*Woodland Paths*) (1963).

Abstraction versus astonishment

Owing to the usual manner in which bureaucracy and mainstream criminology approach an event such as Gary's attack on Pamela, crime's astonishing reality often recedes from view, as it becomes translated into and enciphered as an object or problem. So it is that each form of praxis blithely goes about its business in a matter-of-fact way. As a result of the inexorable drive to attain its pre-determined ends, this approach often conflates the 'subjects' and 'objects' resulting from its practical manipulations with the existential whole from which they have been abstracted and isolated. Moreover, any normative judgment aimed at restricting or overcoming this dynamic eventually conflicts with the self-proclaimed 'neutrality and objectivity' intrinsic to the forms of praxis that it would make subordinate to avowed moral imperatives.

'The bureaucratic paradox'

This conflict unfolds with fateful effects in modern bureaucracy's approach of 'domination through knowledge' (Weber 1978: 225), the perfection of which rests upon a 'dehumanised' stance (*ibid*: 975) that excludes from thought anything not amenable to calculation. Bureaucracy's approach results in a phenomenon that I call 'the bureaucratic paradox', and describe as follows: although it is by virtue of their official roles that bureaucrats initially encounter other human beings, those roles often must be transcended, or made subordinate, in order truly to ameliorate the predicament at hand. In the case of policing, officers struggle to provide transient palliation by way of bureaucratic resolutions imperfectly crafted through the problematisation of human beings and their predicaments. To do more ultimately means relinquishing the bureaucratic mandate. Since bureaucratic praxis ideally occurs '*sine ire ac studio*' (without anger or passion) (*ibid*: 975), factors such as empathy or attentiveness are relegated to the status of happenstance, largely contingent upon ethical notions extraneous to the strict logic of bureaucracy.[5]

Ontology in action

As a bureaucratically conceived 'incident', my encounter with Gary and Pamela epitomised Weber's notion of 'domination through knowledge'. From the moment Pamela telephoned for police assistance, intersecting layers of bureaucracy functioned efficiently to transform her and Gary into the 'subjects' of an investigation. The whole of their being was reduced to the abstract locus of things and properties technically accessible to the grasp of bureaucratic praxis. In this way, their identities effectively disappeared beneath the accreting effects of typification (see Schutz 1962: 20–21). This process occurred through the translation of human presence into 'the matter of fact'. Injuries, emotions, conflicts, predicaments, and memories assumed a univocal, technical significance, as they were abstracted from their existential origins. Anything impeding this dynamic had to be subsumed within it. Ironically, bureaucracy often depends in such circumstances upon the humanity of its agents to obtain from people what pure technique cannot: consider, for example, the success that my colleagues and I had in eliciting 'useful' statements from Pamela and Gary.

---

5   See Weber's notion of *verstehen* (1978: 3–24) and, relatedly, Ferrell 1997 on 'criminological *verstehen*'.

The 'bureaucratic paradox' exists in parallel form and with equally profound consequences in the arena of social scientific praxis. Intellectual reflection undertaken from a naïve stance of detachment, isolated from the very reality that it purports to engage, is merely another form of the abstraction enacted by the bureaucrat, who loses all sense of the profundity of suffering and evil through an unwitting conflation of human existence with the spectre that results from its efficient enciphering. In both cases, thought and praxis at best yield empty banality. At worst, they descend into the kind of 'nihilistic game' (*auflösende Spiel*) that Hegel (1807: 317) identified as a hallmark of self-alienated modern culture. As Hegel made clear, and as subsequent phenomenological and hermeneutic analyses of the structure of understanding have further explained (eg Heidegger 1996 and Gadamer 1989), this dynamic exerts an inestimably powerful influence upon the self-conception of all of its participants.

Evil as an abstract problem

The bureaucratic response to Gary's attack on Pamela illustrates how the universal experience of evil and transgression becomes objectified and problematised through modern modes of knowing. These modes of knowing have altered the pre-modern, mythic conception of evil through a radical and unprecedented transformation of its symbolic meaning: so argues philosopher Paul Ricoeur in calling for a return to language that restores a sense of *astonishment* to the understanding of evil:

> It is in the age when our language has become more precise, more univocal, more technical in a word, more suited to those integral formalizations which are called precisely symbolic logic, it is in this very age of discourse that we want to recharge our language, that we want to start again from the fullness of language. (1967: 349)

According to Ricoeur, modernity has effectively reduced the experience of evil to a pure abstraction, such that its social, moral and sacred meanings have become wholly reconceived on the basis of reductionist interpretations that obscure this plurivocal complexity behind a univocal character. This new character, in turn, takes itself to represent the vindication of thinking that purports to have transcended and overcome the limitations of mythical understanding.

The violence of (rational) abstraction

In a related account that bears directly upon cultural criminology and other metacriminological reflections, Rorty (2001: xi–xvii) considers how modernity has attempted to transform the ontology of evil into a scientific question of criminality and sociopathology. It is, of course, precisely the interpretation of the universal human experience of transgression and evil *as crime* under the regime of modernity that led to the rise of the science of 'criminology' and its allied forms of bureaucratic praxis, such as policing (cf Garland and Sparks 2000). While these developments have been analysed extensively in historical and sociological terms, their underlying philosophical foundations remain virtually unexplored.

Although definitions and understandings vary inestimably across a range of interpretive contexts, human beings universally acknowledge the ontological reality of certain acts that they identify in one way or another as 'crimes', 'misdeeds' and 'transgressions' (see Rorty 2001). In phenomenological terms, this helps to explain why bureaucratic and criminological practitioners necessarily arrive at their respective technical enterprises by way of more elemental notions and experiences of evil, which only later come to be seen as 'crime', and approached as objects or phenomena amenable to instrumental rational analysis and administrative action (cf Heidegger 2001).

The greatest danger inherent in this approach is that once the experience of evil has been reinterpreted as a rationally apprehensible social problem, and translated into an object for scientific analysis and bureaucratic control, it quickly loses its power of primal astonishment and becomes a cipher – a contentless abstraction or nonentity. This phenomenon, which has assumed different forms coincident with wider socio-historical changes, was already recognised as momentous in its nascent stages, during the rise of the Enlightenment and its political incarnation in the French Revolution (see Hegel 1807). Under the sway of abstraction and the absolute negation of symbolic meaning, something so manifestly horrific as a brutal death becomes a contentless event, which has, in Hegel's evocative words:

> no more significance than cutting off a head of cabbage or swallowing a mouthful of water. (1807, 1977 edition: 360)

Still, despite its claim to have rationalised and surpassed mythic conceptions of transgression, the approach common to mainstream criminology and bureaucracy indirectly causes a harkening back to the astonishing nature of evil. From a phenomenological standpoint, this indicates in part the mind's uncomfortable realisation of the inadequacy of its attempts to translate the ultimate profundity of evil into an abstract problem. Indeed, recalling again Gary's attack on Pamela, is it not the palpable revulsion of this act, and our *astonishment* at its wickedness, that first prompts social scientific and juridical reflections upon its meanings, origins and significance? Yet, at the moment that we suppose we have attained a previously impossible analytic self-subsistence, which enables the transformation of the mythical and the symbolic into something wholly apprehensible in rational, scientific terms, we have cut ourselves off from one of the most urgent and astonishing of questions – 'whence come evils?' (Ricoeur 1967: 8). In its refusal to abdicate astonishment, criminological thinking open to this kind of inquiry would truly exemplify criminology 'unleashed'.

The aesthetic retrieval of astonishment

From the ancient stage to the modern street

Broadly defined, 'unleashing' refers to 'letting go' or 'freeing'. Considered from a phenomenological perspective, these definitions indicate the final step needed to arrive at a point from which astonishment might orient our reflections upon evil. This step requires that bureaucracy and mainstream criminology 'unleash' themselves from their commonsense thinking – if only temporarily – and let go of the natural attitude shaping their praxis. Once we have phenomenologically suspended the unexamined notion that an event such as Gary's attack on Pamela is most meaningfully approached through reductionist bureaucratic or social scientific analyses, it becomes possible to imagine otherwise. From this 'unleashed' stance, we may turn to the approach of using aesthetic reflection to disclose aspects of an horrific event that are effaced when it is made into the object of problematisation. Of the numerous aesthetic forms that might restore astonishment to the interpretation of Gary's assault on Pamela, I offer the example of a passage from Sophocles' *Antigone*.

An overview of events and themes in the *Antigone* reads like a list of panel topics from a criminology conference – homicide, suicide, domestic violence, the nature of punishment, and the conflicted relation among law, justice, and tradition. While this congruence suggests the general aptness of the *Antigone* as a basis for understanding a present-day 'moment from the street', the play's distinct value for a phenomenological interpretation rests upon how it reveals the existential foundations of tragedy, violence and evil. The vantage point that Sophocles creates throughout the play, and especially in the famous first choral song (1994: 35–37, lines 332–85), engages human predicaments in immediate relation to their existential origins, from which they might otherwise be misperceived as distantly remote. By applying a few lines from an ancient Greek play to an episode in our own age, we may find compelling evidence of the role of metaphysics in orienting the actions of everyday life. If that role is ignored, and we merely regard an event such as Gary's attack on Pamela as a 'problem' or 'datum', we have failed to comprehend its actual nature and full range of significance.

The astonishing nature of human being

The first choral song interrupts the action of the *Antigone* with a series of extraordinary meditations upon human nature. The song appears in the text immediately after Creon learns that contrary to his decree, someone has performed funeral rites on the body of Polynices. Killed in combat by his brother during a civil war, Polynices was judged by Creon to be a traitor, and therefore unworthy of burial. Readers familiar with the play will recall that it was, of course, Antigone herself who committed the 'crime' of heaping earth on Polynices' corpse.

Against the backdrop of these palpable moments of violence and transgression, the first choral song opens with the following line:

Many things are formidable, and none more formidable than man! (1994: 35)

A different translation reads:

Wonders are many, and none more wonderful than man. (1987: 49)

The two Greek words accounting for the variance between the translations are *'deina'* ('wonders') and *'deinoteron'* ('wonder of wonders', 'the most wonderful'). The root of these words is *'deinos'*, which has an ambivalent meaning that connotes both awe and fear, or tremendous mystery and terrible power (see Sophocles 1969: 486–87; Heidegger 1959: 148 ff; Steiner 1984: 173–76, and cf Burton 1980: 96).[6] In calling human beings the most formidable, terrible, or wondrous of all things, the chorus recognises and evokes this ambivalence, not as a point of abstract speculation, but with the urgent awareness that mankind's existential nature enacts itself to profound effect at every moment of life.

Faced with the tragic events occurring before its eyes, the first reaction of the chorus is to allude to their origins in the nature of human being as *deinoteron* – 'the wonder of wonders'. Juxtaposed as it is with the astonishing reality of suffering and evil, this opening declamation implicitly answers the question, 'how might we truly understand the plights that derive from an ineluctable and tragic aspect of the human condition?'. The words of the chorus suggest that these plights can only be

---

6   The reader may appreciate this ambivalence more concretely by noting the etymological relation of *'deinos'* to the word 'dinosaur' – 'terrible lizard'.

comprehended authentically in and through their ontological relation to our existence.

This message is reinforced as the choral song follows its opening line with an account of the human conquest of nature and the rise of civilisation. The chorus enumerates mankind's amazing capacities for speech, thought, and 'the temper that rules cities' (*astynomous orgas*) – the disposition for sociopolitical order. Although the chorus warns that these capacities provide neither an escape from death, nor the ability to act justly, they remain the means by which man struggles with his own conflicted nature, as

... he advances sometimes to evil, at other times to good. (1994: 37)

Reframing the 'scene of the crime'

On the basis of Sophocles' insights, it follows that the concrete sequence of events defining the bureaucratic encounter with Gary and Pamela manifests the existential nature of the episode's participants, including my colleagues and me. Driven as it was by the logic of problematisation, the official process of gathering and analysing the 'facts' surrounding Gary's attack on Pamela did not approach the situation with such ideas in mind. This is precisely why, in striving to comprehend the wicked act of one human being's trampling on the head of another, bureaucrats and criminologists cannot ignore the kind of ontological truth that is revealed by a work such as the *Antigone*.

At the same time, this is not to suggest that the *Antigone* merits attention because it has 'useful' implications for instrumental rational praxis or social scientific inquiry. Rather, the enduring value of Sophocles' insights lies in the moral and ontological perspective that they create by revealing what is unquestioningly taken for granted when we conceive of trampling on someone's head as a straightforward 'matter of fact'. The *Antigone* shows that the actual scene of the crime is always already more than the bureaucrat or social scientist will ever see. To 'unleash' criminological thought would be to free it to engage this otherwise unseen reality.

Following the lead of the chorus in the *Antigone*, suppose that we were to witness anew the scene of Gary's attack against Pamela, and instead of first regarding it as a set of facts or data, consider it with wilful astonishment. From such a standpoint, our approach ceases struggling to fit human presence into an interpretive framework shaped by the predetermined ends of instrumental rational praxis, and engages it by attending to how it reveals itself as *deinoteron* – the most wonderful and formidable of all things. Rather than effacing human presence by immediately making it the contentless repository of underlying problems or data, we pause, and contemplate it in its fullness and mystery as the centre of meaning.

Pamela now emerges as someone wholly other than an 'unco-operative victim'. We sense that the moment of overwhelming disharmony and affliction in which she finds herself represents the fusion of physical and emotional pain into a kind of turmoil that no police report or scientific analysis could begin to describe adequately. This turmoil is suddenly illuminated with remarkable clarity: consider the layers of meaning discernible within a small detail such as the rivulets of rain-diluted blood and tears that flow down Pamela's face, spreading sorrow over her cold hands, where before there had only been 'facts and evidence' (see Heidegger 2001: 81–83).

To look again at Gary is to see what is ontologically antecedent to 'crime' or 'sociopathology': it is to see vivified the primal, terrifying qualities that exemplify the worst in human being as *deinoteron*. Gary's rage and confusion unfold as elaborate forms of self-presentation traceable to the innermost roots of his existence. Everything from the dynamics of the attack to Gary's capture, unapologetic confession, and oscillating thoughts and emotions manifests a violent ontological disequilibrium. We have thus begun to realise about Gary and Pamela what Sophocles' chorus knew about Creon and Antigone: that to seek the origins of tragedy demands seeing evil events as the violent self-assertions of human presence.

Conclusion: towards a metacriminology

If, in Ricoeur's words (1967: 347), a given comprehension of evil 'leaves everyday reality outside', what is its actual value as a means of understanding human suffering? As our self-ignorant misperceptions grow, our ability to lessen misery contracts in equal measure. Allowed to deteriorate unchecked, a diminished capacity for astonishment results in a numbing of moral faculties. Therefore, the challenge for any approach to crime, transgression or evil is to remain critically aware of its existential relation to the whole out of which its particular 'objects of attention' have been abstracted.

It is here that I envision a potential role for cultural criminology. Unlike mainstream criminology, cultural criminology incorporates a reflexive attentiveness to the socially embedded roots of its disciplinary and analytic structures. By virtue of its alliances with critical criminology and a range of traditions in social theory, cultural criminology from its beginnings has deliberately attended to the symbolic nature of human actions, including not only phenomena of 'crime', but also more crucially, the phenomena of their being-understood as such (see, for example, Ferrell and Sanders 1995 *passim*).

In at least two notable ways, then, cultural criminology offers a uniquely propitious vantage point from which to pursue further the kind of phenomenological approach that I have roughly mapped out and reconnoitred in this chapter. First, phenomenologically grounded philosophy and human sciences might be combined with the specific theoretical concerns of cultural criminology, in order to inaugurate a rigorous *metacriminology*. This project would engage criminology in sustained critical reflections upon its many contingencies – metaphysical, cultural, historical, and otherwise. Second, a phenomenological approach, applied to any of the range of particular inquiries that have become the focus of cultural criminology's investigations, holds forth strong prospects for the development of novel analyses that will continue progress towards more holistic engagements with actions and deeds that should never cease to astonish those who bear witness to them.

References

Arrigo, B and Williams, C (eds) (2005) *Philosophical Foundations of Crime*, Champaign, IL: University of Illinois Press

Burton, R (1980) *The Chorus in Sophocles' Tragedies*, Oxford: Clarendon

Ferrell, J (1997) 'Criminological *verstehen*: inside the immediacy of crime' 14(1) *Justice Quarterly* 3–23

Ferrell, J and Sanders, C (eds) (1995) *Cultural Criminology*, Boston: Northeastern University Press

Gadamer, H-G (1989) *Truth and Method*, 2nd revised edn, Weinsheimer, J and Marshall, DG (trans), New York: Crossroad

Garland, D and Sparks, R (eds) (2000) *Criminology and Social Theory*, Oxford: OUP

Hegel, GWF (1807) [1977] *Phenomenology of Spirit*, Miller, AV (trans), Oxford: OUP

Heidegger, M (1959) *An Introduction to Metaphysics*, Manheim, R (trans), New Haven: Yale UP

Heidegger, M (1963) *Holzwege*, Frankfurt: Klostermann

Heidegger, M (1996) *Being and Time*, Stambaugh, J (trans), Albany: State University of New York Press

Heidegger, M (2001) *Zollikon Seminars, Protocols – Conversations – Letters*, Mayr, F and Askay, R (trans), Evanston, IL: Northwestern University Press

Hogg, R (1998) 'Crime, criminology, and government', in Walton, P and Young, J (eds), *The New Criminology Revisited*, New York: St Martin's Press

Husserl, E (1970) *The Crisis of European Sciences and Transcendental Phenomenology: An Introduction to Phenomenological Philosophy*, Carr, D (trans), Evanston, IL: Northwestern University Press

Husserl, E (1982) *Ideas Pertaining to a Pure Phenomenology and to a Phenomenological Philosophy, First Book, General Introduction to a Pure Phenomenology*, Kersten, F (trans), The Hague: Martinus Nijhoff

Katz, J (1988) *Seductions of Crime: The Moral and Sensual Attractions in Going Evil*, New York: Basic Books

Nelken, D (ed) (1994) *The Futures of Criminology*, Thousand Oaks, CA: Sage

Ricoeur, P (1967) *The Symbolism of Evil*, Buchanan, E (trans), Boston: Beacon

Rorty, A (2001) *The Many Faces of Evil: Historical Perspectives*, London: Routledge

Schutz, A (1962) *The Problem of Social Reality*, Collected Papers, Vol 1, Natanson, M (ed), The Hague: Martinus Nijhoff

Sophocles (1969) [1879] *The Plays and Fragments*, 2nd revised edn, edited with English notes and introduction by Lewis Campbell, Hildesheim: Georg Olms Verlagsbuchhandlung

Sophocles (1987) *Antigone*, Brown, A (ed and trans), Warminster: Aris & Phillips

Sophocles (1994) *Sophocles*, Vol II, *Antigone, The Women of Trachis, Philoctetes*, and *Oedipus at Colonus*, Lloyd-Jones, H (ed and trans), Cambridge, MA: Harvard UP

Steiner, G (1984) *Antigones*, Oxford: OUP

Weber, M (1978) *Economy and Society*, 2 vols, Roth, G and Wittich, C (eds), Berkeley: University of California Press

Chapter 5
Style Matters[1]

Jeff Ferrell

This chapter critically examines that most delicate but resilient of connecting tissues between cultural and criminal practices: style. As will be seen, *style* is considered here not as a vague abstraction denoting form or fashion, but as a concrete element of personal and group identity, grounded in the everyday practices of social life. *Style* is in this sense embedded in haircuts, posture, clothing, automobiles, music, and the many other avenues through which people present themselves publicly. But it is also located *between* people, and *among* groups; it constitutes an essential element in collective behaviour, an element whose meaning is constructed through the nuances of social interaction. When this interaction emerges within a criminalised subculture, or between its members and legal authorities, personal and collective style emerges as an essential link between cultural meaning and criminal identity ...

Style defines the social categories within which people live, and the communities of which they are a part, [serving] as a ready and visible medium for negotiating status, for constructing both security and threat, and for engaging in criminality ... Style defines the lived experience of ethnicity, social class, and other essential social (and sociological) categories ... Ethnicity and social class reside less with skin colour or dollars than they do with participation in various collective styles; they emerge from socially symbolic stances that locate individuals and groups in the larger society. In the moments of lived experience, styles becomes the medium through which social categories take on meaning.

To participate in a community – large or small, ethnic or ideological, criminal or noncriminal – is therefore to participate in style as collective action ... To wear particular clothes, drive certain cars, or listen to distinctive types of music is to make oneself *stylistically visible*, to those both inside and outside the subculture or community. Whether intentionally or not, it is to declare one's membership ... Here, of course, we see a remarkable intersection of individual identity, group interaction, market forces, and meaning – that is, a sort of stylised political economy of everyday life ...

Group styles become in everyday life *epistemic* and *symbolic* markers through which those *outside* the group also 'read' group membership and subcultural identity, and thus come to 'know' who is a gang member or graffiti writer. That is, these styles acquire further layers of meaning in the intricacies of social interaction ... Put differently, style constitutes much of the 'symbolic' in the symbolic interactions of everyday life. When others react to you based on the style you present, and you then react to their reactions, an interactive dynamic has emerged that reinforces and reconstructs the meaning of that style for you and others. This dynamic may carry

---

1   The following is an excerpt from 'Style matters: criminal identity and social control', in Ferrell, J and Sanders, CR (eds), *Cultural Criminology*, 1995, Boston: Northeastern University Press, pp 169–89.

the individual beyond his or her own intentions and create consequences beyond those that could have been anticipated ... Style comes closer to being a causal factor than a casual epiphenomenon; it shapes the nature of social interaction and the meanings that evolve from it.

Style in this sense exists not as a stationary entity but as a negotiated social process. The meaning of style resides not only in clothes and on the body but *between* people, in the interplay of identities, in the reading and counter-reading of stylistic cues. This stylistic process goes on within criminal subcultures – thus creating various stylistic communities – and between subcultural members and those they encounter in their daily lives. And of all these stylistic encounters, certainly the most critical in shaping daily experience and determining crime and criminality are those with legal and political authorities ...

Legal authorities read and respond to the styles of lower-class and ethnic minority kids (and adults), to their collective presentation of self and construction of identity, and in so doing push them into downward cycles of criminalization ... Discriminatory policing or differential enforcement become meaningful not simply as statistical residues of arrest rates, but as interactive dynamics through which authorities pay more attention to one group than another and read (and misread) the stylistic patterns that construct group identity. To put it bluntly, trouble with the police or other authorities comes less from being 'Black' or 'poor' or 'young' as such than it does from particular automobiles, clothes, haircuts, and postures that signify these statuses to those in authority.

Style exists as the *medium* through which disadvantaged groups and legal authorities interact, the *locus* of inequality and power – the place where power relations are played out and resisted – and therefore, the *catalyst* that precipitates the sorts of inequitable interactions that further label and amplify group activities as criminal. The power of subcultural styles is such that they become important cultural currency, not only for those 'outsiders' who develop and adopt them but for legal and political authorities as well ...

The stylistic orientations of disadvantaged groups thus symbolize prior social inequality and group identity, and at the same time propel group members toward further victimization and criminalization. For members of these groups, style carries the history and future of group affiliation and criminalization; it incorporate past encounters with the legal system and precipitates new ones. In the lived experience of identity and inequality, personal and group style exists as a badge of resistance and honor and, at the same moment, a stigmata. It sets in motion and keeps in motion spirals of criminalization and inequality ...

Core concerns of criminology – criminal and subcultural identity, the links between criminality and social inequality, the nature of legal control – are manifest in the stylistic orientations of subcultures and communities ... Stylistic orientations are of concern to criminology because they are the medium through which inequitable legal practices take shape. If style constitutes the connecting tissue between cultural practices and criminal identities, it also forms the connecting tissue between disadvantaged groups and agents of legal control ... Legal authorities read and react to subcultural styles as the stains of prior criminality and the predictors of future crime ... as both the cause and effect of criminality ... Such styles engage legal authorities and subcultural members in spiraling dynamics of interpretive interaction which shape and expand existing inequalities ...

Certainly broad critiques of inequality and injustice are important. But as the many subtleties of style remind us, we must ask, in situation after situation, precisely how and why such inequalities are constructed ... This attentiveness to the lived experience of inequality and injustice moves criminology past the old antinomies of structure and agency, society and small group. It also points, time and again, back to style. For kids, criminals, and legal authorities caught up in a process of symbolic meaning and official reaction, and for criminologists who work to unravel the lived politics of this process, style matters.

Part 2

Across the Borders of
Crime and Culture

Chapter 6
Lombroso and the Birth of Criminological Positivism: Scientific Mastery or Cultural Artifice?

Wayne Morrison

Introduction: learning lessons from the spectacle of seduction

> Visitors to the Palazzo delle Belle Art, Rome in the autumn of 1885 became the witnesses of a most unusual spectacle. On display in one hall was a huge array of objects including well over 300 skulls and anatomical casts, probably several thousand portrait photographs and drawings of epileptics and delinquents, insane and born criminals, and maps, graphs and publications summing up the results of research in the new scientific discipline of criminal anthropology. The exhibition was displayed for only one week next to the assembly hall in which some 130 European criminologists, anthropologists, psychiatrists, jurists and physicians had convened for the First International Congress of Criminal Anthropology between 16 and 20 November. The sight of the place must have been dizzying. Forty-three exhibitors, most of them Italian, some French, German, Hungarian and Russian, showed their personal collections which characterised their individual achievements in the field. Laid out on tables and shelves were series of skulls, demonstrating the typical features of epileptics, street robbers, or suicidels, and individual specimens of special cases: megalocephalics, prostitutes, murderers; brains conserved in alcohol or, after a special method invented by Giacomini, in gelatine, which allowed the fine slicing of the brain for microscopic examination; plaster casts of heads, skulls, faces, ears, and no less than five completely conserved heads, two of nihilists, two of delinquents, and that of the infamous bandit Giona La Gala, which was there in the exhibition of the Genoa penitentiary, complete with his brain, tattoos, and gall bladder stones found during the autopsy.
>
> Maps, diagrams and other graphic displays hung on the walls, illustrating the geographical distribution of various sorts of crimes, the rapport of growing suicide and insanity rates with the rise of crime, or the influence of variations in temperature and grain prices on Italian criminality. Clay and wax figures made by prisoners and mental patients, examples of their writings and drawings, an album with copies of two thousand tattoos, all illustrating aspects of criminal or insane creativity. And in many of the individual collections, second only to skulls, were portraits of criminals, drawings as well as photographs. (Broeckmann 1995: 3)

Positivist criminology was born amidst a dazzling and seductive spectacle. What lessons can we take from this exhibition of material culture 120 years ago? Then, as now, processes operated to establish a discipline, to make visible the 'criminal' as a positive entity and render invisible the cultural suppositions and global reach of those processes as they crossed borders, captured exotic cultural practices and rendered them signifiers of a supposed 'criminality'. This is a broad assertion and in this chapter I will use Lombroso to present certain basic propositions. Firstly, that at the heart of the positivist cannon is performance art – at odds with its official image of neutrally representing facts, positivist criminology is cultural production. Secondly, that 'the late nineteenth-century birth of criminology' was more than what Wetzell (2000: 26–31) describes as 'a general western European phenomenon, taking place in Italy, France, Germany, and to a lesser extent Britain'. These were sites of visible production, but they were informed by flows of information from travellers and their reports of the world beyond Europe, a world that Europeans were shaping in Europe's images and cultural understandings, confidently expecting it to disappear and its forms to exist in the future only in museums of primitive mankind or barbaric practices. We need to reassess this legacy, for if today we seek to develop a 'global criminology', an understanding that criminology has always been structured by global processes is required. The holy grail for criminology has been the production of a secure body of social theory capable of providing a cloak of objectivity, yet the resultant theory is largely the product of the power of certain key nation-states and their defining abilities to render the world knowable to their citizens. Its hidden context was imperialist globalism, a reality that had to be submerged; else too many issues of cultural significance would be raised.

The Italian doctor Cesare Lombroso (1835–1909), the 'father of modern criminology' (Mannheim 1972: 232) and a key figure in the Congress's organisation, brought the largest collection. Lombroso's influence was immense.

> His thoughts revolutionized our opinions, provoked a salutary feeling everywhere, and a happy emulation in research of all kinds. For 20 years, his thoughts fed our discussions; the Italian master was the order of the day in all debates; his thoughts appeared as events. There was an extraordinary animation everywhere. (Dallemagne, a French opponent in 1896, quoted in Gould 1981: 165)

We have forgotten the exhibitory power Lombroso utilised and have difficulty in appreciating that positivism was (and remains) a cultural phenomenon. Its self-image is often accepted, namely that of a rigorous science, founded upon techniques of representation – mapping, cataloguing, measuring – of data purified from the 'cultural'. Certainly the constant refrains of positivism concerning objective representation recall the original claim to locate mankind within its true determinants: 'Criminal anthropology studies the delinquent in his natural place – that is to say, in the field of biology and pathology' (Lombroso's disciple Sergi, quoted in Gould 1981: 166). But that methodology relied upon a cultural practice of presenting and representing which implied that the abnormal and the dangerous could be recognised and mapped in physical space and evolutionary time.

Criminology was born in the transformation of punishment from public spectacle to an activity within the enclosed prison, penitentiary or institutions for the insane. A neglected feature of the transformation was that the legitimacy for this new science was demonstrated by public exhibitions and educational events, practices of organisation and display that demarcated the criminal and insane as something other, entities that were best dealt with by experts in their appropriate professional programmes buttressed by their possession of techniques of identification, measurement and judgment. Rather than the public executions of the old regime, increasingly identified as acts of repression losing their effectiveness, these new practices relied upon seductive spectacles and practices. The strategy had to discredit the culture (in terms of languages, meanings and practices, not to mention sources of intellectual opposition to the new episteme) of those it seized upon as its objects of study – indeed Lombroso's stigmata included both the argot of criminals and the practice of tattooing, both of which were said to be evidence of their atavism.[1] To have considered that the identifiers of criminality (for example, argot or tattoos) were part of cultural practices that may be worthy of respect was anathema to a positivist

---

1   Lombroso argued that criminals had a language of their own with high levels of aonomatoeia and similar to the speech of children and savages: 'Atavism contributes to it more than anything else. They speak differently because they feel differently; they speak as savages because they are true savages in the midst of our brilliant European civilisation' (1887: 476).

ethos that ruled only pure, measurable science as respectable. Yet there were those who realised at the time that Lombroso's science was performance art.

> My father, then a medical student, remembered also that Lombroso's lectures were always attended by overflow crowds of students and admirers and were often accompanied by the presentation of clinical cases. Usually these were derelicts recruited by Mr Cabria, the savvy errand man of the Department, and were selected because they had at least some of the required physical and psycho logic features (not a difficult task given the abundance of choices) and who, for a few lire, would manufacture a suitable criminal record and answer questions about personal and family life with a stream of colourful profanities. (Fo'a 2003: 3)

Lombroso's daughter, Gina Lombroso-Ferrero (1915), reports that when he began his professorship in Turino, Lombroso had to lay out a laboratory at his own expense and found that prisons and asylums denied him entry and thus subjects for analysis. He obtained clients for his psychiatric practice by putting a handwritten note on his door offering free consultations; a successful tactic since his reputation was higher among the general population than within the university. Once he had patients he could teach his course on psychiatry, previously denied him on the grounds that he had no patients to present. Gina admits that obtaining examples of 'living criminals' was more difficult, for they did not readily present themselves at Lombroso's office even when a cash incentive was offered! His assistant Giovasnni Cabria, a bookbinder and lithographer by trade, was enlisted to find criminals, offer them suitable payment, and bring them back to the lab. Gina notes approvingly that Cabria became a 'veritable bloodhound for criminals', searching for them in street arcades and taverns. Cabria also brought to Lombroso's attention hundreds of skulls unearthed by the renovation of Turin that had opened up the cemeteries of criminals, soldiers, Jews, and monks, thus providing an abundance of material for a 'comparative' anthropology.

In time Lombroso overcame the resistance of the medical profession as well as the persons in charge of the prisons and asylums and they came to provide strong support to his project. At the Sixth International Congress of Criminal Anthropology, which was held in Turin in 1906 (Congresses were held every four years until the First World War), Lombroso personally guided a group of male and female delegates to a range of sites for the production of criminological knowledge where he displayed his ability to visually recognise dangerousness. The historian Renzo Villa recounts that while touring the cells of the local prison Lombroso came upon a boy who displayed physical particularities that could be 'catalogued as degenerative stigmata'. After excusing the women, Lombroso had the boy undressed and surveyed his body for other signs of the criminal type, then the delegates watched Lombroso examine other 'specimens' collected by the head guard: a shoemaker convicted of sexual molestation, a recidivist thief, and particularly a second thief whose body was covered with tattoos. Thus Lombroso taught criminological practice, asking his audience to emulate his cataloguing of surface anomalies and pathologies, replicate his measuring and identifying the palpation of the criminal body, interrogating and even diagnosing the subject's handwriting (recounted in Horn 2003: 78).

The delegates would also have been invited to Lombroso's clinic and study the various objects and writings he had collected, for since 1892 Lombroso had founded a specialist museum.

The Museo di Antropologia 'Cesare Lombroso', Turino

We do not know the fate of many of the exhibits at the Congress, but those of Lombroso form the core of the Museo di Antropologia 'Cesare Lombroso', in Turin, Italy. To enter the museum now (my visit was in summer 2003) is to visit a site of exhibition that was intended to be a place of scientific proof. Museums are not passive places, a reflection of facts, but the result of the desire to master, control and order objects, and to celebrate that power in a display.

Today the objects Lombroso collected have lost their seductive power; instead they cause another questioning: How could he and his supporters have thought what they did, or put so much effort into their practices of collection? The museum is testament to the accumulation of criminological facts, but these 'facts' now exist outside any coherent legitimate organising system.[2] There are many sheets of photographs of convicted persons, arranged by offence type, the comparison of which was meant to reveal the underlying criminal type (in addition there are examples of such photographic activity from followers, such as Chinese Prostitutes, Hong Kong 1929). On shelf after shelf lie specimens of skin that have been carefully removed from the bodies of dead offenders, fixed onto cards or boards and displayed to reveal tattoos, often of a sexual nature, but sometimes just containing names and expressions. In a case are presented the full sets of heavy cloths made and worn by an eccentric 'insane' even at the height of summer. Against the wall sits the wooden furniture that inmates of an asylum had created. Examples of the art of the prison and asylum occupy half a room; water jugs with inscriptions, drawings and cartoons provide evidence, Lombroso asserted, of the primitive 'writing' of the criminal and the insane. Plaster models created by prisoners sit side by side with wooden models – all the products of practices that occupied the time of the inmate. Instead of demonstrating creativity or resistance to the power to enclose, to place and fix in a time and place (the prison and asylum), this art, or the act of creating drawings, models, by prisoners and insane, provided proof of degeneracy. In *Genius and Madness* (1864) Lombroso reported that of the 107 mentally ill patients he took as his clinical sample, around half spontaneously painted; this was an atavistic form of representation, paralleling the 'art' of the 'primitive'; both revealed a fixation on the obscene and the absurd. The art of the criminal or his mental patients, we were told, fulfilled no function in the asylum, prison or in the greater world, similarly the art of the savage had no function and no value in itself; instead Lombroso saw it as a spontaneous activity, parallel to the spontaneous act of painting among savages, such as the scratching on rock by the Australian Aboriginals. The insane and the criminal shared with the savage an act that was of interest only for the action of doing, rather than any value in the product.

Then there are the tools of measurement, the camera and other instruments, some of which Lombroso had played a role in inventing. Photos of dried heads of native tribespeople sit opposite images of primates. Everywhere the material objectification of facts is presented, such as the numerous display cases holding the weapons by which robbery or murder was done or attempted. Another room contains many rows of wax and plaster casts of the heads of the condemned. Catalogues of photographs of offenders are presented along with plaster casts of hands and ears; evidence of his search for the representational ear of the offender, the hands of the offender, the mapping of the criminal man. At the side of one room lie rows of skulls, all of which had been the subject of post-mortem (Figure 6.1), and jars

2   For a full account of the Museum (in Italian) see Giorgio 1975, complete with many photographs of items that no longer exist, such as preserved foetuses of deformed children, and the head of Lombroso himself, preserved in a jar. By his will Lombroso directed that his body be subjected to the same processes of analysis he performed on the 'criminal'; today it is kept as a full skeleton.

of brains that once fitted inside those skulls. In another room are instruments of restraint, irons and the wooden beams of a scaffold, the removal of which from the public square and reinstallation in the confines of a museum was itself evidence of progress in penal policy.

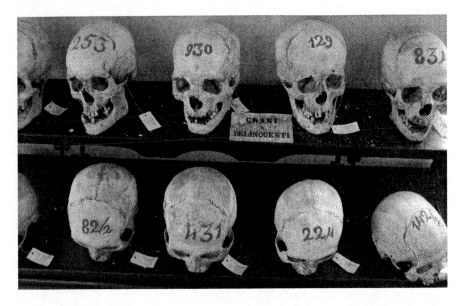

Figure 6.1 Selection of skulls laid out for display, numbered with identification tags (photo Wayne Morrison). Colombo (1975: 76) has a photo of a large pile of skulls taking up half a room as well as preserved heads in large jars. As to the identities and life-stories of the human persons these skulls once formed part of, note this extract from Felice Accame, *Vecchie teste e nuova cattiva coscienza* (Old heads and new bad conscience), in *Rivista Anarchica*, Anno 29, n 252, Marzo 1999:

'Recently, two rather absent-minded and belated delegates discovered the head of Giovanni Passanante preserved in the Museo di Criminologia in Rome. Arousing the cautious compassion of whomever had the awareness to be part of the majority government, they turned to the Minister of Grace and Justice to call for the aforementioned head to be allowed its long awaited burial.

Passanante – classified as an anarchist, perhaps with a little benefit of invention – was a calabrese cook who, in Naples, on the distant 17 November 1878, attempted to plant a knife into King Umberto I, while he was passing by a cheering crowd in the official carriage with the Queen and his child, followed by the President of the Consiglio of the ministries. According to the chroniclers, Passanante went towards the royal carriage with an arm covered in red cloth from which at the crucial moment he drew a knife that presumably in the kitchen he would use skilfully on poultry and quarters of ox. On quarters and insides of nobility, however, it was less able. Once he came close to the King he struck the leg of Benedetto Cairoli, an ex-mazziniano and ex-garibaldino and ex-everything who had found a way to mitigate his populist aspirations by making a political career under the protection of the House of Savoia.

At the legal proceedings that were carried out in March of the successive year, the Ministry called for capital punishment and no one opposed. After the corroboration of the Court of Cassation (reversal) the King, however, benevolently granted the penalty to be switched to forced labour for life.

Some years later, Lombroso paid a visit to Passanante. Lombroso, not dissimilarly to what the defence lawyers had already sustained, declared Passanante mad. Consequently, he was transferred to the criminal mental asylum of Montelupo Fiorentino, where he died in 1910. This declaration was the presupposition for why his body was then treated cruelly – having his head cut off and having who knows what iniquity performed on it – before being displayed to the curiosity of the public as a tangible exhibit of human progress. If one really wants to redress wrongs – wrongs to the entirety of humanity and not only to the poor Passanante – *da fare ce ne* (there is much to do).' (Accame 1999, www.anarca-bolo.ch/a-rivista/252/11.htm. Translated by M Leong)

In pride of place on Lombroso's desk in his reconstructed study is a glass presentation box in which resides the skull of Vilella. In the Introduction to *Criminal Man*, an English edition of his work prepared by his daughter and collaborator, published in 1911, Lombroso explained that his breakthrough came in turning from the abstract study of crime to that of the criminal himself and recognising 'the congenital criminal [as] an anomaly, partly pathological and partly atavistic, a revival of the primitive savage'.

He developed his methodology after he realised that the honest soldier could be distinguished 'from his vicious comrade' by 'the extent to which the latter was tattooed and the indecency of the designs that covered his body'. Having begun to study 'criminals in the Italian prisons', Lombroso was carrying out a post-mortem 'of the famous brigand Vilella' when he found a strange 'depression' located 'as in inferior animals, especially rodents'. Thus he experienced 'a revelation'.

> At the sight of that skull, I seemed to see all of a sudden, lighted up as a vast plain under a flaming sky, the problem of the nature of the criminal – an atavistic being who reproduces in his person the ferocious instincts of primitive humanity and the inferior animals. Thus were explained anatomically the enormous jaws, high cheek-bones, prominent superciliary arches, solitary lines in the palms, extreme size of the orbits, handle-shaped or sessile ears found in criminals, savages, and apes, insensibility to pain, extremely acute sight, tattooing, excessive idleness, love of orgies, and the irresistible craving for evil for its own sake, the desire not only to extinguish life in the victim, but to mutilate the corpse, tear its flesh, and drink its blood. (Lombroso 1911: xi–xx)

Horn (2003: 31) considers that this account, written at the end of Lombroso's life, possesses 'a mythic quality', but also relates that in Lombroso's original 1871 article he had already stressed the importance of that skull.

Amidst the curiosities, this account may also offer us a route into reconstructing the path taken by positivist criminology. Lombroso's actual words tell us how he obtained a knowledge that could link the criminologist into another realm than that of the immediately visible. Not only could Lombroso recognise signs of the criminal (stigmata), but the meaning of these signs is that they enable us to situate the observed subject in an order of being beyond that of the immediately visible: a realm of evolutionary progress and of reversion to a time previous that locates ourselves and the criminal others in evolutionary time and space (corresponding to the civilising process).

But how is this progress made apparent, what of the objects therein located, and what assurances did Lombroso give to those who initially were fearful of his efforts but who then came to support him? Put another way: whose skulls are these that still reside there indicated only by numbers? Who gave them for analysis ... did anyone ever want them returned? Or was that question never allowed to be uttered?

These questions take us onto the nature of European globalisation and Lombroso's immediate context: the unification of Italy. Vilella was a *briganti*, one who resisted the civilising process of Italian unification – what we may otherwise call the colonisation of the Italian south. For centuries Italy had existed only as a conceptual inspiration. The unification of Italy as a nation-state meant the end of numerous petty kingdoms, the defeat of the Hapsburg reign, diminished power for the Catholic Church and the replacement of regional elites by a national governing class. Three groups posed the main problems – peasants, *briganti*, and anarchists.

To the southern peasants unification was a threat to their established traditional social practices; it represented the imposition of a foreign set of customs. Northern

Italians sometimes said that Calabria evoked Africa and the 'Dark Continent' was said to begin respectively at Bologna, Florence, Rome, or Naples, depending on the birthplace of the speaker. The South was cast as a form of other world, racially different, a space to be explored, penetrated, contained and colonised. A unified language containing scientific judgment was essential. As one of Lombroso's followers, Alfredo Niceforo, tells us in *L'Italia barbara*, 'the brigandage of the South and of Sardinia were typical of a more primitive race, and ... the infusion of Arab blood into feudal Sicily was responsible for the Mafia' (quoted in Pick 1989: 114–15). The southerners fought against the new government as they had against their other foreign invaders. In the face of the *briganti* or *brigandage* (a term that covers many actions that could be termed civil wars in the still politically fragile new state as well as being a name given by the new government to any violent local opposition to the laws of Italy) or anarchism, the police and army adopted preventive detention, a strategy in line with Lombroso's arguments. His message to those who ran the prisons and asylums was that they were not involved in a socio-political struggle or culture war; instead they were actors in the civilising process and buttressed by science.

This was the message for the immediate location but it has greater resonance. Evoking the atavisitic and the primitive, Lombroso moves from the political, economic and cultural struggles of a particular nation-state to a realm of the global connected by the idea of an underlying system, namely, an evolutionary sequence that, in practice, renders the original inhabitants of the lands Europe was occupying as of no account, as savages to be superseded. Anthropological criminology employed tactics of rendering visible the criminal that now are dismissed as pseudo-science; but we overlook the fact that those tactics also involved denying or rendering invisible contextual considerations that would have problematised the purity or logic of the object or situation presented as fit for study. Such tactics have been foundational to mainstream criminology, which has been the science of the modern nation-state and thus always bounded, while presenting itself as simply science, as universal. I argue elsewhere (Morrison 2005) that this contradiction lies at the heart of mainstream criminology and renders it unable to come to grips with the problems of the contemporary post-modern or post-European world. To illustrate I take two examples of Lombroso's depreciation of the cultural practices of the natives of the lands now colonised, namely their art and use of tattoos. In both cases Lombroso had seen a demonstrable pathway leading from the European criminal back to the 'primitive' or 'savage'.

The art of the savage as the mark of criminality: who could speak for the Aboriginal?

In spite of the thousands of years which separate him from prehistoric savages, his [the criminal's] art is a faithful reproduction of the first, crude attempts of primitive races. The museum of criminal anthropology created by my father contains numerous specimens of criminal art, stones shaped to resemble figures, like those found in Australia, rude pottery covered with designs that recall Egyptian decorations or scenes fashioned in terra-cotta that resemble the grotesque creations of children or savages. (Lombroso-Ferrero 1911: 132)

In his recent, otherwise excellent, text Horn speaks as a late modern when he says that Lombroso 'worked to link the *cultural* practices of criminals and savages' (Horn 2003: 46; emphasis in original). The problem with this statement is that Lombroso abstracted from cultural practices, presenting what he took to be unproblematic products, while he denied cultural worth to the creative and interpretative practices of native tribespeople and 'earlier races'. That the art of the criminal reasserted the practices of the savage offered a pleasing aesthetic claim and diagnostic tool to identify the misfits in the European civilising process. When Lombroso claimed in a learned journal, however, that criminal songs were confined to the south of Italy, Pitre, a specialist on southern Italian songs, could offer corrected transcriptions and different interpretations of the actual songs as well as refuting the overall claim (see Horn 2003: 172 n 62). But who would, or could, speak for the non-European 'savage', for the peoples of the lands Europe was occupying?

Lombroso collected examples of the handwriting of offenders, inscriptions on the walls of prisons and the asylum, pottery and jugs inscribed by offenders and inmates, to demonstrate that criminals resorted to 'pictography' to express their thoughts and even developed a slang communication technique that was presented in criminal 'hieroglyphs'. This illustrated the atavist link since sketched figures, the first art of mankind, were merely mnemonic devices or aids to memory among savages. They had given way to hieroglyphs and then to the pure alphabet, the mark of civilisation, as only alphabetic writing enabled the 'unfolding of ideas'. It was essential to this evolutionary structure that the art of Australian Aboriginal people was merely 'scratching on rocks', or that the sculptures of the Peruvians and the paintings of the redskins, for example, were at the same level as the 'scrawling of our children' (Horn 2003: chapter 2).

If Lombroso could be corrected when he referred to the cultural practices of the Italian south, there were few to object to his claims as to the non-European other. The dismissal of the art of Australian Aboriginal people, for example, was a commonplace that continued until recently. From the beginning of colonisation Aborigines were denied the status of civilised. They were not recognised as having a complex culture, nor laws; they were no part of the modernity that was to be built in that land (thus the original inhabitants were only granted Australian citizenship in the 1960s!). The depredation of Aborigine 'art' was fundamental to dispossessing them since in their culture art and law intermix. In the 19th century it was widely assumed that Aborigines would become an extinct race. When it was realised that they would survive, the policy became one of absorption or assimilation into the mainstream 'Australian' way of life. This policy was reconsidered in the late 1960s. In the 1970s Aboriginal art gained popularity with collectors and museums and in the 1980s became recognised as expressing both traditional and contemporary culture, involving both reference to sacred times and performance art. Today Aboriginal art is recognised as a mode of expression, cultural production in which the specific meaning, or even identification of subjects cannot be reconstructed without knowledgeable informants, and any specific motif or rock art panel may have many meanings depending upon the particular context of interpretation. Moreover, it is now understood that 'controlling access to esoteric knowledge, including the "stories" encoded in art, was, and is, fundamental to the creation, maintenance and perpetuation of status and decision-making hierarchies in Aboriginal society' (Morwood 2002: 72). The successive revelation of designs formed part of young men's gradual age-grading rituals. 'In the desert, the large ground designs that form the basis of today's acrylic painting movement were progressively revealed to initiates at sacred ceremonies away from the eyes of women' (Isaacs 1999: 6).

Contemporary Aboriginal art is both modern and ancient, intermixing concepts including the relationship to land, ancestral characters and recent social history.

Some pieces can be read as religious works, titles to land, abstract art, or a combination of these. Archaeological records indicate that Aboriginal peoples probably came to Australia by sea from the islands to the north somewhere between 40000 to 100000 BP. In the eyes of the settler society, Australia was empty land (given the legal term *terra nullius*). Thus colonisation was held *not* to involve conquest or a war of dispossession. Rather Aborigines were rendered socially invisible and were presumed to have no recognisable relationship with the land. By contrast, overcoming feelings of alienation towards the vast landscape was foundational to the Aborigines' unique and fragile relationship with the land upon which they lived and died. To fundamental questions of time and creation, of existence and the meaning of life, answers were found in a closely related set of understandings, usually translated into English as the 'dream time' or 'dreaming'. This was their original era, when the great Creation or Spirit Ancestors created the land, its features and the life within it. In the dream time these ancestral beings or forces travelled widely across the land, performing remarkable feats of creation and destruction. The journey pathways or routes along which they travelled are remembered and celebrated wherever they went, at particular sites. Present Aboriginal groups trace their descent directly to these Spirit Ancestors and the dream time is not simply a creative time of the past but a constant and pervasive force in present-day life.

Aboriginal ceremonial items, ceremonies, songs, dances and designs used in bark paintings, body paintings and rock art all take their meaning from the creation stories associated with different parts of the country. Since many of these items and performances serve as tangible charters for land ownership, rights to use them were, and remain, closely guarded. To retain ownership and use their estates, clans had to maintain the sacred law, perform the required ceremonies and pass on the law to succeeding generations. To do this they needed knowledge of the stories, songs and art that encoded the sacred law. The need for people to have localised symbolic knowledge in order to use resources was a way of reducing territorial access. Not knowing the stories for a locality put strangers at a tremendous disadvantage. Introduction to a country meant noting the location of the story places and discovering, for example, the direction in which it was safe to go hunting. The Aborigines mapped land as securely as the modern cartographer; but to appreciate Aboriginal concepts the first step is to understand that the land or earth itself is not static. It is a living thing that can and does interact with human beings, animals, plants, the elements, and the constellations above. The explanations for the ways in which an individual relates to the world contain many unified concepts stressing the way in which land and person interflow. To recognise the land as empty, the coloniser must engage in practices of relegation and dismissal. To have understood Aboriginal art as the product and expression of a dynamic culture would have been to recognise Aborigines as having complex relationships (and hence rights) to land. Since in Western social jurisprudence property and political rights have developed from the relationship and power *vis à vis* land, the dynamic of the civilising process in Australia could have been cast much differently.[3]

---

3   Today their art becomes an object of commercial exchange. Is this another appropriation, or a beneficial entry into the flows of international capitalism? The same question can be raised about *Te Moko*, now worn by pop stars and partially integrated into fashion shows. The former heavyweight boxing champion of the world, Mike Tyson, had a partial *Te Moko* tattooed in an attempt to make him a 'true warrior' (a reference to the successful New Zealand film *Once Were Warriors*, which featured contemporary inner-city Maoris with *Te Moko*).

The tattoo or *Te Moko*

Tattooing is the true writing of the savage, their first registry of civil condition ... Nothing is more natural than to see a usage so widespread among savages and prehistoric peoples reappear in classes which, as the deep sea bottoms retain the same temperature, have preserved the customs and superstitions, even to the hymns, of the primitive peoples, and who have, like them, violent passions, a blunted sensibility, a puerile vanity, long-standing habits of inaction, and very often nudity. There, indeed among savages, are the principal models of this curious custom. (Lombroso 1896: 802)

The publication of *L'Uomo Delinquente* (1876), with a full chapter devoted to the criminological significance of tattoos, established Lombroso as a world expert on the link between tattoos and criminality. Tattoos were a crucial element in the set of stigmata, 'the outward and visible signs of a mysterious and complicated process of degeneration, which in the case of the criminal evokes evil impulses that are largely of atavistic origin'. In his 1882 lecture, 'Tattooing among civilised people', Robert Fletcher simply repeated Lombroso's arguments that tattooing correlated to the atavism of criminals, for 'it is soldiers, sailors, and, above all, criminals, including prostitutes, who most extensively resort to it. ... The criminal classes furnish the most elaborate and most curious examples of tattooing' (1971: 45–47). In Fletcher's analysis of civilised people around the world tattooing was 'mostly confined to the lower classes' and among women it was almost without exception 'confined to prostitutes' (*ibid*: 55).

The practice could serve as an indicator of atavism since the custom itself – as Lombroso rightly stressed – had been introduced into Europe by sailors returning from the South Pacific. Polynesian tattooing was briefly mentioned in European ship logs dating from the 17th and early 18th centuries, but it was the detailed descriptions by Joseph Banks, the naturalist accompanying James Cook on his first voyage, that first brought it to considered attention. Banks was at a loss to explain it. However, some of the sailors allowed themselves to be tattooed and in the following decades many British sailors returned home bearing proof of their travels in the form of exotic tattoos. Some sailors learnt the art and by the middle of the 18th century most British ports had at least one professional tattoo artist.

By 1896 the fashion for tattoos among English upper classes (and the growing fashion in the US) seemed to pose a threat to the assumption of a European civilised body to which the savage was the other. Thus the need for Lombroso to publish a paper in a magazine devoted to *Popular Science*: accepting that those who practised tattooing in their natural surrounding were savages, primitives, could be proof that those who practised it in civilised surroundings had an affinity with the savage or primitive. But the affinity could not be seen as some form of cultural transmission; instead the same savage instincts were said to be at work. The English, it was thought, were different, in part because they lacked scientific understanding of the tattoo. They did not realise that the fashion they were emulating was the true badge of the savage and the identifier of the deviant.

1896 also saw the publication of *Moko – Or Maori Tattooing*, by Horatio Robley (reprinted 1998), a text he wrote to support the specialised record he had drawn of tattoo patterns and of his collection of dried heads that was until recently the major source on Maori tattoos or *Moko*. Robley (1840–1930), who dedicated his text to all those 'who had fought against the warriors of New Zealand', was a soldier, artist and collector of native items. He was stationed in Burma and India before serving in New Zealand from 1863 to 1866. During that time he made many sketches of military campaigns and of Maori life, also learning the Maori language and fathering a child with a Maori woman. He made detailed drawings of many *Moko* and was sympathetic towards understanding their culture.

As well as the drawings he made (one of which is reproduced below as Figure 6.2), he relied upon the study of various dried preserved tattooed heads or *Moko Moki*. The tattooed heads that the Maoris preserved and sold to Europeans were thought to be those of chiefs killed in battle; in fact many were the heads of captured persons tattooed and then killed to provide a valuable item for European 'scientific' consumption in trade for muskets. After retiring Robley decided to acquire as many as he could and built up a collection of 35 heads.[4] Although culturally sympathetic, Robley assumed that the practice of collecting and displaying these heads would be

Figure 6.2 Watercolour by Horatio Robley of Te Kuha, July 1864. Robley wrote on the back of the painting that the assembled Maoris were amazed at the accurate rendering of the *Te Moko*. Courtesy of Alexander Turnbull Library, Wellington, New Zealand (reference no A-080-065).

---

4   We may note the changing cultural sensitivities. In 1908, Robley offered them to the New Zealand Government for £1,000 but they refused his offer. He sold 30 of them later to the Natural History Museum, New York, for £1,250. Today the return of *Moko Moki* is official New Zealand Government policy and a specialist unit for repartition of native remains is part of Ta Papa (the National Museum).

the only remaining evidence of a dead people and witness to their past *mana*. *Mana* was a central concept for Maori – roughly translated it means prestige, power, influence, authority and control. The *mana* of the Maori chiefs, symbolised by the *Te Moko* (in early title deeds, for example, many Chiefs 'signed' by drawing their *Moko*) was widely expected to die – the only hope for the Maori was to become brown *Pakeha* (white New Zealanders of European descent). By the early 20th century virtually no examples of male *Moko* could be found, although the practice continued amongst women in rural areas, usually as a form of cultural resistance to European practices. However, the effects of missionaries and the concern aroused by a male wearing *Moko* had made the practice virtually dead, only recorded by European painters and some photographers.

But Maori did not die out; nor did *Te Moko*. Today there is a cultural renaissance, seen by many *Pakeha* as dangerous. As this chapter was written, the quality daily New Zealand newspaper *The Press* presented images of a 15,000 Maori strong *hikoi*, or protest march, concerning certain proposed legislation affecting perceived Maori rights in terms of photos of 'warriors in traditional dress in central Wellington' that portrayed men with painted *Moko* and body tattoos. Another image was of 'the heavily tattooed … Maori activist Tame Iti' talking on his mobile phone (*The Press*, 6 May 2004). Here, perhaps, we have the ambivalence of recognising resistance to central power; is the contemporary Maori radical the urban savage? Whatever the answer to that question, Lombroso completely misunderstood the function of tattoo in Maori culture. Every *Moko* contained ancestral or tribal messages that pertained to the wearer. These messages narrate a wearer's family, sub-tribal and tribal affiliations and their position within these social structures. *Te Moko* would present the wearer by way of their genealogy, and give recognition to their knowledge or expertise indicating their participation ability within each social level. The power of participation (or authority) of a wearer would be symbolised and it would be clear whether this was because of hereditary bloodlines or arose through acquired qualification or expertise. This was fundamental for the conceptual and practical rituals of encounter. Maori today still give great respect to those with senior birthrights and in earlier times a complex pattern of respect was due to persons on the basis of their birthright. Not granting proper respect was regarded as insult and could easily end in fatalities or, worse, generations of unresolved feuding. *Te Moko* had, then, a practical role in observing and maintaining the hierarchical custom-based structure of authority. Thus ironically – considering Lombroso – *Te Moko* portrayed information pertaining to recognising (the status and rank of) an individual wearer, a practice that aided social control and the cohesion of tribal groupings.

Today we are all too aware that the information about *Moko* symbolism, and the directions and instructions about how to read them, is insufficient and inadequate. There is also the fact that Maori art and its symbolisms are largely suggestive, somewhat ambiguous and fraught with many tribal and sub-tribal variants. To fully understand *Te Moko* would require a comprehensive grasp of the traditional or customary social structures and their inherent hierarchical systems, lifestyles, activities and pastimes, the belief system with its inherent controls, and operative concepts within their arts. Knowledge that Lombroso could not, understandably, invest his time and energy in acquiring, for a criminology interested in supporting the power to dominate could not be culturally sympathetic.

Conclusion

Lombroso invested great effort in collecting material culture and presenting these as 'facts' held together as an objective, scientific enterprise. He sought to catalogue and map the representational characteristics of the criminal as a positive entity in time and place. These procedures and methodologies were intended to be transferable and replicable in whatever society wanted criminological knowledge. Today the items he collected and his methods of representation appear incongruous and illogical, but the structure of positivism remains, as quantitative article after article in leading journals bear witness. In assessing this contemporary legacy we should remember how Lombroso's collecting zeal and presenting zeal, his scientific positivism, was performance art in the service of European power. As he stated: 'nothing is less logical than to try to be too logical; nothing is more imprudent than to try to maintain theories … if they are going to upset the order of society' (1918: 379). It was wise therefore that he 'happily' found that 'scientific knowledge' was 'not at war but in alliance with social order and practice' (*ibid*: 379). Concentrating on positivist practices of active representation and fixing we may neglect other processes of hiding linkages, submerging domination and appropriation. One neglected context was the creation of social order via the practice of colonialism and imperialism.

The crucial act of imperialism was mapping. The world was set out in acts of visualisation that relied upon concepts of fixture – latitude and longitude – that had their bases in a European power of recognition and appropriation. Today much of what was then established is the accepted technology for mapping and locating the features of the world. We see with the gaze that was therein constructed; in part we follow a cultural practice, one that is seen as faithfully representing the crucial features of the natural world, or, put another way, that cultural practice has a performability that gives it continued acceptance. Lombroso worked within that overall logic, applying it to the 'place' of Italy, but the logic, we were told, was universal. The 'natural' sciences may not rely upon their acceptance by their subjects; but criminology was, and is, however, a social science that exists within the realms of culture, and of normative questioning and assertion, of ambiguities and ambivalences. Positivism attempts to 'naturalise' a political and cultural interaction. Against this must be stressed that crime and the reaction to crime cannot but concern sites for the interaction of the many forms of social power, the exercise of forms of power and strategies of resistance.

Earlier I implied that the Museum that Lombroso founded is no longer a living testament to power. I may be wrong, for it may serve as an example of mainstream criminology's continual denial and repression of strategies of resistance that would call into question the power of representation and domination that has been the centre of the process of European globalisation or enlightenment. To walk within the museum is to bear witness to processes wherein Lombroso tried to turn cultural objects into items of plain fact, able to represent the criminal as the other. These relied upon complex strategies of reduction and distancing; wherein Lombroso asked us to enter into his arrangements of visual distinction but hid the fact that they are also ones of deciding cultural worth – that function was pushed into the invisible. The expressions of other cultures were made into something that we can look at as simple fact, and in this there was no sense of human affinity or common capacities. Today, in our post-September 11 world, we may need that sensibility above all. Undeniably, we will have to fight to exercise it.

References

Broeckmann, A (1995) *A Visual Economy of Individuals*, web publication accessed 20 June 2003: www.v2.nl/~andreas/phd

Fletcher, R (1971) [1882] 'Tattooing among civilised people', an address illustrated by photographs and drawings at the 61st regular meeting of the Anthropology Society of Washington, 1882, in *Transactions of the Anthropology Society of Washington*, New York: Kraus Reprint Co

Fo'a, PP (2003) 'Science, pseudoscience and public policy in fascist Italy, physical anthropology, phrenology, constitutional medicine and eugenics: the slippery slope of racism', web publication accessed 4 April 2004: www.reed.edu/~sheaa/primary%20documents/ eugenics_paper.pdf

Giorgio, C (1975) *La scienza infelice: Il museo di antropologia criminale di Cesare Lombroso*, Turin: Bollati Boringhieri

Gould, S (1981) *The Mismeasure of Man*, New York: Norton

Horn, D (2003) *The Criminal Body: Lombroso and the Anatomy of Deviance*, London: Routledge

Isaacs, J (1999) *Spirit Country: Contemporary Australian Aboriginal Art*, Victoria: Hardie Grant

Lombroso, C [1876, 1887] (1972) [*L'Uomo Delinquente*] *Criminal Man: The Heritage of Modern Criminology*, Sawyer, F and Sylvester, SF, Jr (eds), Cambridge, MA: Schenkman

Lombroso, C (1896) 'The savage origin of tattooing', *Popular Science Monthly* (April), pp 793–803

Lombroso, C (1918) *Crime: Its Causes and Remedies*, Horton, H (trans), Boston, MA: Little, Brown and Co

Lombroso-Ferrero, G (1911) *Criminal Man, according to the classification of Cesare Lombroso, with an introduction by Cesare Lombroso*, New York: GP Putnam

Lombroso-Ferrero, G (1915) *Cesare Lombroso: Storia della vita e delle opera narrate dalla figia*, Turin: Bocca

Mannheim, H (1972) *Pioneers in Criminology*, 2nd edn, Montclair, NJ: Patterson Smith

Morrison, W (2005) *Criminology, Civilisation and the New World Order*, London: GlassHouse Press

Morwood, MJ (2002) *Visions from the Past: The Archaeology of Australian Aboriginal Art*, Crows Nest: Allen & Unwin

Pick, D (1989) *Faces of Degeneration: A European Disorder, c 1848–1919*, Cambridge: CUP

Robley, H [1896] (1998) *Moko: The Art and History of Maori Tattooing*, Twickenham: Senate

Wetzell, R (2000) *Inventing the Criminal: A History of German Criminology, 1880–1914*, Chapel Hill, NC: University of North Carolina Press

Chapter 7
Crime, Ethnicity and the Multicultural Administration of Justice

Frank Bovenkerk and Yucel Yesilgöz

After more than a century, the *vendetta* has returned to Western Europe. In the quiet, small Dutch towns of Zevenaar and Velp, two extended families of Kurds are responsible for five deaths. Immigrant families from Diyarbakir in eastern Turkey, they are related to each other. The first death in 1994 appears to have been a simple case of murder: the owner of a pub they jointly ran shot his nephew in the back in the course of a business disagreement. However, five years later and three months after the offender from Zevenaar was released from prison, he in turn was murdered. To this very day, the family in Velp claim they did not hire a hit man to do the job, but at the Kurdish coffee shop, the old men know better: Velp finally took vengeance. Shortly after the second murder, the father from Velp went on holiday to Turkey, where he was murdered. On 8 April 2000 – the larger extended family from Velp had come for a commemoration ceremony – there was a confrontation between the two families in Zevenaar. Two of the relatives from Velp were riddled with bullets, another two wounded, as was one from Zevenaar, probably by a bullet fired by his own group. The relatives from Velp say they didn't even have guns, but the ones from Zevenaar definitely came prepared. To be able to defend themselves, they say, they were armed with pistols and even a Kalashnikov.

What in the world are the Dutch Police and Justice Departments supposed to do about these unusual crimes? There is no time to spare, because there are certain to be new victims before long. In addition to the people from the local Turkish community who know what is going on, anthropological experts can predict who the next victim is likely to be just by doing some genealogical backtracking. Both families nonetheless state that it is not a traditional feud. The folks from Velp are eager to get past archaic customs such as honour and blood vengeance and the ones from Zevenaar say they have no choice but to adequately protect themselves.

Essentially there is little a criminal court judge in the Netherlands can do. The criminal justice system only seems to intensify the conflict. In 2002 the Arnhem Court of Appeals unexpectedly released the gunmen from Zevenaar. The court 'considered it plausible that a vendetta situation can cause so much fear that self-defence is justified'. Ever since, tension between the two families has been on the rise. They meet every day at school, on the market, at the hospital, at the clubs where the youths go. There may be a new victim any day now. The inadequacy of the criminal justice system is painfully obvious. Criminal law might serve any number of functions (retribution, crime prevention, rehabilitation), but settling disputes or dealing with vendettas is not one of them.

The two families are taking matters into their own hands and looking for the kind of solution they are familiar with from the old country and hope will be effective in new circumstances. Peace can be established by restoring the balance. The family that committed the last murder has to offer compensation, for example by allowing one of their girls to marry an older man from the other family. But it won't be much help in Europe nowadays, since the families are so assimilated that it is not likely any of the young daughters would be willing to co-operate. Peace can also be established by having one family give the other a plot of land or pay a substantial sum of money. However, the families are so well integrated that they are aware that the authorities implement ethnic minority policy by granting subsidies. Won't the Mayor of Zevenaar pay fifty thousand euros to appease the wrath of the family in Velp? It might be a short-term solution, but considering the precedent it would be creating, the town authorities can hardly be expected to consider it an attractive option. It wouldn't satisfy the aggrieved party either, since it is the enemy they want to see suffer, not the town authorities. Lastly, efforts can be made to have a third party try to mediate. The family in Velp initially sought the help of the Kurd Parliament-in-exile in Brussels, but to no avail. The politicians listened to their story, but their attention was distracted at the time by the recent arrest of their political leader Öcelan, who was being put on trial in Turkey.

On 9 March 2001 a letter was sent to the Queen of the Netherlands. Couldn't she 'find some influential people who could mediate between the two families in this conflict'? The letter was passed on to the Minister of Justice, who did indeed find a 'wise man' who would fit the bill. Each of the parties had someone in mind similar to what they knew back home in Turkey as the *aga* – a local despot who would use his own armed men if necessary to get people to show the proper respect. He was there but in keeping with Dutch custom he was unarmed. One of the two extended families conceded and allowed the Dutch authorities to arrange for them to move. It meant resettlement for more than 20 nuclear families. Before the local authorities grant final permission, years will have gone by. And how many more deaths will that entail?

Criminal cases like this attract a great deal of European media attention. They are the ones that stand out in the endless list of daily problems generated by the increasing ethnic and cultural pluriformity of modern society. Like the Netherlands, Great Britain, France, Germany, Belgium and other European countries have experienced large-scale immigration since World War Two. It was quite some time before their authorities were willing to face the fact that they had become immigration countries, but they now do. Today more than half the pupils at the schools in many European metropolises are from immigrant families. Institutions in the fields of health care, education and business have to deal with a growing diversity of patients, pupils and customers. The same holds true for the administration of justice. Although not many officials feel free to speak about it openly, we believe every aspect of the criminal justice apparatus in all the countries of Western Europe is under pressure to work towards ethnic diversification. They also look for alternatives to criminal law to solve problems of deviant behaviour.

Criminal court judges may well have been extremely hesitant to allow cultural considerations to play a role in their decisions. There are strict norms of criminal justice procedures and judges attribute a great deal of significance to the principle of equality in special cases that put them in the spotlight. But in the investigation and prosecution stages of criminal justice proceedings as well as the punishment stage, it is already quite common to take the defendants' ethnic background into consideration. So far, the only European country where legal decisions based on cultural diversity have been openly discussed (Poulter 1998) and where the Judicial Studies Board made an *Equal Treatment Bench Book* (1999) available as an aid to judges is Great Britain.

In the Netherlands, we have researched ethnic diversification in the treatment of offenders (Bovenkerk, Komen and Yesilgöz 2003). In fact, a great deal of experimentation is going on. The boards of directors of the institutions and departments involved have discretionary competence to take whatever measures they deem effective and respectful to the culture of their clients. This may not be accepted in theory, but in actual practice taking culture into consideration has long been part and parcel of the proceedings. Let us give one example of cultural exceptions of this kind at each of two stages in the criminal justice chain.

The prosecutor who agrees with an alternative punishment if the offence is not all too severe can close a criminal case in Holland. This keeps youths from having to go through a damaging procedure in the criminal justice system. One precondition for a HALT – ie alternative – settlement is that a confession has been signed. After all, what sense would it make to be punished for something you have not done? The staff at the HALT office are surprised at how few ethnic minority youths they see there, even though they do clearly play a major role in the crime figures. Selectivity in the investigation process? Discrimination? The police have a different explanation. They are clearly under the impression that ethnic minority youths often fail to meet the confession criterion (Wartna, Beijers and Essers 1999). It is not so much that they refuse to confess because it is not clear they committed the crime (the evidence is often technically sufficient and sometimes they were even caught in the act). The problem is that they are following the cultural precept of not admitting having engaged in such a shameful act. The solution opted for by the Public Prosecutor is a pragmatic case for exemption. In these cases the confession is not required: 'Youths who [have to] plead not guilty for reasons of religious faith or cultural background' are now nonetheless eligible for an alternative settlement.

Repeat offences are extremely common among juvenile delinquents of Moroccan descent and since it would be worthwhile to at least examine whether Moroccan social workers do better with them than Dutch ones, an experiment was conducted in Amsterdam in 1993 with a separate penal institution exclusively for Moroccan youths. In *Amal* (the Moroccan word for hope), Moroccan social workers treat their clients in keeping with 'Moroccan norms, values, and customs'. The experiment failed after the youths complained about the personnel beating them.

May or should the ethnic background of criminal offenders play a role in all the steps of criminal justice proceedings? The trend towards ethnic pluriformity in the criminal justice system calls to mind five basic related questions. The first four are of an empirical criminological nature and pertain to the new multicultural societies in Europe. (1) Do ethnic minorities really each have their own crime patterns? (2) Are these crime patterns based on cultural differences? If so, (3) Is there also evidence of differences in their ideas on crime and punishment? (4) To what extent do administrators of criminal justice in the broad sense (from policemen to prison guards) already give in to the pressure generated by these differences and the temptation to treat ethnic minorities differently? What solutions have they come up with? The last question is of a normative nature. It pertains to multiculturalism as a political ideology rather than multiculturality as an empirical fact: (5) Is the introduction of legal pluralism along ethnic lines desirable? Let us address these questions in the same sequence. Although many of our examples are taken from the Netherlands, which we know best and where, for reasons we note below, more experimenting has been going on than in other countries, the issues addressed should be relevant for all modern industrialised immigration countries.

I Ethnic crime patterns

The issue of immigrant and ethnic minority crime, particularly among the second generation, has been noted across Western Europe (Tonry 1997; Haen-Marshall 1997). Multifarious studies have been conducted. There is still, however, little consensus on how to define the problem. Are relatively high crime rates the result of social disadvantage? Are they attributable to the dislocation accompanying the migration process? Do they result from discrimination by the criminal law system? To what degree does it have to do with culture?

In most European countries it is hard to answer these questions, since analysing ethnic specificity in crime is considered undesirable. As each country has its own historical discourse on social problems, each one has its own blind spots of political correctness. In Germany the whole subject of ethnic minority crime is a very emotional matter. Criminologists are hesitant to draw what might be construed as a link to the Third Reich. They object to anyone separately studying the problem of *Ausländerkriminalität* and argue that the offenders (the second generation) were born in Germany and no such distinction should be drawn (Ottersbach and Trautmann 1999). In the United Kingdom the subject has been off limits ever since the aftermath of the London police blunders in the Lawrence case. The black schoolboy Stephen Lawrence was stabbed to death at a bus stop by white racists in 1993, but the police persisted in looking for the killers in immigrant circles. From the moment the committee led by Member of Parliament Macpherson condemned the police shortcomings in 1999, Chiefs of Police in London and Manchester have been openly discussing whether racism is just common among individual police officers, or whether the police force as a whole exhibits institutional racism. It is difficult to discuss the problem of ethnic minority crime in public in Great Britain, and the predominant discourse in criminology pertains to racism among the police and the public (Bowling 1998). In 1999 the Belgian Minister of Justice instructed criminologist Marion van San to conduct a study on crime among ethnic minority youths there. The study was immediately turned into a political issue and was said to promote the interests of the *Vlaams Blok*, an extreme right-wing party on the rise at the time. Even before any of her Belgian colleagues had an inkling of what her study was to entail, they stated in public that ethnicity simply could not be used as explanation because there was too much of a danger of *exoticising* and *essentialising* ethnicity and culture. The monograph on the subject that was published two years later (van San and Leerkes 2001) is still controversial in Belgium. The question was skirted in another way in France. The French conception of citizenship of the Republic assumes that each citizen has an individual relationship with the state, and separate ethnic groups simply do not exist. If there are no separate ethnic groups, obviously there cannot be any such thing as specific ethnic crime problems. The problems that undeniably play a role in the banlieus of Paris, Marseilles and other large cities are not defined as problems of second-generation immigrants, but as problems of slums.

In the Netherlands this *ethnic taboo in criminology* (Karmen 1980) was largely dealt with in the debate following the 1988 leaking of a City of Amsterdam report on Moroccan crime and the dissertation by Marianne Junger in 1990 showing that Moroccan, Turkish and Surinamese youths from the same socio-economic class as Dutch peers really do exhibit far more criminal conduct. After that, interest in the subject mushroomed. The study of ethnic minority crime in the Netherlands is extensive and has generated hundreds of titles. Most of the reports and books are in

Dutch and it will be a while before this output is widely recognised.[1] It is not quite clear why recognition of the problem came so easily. Here we find a possible clue to the Dutch receptiveness of the idea that culture might play a role.[2] The Dutch tradition of accepting cultural differences and the political agreement on non-intervention in religious group cultures – Roman Catholics and various Protestant denominations and the secular segment of the population – was long recognised as the frame of reference in which the Dutch interpret their 'race relations' (Bagley 1973 on *The Dutch Plural Society*). It explains why the Dutch perceive the immigration issue as an ethnic and cultural problem. This may to some degree account for possible selectivity in how the Police and Justice Departments produce such high ethnic minority crime rates as well as the unusual level of interest on the part of Dutch criminologists and politicians.

Another explanation would imply that ethnic minority crime rates are in fact noticeably higher in the Netherlands than elsewhere. Koopmans (2003) ventures into the difficult problem of comparative criminology and is the first to contrast the incarceration rates of minorities in nine European countries. He calculates the degree of overrepresentation of foreign-born inmates, or ethnic or racial minorities if any such data exists, by comparing the percentage of the prison population to their percentage in the total population.[3] It is surprising to see how large the international variation in overrepresentation rates is. Great Britain has the lowest rate of overrepresentation: 2.4 (racial minorities constituting somewhat over 6% of the total population account for 18% of the inmate population), Germany's rate is 4, France's 4.1, Belgium's 4.2 and the Netherlands is highest with 6.3.

2 Ethnic minority crime and culture

The question is of course what is meant in this context by culture or by related concepts such as tradition, orientation or ethnicity. The vendetta example that opened this chapter illustrates how the idea of culture is contested in the courtroom. Most of the ethnographic studies just mentioned adhere to a culturalist definition of the problem and an essentialist conception of ethnicity. Culture is viewed as a set of norms, values and behavioural precepts imported from some distant land. So black youths from Suriname reproduce the hustling culture of Paramaribo, Moroccans bring in an attitude of mutual distrust from the Rif mountain region, criminal Antilleans stab each other with much the same knives they used in the Curacao ghetto and immigrants from Turkey follow the honour rules from back home down to every last detail. An independent and compelling force towards crime and deviance is attributed to the cultures of the countries of origin. If immigrants or their progeny refer to their tradition in these ethnographies, it is as if they have a pure source of culture in their native country.

---

1   However, F Brion, a Belgian professor who reads Dutch, wrote an overview in French with a typically condescending title: '*Une curiosité néerlandaise*', reflecting the politically correct position in Belgium that is noted above (Brion 2003).

2   We are unable to substantiate our impression here that the British discourse on social problems tends to focus on disadvantages stemming from social class differentials whereas the French look at individual psychopathology.

3   This arithmetic is fraught, however, with methodological problems, eg which ethnic groups are included in the statistics and which are not?

According to another and in many ways diametrically opposed constructivist view, however, culture is not a given, it is not a *thing* that shapes human conduct outside the individuals themselves. Instead it should be seen as an analytical notion that constitutes an abstract version of their behaviour and ideas (Baumann 1996: 11). In addition, culture should be considered as the outcome of the process in which people give meaning to their world, and the formation of ethnic groups is a process that develops by way of collective identification (Verkuyten 1997). The formation of ethnic groups is frequently accompanied by drawing ethnic borders and cultivating or even inventing traditions. Conceived in this way, culture and ethnicity are in themselves qualities that require explanation, and not fixed givens of traditions that provide an explanation for whatever phenomena are under examination, such as special forms of crime.

The implication of this view is that ethnically specific crime is in itself also the result of a social construction and the manipulation of ideas and practices. It emerges within a certain social context and in interaction with the environment. Criminals use their culture creatively and manipulate it to get what they want. When they refer to laws or legal conceptions in the countries they come from, they might well have long since ceased to exist, if they ever existed at all. In our own research in the relatively new tradition of cultural criminology as it is conducted at the Willem Pompe Criminology Research Institute of the University of Utrecht, researchers constantly discover examples of manipulation of culture. Coppes, De Groot and Sheerazi (1997) describe young Moroccan offenders who convince the police that they are going to be beaten so viciously by their father or older brother that they ought to be released without informing their family. Zaitch (2002) writes an inside story of cocaine traffickers operating in Holland and his treatment of cultural explanations for crime is more subtle and embedded in a framework of interpretation that is basically economic. He notes that drug dealers strategically refer to the Colombian cartels in order to get the upper hand. Bovenkerk, Siegel and Zaitch (2002) describe the manipulation of criminal reputations by Columbian cocaine dealers, Nigerian prostitutes, Russian mafiosi, Turkish heroin dealers and former Yugoslav bodyguards in the Dutch underworld. The administrators of criminal justice faced with ethnic minority criminals come up against people who make this kind of strategic use of their essentialised *culture*.

'Cultural offences' or 'culturally motivated crimes' (Van Broeck 2001) constitute an intriguing variation of the ethnicity and crime nexus. In keeping with the reasoning of Thorsten Sellin in 1938, crime may result from ethnic minorities following their own conduct norms and violating the law of their new homeland. The most well-known serious crime incidents pertain to avenging blood and honour, kidnapping and abducting, violence as sanction for violating exogamy rules, offences under the influence of magic, the circumcision of girls, funeral rituals and any number of forms of political crime and corruption. The offenders present themselves to the judge as people acting in accordance with their political or religious convictions and they will accept all the consequences. In the eyes of the parties involved, the customs are not viewed as being against the law; in fact if they did not adhere to them they would endanger their position in their own community and perhaps even run the risk of being ostracised. These customs date back to before the time when state law was introduced in their home country and are still more or less accepted or completely permitted by the authorities in various countries or regions. There are numerous examples of criminal justice systems where under certain circumstances, cultural exceptions are permitted or a certain extent of leniency is accepted as a norm. In Iran for example, people participating in a blood feud as a matter of honour are not prosecuted, and in Turkey people who have killed to defend their family honour might get away with only an eighth of the standard sentence for murder. The defendants and their lawyers do not hesitate to refer to the traditional rules if they think that doing so will lead to more lenient treatment or a total acquittal.

Culturally motivated offences present an interesting problem for the criminologist and deserve ample theoretical consideration. If we look at our – ethnocentric – textbooks, cultural offences do not really fall under any of our definitions of crime. Despite the international variety, crime is always defined as undesirable deviant behaviour and usually there are victims. Cultural crimes, however, evoke a great deal of approval in certain communities and the individuals we might view as the victims do not necessarily define themselves as such. Criminologists examine social and psychological or biological conditions causing deviant behaviour. In culture-related crime the offences are committed by individuals who prevent deviance from happening or getting worse. In cases of honour vengeance, the perpetrator seems to have no other choice but to cleanse the sullied reputation of his family (usually involving gossip about the moral conduct of a daughter, sister or mother) and it is evident from his attitude in court that he feels no shame about what he has done. To him and his family, the legal proceedings that ensue are of secondary importance. The main thing is that they can once again hold their heads up in the community, and all they are interested in as far as the court is concerned is damage control. Gambian or Somalian girls who have been circumcised can now expect boys in their circles to want to marry them. Culture-related crime entails the kind of offence people feel obliged to commit because of their cultural background and the immense social and psychological pressure exerted on them by their friends or relatives. In fact they do not view it as a crime at all and want to commit the act for a sacred cause.

Individuals who commit cultural offences do not fit our stereotypical profile of the criminal. Criminals are usually seen as young men from the poorer segments of society, usually unemployed, poorly educated if at all, with no family responsibilities and so forth. They are often repeat offenders, and the first offenders among them are likely to become repeat offenders in the future. Criminals take risks. If they are caught, there is a good chance that they will be registered or punished. Their social position worsens as a result of being punished. This is why criminals use neutralisation techniques or retrospective excuses for their behaviour. However, culture-related crime is mainly committed or ordered by people who are socially strong and in positions of command.

As to their *motivation*, let us follow the reasoning of the criminal inspired by faith. Crime is a bad thing, so under normal conditions people make every effort at home, at school, at work and in their leisure time to stay away from it. If this proves impossible, people who have to break the rules find they have sinned in the eyes of God or Allah. He is the one who will punish them. The authorities are not, however, willing to wait, and have developed criminal law systems and take it upon themselves to arrest and punish criminals. The cultural offender simply has to bear the consequences, though the state's reaction is of secondary importance to him.

Despite their universalist pretension, mainstream theories in criminology have little explanatory power in the field of cultural crime. Theories with the most evident shortcomings are (a) deterrence theory, which criminal law is founded upon, Sutherlans' (b) differential association theory, or (c) Hirshi's control paradigm. (a) People who commit a culture-related crime know in advance that the authorities are going to address the matter and this is not taken into consideration in their thinking. As a consequence, deterrence does not work. In the event of a family feud or vendetta, it can happen that someone is shot just as he comes out of the front gate of a prison after being released. (b) Offenders are not lured into crime by evil friends as differential association would have it, viewing the notion of culture-related crime as a *good friends theory*. They can have a decent life and nice friends and if they want to keep them, they have to restore the honour that has been taken away. At any rate, that is what their *good friends* expect them to do. As soon as the problem is solved, the offender goes back to his respectable life. (c) Culture-related crime is mainly committed or ordered by people who are socially strong and not by those with weak or severed ties with conventional society, as social control theory would have it. The have a status in society, or at any rate with their friends and relatives. This status would be diminished by their not committing a crime.

It is true that cultural offences of this type are not so common and barely exert any influence on ethnic-specific crime rates, but every time they do occur they present criminal justice authorities with a fundamental problem. The courtroom gives the members of the group an opportunity to solicit respect for their ideas and might even serve as a possible forum for collective action.

3 Ethnic diversity in ideas on crime and punishment

In principle, the approach taken by the Police and Justice Departments and other agencies involved in the administration of criminal justice in the broadest sense of the term is based upon the assumption that all their measures affect ethnic minority offenders in much the same way as majority ones. To a certain extent, ideas about good and evil and what is a crime and what is not are universal (Van Dijk and Zvekic 1993), and the same holds true for how seriously certain crimes are viewed in various countries (Newman 1980). A general validity is attributed to the instrumental results of criminal justice, such as general prevention. In some cases and among some ethnic minorities, the state's criminal justice system does not, however, have the intended effect and sometimes its conduct even proves to be counter-productive.

In the first instance this can result from poor communication. The literature on the sociology of law is filled with illustrations of cultural misunderstandings. One example is set in New York, where new immigrants from Russia who are about to be fined for not stopping at a red light give the traffic cops some money, as is their wont. To their surprise they are arrested for attempted bribery (Ryan and Rush 1997: 150). The solution is interesting. The police are given a training course in cultural sensitivity and a special lecture on American police methods is organised for the Russians of Brighton Beach in Brooklyn. Another example is set in Detroit (Hamed and Moore 1999: 113). Immigrants from the Middle East have a hard time comprehending the American system of plea bargaining. Even if the sentence is shorter than the one commonly given for the specific offence, how can they confess to a crime they have not committed? Or so the immigrants tend to reason, and they are not the only ones. A defence attorney comes up with a solution. In the presence of his client, he offers the prosecuting attorney a $20 bill, which of course is returned to him afterwards, just to show that the prosecuting attorney is willing to consider a compromise. The clients recognise and accept the process.

In the second instance, there really are differences in people's legal conceptions and norms. If immigrants and their children rapidly assimilate, this issue of diversity in notions of crime and punishment plays a role only for a short time, if at all. But it plays far more of a role if immigrants do not plan to stay for good or choose to preserve and advance their own cultures, and the continuing influx keeps them well informed on all the latest developments *back home*. Many modern governments implicitly acknowledge immigrants' wishes by adopting multiculturalism as a policy goal. Immigrant public participation agencies express their points of view on the national policy on criminal justice, and more specifically on the policy pertaining to their group. Ethnic minority elites speak out. One would expect a natural tendency in individual criminal cases to plead for cultural leniency. To our surprise, we find many instances of the opposite. Immigrant conceptions of criminal law include a more severe approach rather than shorter sentences. This follows from their general social critique on soft, Western society. A good example is the now famous case of gang rape in Sydney, Australia, that contributed to a heated debate on the links between ethnicity and crime. The 20-year-old second-generation Lebanese leader of the gang was sentenced to a prison sentence of no less than 55 years. Melbourne criminologist Arie Freiberg wrote in the *Sunday Age* of 18 August 2002 that this 'extreme sentence is seen by members of the offender's community as racist, and this may diminish rather than promote respect for the law'. Instead, leaders of the Lebanese community found (in the same issue of the newspaper) that the defendant should be put away for life! 'If the rape had occurred in Lebanon, the offenders almost certainly would have been put to death.'

It is certainly surprising to note that ethnic minority leaders in the Netherlands are in favour of the further investigation of crime in their own communities. One might think that these ethnic minority leaders have been made accessories by the Dutch authorities and this is the result of the typically Dutch ethnic minority policy. The parties note that they themselves, as experts by experience, are in a position to propose better interventions outside as well as within the criminal justice system. In 1991 the Turkish Public Participation Agency published a booklet called *Turkish Youths Between Immigration and Gangs*, citing the role of Turkish gangs in the drug trade and requesting that the authorities implement an integral special approach focused on Turks. In 1994, the National Federation of Chinese Organisations in the Netherlands published a booklet called *Characters in the Lowlands* asking the authorities for help in dealing with extortion in their restaurant sector. In 1988, a Moroccan Youth Commission consisting of prominent members of the Moroccan community proposed a number of measures for combating Moroccan juvenile delinquency in *Moving Confidently Towards the Future Together*. The Antillean community was mobilised by the Antillean Co-Citizenship Advisory Commission in the Netherlands. In its report *Nèt Loke Falta* in December 2001, it demanded co-responsibility in dealing with the crime problem among Antillean youths.

To what extent do various ethnic minorities really have their own ideas on crime and punishment? We can assume that the first generation of immigrants largely adhere to the ideas that prevail in the country or region they come from.[4] But does this still hold true for the second generation, who are the ones exhibiting high crime rates? Do they really consider themselves second-generation immigrants, or do they define themselves as first-generation Dutch, German or French? And what about the

---

4   This might be different for specific immigrant groups such as political refugees.

third generation? Are they totally assimilated, or do they still have their own points of view and their own attitudes? There is a certain consensus on this point in the literature. Although values and norms are certainly shaped in part by the parents, there is a sizeable generation gap, particularly regarding ideas on crime and punishment. The parents were socialised in a different type of society and are only capable of preparing their children for the new land to a limited extent. In a comparative historic study on this problem in the United States, Waters (1999) notes that the second generation is exposed to an unbalanced and inconsistent mixture of influences on their upbringing exerted by the family, the street, the school and the mass media. The multicultural society generates hybrid and multi-layered personalities and this is obvious from the attitude to crime and punishment.

In the Netherlands, Akkas (1999) is the first to have made an effort to research this point using group interviews with Turkish youths. The topic seems extremely conducive to socially desirable responses. In theory of course, all the respondents are against violence, but if the researcher's question pertains to them personally, then, unlike their Dutch peers, they prove quite willing to ruthlessly avenge any offence to the honour of their family. Whatever punishment this might involve for them is of only secondary importance. This first research finding inspires us to further examine the relation between various interpretations of the concept of culture. Even though the constructivist idea of culture seems superior as to flexibility and agency, the deeper levels of the personality might contain some kind of ethnic core identity. Is there space for a combination of the two? Based on insights from the theory of critical realism, Bader (2001) reasons that the points of view need not be mutually exclusive. In describing ethnic identity, it is possible to adjust a double focus by devoting attention to the static as well as the dynamic elements of culture.

4 Multicultural criminal justice

Even if there is still no academically conclusive evidence that ethnic minorities each have their own ideas on crime on punishment, there is no dearth of complaints voiced by criminal justice officials about how the usual approach does not work. Minorities do not take them seriously because these expect a very different kind of behaviour from the police and courts. Dutch alternative sentencing does not have much of an effect on groups they feel have a totally different perception of punishment (Klooster, van Hoek and van 't Hoff 1999).

It is probably the police who have the greatest willingness to experiment. Police officers have been appointed as 'intercultural intermediaries' to improve the poor communication between delinquent youths and their parents. Special projects have been developed such as *Talking to Moroccan Parents* and special contact officials have been appointed to stimulate communication with the local ethnic minority community. The *Neighbourhood Fathers Project* in West Amsterdam, entailing a kind of neighbourhood watch of Moroccans for Moroccans, has even gained international acclaim. The creativity is overwhelming. Police officers organise homework classes, athletic events, sailing weekends and survival expeditions in mountainous regions for ethnic minority youths.

There is little evidence, though, of this kind of cultural experimentation in the course of criminal proceedings themselves. In the courtroom, the Public Prosecutor does sometimes wonder whether to include the issue of ethnic background in his closing statement. He can formulate a relatively lengthy sentence as a warning to other members of the group. In one Dutch court case against the father of a Turkish youth ordered by him to commit a violent act of revenge to defend the honour of the family, the Public Prosecutor formulates a lengthy sentence. 'As far as I am concerned, the message should be very clear. In our society, violent acts of revenge to defend the honour of the family are not tolerated.' Lawyers are faced with the problem of whether or not to present the suspect's culture as an extenuating circumstance. One disadvantage of doing so is that the defendant always has to confess to the offence. In older immigration countries, this problem has long been acknowledged. In the United States the *cultural defence* has even been somewhat diffidently developed, and the culture of members of ethnic minorities is one of the considerations that can work in their favour in criminal cases (Renteln 1995). The same holds true in Australia and Canada, although there it is primarily in relation to the special position and group rights of native peoples. The difficulty is always translating cultural considerations that pertain by definition to a whole category of people into the Western criminal justice system, which is focused in principle on the individual, not the group. In essence, culture can never provide a valid excuse, though it should clearly play a role in how the judge evaluates the personal background of the accused.

The defence lawyer cannot use a cultural defence for his client in Europe, though he can invoke other grounds for exemption from criminal liability. Firstly, he can plead that the defendant used force in self-defence. The social or internally perceived pressure is so great that the accused is unable to withstand it, as in the case of the vendetta at the beginning of this chapter. Secondly, lawyers can plead *provocation*. They can refer to severe aggravation in the event of a public offence to their client's honour. Thirdly, the perpetrators of cultural offences can be declared *insane* so they are not held responsible if the judge fails to understand the nature of the act or if he wishes to consider extenuating circumstances without explicitly citing the cultural background of the accused in the sentencing. We can expect cases of insanity plea to occur increasingly in Europe, for example in crimes involving people possessed by demons. Fourthly, it is possible in principle to plead innocence in cases where members of ethnic minorities are not familiar with the law. This can for example be the case when they send money home via informal banking systems. People from countries without a banking infrastructure think all you need to do is go to a banker who calls a relative or some trusted person and tells him to give the money to the beneficiary. This can mean a violation of the law rendering underground banking a punishable act. This law has been formulated to combat organised crime or terrorism, but this form of informal banking is an everyday thing for people from some Third World countries.

Judges tend to cling to the rules and generally hold their tongue. They are, however, facing a dilemma in that they want to consider the defendants' sense of justice and sometimes do allow cultural background to play a role in their judgment. In the final sentencing, at most this can be found in the form of a covert allusion. Other officials in criminal proceedings face the same dilemma. The forensic report to the court by psychiatrists, which is drawn up from a Western point of view, leads to bizarre problems when dealing with suspects from other cultures. Child Care and Protection Boards and Probation and After-care Councils, which also make recommendations, would prefer not to diversify but in their day-to-day practice they have no choice. This issue also plays a role in the last stage of the criminal justice chain, the enforcement of sentences. Clear efforts are made to take the matter of religious diversity into consideration (Moerings and Post 2003). Measures have been taken to respect religious precepts, there are opportunities to celebrate various religious holidays, which are not automatically included in the existing laws on compulsory labour, various types of meals are prepared, and convicts are permitted to receive religious guidance from their own clergymen.

For more than a decade, efforts have been made at all the country's prisons and penitentiaries to cope with the issue of ethnic diversity. What is the right response? The conduct of the authorities should be understood by the suspects and their communities, it should be in keeping with their sense of justice and it should be effective in that it prevents recidivism. The theoretical question underlying these practical problems is: To what extent should society's ethnic diversity be expressed in judicial diversity? The officials at all the various links in the criminal justice chain are faced with the same dilemmas: Should members of ethnic minorities be treated differently? Where are the boundaries of this special treatment? The principle of equality is deeply embedded in criminal law, and this principle is more crucial than anywhere else in matters of race (in Anglo-Saxon countries) and ethnic or national descent (in Continental Europe). The civil rights movement in the United States and ethnic minority and anti-discrimination organisations in Europe all want the formal equality of procedures for minorities to really lead to material equality. According to ample research, there is still a long way to go before this goal is reached. The police in the United States definitely do discriminate in their investigation methods, Public Prosecutors get very tough when it comes to users of the black drug crack cocaine, judges are less lenient with black defendants, as is also clear from the disproportionately high percentage of blacks condemned to death (Kennedy 1997). Inequality of this kind has also been revealed in studies conducted in Europe.

Matters become even more complex if the social categories ethnic minorities belong to differ as regards a criterion relevant to the administration of criminal justice. The reasoning might then be that it is precisely the inequality in treatment that produces equality. In the United States, this *culturally sensitive approach* is supported by numerous studies in actual practice and included in police, criminal justice and social work training courses. Textbooks discuss 'strategies for peacekeeping in a diverse society' (Shusta *et al* 1995) and the 'culturally sensitive treatment of minority crime victims' (Ogawa 1999). There is an abstract criterion for drawing distinctions that is relevant to the administration of criminal justice. Ethnic minorities can claim a right to special treatment on the grounds of their right to their own culture. Article 27 of the International Covenant on Civil and Political Rights guarantees respect for minorities and their culture. In the judicial system, the discrepancy between the two basic rights, equality and special treatment, can be resolved by making the law more complex, liberalising regulations or applying the principle of discretionary powers. Any number of family law or religious questions can relatively easily be settled using these instruments because it is primarily private life that is entailed and there are no serious consequences for the majority population. This also holds true as regards the social fields that are only weakly institutionalised. The expansion of the Burial and Cremation Act does not generate many problems, nor do days off from work or school on other groups' religious holidays, or greater ritual slaughter options. As regards other issues, though, the ideas and customs of ethnic minorities differ too much from the existing legal rules; polygamy is prohibited and so is female circumcision, compulsory education requirements also apply to girls, supporting a *fatwa* such as the one against Salman

Rushdie is unacceptable, and neither blood feuds nor abduction can be tolerated. General human rights pretty much demarcate the borderline (Poulter 1998; Foblets 2002).

5 Is ethnic pluralism in criminal law desirable?

Is it politically and socially desirable to admit elements of pluralism to the criminal law chain? There are arguments for and against doing so. The ones in favour derive from the political philosophy of multiculturalism. According to the multicultural line of reasoning, cultural diversity ought to be acknowledged and appreciated in modern, liberal democratic societies. The people maintain their relations with the government via the intermediary of the cultural community they are part of. This obliges the state not only to tolerate the cultural identity of individuals and groups, but actively to protect it (Kymlicka 1995). This not only holds true for the pleasing aspects of diversity, it holds true even more for the ideas and customs that tend to evoke irritation and disapproval. This category includes cultural offences generally committed within the group as well as ideas about how the community itself ought to prevent and combat crime. In the administration of criminal justice, taking the cultural background of defendants into consideration inevitably leads to a certain form of legal pluralism.

We have noted the most important instrumental argument in favour of a certain extent of pluralisation in the criminal justice system: taking ethnic specificity into consideration can contribute towards the effectiveness of criminal law and other interventions and thus the reduction of crime. We do not know whether this specificity in the approach really helps. As far as we know, no evaluation studies are available on projects of this kind (*what works?*) that can withstand the test of academic criticism.

Another argument in favour of diversification is that it puts ethnic minorities in a better position to accurately see their own place in the criminal justice system, which gives it an extra element of legitimacy. Something should be said here to counter the obvious argument that taking the defendant's cultural background into consideration works against the social integration of immigrants. Wouldn't immigrants feel more at home in a society that acknowledges their culture and where their views are taken seriously than in a society where unconditional assimilation is required? There are ethnic minority parents who send their children back to their country of origin to get a decent – religious – education there. It is their way of protesting against what they see as the sick Western mind-set and getting their children away from its immorality. After a questionnaire survey, Veenman (1996) concludes that many Turks and Moroccans in the Netherlands send their children *home* for a year, causing them to lag behind in the Dutch school system and on the Dutch labour market.

Now the arguments against diversification. Firstly, the pluralisation of criminal law and its enforcement can reduce the internal cohesion of the law and produce an inconsistent and contradictory conglomerate (Smith 1994). This goes in turn at the expense of its legitimacy and can cause discrimination. A development of this kind can perhaps be avoided if the adaptations follow the logic of a multicultural criminal law theory. As long as no theory of this kind has been developed, it is difficult to state which parts of criminal law can or cannot be adjusted, expanded and sharpened.

This similarly holds true for all the diversification in the approaches of agencies that enforce criminal law. Pluralisation that is not driven by anything but the needs of the day and the latest fashions of the moment produces a shaky entity that contributes in the last instance to the disintegration of society.

The second disadvantage is that the power factor is overlooked. The multiculturalist ideal creates exaggerated expectations on the part of ethnic minorities. Respect for culture is wonderful, but as long as the minorities are so limited that they only constitute a small percentage of the population and as long as they are less privileged in a socio-economic sense, there is little reason to expect them to be able to make any real demands in this connection. Only very marginal adaptations are to be expected, and they have more to do with the nuisance value of ethnic minority juvenile delinquency than real status and esteem acquired via cogent arguments.

The third disadvantage has to do with multiculturalism's virtually inevitable culture fixation and adherence to ethnic stereotypes. In discussing the issue of ethnic causes of crime, we have referred to the reifying and reductionist use of the concept of culture. Anyone wishing to qualify for special treatment based on ethnic exception has little use for a constructivist and consequently relativist concept of culture. Expert witnesses in the courtroom have little choice but to very concisely present highly complicated ideas and practices to judges who need simple information in order to make a decision (Wiersinga 2002). Use is recurrently made of culturalist opinions and in the Netherlands, cultural anthropologists speak in court who reproduce traditional ethnic criminology studies. The culturalist reporting style is similarly dominant in the work of Justice Department agencies such as the Child Care and Protection Boards, the Probation and After-care Councils and the Forensic Psychiatry Department (Bovenkerk, Komen and Yesilgöz 2003). It is primarily the enormous pressure Justice Department staff members – street-level bureaucrats, as Lipsky (1980) calls them – are under at work that leads them to turn to the stereotype pattern as recommendation. In the advice and information provided at all the criminal law agencies now and then, in the numerous training courses on interculturalisation and against racism and in the curriculum at the police academies, we feel that a static and uniformity-oriented depiction of the various ethnic minorities and their culture is presented, or simplified versions of anthropological interpretations of it. The hybrid and multi-layered culture of the second generation of immigrant youths goes against the norms and values of their own group and is not suitable to be incorporated in any way into the national administration of criminal law. When culture is being invoked it alludes back to the Great Tradition in the country of origin, the official conception in the native country, the holy books, unwritten law. The Police and Justice Departments turn to today's religious leaders in the ethnic communities for advice and co-operation in dealing with second-generation crime, even though they are sometimes barely aware of what the day-to-day lives of second-generation youths are like. They consult with the official leaders of the ethnic community, who are often traditional members of the first generation. It has already been noted in American cases where the cultural defence is used that defendants sometimes appear in court in traditional attire. The impression so easily given this way is of a static culture with a high degree of 'orientalism'. There is a good chance that youths' more Western standpoints, the programme of the women's emancipation movement or the more progressive groups will not enter the picture in deliberations. The authorities might be aware of this danger, and wonder which other ethnic minority community leaders they ought to approach instead. There is a good chance that they will opt for more progressive leaders, whose authority in the community is extremely limited and who mainly use their positions to further their own interests. Anyone claiming to represent the entire ethnic community will present it as being more homogenous and exhibiting greater solidarity than is actually the case.

The fourth danger is closely linked to the previous ones. Granting a certain exemption for cultural offences generally has the effect of reinforcing traditional power relations in the ethnic community. The victims of crimes linked to matters of honour or magic are often women or children. Nowadays the most severe criticism of multiculturalism comes from the movement of ethnic minority women (cf the discussion with Susan Okin in *Is Multiculturalism Bad for Women?* (1999)).

Finally, in the practice of criminal justice there is a risk of defendants using their culture as an excuse for the crime they have committed. Bringing culture into the picture is like building on quicksand. Who has a special culture and who doesn't? How many people have to share a set of values and norms for it to be a culture? Where is the moral borderline of admissibility? There are also cultures of tax evaders or drug users. Should we accept Mafia murders because they are part of the Mafia culture? Accepting the cultural defence also means that any number of other suspects can do the same – *me too* – flooding the courts with their exemption claims.

Closing comments

In closing, let us just say that the actors generally assume clear-cut positions in the debate on multiculturalism. We do not do so here because so much can be said for either of the positions, for or against multiculturalism. Of course it is only right that the cultural diversification of modern-day Europe should have certain effects on all the state agencies, including the criminal justice system, and how they work. However, this does not in any way mean that special rights should be granted to groups of people who share a culture or say they do. It does mean, though, that the individual backgrounds of offenders should be taken into consideration, and their cultural orientation can be part of that. Up to now, crime and punishment in multicultural societies has primarily been a field of study in the anthropology of law and the main focus there has been on questions of legal pluralism and settling disputes. We feel that cultural criminology would be able to contribute a great deal towards understanding crime in modern-day society by putting the relation between culture, crime and the administration of criminal law on the research agenda.

References

Akkas, S (1999) '*Maar de hoop is niet gebroken*', *Rechtsopvattingen van Turkse jongeren over het Nederlandse strafrechtsysteem en over bepaalde soorten criminele handelingen*, Scriptie, Utrecht: Willem Pompe Instituut voor Strafrechtswetenschappen

Bader, V (2001) 'Culture and identity' 1(1) *Ethnicities* 139–72

Bagley, C (1953), *The Dutch Plural Society. A Comparative Study in Race Relations*, Oxford: OUP

Baumann, G (1996) *Contesting Culture; Discourses of Identity in Multi-Ethnic London*, New York: CUP

Bovenkerk, F (2003) 'Over de oorzaken van allochtone misdaad', in Bovenkerk, F, Komen, M and Yesilgöz, Y (eds), *Multiculturaliteit in de strafrechtspleging*, Den Haag: Boom Juridische Uitgevers, pp 29–58

Bovenkerk, F, Komen, M and Yesilgöz, Y (eds) (2003) *Multiculturaliteit in de strafrechtspleging*, Den Haag: Boom Juridische Uitgevers

Bovenkerk, F, Siegel, D and Zaitch, D (2003), 'Organized crime and ethnic reputation manipulation' 39(1) *Crime, Law and Social Change* 23–38

Bowling, B (1998), *Violent Racism. Victimisation, Policing and Social Context*, Oxford: OUP

Brion, F (2003) 'Une curiosité néerlandaise. La recherche sur la criminalité des allochtones', *Revue de droit pénal et de criminologie*, June, 767–98

Broeck, J van (2001) 'Cultural defense and culturally motivated crimes' 9(1) *European Journal of Crime, Criminal Law and Criminal Justice* 1–32

Coppes, R, de Groot, F and Sheerazi, A (1997) *Politie en criminaliteit van Marokkaanse jongens*, Deventer: Gouda Quint

Dijk, JJ Van and Zvekic, U (1993) 'Surveying crime in the global village: assumptions, experiences, and ultimate goals', in *Understanding Crime: Experiences & Crime Control*, Rome: UNICRI, pp 365–77

Foblets, M (2002) 'Recht als cultuur, cultuur als recht. Denkpistes voor de multiculturele samenleving' 81(3) *Proces* 35–39

Haen-Marshall, I (ed) (1997) *Minorities, Migrants, and Crime*, Thousand Oaks, CA: Sage

Hamed, M and Moore, JI (1999) 'Middle Easterners in American courts', in Moore, JI (ed), *Immigrants in Courts*, Seattle and London: University of Washington Press, pp 112–16

Judicial Studies Board (1999) *Equal Treatment Bench Book*, downloaded at www.jsboard.co.uk

Junger, M (1990) *Delinquency and Ethnicity. An Investigation on Social Factors Relating to Delinquency among Moroccan, Turkish, Surinamese and Dutch Boys*, Deventer and Boston: Kluwer

Karmen, A (1980) 'Race, inferiority, crime and research taboos', in Sagarin, E (ed), *Taboos in Criminology*, Beverly Hills and London: Sage, pp 81–84

Kennedy, R (1997), *Race, Crime, and the Law*, New York: Vintage

Klooster, EM, van Hoek, AJE and van 't Hoff, CA (1999) *Allochtonen en strafbeleving*, The Hague: Minsterie van Justitie

Koopmans, R (2003) 'Het Nederlandse integartiebeleid in international vergelijkend perspectief; etnische segregatie onder de multiculturele oppervlakte', in Pellikaan, H and Trappenburg, M (eds), *Politiek in de multiculturele samenleving*, Amsterdam: Boom, pp 64–100

Kymlicka, W (1995) *The Rights of Minority Cultures*, Oxford: OUP

Lipsky, M (1980), *Street-level Bureaucracy, Dilemmas of the Individual in Public Services*, New York: Russell Sage Foundation

Moerings M and Post, M (2003) 'In detentie', in Bovenkerk, F, Komen, M and Yesilgöz, Y (eds), *Multiculturaliteit in de strafrechtspleging*, Den Haag: Boom Juridische Uitgevers, pp 151–66

Newman, GR (1980) *Crime and Deviance: A Comparative Perspective*, Beverly Hills, CA: Sage

Ogawa, BK (1999) *Color of Justice*, Boston, MA: Allyn & Bacon

Okin, S (1999) *Is Multiculturalism Bad for Women?*, Princeton, NJ: Princeton UP

Ottersbach, M and Trautmann, SK (eds) (1999) *Integration durch soziale Kontrolle?*, Cologne: Edition Der andere Buchladen

Poulter, S (1998) *Ethnicity, Law and Human Rights. The English Experience*, Oxford: Clarendon

Renteln, AD (1995) 'Culture and culpability: a study of contrasts', in Renteln, AD and Dundes, A (eds), *Folk Law, Vol II*, Madison, University of Wisconsin Press, pp 863–80

Ryan, PJ and Rush, GE (eds) (1997) *Understanding Organized Crime in Global Perspective: A Reader*, Thousand Oaks, CA: Sage

San, M van and Leerkes, A (2001) *Criminaliteit en criminalisering. Allochtone jongeren in België*, Amsterdam: Amsterdam UP

Shusta, RM *et al* (1995) *Multicultural Law Enforcement*, Upper Saddle River: Prentice-Hall

Smith, DJ (1994) 'Race, crime, and criminal justice', in Maguire, M (ed), *The Oxford Handbook of Criminology*, Oxford: OUP, pp 1041–18

Tonry, M (ed) (1997) *Ethnicity, Crime, and Immigration*, Chicago: University of Chicago Press

Veenman, J (1996) *Heb je niets dan ben je niets. Tweede generatie allochtone jongeren in Amsterdam*, Assen: Van Gorcum

Verkuyten, M (1997) 'Discourses of ethnic minority identity' 36 *British Journal of Social Psychology* 565–86

Wartna, BSJ, Beijers, WMEH and Essers, AAM (1999) *Ontkennende en bekennende verdachten. Over de proceshouding van verdachten van strafzaken tijdens het politieverhoor*, WODC-onderzoeksnotities No 5

Waters, T (1999) *Crime and Immigrant Youth*, Thousand Oaks, CA: Sage

Wiersinga, HC (2002) *Nuance in benadering. Culturele factoren in het strafproces*, The Hague: Boom Juridische Uitgevers

Zaitch, D (2002) *Trafficking Cocaine. Colombian Drug Entrepreneurs in the Netherlands*, The Hague: Kluwer Law International

Chapter 8
Cultural Criminology and Engagement with Race, Gender and Post-colonial Identities

Chris Cunneen and Julie Stubbs

Introduction

This chapter explores the potential of cultural criminology as a theoretical and methodological paradigm with reference to some earlier research in which we examined the high victimisation rates of Filipino women in cases of spousal homicides compared to other Australian women. Our research considers the interplay of gender, ethnicity and first world/third world relations, both materially and symbolically, in seeking to understand the women's experiences as immigrants, their postcolonial identities and their victimisation. The gendered and racialised nature of the movement of women across national boundaries, and their subsequent exposure to more extreme levels of violence, gives the research a broader focus than simply the experiences of Filipino women in Australia. While cultural criminology provides useful insights into the construction of this symbolic world surrounding violence against women, we argue that it cannot ignore the broader global political economies of labour, capital and communications which are closely connected to the construction of apparently 'localised' cultural expressions. We also demonstrate the importance of specificity in explaining how post-colonial identities and representations are constructed, and in understanding practices such as violence against immigrant women.

Cultural criminology explores 'the common ground between cultural and criminal practices in contemporary social life – that is, between collective behaviour organized around imagery, style, and symbolic meaning, and that categorized by legal and political authorities as criminal' (Ferrell and Sanders 1995a: 3). However, this relationship between cultural and criminal practices, within particular parameters of gender, class and 'race', is also significant in rendering some activities as 'justifiable' although criminal, particularly where the offending behaviour involves serious violence against vulnerable groups. Becker's injunction to study not only criminal subcultures but also the legal and political authorities who construct subcultures as criminal has been a powerful influence on the development of cultural criminology (*ibid*: 6). However, it is equally important for cultural criminology to study and understand how power constructs and legitimises forms of social harm. In this chapter our focus is the harm caused through inequalities generated by powerful international relations of political economy and unequal gender relations, particularly within global markets for labour and sex. In examining that harm, we engage with identity (of self and Other), sexuality (and desire), social space (crossing literal space as well as virtual space) and with the creation and consumption of images and discourses.

An important part of our research has been the Internet, which is a significant global site for the representation of women and a marketplace for buying and selling women. The Internet also exemplifies the manner in which economic privilege and access to technological knowledge and resources reinforces hierarchies based in 'race' and gender, and reproduces inequality within and through cyberspace. We show that there are essentialised images of these women as objects of desire which are common to Internet marriage marketing sites. Further, these images are readily deployed and at times inverted by former partners, media outlets and sometimes courts when men convicted of homicide seek to justify or excuse their behaviour.

Researching violence against Filipino women in Australia

Filipino women are almost six times overrepresented as victims of homicide, as compared with all women in Australia (Cunneen and Stubbs 1997). They are more likely to be victims of homicide than Filipino men in Australia, a pattern that is contrary to that for almost all other immigrant communities in the country: it is usual for homicide rates to be higher for men than for women (Kliewer 1994). At the request of the Australian Human Rights and Equal Opportunity Commission, and with the assistance of the Filipino community in Australia, we sought to identify factors that might contribute to the overrepresentation. Official data on homicide was supplemented by analysis of media reports of deaths of Filipino women and consultations with Filipino communities and relevant agencies in both Australia and the Philippines. The promotion of international marriages with Filipino women was identified in consultations as a key concern. Given the role of the Internet in promoting such marriages we undertook a search of the Internet using conventional search engines to locate sites that focused on Filipino (or Asian) women as marriage partners.

We identified 27 homicide cases, but this is likely to underestimate the total number of deaths of Filipino women because sources of official data concerning the country of birth, race or ethnicity of homicide victims are limited and incomplete (Cunneen and Stubbs 1997: 29–31). Where there was a known offender, all but one of the homicides had been committed by a man who had been married to, or in an intimate relationship with, the victim. None of the men were themselves Filipino, and with few exceptions they were Australian citizens. Consistent with the ethnic diversity of Australia, the offenders came from a wide range of ethnic backgrounds. By contrast, spouse homicides within Australia typically involve victims and offenders from the same country of origin. The different pattern for Filipino women homicide victims reflects immigration and marriage patterns for Filipino women in Australia. Australian immigration policy is restrictive and the primary mechanism by which women qualify for entry is through their relationships with men (Fincher et al 1994: 54, 80). Migration from the Philippines to Australia is biased in favour of women, and approximately 70% of Filipino women come as spouses or fiancées of Australian residents (Bureau of Immigration and Population Research 1994).

There were large age differences between the victims and the men with whom they had been in relationships: the average age difference was almost 13 years and in a third of cases the age difference was 20 years or greater. Other studies have found that Australian men sponsoring Filipino women as spouses or fiancés tend to be much older than the women (Robinson 1996: 59). However, in some of the homicide case studies the age differences seemed exceptional; for instance, one of victims was 15 years old when married in the Philippines to a 38 year old Australian male. Male perpetrators in this study also tended to be older than those in other comparable Australian homicide data (Polk 1994: 2): the oldest was 62 and the average age was 44. The substantial difference in age is discussed below in our analysis of markets for marriage and sex, and constructions of masculine desire. It is commonplace for Internet sites promoting marriage or sex with Filipino women to stress the youthfulness of the women and that the age of the man is no barrier to the relationship.

In some cases it was possible to determine that the couples had met through agencies promoting marriage, 'pen pals' or domestic help. One man went to the Philippines with three male friends after a popular television program depicted the ease with which Australian men could find wives in the Philippines. Another man, later convicted of manslaughter, had made contact with an introduction agency seeking another Filipino partner in the days immediately before he killed his then current Filipino wife. Many of the men had previously been married and two had previously been married to Filipino women. Given that the homicides we studied occurred during the 1980s and 1990s, the Internet was not used as a means to locate a Filipino partner. However, we note that the various mechanisms that were previously utilised have been supplanted by the Internet. For instance, commercial international marriage brokers are now illegal in the Philippines.

In two thirds of the homicides where information was available there was evidence of previous violence by the offender towards the victim, and in several cases there had been escalating violence leading up to the homicide. Several women had separated from their partner or were in the process of doing so at the time of their deaths, a factor that is common in spousal homicides (Wallace 1986; Polk 1994: 36). However, women's attempts to leave their partners commonly were presented negatively in media coverage of the event, and/or in court hearings concerning the homicide. Their actions were painted as licentious and immoral, they were represented as the (morally) *abusive* partner because they had left the relationship, and the men were re-presented as victims. The desire for 'life in the fast lane' became a popular media phrase, drawing on constructed images of Filipino women. In other words, there was a distinctly racial or ethnic interpretation given to the actions, and the violence the women were attempting to escape was largely ignored.

A theoretical framework

One common approach to examining victimisation and/or offending by immigrants has been derived from Sellin's (1938) argument that primary cultural conflicts may arise from migration (see for instance the influence of this approach in Freilich *et al* 2002). Our research demonstrates the inadequacy of such a singular approach. Filipino women's heightened vulnerability to violence is not shared by Filipino men or by other immigrant women. This shows the complexity involved in understanding a term like 'culture'. A construct like 'cultural conflict' is completely inadequate to capture the multiple layers at play. Our study suggests the importance of identity, sexuality, social space, and the creation and consumption of images and discourses set against the profoundly unequal relations between the 'first world' and the 'third world'. All of this is, or should be, the stuff of cultural criminology (Ferrell 1999: 397).

Gender has both a symbolic meaning (the particular representations of Filipino women as desirable for first world men) and a relationship to the developing political economy of the Philippines within the global sphere (Filipino women as important foreign exchange earners) (see also Ong and Peletz 1995: 2). The different forms of power and knowledge which define the position of Filipino women in relation to first world (Australian) men are also sites of broader social, economic and political transformations along the axis of gender within a postcolonial framework. Within international markets for labour, marriage and sex, those privileged both by their place in raced and gendered hierarchies and by economic resources are well placed to dominate in both the material and symbolic realms. While culturally dominant discourses do not necessarily determine masculine and feminine behaviour (Messerschmidt 1997: 10–11), the intersection of race, gender and international relations situates the immigrant Filipino woman in such a way that she has limited prospects for resistance or opposition.

It is particular racialised and gendered cultural constructions of Filipino women that contribute to their commodification and render them accessible to men with economic power. Pettman has demonstrated the importance of identifying 'how Asian women's sexuality is packaged and sold internationally, and how this feeds off and into representations of colonial and third-world women as passive/exotic' (1996: 195). At a more general level, cultural criminology needs to consider this interconnectedness of the material and symbolic realms, that the symbolic realm of the cultural does not exist independently of the material world of economic and political power.

Migration, gender and political economy

Migration by Filipino women to Australia for marriage cannot be understood simply as a matter of individual or family choice. The Philippines government actively promotes migration. Poor economic performance in the Philippines has been associated with a legacy of dependency and subservience to the IMF, World Bank, foreign banks and transnational corporations (Boer 1988; Pettman 1996). Emigration and the export of labour are acknowledged as part of the country's national employment policy. Incentives exist to lower the cost of emigration and the government provides mechanisms through which remittances are sent back to the Philippines (Raj-Hashim 1994: 122–23); these remittances are the country's top foreign exchange earner (Cahill 1990: 30).

Such strategies are endorsed by international agencies that have a role in promoting structural adjustment. These 'adjustment' policies and the deregulation of trade have had a particularly negative impact on women, in both the formal and informal economies, and have entrenched an international order in which women from developing countries are themselves 'traded' as workers, or wives. The pattern through which some countries acquire brides or domestic workers, and others supply them, reflects relative positions within the international political order (Pettman 1996: 194). Further, 'the state, at its most benign, is a fiscal beneficiary of the exploitation of women, and at its least benign, an active agent structuring the exploitation itself' (Heng 1997: 32).

International relations also have a significant effect on internal migration and on gender relations within the Philippines. For instance, the large US military bases that operated in the Philippines until 1992 attracted a large workforce of men and women to service its needs, including through prostitution. The decline of agricultural employment in rural areas also resulted in many Filipino women migrating to the areas around the bases to work in prostitution and the entertainment industry. The closure of the bases resulted in economic hardship for many workers, especially women, and no planning was in place to address their needs (Enloe 1993: 158). Sex tourism was actively promoted in the name of national development around former military bases. Thus the 'international politics of Third World debt and the international pursuit of commercial sex have become deeply entwined' (McClintock 1992: 92). According to Barry, 'sex tourism and mail-order bride marketing are the two major sex industries built up from military prostitution' (1995: 138).

Thus there are clear connections between what, on the surface, may appear to be distinct practices: prostitution; tourism; overseas contract work especially in the form of domestic service; and the export of women for marriage. Each of these practices is often state authorised or sponsored in the pursuit of 'development'. The fact that such strategies are viable reflects more than just the demand by rich countries seeking domestic workers, entertainers or wives from poorer countries. Such strategies also work because they are consistent with profoundly raced and gendered cultural constructions around the 'nature' of Filipino women, and Asian women more generally.

Representations of Filipino women

The racialised and sexualised representation of Filipino women and other Asian women has had important effects on how they are seen in Australia, both by their marriage partners and by the criminal justice system. As Truong has recognised, 'emphasising the "otherness" of the East, the sexual availability of Eastern women and the culture of their poverty' has two important effects. It 'creat[es] a distinct national identity to attract consumers' and 'legitimi[ses] oppressive practices by relegating them to the culture of a particular ethnic group and thereby helping to ease the conscience of the consumers' (1990: 200). Myths about 'naturally' submissive and sexually accommodating Filipino women act to authorise particular forms of masculine power and control over women. The process of racialisation functions to obscure the oppressive role of particular forms of international relations, and gender relations.[1]

The body is a site of shifting historical and cultural inscriptions of power and knowledge, and the bodies of Asian women are inscribed with characteristics which position them within a particular postcolonial context (Ong and Peletz 1995: 6). Cho (1997: 205) has argued that there is an interweaving of colonial and military domination with sexual domination in the representations of Asian women that creates the 'ultimate western male fantasy'. The various features inscribed on Asian bodies are directly connected to the construction and marketing of national (female) identities. For example, Boer (1988: 7) makes reference to constructions of images of Filipino women in Philippine Airways brochures and other commercial publications:

Most Filipino women have a natural femininity and beauty unequalled by any other race. They are indeed fiercely loyal, very industrious and extremely dedicated to their families. They are not materialistic. Money is not their God. They enjoy a good yarn, a laugh and

---

1   The racialising process is not simply patterned through 'East/West' relations. It is also shaped, fundamentally, through economic power. See, for example, the representation of Korean women by Japanese men as racialised 'other', allowing the commodification of Korean women for sex by promoting their alleged submissive qualities (see Mitsui 1984: 66). The movement within Asia of domestic workers from poorer to wealthier countries may also employ racial stereotypes in determining preference for particular women (Pettman 1996).

a happy song. They love having babies, they make wonderful mothers, great lovers and companions. Western women cannot compete with them in any of these qualities! (Cited in Boer 1988: 35)

The representation of Filipino women as submissive and obedient can have a number of effects, including providing an 'excuse' for exploitation by brothel owners, and the exploitative work practices of transnational corporations (Boer 1988: 7). Such representations also contain the contradictory elements of fear and desire that characterise Western male imaginings of Asian women (Robinson 1996: 54). In this reading, desire is represented in the image of 'luscious compliant beauties who are sex slaves to first world men'. Fear is evident in the prophecy of marriage failure, duplicity on the part of the woman and miscegenation (*ibid*). At one level, the representations of Filipino women fit within the concept of 'emphasised femininity' developed by Connell (1987) that stresses fragility, compliance, acceptance of marriage and so forth. Yet these idealised representations of women are also deeply racialised, and as a result heterosexual masculine desire is itself established within culturally signified racialised boundaries.

Since the late 1970s a discourse has been evident in Australia and elsewhere concerning 'mail-order' brides, a term specifically rejected by many Filipino groups as misleading and offensive, in which Filipino women are presented as 'meek, docile slaves, oriental beauties with shady pasts, passive and manipulable, but also grasping and predatory, using marriage to jump immigration queues' (Robinson 1996: 54). Our analysis of media reports surrounding the murder of Filipino women in Australia shows the use of these cultural stereotypes. In one case a media report referred to the murdered woman as 'vivacious, glamorous and never short of boyfriends'. M had been found handcuffed and stabbed to death. There was no suspect in this case and no apparent connection between her death and reported 'lifestyle' (Cunneen and Stubbs 1997: 75–76). In other murder cases, media reports represented the male perpetrator as the victim and ignored evidence of ongoing domestic violence as a major issue (*ibid*: 69–71).

Gender and 'race' in cyberspace

One way of unpacking the dynamics surrounding the disproportionate use of violence against Filipino women in Australia is through a consideration of the relationship between masculinity and the culturally specific fantasies of power, desire and sexuality. How do *representations* of gender and 'race' intersect within these constructed fantasies and work to inscribe the bodies of women with particular male-defined characteristics? What is the relationship between representations of the fantasised 'other' and the use of male violence? In other words, following Messerschmidt (1997), how do some men use violence to 'accomplish gender'; and, further, how is the accomplishment of gender better understood through an analysis which considers specific cultural and subcultural constructions?

The commodification, marketing and sale of Filipino women for sex or marriage provides an insight into this process. There is a common construction of Filipino women as perfectly fulfilling the desires of male fantasy. We have explored this issue further through the marketing schemes available on the Internet. The Internet is both a marketplace in which commodities and their symbolic attributes are exchanged, as well as a medium through which communication occurs. A simple search of the Internet using the term 'mail-order bride' demonstrates the significance of the

Internet to the promotion and marketing of international marriage: it yielded a staggering 835,000 hits.[2] A check of the first 100 hits revealed that most were introduction or marriage marketing agencies and that many sites specialised in or highlighted particular ethnic or racial groups: Russian, Filipino and Asian were the most common categories.

Some Internet sites offer detailed information on how to go about meeting 'foreign women' for the purpose of marriage, and offer advice about the quality and cost-effectiveness of the many introduction agencies that are available internationally. Several 'mail-order bride resource guides' are available that provide a directory of 'the World's Best introductions agencys' (sic),[3] and advice about travel, immigration and costs. Other Internet sites operate as introduction agencies with extensive catalogues of women to choose from. Many Internet services specify that they offer inter-racial introductions. Some sites focus on Asian women and many are specific to Filipino women. For instance, the Best Filipinas site offers 'Sexy & Beautiful! Hot Bikini Photo's [sic], Young Philippine ladies seeking love, romance and marriage'; E-Cebu Online Introduction Service offers 'Beautiful Filipina girls with old fashion values and beliefs seeking foreign men'; and EverLasting Love offers 'young pretty Filipina girls that passed medical and background checks'. The youthfulness of the women and their availability to older men is a common marketing tool: Age is just a number is just one of the sites offering 'young, educated, attractive Asian ladies for mature, serious minded men'.

The representation of Asian and Filipino women as 'perfect partners' is a common feature of sites promoting sex tours and marriage introduction agencies, and these are in fact different sides to the same phenomenon (see also Cahill 1990: 65). Sites offering introductions to women seeking marriage partners commonly have links to other sites offering 'erotica', sexualised images of Asian women, and sex tour information. Some sites offer both sex and marriage introductions. Nor is it unusual for sites to have multiple categories of service, including sex tours, marriage introduction, general sightseeing, and diving tours. Sites are becoming increasingly sophisticated and some include language classes, translation services, cheap international phone rates and video clips.

Some of the Internet sites provide information on prostitution, the age of consent and the legislation governing paedophilia, and some provide guidance concerning how to access Internet services anonymously and how to access sites barred by net administrators.

Masculine fantasy, violent reality

The use of violence against a partner or a person with whom one is in an intimate relationship is an example of what has been termed a 'masculine scenario of violence' (Polk 1994: 1). A number of studies have reinforced the view that masculine power and control are central features in spouse homicides and that 'separation, or the threat of separation, and sexual jealousy were the major precipitating factors in wife-killings' (Wallace 1986: 108; see also Polk 1994: 56).

---

2   The search was conducted in March 2004 using Google. The number of such sites seems to
     have grown exponentially since we first began research on this topic in 1997 (Cunneen and
     Stubbs 1997).
3   www.bridesbymail.com, accessed March 2004.

The homicides of Filipino women share many of the characteristics of spouse homicides more generally, but they are also distinctive. The difference becomes apparent when we integrate the fantasised images of Filipino women back into the relationships that resulted in the deaths and disappearances of women whose cases we have examined. Cultural criminology promotes a focus on the way in which the symbolic representations of the women underpin masculine fantasies that in turn may feed back into real relationships when violence is used in an attempt to secure the women's compliance. In other words, the use of a 'cultural criminology' approach can significantly deepen our understanding and explanation of masculine violence and homicide.

What happens when men attempt to live out these fantasised relationships? We noted above that Filipino women are not in a position to contest the representations of themselves on the Internet or other forms of the international marriage market. However, in relationships they are in a position to contest and resist. At one level we can understand the resort to violence as a means of 'doing gender', as a means of accomplishing masculinity in situations where women challenge the position in which they find themselves, and the 'material resources' which men rely on is the use of escalating violence (Messerschmidt 1997). However, we would add that 'doing gender' in these cases is bounded by specific cultural understandings of the apparent 'nature' of Filipino women.

Two interwoven processes become apparent in many of the homicide case studies. First, violence emerges as a resolution to conflict when the male attempts to assert absolute dominance and authority and the women resist. Secondly, the Filipino women become re-invented as manipulative and self-seeking women who simply marry Western men to leave the Philippines. The women's actions are reinterpreted through a stereotype of Filipino women as sexually promiscuous 'gold diggers' seeking foreign nationalities. They are seen as complicit in the violence against them, or even as the cause of the violence. The men are constructed as victims.

We have chosen one of the homicide case studies to illustrate these issues (for discussion of other cases see Cunneen and Stubbs 1997, 2003). A 17-year-old Filipino teenager was killed by her 41-year-old husband ('JS') who shot her several times and beat her head with a rifle butt. She had left her husband because of significant prior incidents of domestic violence. She was 15 years of age when she met and married JS. He had been divorced from his first wife one month previously and there was evidence of previous domestic violence.

JS pleaded guilty to manslaughter with diminished responsibility and was sentenced to a minimum term of six years. In general, the sentencing comments accept the depiction of the young Filipino woman as being at fault in her own death. She was presented as a bad mother. 'To a large extent his wife had left the care of their small child to the prisoner.'[4] She was presented as manipulative. 'He is said to have worked at a second job in order to earn enough money to send a monthly sum ... to her family in the Philippines. He sometimes took the child with him to cleaning work.' She was presented as self-seeking. The sentencing judge noted that 'a friend of [the defendant] ... said the prisoner told him that if he stopped paying the money, which was being sent to his wife's family in the Philippines, she threatened to leave

---

4   R v Sokol, unreported, Supreme Court of New South Wales, 19 February 1988.

him ... [he] told me of how he had to sell a lot of his assets in order to keep [her] happy'.

In various statements to the court the victim was presented as unfaithful, unloving and uncaring. The sentencing comments again cite the defendant's friend: '[he] told me that [she] had told him he was too old and boring.' A psychiatrist's report reinforced the view of the dead woman as unloving. 'He craved warmth and security but did not get much of that from her.'

The assessment of the victim was derived completely from statements and views of the man who had killed her. Perhaps not surprisingly, she was re-presented as unreasonable and his ongoing violence was absent from the account. By contrast, the defendant was re-presented as a victim. Consider the following sentencing comments.

> [He] presented as a slightly built, very vulnerable looking man with thinning hair and intense appearance.
>
> The prisoner was born in Germany of Polish parents. He came to Australia when he was very young. His father was a most hard-working man but was also harsh, demanding and authoritarian. His mother died when he was seven in sad circumstances. There was no-one else to fill her place. (Statement by psychiatrist to New South Wales Legal Aid Commission, 7 October 1987, pp 2 and 6)

While remanded in prison, JS was diagnosed with a longstanding personality disorder characterised by intense feelings of insecurity and loneliness and a craving for closeness and intimacy. He was described as having immense emotional and maternal needs. The psychiatrist's assessment of JS noted the following:

> The relationship with RS was doomed from the start. I suspect that by choosing a young woman from another culture he felt some security in the relationship because he was in the dominant position ... [However] she was not much interested in being a mother and certainly not interested in responding to the immense maternal needs JS had. (Statement by psychiatrist to New South Wales Legal Aid Commission, 7 October 1987, p 5)

What is of interest here is not the clinical assessment *per se*, but rather the gendered nature of the response to the illness, both in terms of the desire for a Filipino bride and all that such a relationship promised, as well as the resort to violence in an attempt to maintain the relationship when it began to fail. There is little in the sentencing comments that reflects the escalation of violence by JS against the young woman despite independent evidence of that violence.[5]

According to the psychiatric assessments, the violence arose in an attempt to maintain the 'security' offered by the relationship. Yet that promise of security was one constructed within the parameters of what introduction agencies offer, specifically, fantasised versions of Filipino women as 'ideal marriage partners'. It is clear that JS accepted the constructed image of Filipino women. Police noted that the perpetrator had remarked, 'So much for Filipino women being faithful and looking after you'. Indeed, the day before the murder of the young woman, JS was already making arrangements through an introduction agency for another 'Filipino bride'.

In the *Sokol* case, as in many of the other cases we examined, violence against women becomes a way of enforcing compliance with what is, in the end, a masculine

---

5   The other administrative and legal aspect to this case is the issue of how JS could so easily marry a 15-year-old girl and bring her back to Australia, given his previous psychiatric history, his earlier failed marriage, an outstanding domestic violence order by his previous wife, and the removal of his two children by the authorities.

construction of appropriate female behaviour. In these cases images of women are overladen with racialised and sexualised fantasies about Filipino women as perfect partners. The women who are killed are recast as being complicit in their own demise when they fail to fulfil the requirements of male fantasy. A new racialised and sexualised image then emerges: Filipino women are seen as permissive and grasping 'gold diggers'. The men are reinvented as doubly victimised because they are naïve or unstable enough to believe in the possibility of fulfilling their desires through these marriages, and because they are the victims of women who manipulate their desire.

Filipino women (and 'Asian' women more generally) are created as the apotheosis of male desire, as 'perfect partners'. The extent and the intensity of the violence perpetrated against them by non-Filipino men needs to be understood within this context. The violence can be understood at one level as male violence against women. However, it is also mediated through specific cultural understandings of the relationship between first world men, what some first world men understand to be *Filipino* women, and, by implication, what some first world men understand as their own masculinity.

Conclusion

'Shared symbolism and mediated meaning, subcultural style and collective imagery define the nature of crime, criminality, and social control not only for criminals ... but for everyone caught up in the larger social processes of constructing and perceiving crime and control' (Ferrell and Sanders 1995b: 298). We have sought to demonstrate in this chapter that this basic standpoint of cultural criminology is equally true for defining victims. The shared symbolism of 'Asian women', the mediated meanings of why they seek life in wealthy capitalist nations, the collective imagery of 'mail-order' brides and their relationship with 'western' men, all speak to the larger social processes which redefine male violence against these particular women as somehow justified.

Racialised femininities and particular understandings of masculine desire underpin the conditions within which Filipino women in Australia become vulnerable to violence. Cultural analysis of the representations of Asian and Filipino women on the Internet shows the construction of *desire* in terms of perfect partners for marriage and sex. These images have a powerful position within masculine fantasies about 'exotic' women. However, the other side in this dichotomy is the *fear* of the exotic 'Other'. The parameters of that fear are made explicit in the construction of Filipino women in Australia as manipulative and exploitative of (first world) men's emotions and good natures.

More generally our analysis shows the importance of understanding the culturally defined and racialised concepts of masculinity and femininity within the context of increasingly globalised markets for marriage and sex. Following Connell (1998: 7), we view such a broader project as essential for understanding how 'locally situated lives are ... powerfully influenced by geopolitical struggles, global markets, multinational corporations, labor migration, [and] transnational media'. It is our argument that the understanding of symbolism, style and subcultural meaning needs to be situated within postcolonial and global political economies which increasingly structure relationships between individuals.

References

Barry, K (1995) *The Prostitution of Sexuality*, New York: New York UP

Boer, C (1988) *Are You Looking For a Filipino Wife? A Study of Filipina-Australian Marriages*, Sydney: General Synod, Anglican Church of Australia

Bureau of Immigration and Population Research (1994) *Community Profile 1991 Census: The Philippines Born*, Canberra: AGPS

Cahill, D (1990) *Intermarriages in International Contexts: A Study of Filipina Women Married to Australian, Japanese and Swiss Men*, Quezon City, Philippines: Scalabrini Migration Centre

Cho, SK (1997) 'Converging stereotypes in racialized sexual harassment: where the model minority meets Suzie Wong', in Wing, AK (ed), *Critical Race Feminism*, New York: New York UP

Connell, RW (1987) *Gender and Power*, St Leonards: Allen & Unwin

Connell, RW (1998) 'Masculinities and globalisation' 1(2) *Men and Masculinities* 3–23

Cunneen, C and Stubbs, J (1997) *Gender, 'Race' and International Relations: Violence Against Filipino Women in Australia*, Sydney: Institute of Criminology

Cunneen, C and Stubbs, J (2002) 'Migration, political economy and violence against women: the post immigration experiences of Filipino women in Australia', in Freilich, JD, Newman, G, Shoham, SG and Addad, M (eds), *Migration, Culture, Conflict and Crime*, Aldershot: Ashgate Advances in Criminology

Cunneen, C and Stubbs, J (2003) 'Fantasy islands: desire, "race" and violence', in Tomsen, S and Donaldson, M (eds), *Male Trouble: Looking at Australian Masculinities*, North Melbourne: Pluto

Enloe, C (1993) *The Morning After: Sexual Politics at the End of the Cold War*, Berkeley: University of California Press

Ferrell, J (1999) 'Cultural criminology' 25 *American Review of Sociology* 395–418

Ferrell, J and Sanders, C (1995a) 'Culture, crime and criminology', in Ferrell, J and Sanders, C (eds), *Cultural Criminology*, Boston: Northeastern University Press

Ferrell, J and Sanders, C (1995b) 'Toward a cultural criminology', in Ferrell, J and Sanders, C (eds), *Cultural Criminology*, Boston: Northeastern University Press

Fincher, R, Foster, L and Wilmont, R (1994) *Gender Equity in Australian Immigration Policy*, Canberra: Bureau of Immigration and Population Research and AGPS

Freilich, JD, Newman, G, Shoham, SG and Addad, M (eds) (2002) *Migration, Culture Conflict and Crime*, Aldershot: Ashgate Advances in Criminology

Heng, G (1997) 'A great way to fly: nationalism, the state and varieties of third-world feminism', in Alexander, MJ and Mohanty, C (eds), *Feminist Genealogies, Colonial Legacies, Democratic Futures*, London: Routledge

Kliewer, E (1994) 'Homicide victims among Australian immigrants' 18 *Australian Journal of Public Health* 304

McClintock, A (1992) 'Screwing the system: sexwork, race and the law' 19(2) *Boundary* 70

Messerschmidt, J (1997) *Crime as Structured Action*, Thousand Oaks, CA: Sage

Mitsui, Y (1984) 'Why I oppose Kisaeng tours', in Barry, K, Bunch, C and Castley, S (eds), *International Feminism: Networking Against Female Sexual Slavery*, New York: International Women's Tribune Centre

Ong, A and Peletz, M (eds) (1995) *Bewitching Women, Pious Men: Gender and Body Politics in Southeast Asia*, Berkeley: University of California Press

Pettman, JJ (1996) *Worlding Women: A Feminist International Politics*, Sydney: Allen & Unwin

Polk, K (1994) *When Men Kill*, Melbourne: CUP

Raj-Hashim, R (1994) 'A review of migration and labour policies in Asia', in Heyzer, N, Lycklama, G and Weerakoon, N (eds), *The Trade in Domestic Workers: Causes, Mechanisms and Consequences of International Migration*, London: Zed

Robinson, K (1996) 'Of mail-order brides and "boys' own" tales: representations of Asian-Australian marriages' 52 *Feminist Studies* 53–68

Sellin, T (1938) *Culture, Conflict and Crime*, New York: Social Science Research Council

Truong, TD (1990) *Sex, Money and Morality: Prostitution and Tourism in Southeast Asia*, London: Zed

Wallace, A (1986) *Homicide: The Social Reality*, Sydney: NSW Bureau of Crime Statistics and Research

Chapter 9

Crime, Media and Community: Grief and Virtual Engagement in Late Modernity

Chris Greer

Introduction

As media proliferate and become more integral to social existence, so too, it might be suggested, their role becomes more complex and contested. Media forms and representations are instrumental in the creation of deviant identities and the subsequent stigmatisation and demonisation of whole groups of individuals. They are a driving force behind the nostalgically reactionary discourse that rails against the so-called 'culture of permissiveness', decrying the decline in respect and the loss of community. Yet they are also an important conduit for the celebration of diversity and the articulation and advancement of alternative discourses, counter-definitions and marginalised views and interests. Finally, they present opportunities to be 'social' in new and novel ways. They offer a source of virtual collectivism and identity in an uncertain physical world; what one might describe as a source of imagined community. This chapter begins to explore some of the interconnections between crime, culture and community as they are played out in old and new media.

Crime, culture and community: the late modern context

In the past three or four decades, western society has undergone profound changes to its social, cultural and economic structures. De-industrialisation, the globalisation of the manufacturing industries and the growth in service industries threaten to eradicate traditional forms of industrial labour. The emergence of new markets and economies has presented exciting opportunities, but also considerable problems. While sections of the traditional working class have been absorbed into the lower echelons of the middle class, others have fared less well and now face long-term unemployment and economic uncertainty. The felt sense of insecurity may be sharpest among the most socially and economically marginalised, but the middle classes are not exempt. Much of the labour force is subject to short-term contracts, and rationalisation and redundancy are a constant lingering threat. Meaningful planning for the future becomes more difficult and, for some, all but pointless. The anxieties engendered by economic precariousness in a destabilised job market are experienced by all but the luckiest few (see Hall and Winlow, this volume). As Bauman points out, the late modern human condition is characterised by 'freedom of unprecedented proportions – but at the price of similarly unprecedented insecurity' (2001: 159).

Pratt (2000: 431) notes that 'in a climate of scarce resources, in juxtaposition to the offers of high rewards to successful risk takers, one's neighbour or colleague becomes a rival or competitor; one's social habitus comes to reflect less tolerance and self-control, and a greater likelihood of aggression'. Certainly, traditional conceptions of 'community' – based around geographical and territorial borders, shared values, identities and belief systems, collective politics – seem less applicable across much of the urban landscape. Societies are openly and expressively diverse. Identity and membership are fluid. Populations are often transient, and constantly in flux. As Hancock and Matthews (2001: 111) note:

> In the context of increasing contingency, ambivalence and fragmentation the search for 'community' appears more hopeless and unrealistic. The identification of consensus becomes more elusive and the ability to mobilise universal truths in order to sanction, humiliate or stigmatise becomes increasingly difficult. The construction of order begins to look more artificial and fragile.

The problem of crime cannot easily be isolated from society's other problems (Young 1999). Definitions of and tolerance toward deviance and criminality interact closely with shifts in the wider economic, political and cultural environment. Individualism, competition and insecurity in the labour market, for example, are intimately related to the widely observed suspicion, mistrust and intolerance of the unknown other. The development of gated communities and the relentless monitoring and surveillance of public space establish clear boundaries between those included in and excluded from mainstream social and economic life (Davis 1990, 1994; Ferrell 2002). Whole categories of individuals are stigmatised, criminalised and excluded on the basis of their look, their style, their demeanour – their perceived 'risk' or 'dangerousness'. Citizens are anxious and untrusting, acutely aware of and concerned about threats (both real and imagined) to their well-being and personal safety. Crime consciousness and fear of crime run high.

Fragmentation, surveillance, dangerousness, risk, exclusion – prominent features of late modern existence – may all be said to discourage social engagement and threaten traditional forms of 'community'. Yet, paradoxically, it is precisely the atomising and isolating influence of these conditions that makes the need for unity so vital. It is in this context that the role of media forms and representations is of particular theoretical and empirical interest. Amid widespread ontological insecurity, individual life histories are structured, shaped, and made sense of within frames of reference provided, to a significant degree, by mass media, to the extent that a sense of shared (popular) culture generates 'imagined community' (Anderson 1983). One important way in which people are afforded a sense of collective identity and social cohesion is via the mediatised construction of deviant and idealised identities. These constructions achieve much of their potency through the selective creation of binaries – the 'idealised victim' and the 'absolute other', a 'utopian' past and a 'dystopian' future. Both old and new media technologies present opportunities to engage collectively in the affirmation of virtuous identities through insisting on the non-identity of those 'not like us'. These are the social conditions that serve as the starting point for this chapter.

Media, crime and the deviant other

The popular press, more than any other form of mass communication, seem obsessed with 'traditional' conceptions of community and order, routinely employing nostalgically reactionary language and narrative forms to hark back to a bygone age of better times. Stories are replete with romanticised images of the family, the school, the institutions of criminal justice, and indeed, the state. Permissiveness and a general decline in values – falling moral standards, a lack of respect for others, individual selfishness – are advanced unproblematically as the 'cause' of society's ills, while any reference to the impact of economic restructuring and destabilised labour markets is notable by its absence. Even the most cursory search through the headlines of both tabloids and broadsheets offers up a rich trawl of populist soundbites decrying the present, dreading the future and lionising the past, while ignoring all that was harmful, unfair, discriminatory or prejudiced. This perspective was encapsulated in an editorial by the conservative *Daily Mail's* Simon Heffer (20 August 2002):

> This Government has done nothing to reverse the trend towards lethal permissiveness. It has relaxed laws about censorship and legalised acts of gross indecency with young men and women. It has relaxed the drugs laws. It has made a virtue of 'alternative lifestyles'. Its permissiveness erodes the respect of individuals for others, cheapens human life, and results in a culture where the pursuit of gratification prevails, without any sense of responsibility for its consequences.

The *Daily Telegraph* (9 January 2003), the UK's best-selling daily broadsheet newspaper, insisted that society today is a much less civilised place than it was in 'golden age' of the immediate post-war era, and listed the following evidence as proof:

> One marriage in three now ends in divorce. Almost 40 per cent of children are now born out of wedlock, the highest figure in Europe. Since the 1967 Abortion Act, more than six million unborn children have been aborted. The legalisation of homosexuality has not been the end of the chapter, but merely the beginning, with an aggressive 'gay rights' lobby demanding more and more concessions. The policy of early release of prisoners has had a catastrophic effect on the safety of the general public ... In addition to this, we must add the hundreds of innocent lives lost as a result of the abolition of capital punishment. The self-restraint and taboos of the 1950s have all gone.

Located at the heart of the putative problem of social decline are various categories of deviant 'other'; enemies 'without' and enemies 'within'. On the one hand, the most allegedly serious and dangerous offenders – paedophiles and fundamentalist terrorists – are the 'absolute others', portrayed as being *in* society, but not *of* it. On the other hand, there are those whose transgressions may scarcely border on illegality, whose actions and behaviours are criminalised on the basis of some failure to conform to the 'proper way of doing things' – dole scroungers, drug addicts, immigrants and asylum seekers, homosexuals, single mothers and feckless fathers. These are the 'stigmatised others', portrayed as being *of* society, but not *in* it. I have explored elsewhere the enthusiasm with which sections of the press merge these criminalised identities in order to tar whole categories of individual with the same deviant brush (Greer and Jewkes 2004). The key point to make here is that the deviant categories that feature so heavily are themselves often mythical constructions, created by and contained within a cyclically reproduced, reactionary media narrative which becomes self-perpetuating in its vitriol against marginalised groups.

Columnist Peter Hitchens gave full vent to this style of reportage. With some considerable journalistic dexterity, he managed to link sexual permissiveness, single mothers, Islamic fundamentalism, crime and disorder, and the loss of community, all in the same article. The author began by lamenting the trajectory of a once great society careering 'ever more rapidly down the path of permissiveness which began so gently in the sixties and now slopes ever more steeply downwards toward sexual chaos, drunkenness, family breakdown and the epidemic use of stupefying drugs' (*Mail on Sunday*, 2 November 2003). He went on to stress the dangers of the rising Islamic population in Britain, proposing that:

> Official Islam may disapprove of such things but there have even been signs of the Muslim intolerance towards Christianity that is a nasty feature of so many Islamic societies ... [A] Brownie pack leader was attacked ... by young men who snarled 'Christian bitch' at her. An isolated and meaningless incident? You might hope so, but it would be unwise to be sure.

Conservative disapproval is ubiquitous in the popular press, and the impact of its unremitting articulation cannot be dismissed lightly. It is also important, however, to acknowledge that there are those who are trying to tell a different story, and that alternative viewpoints do find resonance. *The Independent*, for example, a liberal British daily newspaper, recently declared, 'Newspapers Can be Dangerous at Times Like These ... A Xenophobic Agenda Means Twisting Almost Any Story – And it's Getting Worse' (4 April 2004). The narrative beneath this headline cautioned that linkages between issues like race, crime and immigration are often 'tenuous and even dangerous' and, further, they can create 'an overall tone which can stick in the public consciousness, particularly if there is an inclination there to make unjustifiable connections'.

In stark contrast to Peter Hitchens' representation of all Muslims as potential thugs, criminals and terrorists, some journalists highlight the experience of Muslims as victims. 'The Rising Tide of Islamophobia in Britain' (*The Independent*, 3 June 2004) called attention to the 'upsurge in attacks on Muslims and their places of worship'. The article was critical of the 'sensationalist press' for fuelling animosity, and of the police for being 'quick to claim credit for foiling terror attacks, but when all the suspects are released without charge ... they seem to have little interest in setting the record straight'. It continued, 'while Osama bin Laden and his acolytes may consider themselves devout Muslims, there is nothing Islamic about the carnage they have caused. Britain's Muslims know this to be true, and it is high time everyone else accepted it too'.

This level of media reflexivity provides a useful corrective to the reductionist stance – the construction of deviant identities, and promotion of simplified binaries – evident in so much reportage. Alternative discourses create a vital space within which counter-definitions can compete and find resonance in the public imagination. They encourage the selective celebration of diversity and difference, rather than its fearful condemnation. In a climate of heightened sensitivity to the risk of terror attacks, the issues of immigration and asylum, crime and disorder, and wider social decline are all too easily linked in stigmatising and exclusionary polemics, and in the public imagination. Those commentators who would present alternative views, including those who themselves are the focus of stigmatisation and exclusion, continue to face an uphill struggle. But it is in precisely this context that the importance of their contributions increases.

Media, crime and victims

The media stigmatisation and demonisation of marginalised groups is not a new phenomenon, though the characteristics of particular deviant categories and how they are constructed and merged may vary over time (Pearson 1983). The increasing focus on victims of crime, however, is comparatively recent. Over the last 20 years in the UK, victims have moved from the margins to centre stage in political and media discourses. The victim-centricity of current crime talk and policymaking reflects the general rise in crime consciousness and concern about personal safety. It also reflects the wider social and political concerns about victims' needs and rights which gathered momentum throughout the 1980s and 1990s (Garland 2000; Maguire and Pointing 1988).

The foregrounding of crime victims in the media is one of the most significant qualitative changes in representations of crime and control in the postwar period (Reiner *et al* 2000a, 2000b). Contemporary narratives, whether print or broadcast, broadsheet or tabloid, conservative or liberal, not only invite, but actively encourage consumers to identify and empathise with victims of crime: to see what they are seeing and feel what they are feeling; to become involved emotionally and join in the condemnation and punishment of the offender, who is increasingly portrayed as evil and beyond redemption. These emotional and expressive adaptations – empathising with the victim, demonising and denouncing the other, both articulated and reinforced in mediatised discourses – comprise key constituents of the repertoire people use to negotiate the problem of crime, and the wider and inseparable problems of anxiety and uncertainty, that late modernity throws up. The playing out of these adaptations in the context of an uncertain physical world raises interesting questions about membership, identity, collectivism, and community.

The current phase in our history, as a number of commentators have observed, is characterised by people living together in segregated fashion, mixing but not socialising, sharing physical space (to a point), but little else. Sennett (1991) describes the indifference with which urban dwellers regard one another, the palpable sense of detachment and separation as they go about their daily lives. Taylor (1999: 64) has noted the 'startling decline in the level of any form of voluntary activity (and indeed any kind of shared public activities other than sport) "in the community"'. The rugged individualism of neocapitalism, it is suggested, has contributed to the creation of societies inhabited by 'lightly engaged strangers' (Young 1990). To the extent that this is true, the collective expressiveness and emotionality essential to social interaction – and the empathising with crime victims actively encouraged in media discourses – would seem to risk suffocation beneath insecurity, indifference and social withdrawal.

Media, crime and collectivism

That there are new and emerging relationships between people and the spaces they both produce and inhabit is undeniable. Yet to suggest that people no longer take an interest or demonstrate any active involvement in their geographical communities is to overstate the case. The thesis of the 'stranger society' should not be taken too far. In a climate of uncertainty, people tend to congregate around those issues which offer them some sense of unity and cohesion. Sport is one obvious example. Crime is another. While the identification of consensus and the ability to mobilise universal truths in order to sanction and stigmatise may appear increasingly difficult (Hancock and Matthews 2001), some crimes are viewed as so utterly and unconditionally heinous that they take on an almost sacrilegious status. Child sexual murders are an interesting case in point.

Though all cases of child sexual murder are horrific, most capture neither media attention nor the public imagination with any force or longevity, and some barely register at all. Jewkes (2004), for example, notes that during the search for missing 14-year-old Milly Dowler in 2002, the body of a teenage girl was recovered from a disused quarry. Just as sections of the press were speculating that Milly had been found, the body was identified as 14-year-old Hannah Williams, who had disappeared a year earlier. Yet it was Milly who still continued to dominate the headlines, while Hannah was forgotten almost immediately. Milly matched the profile of the 'ideal' middle class teenager. Hannah was working class and had run away before. According to a police spokeswoman, her mother – a single parent on a low income – 'wasn't really press-conference material'.

It is only those cases featuring a particular type of victim that will attract sustained media attention and collective public outcry. Those cases that journalists feel do not communicate the binaries of 'innocence' and 'guilt', 'purity' and 'evil' with sufficient force and clarity – even in the absence of a known offender – may scarcely feature in media discourse. Those child sexual murders that do, however, have the capacity to invoke in media, public and politicians alike an intensity of reaction unrivalled by most other crime types. High profile and highly mediatised crimes of this nature provide a focal point around which people can unite to express collective feelings of empathy and suffering, sadness and hatred. In so doing, they present opportunities to establish a sense of membership and belonging – underpinned by the affirmation of virtuous and deviant identities – through the collective mourning of the 'idealised victim' and denunciation of the 'absolute other'.

The murder in 2000 of eight-year-old Sarah Payne – a bright, photogenic girl from a stable and loving family – by convicted sex offender Roy Whiting invoked near-hysterical media outpourings, and resulted in public protests and a series of vigilante-style attacks on suspected paedophiles (Silverman and Wilson 2002; Evans 2003). The killing in Soham in 2003 of Holly Wells and Jessica Chapman – school friends, again highly photogenic, with similarly bright futures and stable pasts – by school caretaker Ian Huntley also attracted sustained media coverage and public outcry. This tragic event is most notable not for ensuing public violence, but for the sober observation of a semi-official minute's silence nationwide. In both cases, many who were physically proximate left flowers and gifts, queued to sign books of condolence, and gathered in remembrance of the loss of sacred life. When the journalists and camera crews eventually decamped, physical artefacts of shared suffering defiantly proclaimed the togetherness of a community torn apart by tragedy. But messages of anger and sadness came from much further afield. In the midst of these tragic events those so inclined could go online to collectively offer their sympathies and support, and express their outrage, through specially established websites. Contributions came from around the world.

Media, crime and imagined community

Anderson (1983: 18) proposes that 'All communities larger than primordial villages of face-to-face contact (and perhaps even these) are imagined'. At a time when face-to-face interactions in physical space and time appear to be negotiated with growing caution, notions of imagined community are especially resonant. The advancement and proliferation of communications technologies presents opportunities to be social in new and novel ways. In the network society (Castells 1996, 2004), members of the 'global village' can engage instantaneously and continuously, sharing interests, building relationships, challenging or reinforcing values and belief systems, both marginal and mainstream. McLuhan (1964) predicted that new electronic media, and the global flow of images, texts and meanings that they permit, would lead to the restructuring and reconceptualisation of relationships, and the re-evaluation of how people interact (see also Feenberg and Bakardjieva 2004). It is now possible to create virtual networks of connectedness neither bounded by geographical borders nor subject to conventional restrictions of space and time (Rheingold 1994). New forms of closeness and proximity are generated. New forms of collectivism and community are established.

In cyberspace, the negotiation of crime, fear and uncertainty merges with new media technologies in the creation of imagined communities structured around collective expressiveness, emotionality and identity. Of particular salience here are commemorative websites and global Internet books of condolence, and online petitions and discussion boards, established in response to high-profile murders of 'idealised victims' by 'absolute others'. Valier (2004) notes that online discussion sites established in response to notorious UK and US murders are characterised by calls for excessive punitive justice and, not infrequently, threats of violence and even death to the perpetrators. Consideration of virtual engagement in the wake of those murders considered in this chapter adds further weight to this claim. When Ian Huntley was sentenced to life imprisonment for the murders of Holly Wells and Jessica Chapman, contributors to online discussion boards declared: 'He will receive the treatment a "nonce" deserves'; 'I hope Huntley rots, may the bastard die of cancer'; 'Let the justice commence'; and 'Kill him'.[1] These online bulletin boards are also accessible to those who would challenge the promotion of vengeance and vigilantism and offer an alternative interpretation of the 'appropriate' response to tragic murders. Oppositional sites are posted with a view to promoting, in the words of one website seeking to counter the dissemination of excessive online punitivism, 'reason and common sense in the UK', and to 'stop the madness'.[2] Even more than in the physically constrained, agenda-based world of the print media, messages transmitted in cyberspace are open to contest and debate. The challenge is to be heard above the resounding clamour of virtual fear and loathing.

These virtual discussion forums exist in parallel with and frequently, it would seem, in stark contrast to online books of condolence and memorial websites built around the shared suffering with and caring for victims and victims' families. 'Guestbooks' established in memory of Sarah Payne, Holly Wells and Jessica Chapman, and the victims of other recent tragic murders,[3] invite members of the global village to pass on their sympathies and pay their respects. As with online demands for punitive action and vigilante justice, passions and emotions run high. But what is most striking about these cyberspatial communications is the profound sense of loss that contributors themselves – essentially complete strangers – claim to feel: 'Words cannot express our sadness' (UK); 'They are candles in the darkness – their wee lives have touched the world' (Australia); 'I feel I have no words to express just how I feel' (UK). The intense hostility and vengefulness invoked in so many by the tragic murder of 'idealised victims', while disconcerting, does seem to 'make sense' within the context of the wider punitive culture and penal escalation of recent decades. Why, though, in a society in which people are less inclined to engage and

---

1   See, for example, http://forums.armageddononline.org/archive/index.php/t-1281.html; www.analogsf.com/discus/messages/1/671.html?1082546353.
2   See, for example, rationalism.org.uk.
3   Websites were also established, with varying degrees of contemporaneity, following the fatal shooting of 16 school children and one teacher in Dunblane, Scotland, in 1996 by Thomas Hamilton, who then turned the gun on himself, and the murder of toddler James Bulger in 1993 by two 10-year-olds (see also Appleton 2002; Brown 2003; Valier 2004).

interact in physical space, and more inclined to be aggressive when they do, would so many wish to share in the pain and suffering of those they had previously never heard of, still less met?

Becoming emotionally involved with the victims of high profile, mediatised murders, participating in their suffering and sharing in their grief, is one way of outwardly and expressively demonstrating one's depth of feeling – of proving one's humanity – in a cynical and fragmented society. That compassionate empathy is being directed at strangers serves to amplify the expression of humanity still further. The sheer quantity and geographical diversity of contributions to memorial websites would appear to reinforce the visions of McLuhan (1964) and Rheingold (1994) of cyberspace as a forum for global interconnectedness and community based on mutual compassion, empathy and support. Indeed, virtual expressions of shared suffering may well constitute an invaluable source of strength and support for those who actually knew the victim. But while the majority of contributions are no doubt sincere, their authenticity bears greater scepticism.

Appleton (2002) likens collective involvement in mass mourning to a 'grief roadshow', and finds it deeply troubling that 'it is not enough to feel upset – you have to show other people how upset you are, and to join in with others who are feeling the same'. Collectively engaging and expressively sharing in the intense anguish of others – unknown others – conduces the development of an economy of suffering and pain in which members may compete to appear the most hurt and, therefore, the most human. It contributes to the ritualisation and commodification of grief, where grief becomes something to be conspicuously consumed, and then discarded; another commodity in an aggressive neocapitalist economy. Signing the book, visiting the website, leaving the message, all these things provide a fast-working but short-lived antidote to the uncertainty and anxiety that characterises the late modern human condition – temporarily satisfying, but ultimately unfulfilling. The emotions diffuse, the murders are forgotten, the books of condolence close, and the 'imagined community' dissolves away into cyberspace, only to be recreated, re-established, reconnected in the wake of the next murder featuring 'suitable' victims and offenders.

Imagined communities established in the wake of high profile child sexual murders provide a source of identity and belonging, however superficial and ephemeral, in an age of uncertainty. It is scarcely surprising that so many want to 'belong'. Yet the extent to which this new collectivism constitutes social interaction is questionable. Cyberspatial communications, as Wallace (1999) points out, retain a perception of anonymity. Messages of condolence and contributions to discussion boards may be signed 'Tom, US' or 'Karen, Australia', but seldom include more personal detail than that, and often include less. The virtual expression of shared suffering provides a way of touching a stranger's life, of leaving a trace, without having to endure one's own life being touched back by strangers in any palpable way. It corresponds with a particular conception of proximity and closeness, but it is closeness at a distance. It is individualised sociality, anonymous and largely faceless, resonating with Agger's (2004: 47) observation that 'the postmodern condition is communicating with people whom you can't see, but can imagine'. It is indicative – in keeping with discussions of social engagement, identity and collectivism in late modernity – of a climate in which people want some level of contact, and some form of interaction. But not too much.

Conclusion

As identities and meanings become more fluid and contested, populations become more transient, and citizens become more wary of face-to-face interaction, traditional forms of collectivism, sociality and community appear to fragment and disintegrate. New media technologies provide a means of achieving a sense of identity, belonging and community in this climate of uncertainty. One example of this new collectivism is the emergence of imagined communities in the wake of child sexual murders involving 'idealised victim' and 'absolute other'.

Notions of 'community' – whether relating to the physical and traditional or the imagined and virtual – are, fundamentally, about membership and identity. As such, they are inscribed with notions of inclusion and exclusion. In the context of those issues discussed in this chapter – conservative and liberal counter-discourses about permissiveness and decline, and high profile child sexual murders – community derives from the collective affirmation of virtuous identities through the distancing from, and insistence upon, the non-identity of others. The distinction between identity and non-identity, however, and the process – both symbolic and physical – of inclusion and exclusion, is not simply the distinction between victim and offender.

Imagined communities only emerge around particular types of victim. Those victims who cannot be 'idealised' – because their image or background does not match the preferred profile – will generally attract neither sustained media attention nor widespread public and political outcry. Their deaths may scarcely result in national recognition in the physical world, still less global commemoration and remembrance in virtuality. Notions of exclusion, then, do not only apply to those vilified in the press and condemned in online discussion boards. They apply equally to those child victims who do not fit the right profile or tick the right boxes, and who are therefore overlooked, ignored, denied. Thus imagined communities are created around binaries first established in news media discourses, and, in this sense, form part of a wider process of inclusion and exclusion in which whole categories of individual may be legitimated or marginalised on the basis of such arbitrary factors as background, colour, or class.

By vicariously participating in the suffering of those affected or afflicted by child sexual murders – by sorrowing with their loss, and sharing in the anger that loss may invoke – people garner a sense of community, a sense of membership and belonging, in a world where the notion of community and community membership has changed fundamentally. Though these imagined communities are based on highly selective and exclusionary premises, they can constitute a space for the promotion of compassion and empathy, and measured penal debate. But they can also stimulate the dissemination of vengeful hate, and contribute to the generation of an economy of grief in which humanity is measured competitively and demonstrated through highly expressive, yet faceless, ephemeral and, ultimately, inauthentic gestures of suffering and loss. As such, being excluded is perhaps not so bad.

References

Agger, B (2004) *The Virtual Self: A Contemporary Sociology*, Oxford: Blackwell

Anderson, B (1983) *Imagined Communities: Reflections on the Origin and Spread of Nationalism*, London: Verso

Appleton, J (2002) 'Grief roadshow moves on', *Spiked*, at spiked-online.com

Bauman, Z (2001) *The Individualized Society*, Cambridge: Polity

Brown, S (2003) *Crime and Law in Media Culture,* Buckingham: Open University Press

Castells, M (1996) *The Rise of the Network Society,* Oxford: Blackwell

Castells, M (2004) *The Power of Identity,* 2nd edition, Oxford: Blackwell

Davis, M (1990) *City of Quartz: Excavating the Future in Los Angeles,* London: Verso

Davis, M (1994) *Beyond Blade Runner: Urban Control. The Ecology of Fear,* Open Magazine Pamphlet Series, Pamphlet 23

Evans, J (2003) 'Vigilance and vigilantes: thinking psychoanalytically about anti-paedophile action' 7(2) *Theoretical Criminology* 163–89

Feenberg, A and Bakardjieva, M (2004) 'Virtual community: no "killer" implication' 6(1) *New Media and Society* 37–43

Ferrell, J (2002) *Tearing Down the Streets: Adventures in Urban Anarchy,* London: Palgrave

Garland, D (2000) *The Culture of Control: Crime and Social Order in Contemporary Society,* Oxford: OUP

Greer, C and Jewkes, Y (2004) 'Extremes of otherness: media images of social exclusion', *Social Justice* (special edition)

Hancock, L and Matthews, R (2001) 'Crime, community safety and toleration', in Matthews, R and Pitts, J (eds), *Crime, Disorder and Community Safety,* London: Routledge

Jewkes, Y (2004) *Media and Crime,* London: Sage

McLuhan, M (1964) [2002] *Understanding Media: Extensions of Man,* London: Routledge

Maguire, M and Pointing, J (eds) (1988) *Victims of Crime: A New Deal?* Buckingham: Open UP

Pearson, G (1983) *Hooligan: A History of Respectable Fears,* London: Palgrave

Pratt, J (2000) 'Emotive and ostentatious punishment: its decline and resurgence in modern society' 2(4) *Punishment and Society* 417–39

Reiner, R, Livingstone, S and Allen, J (2000a) 'Casino culture: media and crime in a winner-loser society', in Stenson, K and Cowell, D (eds), *Crime, Risk and Justice,* Devon: Willan

Reiner, R, Livingstone, S and Allen, J (2000b) 'No more happy endings? The media and popular concern about crime since the Second World War', in Hope, T and Sparks, R (eds), *Crime, Risk and Insecurity,* London: Routledge

Rheingold, L (1994) *The Virtual Community: Finding a Connection in a Computerized World,* London: Minerva

Sennett, R (1991) *The Conscience of the Eye,* London: Faber & Faber

Silverman, J and Wilson, D (2002) *Innocence Betrayed: Paedophilia, the Media and Society,* Cambridge: Polity

Taylor, I (1999) *Crime in Context: A Critical Criminology of Market Societies,* Cambridge: Polity

Valier, C (2004) *Crime and Punishment in Contemporary Culture,* London: Routledge

Wallace, P (1999) *The Psychology of the Internet,* Cambridge: CUP

Young, I (1990) 'The ideal of community and the politics of difference', in Nicholson, L (ed), *Feminism/Postmodernism,* New York: Routledge

Young, J (1999) *The Exclusive Society,* London: Sage

Part 3

Marginal Images

Chapter 10

Collisions of Culture and Crime: Media Commodification of Child Sexual Abuse

Karin Schofield

Introduction

The idea of 'child sexual abuse' was first presented in the 1970s as a scientific concept to describe and classify certain actions and behaviours between adults and minors (see Best 1990). Since then, issues surrounding the phenomena of paedophilia and child sexual abuse have evolved into a highly charged socio-political cause, attracting widespread media attention, academic research and political debate. Against this climate of heightened societal concern with child sexual abuse, the paedophile has, in recent years, emerged as arguably the most feared and vilified of all 'predatory strangers'.

Everyday understandings of paedophilia and child sexual abuse have been conventionalised through established norms and values. This chapter draws on the framework of cultural criminology in order to critically examine this process. Cultural criminology advocates the blending of ideas and approaches from a range of theoretical orientations, most notably media and cultural studies, through which the social construction of crime and criminal behaviour(s) can be interrogated and theorised. Proceeding from this perspective, the specific aim here is to interrogate the collisions of culture and crime through which the discourses and understandings about paedophilia and child sexual abuse have been constructed. The chapter therefore considers the changing representation of these phenomena within cultural texts, complex notions of 'style' and situated meaning (see Ferrell's 'Style Matters', this volume), shifting notions of acceptability, and the 'commodification' of crime and transgression (see Presdee 2000; Hayward 2004). It concludes by considering how the cultural criminological framework might be further developed in the future. More specifically, it advocates the development of a 'multi-modal framework' that places emphasis on specific approaches, methods and procedures that, in turn, reflect the multi-mediated nature of crime and criminal behaviour(s).

Some may think that the notion of such a cultural criminological approach to the examination of child sexual abuse and paedophilia is unnecessary, even quite frivolous. Why examine phenomena that have undoubtedly harmed and affected many people in a manner that does not seek to explain the causes, reduce the risk, or offer counsel for the victims? My response is straightforward. It is my belief that prevailing social norms surrounding sex offenders have not only served to heighten the risks to potential victims of child sexual abuse, but have also had far-reaching societal and organisational implications. Increasingly, for example, community fears and understandings about sex offenders – and community responses to them – are understood by professionals and academics to be potentially detrimental to the effectiveness of the work of criminal justice practitioners. Community responses can potentially put at risk both the impact and effectiveness of child protection strategies, and the interventions aimed at reducing the risks posed by convicted child sex offenders. West, for example, asserts that 'Assumptions of incorrigibility impede the rehabilitation of [child sex] offenders through vigilantism, stigmitization and barriers to employment. This amplifies deviance and does not protect children' (2000: 511).

Going even further, sociologist Frank Furedi (2001) suggests that everyday public understandings of child sexual abuse have led to a growing distrust of adult motives. He describes a society estranged from its children, where adult collaboration in raising children is fast diminishing. Not only are parents increasingly reluctant to involve grandparents, neighbours and friends in the general care of their children, but also many adults, fearful of accusations of misconduct, are now refraining from offering to assist in child supervision. This pervasive 'climate of suspicion' has led to what Furedi describes as the 'stigmatisation of one-to-one contact between adults and children'. He charts, for example, how voluntary organisations such as the British Scout Association and St John's Ambulance, along with more general sporting bodies and religious groups, are now suffering from a shortage of members due to adult fears – particularly male fears – about undertaking volunteer work with children: 'Where once there would have been an assumption of goodwill, dangers are now seen to lurk' (ibid: 3). Furedi suggests that this predicament has led ultimately to the social isolation of parents, a distancing between the generations and a diminished sense of community.

For Furedi the message that parents should be wary of the integrity of adults – particularly professionals entrusted with the care of their children – is conveyed, in part, through television and popular culture. In general, this chapter supports this proposition and thus seeks to outline how these media messages have been historically and culturally shaped through various collisions of culture and crime. In recognising the breadth of the concerns and methods that have constructed contemporary understandings of paedophilia and child sexual abuse, it is clear that enquiries regarding such phenomena require careful examination beyond the traditional criminological boundaries of investigation. The cultural criminological approach allows us to consider not just how crime is realised but how it is represented in our culture and constructed through moral and discursive frameworks.

Abuse as entertainment

In his book *Cultural Criminology and the Carnival of Crime*, Mike Presdee (2000) describes the interrelationship of crime and culture through cultural texts as the 'commodification of crime'. This practice is best illustrated by the popularity of the genres of crime and deviance within film, television and literary texts. Through such media, crime becomes a commodity enabling us to consume and experience criminal acts and behaviour as pleasure. Police camera footage and real life crimes captured on closed circuit television, for example, are commodified and distributed as television programmes or videotapes to be pleasurably consumed in our homes. Likewise, television dramas such as *The Bill* (ITV1) and *Inspector Morse* (ITV1) are a staple feature of prime time TV schedules, while crime-related 'documentary' programmes have also proliferated in recent years. The cultural contradictions of contemporary society allow phenomena that provoke reactions of anger and disgust to become intermingled with pleasure, fun and performance through the multimedia industry (see relatedly Williams 1974: 59; Kilborn and Izod 1997). As with other criminal acts and behaviours, paedophilia and child sexual abuse have also been objectified and commodified and can be pleasurably consumed through a variety of media.

The issues surrounding paedophilia and child sexual abuse have regularly featured in a number of televisual forms of programming. In 2001, the UK's two most popular soap operas, *Coronation Street* (ITV1) and *EastEnders* (BBC1), both dealt with issues surrounding these subjects. *Coronation Street* featured a storyline based around the emerging issue of the use of the Internet by paedophiles as a 'grooming' tool to establish relationships with children. Likewise *EastEnders* featured a story about inter-familial adult-child sexual contact. Such storylines raise mixed reactions. They are often seen to be 'well intentioned cautionary tales', or regarded as useful in contributing to public knowledge (*Sunday Mirror*, UK, 15 July 2001). In contrast, others claim that such portrayals over-simplify the issues they tackle, instilling fears amongst viewers (*The Guardian*, UK, 10 July 2001).

However, dramatic simulation is not just used within fictional programmes. In recent years, the 'true story' has become a 'trusted weapon in the [TV] schedulers' armoury' (Kilborn and Izod 1997: 137). Indeed, it is perhaps through 'real-life' crime documentaries that the media commodification of crime is best illustrated. Television crime documentaries operate in two formats: crime reconstruction programmes, or more in-depth 'documentaries' that focus on one particular offender or type of crime. Series such as *Crimewatch UK* (BBC1) and *Most Wanted* (ITV2) are crime reconstruction or 'armchair detective' (Soothill 1998: 155) programmes. They show footage of a number of unsolved crimes, either captured on CCTV or reconstructed, and ask the audience for assistance in the investigation of them. Such shows package real instances of crime as entertainment whilst purporting to be a useful public service.

The worthiness and consequences of reconstructing unsolved crimes has been questioned (Soothill 1998; Farrell and Soothill 2001). In Farrell and Soothill's examination of the television documentary, *The Real Story of the DJ Rapist* (Channel 4, 17 June 1999), which profiled the story of the convicted serial rapist, Richard Baker, the authors question whether the television crime documentary makers, in pursuit of entertaining audiences, may actually be fuelling further similar crimes. They argue that the dramatic imperatives of television documentary programmes have meant that 'such programmes do not enlighten, they endanger. They endanger by pandering to the requirement of the sensational, whilst giving clues to potential rapists' (2001: 67). Other television documentaries which have focused on child sex abuse crimes might also be viewed as educational tools for similar would-be offenders. Recent documentaries concerning child sexual abuse have either focused on a particular case, such as Roy Shuttleworth's conviction (as examined in *In the Name of the Children*, BBC1, 26 November 2000), or on the investigation of a number of similar crimes, such as *The Hunt for Britain's Paedophiles* (BBC2, 6 June 2002; 13 June 2002; 20 June 2002). In dealing with crimes where the offenders have been arrested and/or prosecuted, these programmes highlight both the mistakes the offenders made and the police investigation procedures that led to the offender being identified.

The Hunt for Britain's Paedophiles was a three-part documentary that purported to profile 'Operation Door Knock', an investigation into paedophile criminal activity by Scotland Yard's Paedophile Unit. Within the three programmes, the technique of merging documentary footage with dramatic components is clearly evident. All stories or events featured in the programme were accompanied by camera footage of the offenders and photographic or video evidence of child sexual abuse crimes taking place. The programme makers' use of salacious photographs and scenes from videos owned by paedophiles contributed to the sensational appeal of the programme. Although the images of the victims were obscured to protect their identity, the nature of the event that the image had captured was clearly apparent. The repetitive use of the same images throughout the programmes seemingly contradicted the programmes' condemnatory narration. The acceptability of the existence and use of such images changed, as they became dramatic tools, emphasising the 'true-life' drama of the stories. The narrative of the documentary also served to sensationalise the events it documented. For example, at the end of the first programme the audience is informed that the Scotland Yard Paedophile Unit had received further evidence of paedophile activity and that the Unit was to continue its investigation. The narrator then added that the investigation that followed led to the discovery of a body. This sensational piece of information was undoubtedly used as a dramatic lure to persuade the audience to watch the subsequent episodes in the series.

The details of the further investigation referred to at the end of the first programme formed the focus of the final programme in the series. At the start of the episode the viewers were once again informed that the investigation led to the discovery of a body. This salacious detail presented the viewer with the idea that a dramatic spectacle was about to unfold. Much of the footage contained in the programme was of the police searching the premises of a known child sex offender, looking for evidence that he was an active paedophile. Through the presentation of the footage a significant focus was made on the police detectives' remarks regarding the smell of the premises. At one point a detective likened the smell to the odour of a dead body. The narrator's communication at the start of the programme informing the viewers that a body was found as part of this investigation, coupled with the programme's emphasis on the police search and the apparent smell, would lead the viewer to imagine that the body of a victim was about to be uncovered. The idea that a police detective was about to make a gruesome discovery whilst he searched the offender's flat dramatised the otherwise mundane and repetitive footage. It was not until the end of the programme that it was revealed that the body found was that of the offender, who had committed suicide following the Paedophile Unit's discovery of his paedophile activity.

The Hunt for Britain's Paedophiles' sensational narrative dramatised the events and moulded the documentary into a format more associated with fictional crime dramas. The seemingly routine investigation into a crime that often provokes anger and disgust had been transformed into an entertaining and dramatic spectacle to be pleasurably consumed in homes across the UK. The programmes' dramatic imperatives meant that the activities of the Paedophile Unit were not so much profiled, as were the crimes they were investigating. Moreover, it is not just the criminal acts and behaviours of child sex offenders that were commodified by the documentary makers – it was also the public responses to them. Paedophilia and child sexual abuse not only produce responses of disgust and anger, but also more pleasurable ones of intrigue and fascination. Under the guise of investigative journalism the documentary was designed to stimulate viewers through its sensationalist approach.

Such criticisms regarding the sensationalism of paedophilia would appear to vindicate the much-criticised Channel 4 broadcast of a special edition of its satirical comedy series, *Brass Eye* (26 July 2001). The programme, devised by Chris Morris, satirised hysterical media responses to child sex abuse via a spoof documentary. Well known figures from sport, music, film and politics were duped into making outlandish and false statements about paedophiles and paedophilia, believing that they were endorsing a 'charity campaign'. Many organisations and Government ministers voiced concerns over the placement of the emotive issue of child sexual abuse within a comedy broadcast. The public lodged complaints with the Independent Television Commission, the Broadcasting Standards Commission and Channel 4, making the special edition of *Brass Eye* the most complained about programme in British television history. Much of the press's reactions to the spoof documentary included accusations that the programme was trivialising issues surrounding paedophilia (*The Sunday Telegraph*, UK, 29 July 2001). There were also sustained calls for those responsible for the programme to be sacked (*News of the World*, UK, 29 July 2001), the *Daily Mail* calling it 'The sickest TV show ever' (28 July 2001).

Following the broadcast of *The Hunt for Britain's Paedophiles*, an article in *The Telegraph* argued that:

> Chris Morris, the man behind the *Brass Eye* programme ... brilliantly satirised exactly this sort of television. If ever there was a case of life imitating art, this was it ... There was a serious point behind Mr Morris' programme – to highlight the crude tactics behind such programmes as *The Hunt For Britain's Paedophiles*, where presenters are supposedly exposing some vice or other, in the full knowledge that the appeal of the programmes depends on the viewers' salacious interest in that vice. (8 June 2002)

Brass Eye was not the first media forum to draw attention to media sensationalism of the issues surrounding paedophilia. The events surrounding the abduction and death of eight-year-old Sarah Payne in 2000 allowed for sustained media coverage, fuelling sensationalised stories, debates and media campaigns amongst the tabloid print media. The media hysteria that followed drew criticism from politicians, criminal justice practitioners and other media forums. However, this time it was not just the public responses of fascination and intrigue that were being commodified, but also parents' fears. In doing so the print media drew on an already established interpretative repertoire surrounding the predatory paedophile to express prevalence and danger. Dominant discourses represented the paedophile as irrational 'other' and constructed the victim as innocent and vulnerable. Expressions of perpetrators' 'otherness' were expressed in terms of the moral discourses of evil, sin, monstrosity and perversion, coupled with medical models of sickness, pathology and incurability: 'Monsters who have lost their right to go on living' (*Daily Mail*, 19 July 2000); '... evil bastard's perverse sexual desires' (*The Mirror*, 19 July 2000); 'The most reviled and recidivistic of criminals ... with neither the intention nor the ability to change their ways' (*Daily Express*, 4 August 2000); 'Smallpox was once another incurable killer of infants but it has now been eradicated. Child abusers are incurable germs too, and must also be taken out of circulation forever' (*Sunday People*, 30 July 2000).

Defensive rhetoric, in the form of erroneous statistical evidence or the framing of Sarah Payne's abduction as the latest in a series of similar attacks, was employed in a bid to corroborate and bolster the press's discursive constructs. Such tactics served to amplify the prevalence of sexual attacks on children, further playing to parents' fears: 'There are 110,000 child sex offenders in Britain ... one for every square mile' (*News of the World*, 23 July 2000); 'There are paedophile rings in every town' (*Daily*

Mail, 19 July 2000); 'The pattern was chillingly familiar from the start' (*The Mirror*, 19 July 2000); and 'For too long the nation has endure the pain of seeing little innocents such as Sarah Payne snatched from streets to become victims of paedophiles' (*News of the World*, 23 July 2003).

Filmic and literary representations

Representation of child sexual abuse, paedophilia and adult-child sexual relationships is not limited to journalistic media forms. The commodification of the phenomena (and the public reactions of intrigue and fascinations to them) can also be identified within a small number of filmic and literary texts. Within filmic productions, childhood sexuality and adult-child sexual relationships have been dealt with by a number of cinematic producers. Prominent examples include: Jody Foster playing a child prostitute in Martin Scorcese's *Taxi Driver* (1976); and Luc Besson's *Leon* (1994), in which Natalie Portman plays Mathilda, a 13-year-old girl who (we assume) seeks a sexual relationship with the eponymous hit-man. However, the film adaptations of Vladimir Nabokov's modern classic *Lolita* (1959) directed by Stanley Kubrick (1962) and Adrian Lyne (1998) are perhaps most unusual in that they explore paedophilic desires specifically. The story of Humbert Humbert, a man who starts a sexual relationship with his stepdaughter, Lolita, after her mother dies, came under renewed attack when Adrian Lyne's remake of the film was released in 1998. Placing paedophilia within a fictional cultural text presented problems for the producers. Against the backdrop of heightened societal concern with child sexual abuse, the film was unable to find a distributor in the USA, due to distributors' fears of being seen to be supportive of paedophilia. *Lolita* was, however, released in the UK, drawing widespread media attention, much of which suggested that the release of the film would 'normalise' paedophilia and put children at risk.[1]

Nabokov's novel *Lolita* explored adult-child sexual relationships long before child sexual abuse and paedophilia had been established as the prominent social issue that it is today. However, it is not the only literary text to have done so; Sadleir's *Fanny by Gaslight* (1940) includes details of sexual attractions and relationships between adults and minors, whilst Metalious' *Peyton Place* (1956) offered a glimpse of child sexual abuse before the term was even coined by medical and social practitioners. In the denouement we read that Lucas, the father of Selena:

> was a drunkard, and a wife beater, and a child abuser. Now when I say child abuser I mean that in the worst way you can think of. Lucas began to abuse Selena sexually when she was fourteen, and he kept her quiet by threatening to kill her and her little brother if she went to the law. (Metalious 1956: 347)

More recently, Vachss' *Strega* (1987) tells the story of an ex-offender asked to find a piece of child pornography. The story centres around the pursuit and destruction of a paedophile ring involved in exchanging child pornography images via the Internet. Interestingly, Vachss' novel was written long before social concern with this practice had become widespread. In an interview with *The Spectator*, Vachss is quoted

---

1   It does appear, though, that the directors of both film adaptations of *Lolita* were conscious of the likely reactions to the relationship between Lolita and Humbert. In the novel Lolita is 12 and a half; however, in Kubrick's adaptation Lolita looks 16 or 17 years old, while Lyne raised the age of Lolita to 14. The closer Lolita appears to approach full sexual development, the more 'natural' Humbert's infatuation with her is likely to seem.

as saying, 'When I wrote about predatory paedophiles trading kiddie porn over modems in 1987, book reviewers were unanimous in telling me what a sick, fevered, crazy imagination I had' (9 April 1998).

In recent years the social concern regarding paedophilia and child sexual abuse has been instrumental in the publication and success of a number of other literary works, both fictional and non-fictional. In 2001, Thornton published *Nanin*, a non-fictional book that catalogues the sexual abuse inflicted on him by his father and later by his uncle, who also 'lent' him to other men. *Nanin* follows the recent success of other similar non-fiction best sellers, such as Pelzer's autobiographical trilogy, which graphically describes the abuse he experienced during his childhood, and McCourt's memoir, *Angela's Ashes* (1996), which provides an account of childhood as part of an impoverished family living in Limerick, Ireland. Originally written by Thornton as a form of therapy, *Nanin* offers child sexual abuse in a form that can be pleasurably consumed. The memoirs essentially outline the ramifications of being sexually abused as a child on the author's later life. However, they also offer detailed accounts of sexual abuse, including the erotic excitement experienced by Thornton during the abusive acts. These accounts, in their graphic and titillating detail, may act as sexual triggers, making the violent and shocking acts endured by the author pornographic and enthralling. Such detailed accounts led the *Observer* columnist, Geraldine Bedell, to question 'whether the most enthusiastic readers of this book might, in fact, be paedophiles [and] whether by describing his childish pleasure in these things, Thornton isn't in some sense normalising abuse' (2 September 2001). Had Thornton's work been a piece of fictional literature, or the script for a play or film, it is likely that much attention and criticism would emanate from its placement in the public domain. Yet, Thornton is a victim who presents *Nanin* as a truthful account, and therefore the level of criticism against *Nanin* is likely to be small, as it is less acceptable to be critical of the truth and a victim. However, it may be argued that, through the packaging and retailing of the sexual abuse he endured as a child, Thornton has commodified child sexual abuse into a form that can be pleasurably consumed by *Nanin's* readership.

Walters' *Acid Row*, a fictional account of a neighbourhood's growing disquiet at the housing of a convicted paedophile on their residential estate in the wake of the abduction of a young girl, is purposefully based on the lack of public understanding of the risks posed by paedophiles (Walters, Radio 4, 5 November 2001). Walters not only describes a community's false assumptions about child sexual abuse, but also illustrates how even innocent events can be re-interpreted or labelled differently in light of the current hysteria surrounding paedophilia. By the end of the fictional account it is apparent that no sexual acts against a child actually took place, leaving us to ponder on the fact that it is not so much the crimes of child sexual abuse and paedophilia that are commodified by Walters, but the societal understandings and responses to the phenomena.

Shifting notions of acceptability: controversy and concern

Ferrell and Sanders note that 'In the same way that everyday crime and criminalization operate as cultural enterprises, everyday popular cultural undertakings … are regularly recast as crime' (1995: 7). Ferrell argues that much of what is produced in the worlds of art, music, literature and fashion gets caught up in controversies over 'good taste', public decency and the alleged influences of popular culture (Ferrell 1995). Such conflicts not only promote controversy but also reconstruct cultural undertakings as criminal. Ferrell and Sanders' examples of conflicts between crime and the consumption of cultural artefacts include Robert Mapplethorpe's photographs of nude children, which stoked controversy in the USA and the UK, and the reaction to punk music's association with sadomasochism and anarchy.

Cultural forms and expressions have also been recast as crime in light of the controversies over 'good taste' and decency that have arisen through the development of understandings of paedophilia and child sexual abuse. In a society sensitive to the subject of child sexual abuse, standards of acceptable images and representations of children have changed. Greater public knowledge and understandings of paedophiles and their behaviour have undoubtedly led to increased concern regarding the representation of children's bodies and relationships between adults and children. In this relatively new cultural context, standards of acceptability have shifted in the realms of popular culture, fashion and advertising, rendering some images and literature obscene and distasteful.

While there is evidence of an increasing tolerance towards other forms of sexual representation, such as homosexuality, contemporary culture shows 'a tremendous sensitivity to depictions of nudity where children or even adolescents under the current age of consent are involved' (Lucie-Smith 2001: 1). Many images, innocuous at the time, may provoke sentiments today that did not exist when they were produced. From the 15th to the 18th centuries the image of the naked child personified innocence. Later in the 18th century it became fashionable to depict naked children kissing or embracing, intended as harmless frolics. Later still, painters were not afraid to confront the sexuality of young subjects (*Puberty* (Edvard Munch, 1894); *Thérèse* (Balthus, 1938); *Untitled* (Pierre Louys, 1885); *The Awakening Conscience* (William Holman Hunt, 1835)).

The development of photography in the 19th century opened up new debates regarding the aesthetic of photographic images. In contrast to paintings and drawings, which are understood to be fabricated and constructed objects, photographs, although mediated representations, appear to capture the real. As a result of widespread knowledge and concern about child sexual abuse and child pornography, photographic images of naked or partially clothed children have gained extensive public controversy. Robert Mapplethorpe's *The Perfect Moment* exhibition at the Contemporary Arts Center in Cincinnati became the focus of a legal dispute due to its inclusion of two photographs of children that were branded obscene (*Jesse McBride* (1976) and *Rosie* (1976)).

Further anxieties about the way children and childhood are represented through photography were expressed when photographs by Tierney Gearon of her two children were exhibited as part of the *I Am the Camera* (2001) exhibition at the Saatchi Gallery in London. One photograph was of her two children, aged four and six, playing on the beach dressed only in masks, and the other was of her son urinating in the snow. Gearon's exhibition was intended as a photographic documentary account of family life. To some, the images look like family snapshots, lacking in formal qualities, not posed, spontaneous and not unlike those treasured in family photo albums. However, their placement in the public domain as cultural undertakings led to complaints to the police and an investigation by the Obscene Publications Unit. There was, however, no prosecution with regard to the photographs as there was deemed to be no sense of lewdness or sexual provocation. It seems that controversy was stoked simply because the subjects were unclothed.

These reactions to Gearon's and Mapplethorpe's images are indicative of the confusion surrounding what is now acceptable imagery of children in a world subject to rapidly shifting understandings of 'good taste' and decency.

Conclusion: developing the cultural criminological approach

Traditionally, when examining criminal or deviant behaviour, mainstream criminologists look to established sources of criminological information to inform their ideas and understandings (ie criminal statistics, established criminological theories, psychological research and legislative documentation). Cultural criminology advocates a useful expansion of these conventional channels of information used to study crime, arguing for the merging of theoretical orientations, most notably cultural and media studies. This trans-disciplinary approach is perhaps the greatest strength of cultural criminology, as it reflects the multi-mediated nature of much criminality in late modernity. The cultural construction of child sexual abuse and paedophilia is clearly illustrative of the need to adopt a trans-disciplinary approach, with the approaches of criminology, psychology, sociology, criminal justice policy, media studies, cultural studies, legal studies, social history, and linguistics all providing insight.

This chapter urges that this multi-modal approach should be recognised more fully and thus be treated as a more distinctive methodological approach within cultural criminology. Cultural criminologists should not look to an accepted staple literature. Rather they should look towards interweaving ideas and understandings from all relevant tangential literatures. What is relevant should be subject-led, and this should become a more distinctive feature of cultural criminological research. However, if this subject-led approach is to succeed, a recognised multi-modal approach with named inter-linked modes of analysis should be identified. Modes would encourage seemingly diverse intellectual dimensions to be linked to ensure critical and multi-faceted studies of the social construction of crime and deviance. By way of a conclusion to this chapter I have identified a series of tentative modes that could help to augment current cultural criminological thinking.

A 'Communicational Mode' would build upon Ferrell and Sanders' (1995) theme of 'media', but would extend it to incorporate broader understandings of communication activities. Communication activities such as broadcast, print media, fiction, film, theatre, art, photography and public debate can be used as barometers of social process and change and are indicative of behavioural and societal attitudes (see O'Neill, this volume).

An 'Investigative and Illuminative Mode' would incorporate the parameters of Ferrell and Sanders' (1995) 'critical cultural criminology'. This critical and investigate mode is so named because it draws on the ideas of power, conflict and insubordination to help explain the relationship between culture and crime. Through this mode the particular relationships between legal and moral authorities and subversive criminalised (sub)cultures could be investigated. It places a critical focus on the complex interplay between these elements in an effort to understand how power is both enforced and resisted, leading to social inequalities through which criminal and deviant understandings are constructed.

An 'Enactional Mode' would draw on ideas of style and imaging as shaping criminal identities, analysing how criminal behaviours and deviance are performed and displayed. The enactional mode looks to the collective imagery and the production of shared symbolism and meanings within criminal and deviant subcultural groups. It also considers legal and moral stylistic and aesthetic assumptions as informing the criminalisation of certain behaviours and undertakings. Ferrell and Sanders (1995) have already set out their understanding of 'style' in shaping crime. However, the criminal behaviour(s) of a paedophile highlights that the concept of 'style' in shaping crime and criminal identities may not be as straightforward for some criminal groups. Society's attempt to label cultural undertakings as criminal and deviant, such as the art and photographic forms discussed earlier, is clearly illustrative of Ferrell and Sanders' understanding of 'style' whereby legal and moral stylistic assumptions lead to the criminalisation of behaviours. However, Ferrell and Sanders also draw attention to the role of shared styles shaping criminal identities. Hebdidge's (1979) notion of subcultural style, defined as collective symbolism and shared meanings within subcultural groups, may have apparent applications for cultural criminologists examining criminal subcultural groups such as graffiti artists. Their subcultural style may be played out through their argot, appearance and aesthetics and stylised presentation of self (Ferrell 1995). Paedophiles and child sex offenders, however, seem to present a far more complex task. O'Carroll states that 'being a paedophile is a very hazardous business' (1980: i). The danger in being identified as a paedophile or child sex offender is clearly illustrated through the many news media stories of violent attacks on convicted child sex offenders, or those thought to be paedophiles. Such high profile negative consequences of being identified as a paedophile undoubtedly mean that easily distinguishable symbolic codes that identify paedophiles are unlikely to exist. It is doubtful that shared styles, similar to the 'dressing down' of gang members (Miller 1995), can be detected among paedophiles. However, paedophiles may be considered to be similar to other deviant or criminal groups, which, because of their behavioural nature, are also spatially dislocated, such as computer hackers (Ferrell and Websdale 1999). The 'style' of paedophiles may be located within the practices of producing and distributing child pornography, which is one form of paedophilic behaviour, indicating that although paedophiles are often spatially dislocated, there are shared normative symbolic codes. It may be argued therefore that paedophile style may be situated within the aesthetics of the images they choose to produce and consume, and the argot employed when attempting to distribute or receive criminalised images undetected. There is perhaps a 'covert paedophile style'.

A 'Representational Mode' incorporates issues of discourse, narrative and representational strategies. Analysis should pay attention to the ideas, beliefs, values, theories, propositions and ideologies that construct portraits of crime within social texts, and, by extension, the public perception of the social problem.

Finally, an 'Epistemological Mode' emphasises the trans-disciplinary nature of cultural criminological research by highlighting the wealth of literature, encompassing a variety of disciplines and methodological approaches. Drawing on trans-disciplinary literature brings together grounds of knowledge, which may include ethnographical and biographical accounts, psychological and philosophical work, traditional criminological accounts and historical accounts. The parameters from which texts might be drawn should not be seen to be established; rather, the importance of identifying topic-led boundaries should be recognised.

These five modes have all been drawn upon in the development of content and discussion within this chapter. Doing so illustrates that by establishing a multi-modal framework, emphasis is placed on approaches, methods and procedures of cultural criminological study, rather than the more subject-based themes previously offered by those who have sought to establish and define cultural criminology so far. This serves to highlight, and make more distinctive, the multi-disciplinary nature of cultural criminological research that is required for an area of study that encompasses a diverse range of behaviours, activities and influences.

References

Best, J (1990) *Threatened Children: Rhetoric and Concern about Child-Victims*, Chicago: University of Chicago Press

Farrell, P and Soothill, K (2001) 'Television documentaries on sex offenders: the emergence of a new genre' 74 *The Police Journal* 61–69

Ferrell, J (1995) 'Culture, crime and cultural criminology' 3(2) *Journal of Criminal Justice and Popular Culture* 25–42

Ferrell, J and Sanders, C (eds) (1995) *Cultural Criminology*, Boston: Northeastern University Press

Ferrell, J and Websdale, N (1999) *Making Trouble: Cultural Constructions of Crime, Deviance and Control*, New York: Aldine de Gruyter

Furedi, F (2001) *Paranoid Parenting*, Harmondsworth: Allen Lane/Penguin

Hayward, KJ (2004) *City Limits: Crime, Consumer Culture and the Urban Experience*. London: GlassHouse Press

Hebdidge, D (1979) *Subculture: The Meaning of Style*, London: Methuen

Killborn, R and Izod, J (1997) *An Introduction to Television Documentary: Confronting Reality* Manchester: Manchester UP

Lucie-Smith, E (2001) 'Eros and innocence', Index On Line Issue 297: www.oneworld.org/index_oc/Issue297/lucie-smith.htm

McCourt, F (1996) *Angela's Ashes*, London: HarperCollins

Metalious (2002) [1956] *Peyton Place*, London: Virago

Miller, J (1995) 'Struggles over the symbolic: gang style and the meanings of social control', in Ferrell, J and Saunders, C (eds), *Cultural Criminology*, Boston: Northeastern University Press

Nabokov, V (1959) *Lolita*, London: Weidenfeld and Nicolson

O'Carroll, T (1980) 'Paedophilia: the radical case' 12 *Contemporary Social Issues Series*, London: Peter Owen

Presdee, M (2000) *Cultural Criminology and the Carnival of Crime*, London: Routledge

Sadleir, M (1940) *Fanny by Gaslight*, London: Constable and Co

Soothill, K (1998) 'Armchair detectives and armchair thieves' 2 (LXXI) *The Police Journal* 155–59

Thornton, T (2001) *Nanin*, London: Book Guild

Vachss, A (1987) *Strega*, Boston: Vintage

Walters, M (2001) *Acid Row*, London: Macmillan

West, D (2000) 'Paedophilia: plague or panic?' 11(3) *Journal of Forensic Psychiatry* 511–31

Williams, R (1974) *Television, Technology and Cultural Form*, London: Chatto and Windus

Chapter 11
Cultural Constructions of the Hillbilly Heroin and Crime Problem

Kenneth D Tunnell

Introduction: constructing the problem

OxyContin (trade name), an oxycodone drug, was approved by the United States Food and Drug Administration (FDA) in 1995 and first marketed in 1996 by Purdue Pharma of Stamford, Connecticut. Among the most powerful analgesics currently manufactured, OxyContin is a synthetic opioid. Opioid drugs (which include opium, heroin, morphine, codeine, hydrocodone, and oxycodone) are produced from the opium poppy. Opiate agonists, such as OxyContin, provide pain relief by acting on opioid receptors in the brain, the spinal cord and directly on tissue (OxyContin Diversion and Abuse 2002). OxyContin is a single-entity product unlike most oxycodone products (eg Percodan and Percocet) that typically contain aspirin or acetaminophen. A marked improvement over other drugs, OxyContin reportedly is 16 times more powerful than similar narcotics (Sappenfield 2001). Designed as an orally administered, time-release analgesic, OxyContin provides significant and sustained pain relief and, due to its addictive propensity, is listed as a Schedule II narcotic (ie drugs approved for medical use and that have a high potential for abuse) under the Drug Enforcement Administration's (DEA's) Controlled Substances Act.

OxyContin abuse first surfaced in Maryland, the eastern part of rural Maine, eastern Ohio, the rust-belt areas of Pennsylvania and the southern Appalachian region of West Virginia, Virginia and Kentucky. During the year 2000 (the most recent data), the 10 states with the highest OxyContin prescription rates (per 100,000 population) and those areas with problems of abuse were, in descending order: West Virginia, Alaska, Delaware, New Hampshire, Florida, Kentucky, Pennsylvania, Maine, Rhode Island and Connecticut (Hutchinson 2001). West Virginia, particularly its southern region, and Kentucky have long histories of pharmaceutical abuse (DEA briefs and background 2002).

This chapter describes this new drug of abuse and its constructed mediated images. It also details public officials' efforts at linking this new abuse problem to increases in crime rates locally and nationally. Finally, the chapter describes the bigoted rhetoric found in media reports about this drug and its rural Appalachian users.

OxyContin was first recognised as a drug of abuse during the late 1990s with frequent front-page news stories detailing the problem. News articles consistently increased in number and fuelled a new moral panic (Goode and Ben-Yehuda 1994). Table 11.1 illustrates the media's frequency of reporting on OxyContin abuse.

Table 11.1: OxyContin keyword search by year and frequency, 1998–2003

YEAR	1998	1999	2000	2001	2002	2003
Major papers	0	0	10	312	158	166
Magazines & journals	0	0	3	16	10	12
Legal news	0	0	1	20	33	22
Health & medical news	0	0	3	56	32	47
TOTAL	0	0	17	404	233	247

Source: Lexis-Nexis Search by keyword OxyContin

Abuse methods vary. In some cases tablets are crushed and snorted. In others, the powder is diluted and intravenously injected. A less often-used delivery style is to peel off the outer coating and chew the tablets (eg Sullivan 2001). These abuse methods result in the sudden absorption of the analgesic rather than as designed – slowly and continuously over several hours. Not surprisingly, overdoses and deaths have occurred, although no one knows just how many. The actual number of overdose deaths caused by OxyContin is difficult to disaggregate and likely will never be known with any degree of certainty. This is due in part to poly-drug use since OxyContin is often mixed with alcohol and other depressants. Furthermore, data do not distinguish accidental deaths from suicides. Nonetheless, the media and office holders have published all sorts of numbers.

Unsubstantiated rhetoric about this drug is pervasive. For example, Joseph L Famularo, the US Attorney for the Eastern District of Kentucky, claimed, '[I have] personally counted 59 deaths since January of last year that local police attributed to addicts using the drug and I suspect that's pretty conservative' (Clines and Meier 2001). *The Guardian* (UK), reporting on the 'scores of deaths in the [southern Appalachian] region in the form of overdoses, suicides and car wrecks', blindly accepted the grisly depiction of a Kentucky prosecutor who claimed that 'bodies are stacking up like cordwood' (Borger 2001). Hazard, Kentucky (located in Perry County) was a featured *Newsweek* cover story with the sensationalistic reporting that: 'These days, nearly everyone in Hazard has an OxyContin horror story to tell. Even grandmothers peddle their prescriptions for quick cash' (Rosenberg 2001: 49). And from the Harlan County Sheriff's Congressional Testimony:

> Today [Harlan County's] picturesque beauty is marred by a terrible blight ... It affects the young, middle-aged, and senior citizens alike. It affects both rich and poor. The blight I am speaking of is the drug OxyContin and it has left a huge path of destruction in its wake. (Dangers of OxyContin 2001)

In the midst of a developing moral panic, the DEA requested autopsy, toxicology and medical examiners' reports on all deaths 'induced by, associated with, or related to oxycodone and/or specifically the oxycodone product, OxyContin for 2000 and 2001' from 775 medical examiners across the country. The DEA was sent 1,304 reports from 32 states that were pared down to 949. From those, 146 deaths (15%) were OxyContin verified deaths. The majority of the deaths could not be traced solely to OxyContin. Rather, they resulted from poly-drug interactions although only 19% resulted from oxycodone and alcohol interactions. Nine deaths were associated with injecting an oxycodone and only one death was associated with snorting. The vast majority of oxycodone deaths resulted from oral consumption rather than illicit and widely propagated modes of abuse (*Drugs and Chemicals of Concern* 2002).

The *Cleveland Free Times* questioned information on reported OxyContin-related deaths in Kentucky and contacted the state's Medical Examiner. According to the *Cleveland Free Times'* report there were 27 oxycodone (not OxyContin) deaths in all of Kentucky during the year 2000. Of the 27, two deaths were attributed to a combination of oxycodone and alcohol. Twenty three deaths resulted from multiple drugs (viz Dilaudid, Fentanyl, cocaine and heroin), including oxycodone, found in victims' blood. The result – two deaths statewide resulted from oxycodone use alone (Kaushik 2001).

Drug scares, it has been noted, 'are independent phenomena, not necessarily related to actual trends or patterns in drug use or trafficking' (Brownstein 1995: 55). In the midst of this recent scare, a Hazard, Kentucky woman was sentenced to 10 years in prison for selling four OxyContin pills. The sentencing judge declared Oxycontin 'a pure scourge upon the land ... demonic fire' (Rosenberg 2001: 49). An Eastern Kentucky US Attorney who headed a major OxyContin drug sting made the unsubstantiated claim that 'we caught 207. We didn't catch half of them; that's how pervasive this thing is' (Clines and Meier 2001).

The oxycontin-crime connection

During the most hysterical period in the OxyContin scare, the Hazard, Kentucky police chief reported that 90% of thefts and burglaries in his area were to get money to buy OxyContin (Alford 2001). He offered no explanation for thefts and burglaries prior to 1996 (when OxyContin was first marketed) or for relatively *stable* crime rates since then. For example, the year before OxyContin was manufactured, Perry County (which includes Hazard) had 303 crimes per 10,000 population. In 1996, it had 260 per 10,000 population; in 1997, 251; in 1998, 272; in 1999, 264; and in 2000, an increase to 382 per 10,000 population. A less sensationalistic interpretation is that crime rates in Perry County, like nearly everywhere, fluctuate with some years experiencing increases and others decreases. Yet this universal feature of crime goes unreported by media and public officials. Statewide crime rates in Kentucky, as Table 11.2 overleaf illustrates, have also fluctuated, with lower rates in 2000 than in 1996.

According to an article in the *Washington Times*, a former OxyContin dealer claimed that 'selling one 90 pill prescription of 80 milligram OxyContin is more profitable than selling a kilogram of cocaine on the black market when the risk factor is weighed' (Taylor 2003). This statement lacks face validity. Furthermore, the *Washington Times* pays no attention whatsoever to how one goes about weighing, operationalising, or measuring 'risk factor' to make such a comparison. Rather, the exaggerated claim is simply accepted and reported to a gullible public.

Table 11.2: Kentucky crime index rates per 100,000 inhabitants, 1996–2000

Year	Violent crime	Property crime	Murder	Rape	Robbery	Assault	Burglary	Larceny	Vehicle theft
1996	320.5	2845.8	5.9	31.7	93.8	189.2	688.4	1896.3	261.1
1997	316.9	2810.1	5.8	33.4	90.7	187.0	681.6	1880.4	248.1
1998	284.0	2605.3	4.6	29.3	75.4	174.7	637.4	1750.1	217.8
1999	308.3	2645.1	5.1	29.0	78.4	195.8	635.7	1785.5	223.9
2000	294.5	2665.2	4.8	27.0	80.6	182.2	626.2	1809.6	229.5

Source: Crime in Kentucky

The *Washington Times* quoted an ATF agent assigned to Southwest Virginia who said that 'every year from 1996 to 1999, the crime rate doubled directly because of the influx of OxyContin' (Taylor 2003). This is irresponsible journalism. Not only did the crime rate not double, these numbers were published without verification when they are a matter of public record. The story also naïvely accepts a mono-causal relationship asserted by law enforcement who, along with the press, has a vested interest in publishing these alarming figures. The three largest counties in Southwest Virginia did indeed witness some increases (and also some decreases) between 1996 and 2002, but increases were mainly due to hikes in larceny (which in the United States is the most frequently occurring and least serious index crime).[1]

From the *Boston Herald* comes the report that '[OxyContin] is seen as fueling a crime wave around the country, particularly in poor areas where it is dubbed Hillbilly Heroin' (Lasalandra 2003). In this case, a national crime wave is associated with the use of this one drug. No such crime wave exists. Property crime (the type most commonly associated with drug abuse) decreased from a high of 5,140 per 100,000 population in 1991 to 3,624 per 100,000 in 2002. For the first half of 2003 (the most recent data), property crimes decreased 0.8% indicating that the downward trend of the past 12 years is continuing. The percentage of households experiencing any type of criminal victimisation steadily decreased from 25% in 1994 to 16% in 2000. The raw number of households experiencing crime likewise shows steadily decreasing trends (Uniform Crime Report 2003; *Sourcebook of Criminal Justice Statistics* 2002). Furthermore, the 10 states with the highest per capita OxyContin use have lower crime rates than the 10 states with the lowest per capita OxyContin use. Not only is a national crime wave a fabrication, but those very states that have the highest OxyContin use per capita have experienced declining crime rates since OxyContin was first marketed and rates under those states with the lowest OxyContin use.

---

1   Larceny is the unlawful theft of property (other than motor vehicles) by stealth rather than by force. Larceny is one of the Federal Bureau of Investigation's (FBI's) index crimes and its rates are reported annually. Distinctions between petty and grand larceny vary greatly across states in the United States.

Henry Brownstein's (1995) observations on the social construction of New York City's crack and violent crime problems are useful here. Brownstein's data suggest that the crack-violent crime relationship was exaggerated by the media and local and state politicians, including then-governor Mario Cuomo, who reported that the state's three biggest problems were 'Drugs, drugs, and drugs'. Crack, as we know and knew then, is a highly localised problem, at that time specific to isolated pockets of New York City. Propagating crack as a problem for the entire state (and a state that is mainly rural) exaggerated its impact. The media's uncritical acceptance and reproduction of the crack and violent crime problem in New York skewed the impression for countless state residents. The crack problem, much like the current OxyContin problem, was socially constructed within a political context. In both cases, the media respond to descriptions of 'epidemics' and reproduce them by relying on their 'credible authorities'. A hierarchy of credibility undoubtedly shapes the news and in the case of crack and OxyContin, governors, local politicians and police chiefs receive far greater media coverage than those who are just as informed (if not more so) but who occupy a lower strata. Without state-corporate recognised clout, spokespersons rarely appear in the media no matter how well informed they may be. Consider how few academics appear on the nightly news and engage in discussions about drug abuse and crime. With such informed voices absent from the debate, moral panics, such as an OxyContin-crime scare, are easily constructed (see eg Goode and Ben-Yehuda 1994).

Bigoted media depictions

From 2001 through February 2004, according to two electronic databases, between 82 and 125 published newspaper and magazine articles used the term 'Hillbilly Heroin' when describing OxyContin abuse or the OxyContin-crime relationship (Highbeam Research; Lexis-Nexis). Given the inadequacies of electronic databases, in all likelihood more than 125 articles appeared during that period. Consider the following statements from various news sources:

- The *Washington Times* reports that 'Oxy, Hillbilly Heroin and Killer are a few of the street names for the prescription pain pill OxyContin' (Taylor 2003: 1).

- A 2001 *San Francisco Chronicle* headline reads 'Hillbilly Heroin Brings Robbers to Pharmacies'.

- A CNN interview with an addiction specialist medical doctor opens with the interviewer's first words: 'They call it Hillbilly Heroin in some parts of the country ...' (CNN, 10 October 2003).

- A FOX news story claims that 'Unverified media reports of deaths attributed to OxyContin abuse surfaced, leading to a new species of victim: the hillbilly heroin addict' (Milloy 2001).

- The *New York Daily News,* reporting on talk show host Rush Limbaugh's OxyContin abuse, concludes that the drug does not recognise class boundaries. 'This synthetic version of morphine is by no means sought after only by the rich and famous. In Appalachian states, where its use is rampant, it's known as hillbilly heroin' (Shin 2003).

- A *Knight Rider* article speculates on the origin of the hillbilly heroin label: 'OxyContin picked up the hillbilly heroin nickname because its abuse first proliferated in rural and suburban areas of Maine, Virginia, West Virginia, Kentucky, Pennsylvania and Massachusetts' (Johnson 2003).

- The *Los Angeles Times* reports that the label 'hillbilly heroin' was actually earned as it 'ravaged poor parts of Appalachia' (Mehren 2001).

- A *Guardian* (UK) writer on assignment in West Virginia reports that 'in this part of West Virginia and the neighbouring hill counties of Virginia and Kentucky, they call it hillbilly heroin or poor man's heroin' (Borger 2001).

- *The Christian Science Monitor* reports that OxyContin 'swept through the vales of ... Appalachia like crack cocaine saturated inner cities in the 1980s. Folks call it hillbilly heroin' (Sappenfield 2001).

- FOX Network's talk show host, Bill O'Reilly, refers to OxyContin as 'liquid heroin' [which makes no sense whatsoever since it is manufactured in pill form] (Satel 2003).

- The *Pittsburgh Post-Gazette* claims that 'Many in Appalachia call OxyContin Hillbilly heroin' (Breed 2001).

- The *Lexington Herald-Leader* claims that 'hillbilly heroin [is] coveted by Appalachian junkies' (Camp 2003).

- British rock and reality TV star Ozzy Osbourne, commenting on his son's OxyContin problems, said: 'When I found out the full depth of him getting into OxyContin, which is like hillbilly heroin, I was shocked and stunned. The thing that's amazing was how rapidly he went from smoking pot to doing hillbilly heroin' (MTV News 2003).

- From Nova Scotia comes the news that 'police in the US began to use the term hillbilly heroin because oxycodone is less expensive to buy than heroin and more available in rural states' (Richer 2003).

- From *The Observer* (UK) comes a story that begins: 'A lethal drug dubbed Hillbilly Heroin that has been responsible for hundreds of deaths in America has surfaced in Britain' (Thompson 2002).

- And from Canada, the *Calgary Sun* uses the label 'Hillbilly heroin ...' (Seskus 2001).

A commission from Washington County, Maine was formed to determine, among other things, 'What made OxyContin the so-called Hillbilly Heroin?'. The social construction of a drug of abuse and of rhetoric that belittles poor, rural Americans was not the Commission's concern. From the same report: 'Maine had been identified as the first state with a problem with OxyContin abuse, but it was quickly followed by Kentucky, rural parts of Virginia, and West Virginia leading to the creation of the moniker Hillbilly Heroin for OxyContin' (Substance Abuse Services Commission 2002). No mention is made of the process of creating the moniker, to its belittling symbolism, or to its northeastern imposed association with rural Southern Appalachia.

The DEA's street terms for OxyContin include Hillbilly Heroin and Poor Man's Heroin, Oxy, Oxycotton, Killers and Ocs. 'Hillbilly heroin' is a term used almost solely by non-Appalachians. Despite some news reporters' claims that 'many in Appalachia call OxyContin hillbilly heroin' (Breed 2001; cf Gillespie 2001), the term is rarely used by Appalachian residents who, during this research, consistently dismissed it as derogatory. Some in the region proudly embrace a 'hillbilly' image of themselves as part of their self-identity. The vast majority, however, are offended, and have been for decades, by the prejudiced label.

Satirising Appalachians, depicting them in stereotypical ways and exaggerating their cultural traits (including drug use and abuse) are the last bastions where public bigotry is acceptable. Even well educated men and women feel comfortable belittling hill country people. For example, during a recent lecture (6 February 2004) at the University of Tennessee, a pharmacology professor (originally from Florida) who teaches at East Tennessee State University opened his presentation with: 'I teach up in the hillbilly corner of the state.' Commentators have observed that bigoted jokes or comments about blacks, Jews, women, gays, immigrants and so on do more than simply offer a laugh at others' expense or place a distance between themselves and their subjects. They also dehumanise and reduce their subjects and, as a result, 'dismiss legitimate complaints about discrimination ... to deflect potentially disturbing questions about who has money and power, who doesn't and why' (Shelby 1999: 158). Given this stratified view of 'the other', it is easy to understand that the social response, and especially to urban and rural drug users and criminal actors, is most often simplistic, cavalier and punitive. Rather than seeking understanding of root causes and solutions, entrenched social problems are easily dismissed and the subjects ignored. It has become much easier to imprison than to treat, to dismiss than to understand, to pontificate than to question. In Central Kentucky, although drug treatment policies are often supported, news reporters, creating the news themselves, publish their own questions as to why more OxyContin users are not receiving prison time. Consider these facts bemoaned in a recent newspaper article:

> Courts in 32 counties had conviction rates of 50 percent or less in drug cases. Courts in 18 counties dismissed 20 percent or more of their drug cases. Courts in 25 counties granted probation to more than 60 percent of the people convicted of drug crimes. And courts in 18 counties allowed at least 20 percent of their cases to linger 18 months or more without resolutions. (Estep *et al* 2003)

The *Lexington Herald-Leader*, in one issue (2 February 2003), ran articles with the following titles:

Prosecutors' misunderstanding produces parade of probations

Courts' confusion aids the accused

Wrong interpretation of law leads to 40 cases' dismissal

Evident from these statements made by some members of the media is a particular worldview or bias that embraces a dehumanisation of the subjects and an acceptance of punishment over treatment and individual responsibility over social imagination.

In 1900, the *New York Journal* defined a 'hill-billie' as 'a free and untrammeled white citizen of Appalachia who lives in the hills, has no means to speak, dresses as he can, talks as he pleases, drinks whiskey when he gets it, and fires off his revolver as the fancy takes him' (Green 1968: 204). During a 1975 interview, Bill Monroe, the Kentuckian who originated Bluegrass – an entirely new form of music – articulated his feelings about the hillbilly label:

> I have never liked the name, the word, 'hillbilly'. It seemed like maybe another state out west would call you hillbilly if they thought that you'd never been to school or anything. I've never liked that and I've never used it in my music. (Wolfe 1975: 6)

Denise Giardina (1999: 161) relates the writing of English historian Arnold Toynbee (1934) who boldly claimed that 'the Scotch-Irish immigrants who forced their way into these natural fastnesses have come to be isolated from the rest of the World. They have relapsed into illiteracy and witchcraft. The Appalachian "Mountain People" at this day are no better than barbarians'. Toynbee continues with the belief that barbarism will disappear as Appalachians assimilate and change their ways of life as wage earners in the North Carolina cotton mills. Examining old photographs of her Appalachian ancestors, Giardina looks for 'signs of encroaching barbarism' and discovers that 'mountain people looked normal' (*ibid*: 163). Countering Toynbee's assertion that vast areas of Appalachia were isolated (indeed vast areas were *not* isolated, see eg Lewis 1999), Giardina presents the well-supported argument that it and its people suffered from economic exploitation, capital flight, the devastation of land from timbering and coal mining, thefts of minerals through legal shenanigans and broad form deeds, and violence from company and criminal justice thugs in the mines and mills. These explanations (and current policies and practices) remain salient ones for concentrated poverty in the region. For example, Kentucky's newly elected Republican governor proposes eliminating two agencies that promote Kentucky's Appalachian region and its economic development – the Kentucky Appalachian Commission and the Kentucky Coal Council. The governor's budget plans for $695 million in capital projects across the state, with the exception of Appalachian southeastern Kentucky which includes some of the state's poorest counties (Cheves 2004: A1).

Anne Shelby (1999: 154) recognises that 'Appalachians have been objecting to the stereotypes for well over a century now, seemingly to no avail'. Although she lives in rural Appalachia and knows many hillbilly jokes, she never hears them in her community. Local people simply do not appreciate them. She does hear them, however, in major cities or when encountering lawyers and business people in the county seat. Even people who seem to understand that there is little acceptance for jokes that belittle ethnic groups, women or sexual orientation 'feel perfectly free to stereotype rural southerners' (*ibid*: 158).

In early 2002, CBS, the leading television broadcasting company in the United States, proposed *The Real Beverly Hillbillies*, a reality show depicting a family of *real* Appalachians who would be moved from the hinterland and plopped down in the middle of Beverly Hills, California. An ugly reality extension of the 1960s television show, *The Beverly Hillbillies*, this programme would use non-actors. The real, authentic, live hillbillies would move from their impoverished communities to the lap of luxury and glitter of a Beverly Hills mansion. CBS executives giddily tried selling the show by imagining particular episodes such as the one 'where they have to interview maids' (*The Guardian* 2003). A Kentucky-based citizens' action group, the Center for Rural Strategies, reacted strongly to the proposal. Denying rumours that they 'can't take a joke', the Center objected to CBS' plans to select a 'particular group of Americans for ridicule ... and to make fun of and commercialize low-income rural folks'. Hoping to convince CBS to abandon its idea, the Center placed quarter-page ads against the programme in *The New York Times*, *The Washington Post* and *The Cincinnati Enquirer*. The cost of the ads totalled $75,000. A conservative online website published individuals' opposition to the Center's decision to criticise CBS. Consider these messages posted at www.freerepublic.com:

It is rather insane that this Hillbilly advocacy group is spending so much money on these ads.

That could have provided a lot of social services. I wonder how much of that was taxpayer money?

The staff of the Center for Rural Strategies consists of your usual collection of career leftist non-profit workers with histories of working on women's issues and environmental gripes.

Pearl! Run n git me Paw's gun. Ah'm gonna hunt me some city folks! Make fun of me, bygawd!

It is no longer considered polite to refer to them as 'hicks'. The appropriate term is 'Rustic Americans'.

Dang, ma, we're gonna be on TV!

Conclusion

Socially constructed images of criminals are typically those of urban, drug-using, non-white males. A very different mediated image has taken shape about southern Appalachia. Depictions of criminals in that region are of rural, white, 'hillbilly' males. Likewise, from the mediated entertainment and news industries the crime problem generally is described as an urban nightmare, lurking and swiftly preying on unsuspecting victims. In Appalachia, the crime problem is depicted as a slow-witted adventure of country bumpkins. Yet in each case, mediated images of criminal actors generally instill fear. The urban image is one of a wild-eyed, crack-driven, pistol-wielding, violent, young, black male. The Southern Appalachian image is one of a wild-eyed, moonshine (or today, OxyContin)-crazed, shotgun-toting, toothless, white male straight from the set of *Deliverance*. The literature is abundant on the social construction of the mythical, drug-crazed urban predator and seems relevant to its rural counterpart. Specific and skewed images of both types pervade popular culture and especially news and entertainment industries, as is evident from the exaggerated claims about the OxyContin-crime connection and the bigoted rhetoric used when describing Appalachians and rural social problems.

References

Alford, R (2001) 'Across the east, abuse of painkiller meant for cancer patients is rising', *Inquirer*, 10 February, p A5

Borger, J (2001) 'Hillbilly heroin: the painkiller abuse wrecking lives in West Virginia', *The Guardian*, 25 June, p 2

Breed, AG (2001) 'Painkiller hooks legion of addicts in Appalachia', *Pittsburgh Post-Gazette*, 17 June, p 3

Brownstein, HH (1995) 'The media and the construction of random drug violence', in Ferrell, J and Sanders, CR (eds), *Cultural Criminology*, Boston: Northeastern University Press, pp 45–65

Camp, CB (2003) 'Millions sold, office by office', *Lexington Herald-Leader*, 17 August, p A-1

Cheves, J (2004) 'Fiscal ax falls on southeastern Kentucky', *Lexington Herald-Leader*, 28 January, p A1

Clines, FX and Meier, B (2001) 'Cancer painkillers pose new abuse threat', *New York Times*, 9 February, pp A1 and 21

Dangers of OxyContin (2001) *Federal Document Clearing House Congressional Testimony*, 11 December

Drugs and Chemicals of Concern (2002) 'Summary of medical examiner reports on oxycodone-related deaths', Drug Enforcement Administration Diversion Control Program, Washington, DC: US Department of Justice

Estep, B, Lasseter, T and Johnson, LJ (2003) 'Trying public trust', *Lexington Herald-Leader*, 2 February, p A1

Giardina, D (1999) 'Appalachian images: a personal history', in Billings, DB, Norman, G and Ledford, K (eds), *Confronting Appalachian Stereotypes: Back Talk from an American Region*, Lexington: University Press of Kentucky, pp 161–73

Gillespie, C (2001) 'Chronic pain sufferers seek OxyContin', OxyContin information site: www.leflaw.net

Goode, E and Ben-Yehuda, N (1994) 'Moral panics: culture, politics and social construction' 20 *Annual Review of Sociology* 149–71

Green, A (1968) 'Hillbilly music: source and symbol' 78 *Journal of American Folklore* 204–28

Highbeam Research (2004): www.highbeam.com/library

Hutchinson, A (2001) Statement of Asa Hutchinson, Administrator, Drug Enforcement Administration Before the House Committee on Appropriations Subcommittee on Commerce, Justice and State, 11 December, DEA Congressional Testimony, Washington, DC: US Department of Justice

Johnson, C (2003) 'Hillbilly heroin', *Knight Rider*, 23 November

Kaushik, S (2001) 'An Oxy con job?', *Cleveland Free Times*, 2 May, p 1

Lasalandra, M (2003) 'Harvard, drug maker skirt pain-center controversy', www.bostonherald.com

Lewis, RL (1999) 'Beyond isolation and homogeneity: diversity and the history of Appalachia', in Billings, DB, Norman, G and Ledford, K (eds), *Confronting Appalachian Stereotypes: Back Talk from an American Region*, Lexington: University Press of Kentucky, pp 21–43

Mehren, E (2001) 'Hooks of hillbilly heroin', *Los Angeles Times*, 4 October, p 2

Milloy, S (2001) 'Scare-mongering over hillbilly heroin deprives the rest of us', FOX News, 5 August

MTV News (2003) 'Ozzy says he now believes pot leads to other addictions', 8 July

OxyContin Diversion and Abuse (2002) *Information Bulletin*, National Drug Intelligence Center, Johnstown, PA: US Department of Justice, January

Richer, S (2003) 'Hillbilly heroin hits Cape Breton', www.globeandmail.com

Rosenberg, D (2001) 'How one town got hooked' 137(15) *Newsweek*, pp 48–52

Sappenfield, M (2001) 'Rise of hillbilly heroin creates alarm in east', *Christian Science Monitor*, 12 July, p 3

Satel, S (2003) 'OxyContin half-truths can cause suffering', *USA Today*, 26 October, p 2

Seskus, T (2001) 'Police fear spread of hillbilly heroin', *Calgary Sun*, 27 November, p 1

Shelby, A (1999) 'The "R" word: what's so funny (and not so funny) about redneck jokes', in Billings, DB, Norman, G and Ledford, K (eds), *Confronting Appalachian Stereotypes: Back Talk from an American Region*, Lexington: University Press of Kentucky, pp 153–60

Shin, PHB (2003) 'Hillbilly heroin spurs abuse', *New York Daily News*, 5 October, p 3

Sourcebook of Criminal Justice Statistics (2002) Washington, DC: United States Bureau of Justice

Substance Abuse Services Commission (2002) 'OxyContin abuse: Maine's newest epidemic', January

Sullivan, P (2001) 'OxyContin-abuse problem appears limited to US' 165(5) *Canadian Medical Association Journal* 624–25

Taylor, G (2003) 'OxyContin a scourge for users in rural areas', *The Washington Times*, 2 September, p 1

The Guardian (2003) 'Southerners rebel over hillbilly reality TV show', 11 February

Thompson, T (2002) 'Epidemic fear as hillbilly heroin hits the streets', *The Observer*, 24 March, p 2

Toynbee, A (1934) *A Study of History*, Oxford: OUP

Uniform Crime Report (2003) Washington, DC: US Department of Justice

Wolfe, C (1975) 'Bluegrass touches: an interview with Bill Monroe' 16 *Old Time Music* 6–12

Chapter 12
Criminalising Marginality and Resistance: Marilyn Manson, Columbine and Cultural Criminology

Stephen L Muzzatti

Introduction

Despite lofty sentiments and rhetorical flourishes, America has never been particularly tolerant of dissent, dissenters or others who are unwilling/unable to march in lockstep to hegemonic cadences. While the foci of this intolerance are numerous, this chapter addresses one set of domestic cultural targets: youth music culture, with particular attention to Marilyn Manson and their young fans. As such, it examines the ways in which epistemic bricoleurs transform discontent, alienation, and 'sociological' critiques embedded in style, imagery and artistic production into criminality through mass-mediated deligitimisation and Othering.

Life in the United States is hard, and for many it is getting harder. To be sure, the poor, immigrants, gays and lesbians, women, people of colour, and a host of other marginalised masses of people have long languished under oppressive conditions in the US. In fact, many of the same structural conditions that facilitate the crimes by the capitalist state abroad (such as neo-imperial wars) also contribute to the social harms it inflicts on people in America (Tifft and Sullivan 1980; Barak 1991). However, for the past few years, the list of targeted groups has grown exponentially and the US has become an increasingly militarised society. While it is certainly true that both repressive and ideological state apparatuses have long worked in the interests of conservative, and more recently neo-conservative, forces bent on deligitimising, marginalising, quelling and ultimately silencing dissent, several events of the last few years have provided great impetus to these forces, and have acted as catalysts for increased control and surveillance of populations designated potentially troublesome. The shooting at Littleton, Colorado's Columbine High School just outside of Denver on 20 April 1999 was one such event.

Since the late 1960s, 'war' has become a metaphor and strategy for dealing with a host of open-ended referents and perceived 'social problems' in the US. Wars are no longer waged solely against nations. America, we are now told, wages wars against 'terror', 'drugs', 'crime', and a host of other constructions defined as a potential threat to public order. War has become a permanent condition adopted by the criminal and repressive State. The US is involved in two wars in the Middle East. It is also involved in wars at home; one of which is a war against youth and some elements of youth culture that in shape or content resist easy appropriation to the service of homogenising 'Walmart-culture'. Like wars of neo-imperial aggression abroad, the culture wars at home are waged both with Benjamin's (1968) beautiful machinery and the tools in the propagandist's arsenal, and on several fronts: in the legislatures, school board offices, and in the media. In this sense the corporately owned mass media's attempts to recast youth culture practices and actors such as Marilyn Manson and 'Goth'[1] as criminal, and to define social effects of music style as

---

1   Throughout the paper, the term 'Goth' will be used loosely (and problematically – as it is by the corporately owned mass media) to refer to a host of loosely and sometimes tenuously connected youth subcultural tribes, practices and artefacts.

criminogenic, constitutes an attempt to control ontology and epistemology (Ferrell 1996, 1998) and to neutralise an entire generation of potential dissenters.

Ground Zero – Columbine

The Columbine shooting shocked the nation. While shootings in US high schools have occurred for decades, the Columbine killings of 20 April 1999 stood apart. It was the bloodiest episode of its kind (resulting in the deaths of 14 students and a teacher, and the wounding of 23 others) and was one of about a dozen such incidents to occur during an 18-month period. Furthermore, unlike the shootings that have plagued urban high schools for decades, this one (and others during the period) occurred in a relatively affluent, mostly white, suburban community. CNN and other national news media interrupted their regular programming to broadcast highly charged, emotional camera footage of anxious teachers and tearful parents behind police barricades, and terrified students (many of them with their arms raised over their heads – presumably to indicate that they were not threats)[2] being escorted away from the school by paramilitary police units. Similarly, many of the major television networks carried images of a misty eyed and obviously distraught President Clinton, temporarily torn away from the business of ordering the bombing of civilian populations,[3] stating:

> We all know that there has been a terrible shooting at a high school in Littleton, Colorado. I hope that the American people will be praying for the students, the parents and the teachers. And, uh, … we'll wait for events to unfold and then uh, ... there'll be more to report. (NBC 1999)

Because this event was so horrifying and tragic, it could easily have served as an impetus for discussions to promote progressive social change. Sadly, as often happens with the mediated reality of crime, outside of the somewhat limited discussion to emerge more recently from the release of Michael Moore's film, *Bowling for Columbine*, little of this discussion actually occurred. While there was some discussion about gun control,[4] there was little, if any, about broader issues of a culture of fear and violence, alienation, hyper-masculinity, frustration, marginalisation or a host of other issues more salient to the shooting. Instead – there was scapegoating. Instead of an open and honest discussion, Americans were served up an almost constant dose of fear mongering, and vile, vituperative, Nuremburg-esque rants about teen-super-predators, poor parenting, violent video games and the moral bankruptcy of Hollywood and the music industry. Certainly, the target most

---

2   As late as 2:30 pm local time, more than two hours after Eric Harris and Dylan Klebold ended their own lives with self-inflicted gunshot wounds, police SWAT teams were still leading students away from the school building as they would suspects, frisking and questioning them before offering medical care and transporting them from school grounds (*Boulder News* 1999).

3   As Michael Moore powerfully illustrated in his film *Bowling for Columbine*, 20 April 1999 marked the largest bombing campaign of the Kosovo War.

4   While the shooting was used by some as a conduit through which to address the proliferation of guns in America, others in the pro-gun lobby, most notably the National Rifle Association (NRA), seized upon it (as they did other such incidents, both before and after Columbine) to argue that guns are not the problem.

frequently designated by politicians, religious leaders, and the news media was Marilyn Manson and more generally 'Goth' youth culture.[5]

Beginning with post-World War Two youth subcultures and accelerating through the 1980s and 1990s into the 21st century, teens and young adults have become increasingly defined as a threat to be feared and a problem to be contained. Hence it stands to reason that youth cultural forms, particularly variants of hard rock, rap, metal and punk, became the nexus of control strategies. Ironically, these cultural forms – symbolic representations of social ills (Hebdige 1979) – are now largely portrayed as the source of them.

Marilyn Manson, Goth and Columbine

Like many of the most notorious accusations made in the wake of Columbine,[6] the allegations that Klebold and Harris were Marilyn Manson fans and the overly simplistic cause-effect relationship between Goth and the school shootings were quickly revealed as, at best, misguided and spurious, if not outright malicious. However, while Goth and Marilyn Manson clearly had no part to play, they were quickly and continuously indicted and criminalised in the mass media, '... through their re-presentation as criminal in the realm of soundbites, startling images, news footage and newspaper headlines' (Ferrell 1998: 75). The evening following the shooting ABC's news magazine '20/20' televised a segment on Marilyn Manson and Goth, Satanism and cults as part of their Columbine special report programme. Similarly, the *New York Post* ran an article entitled 'Telltale signs your kids might be ready to explode' with photos of Marilyn Manson, teens in Goth make-up, a man with multiple face piercings and Adolf Hitler (O'Connor 1999). On CNN's webpage entitled 'Are US schools safe' the network solicited email comments from the audience. Among the literally thousands of emails that poured in, the network selected the following as the lead:

> To all decent Americans,
>
> The students, and their associates, that were involved in the shootings in Littleton, Colorado were members of an anti-culture clique ... you know the type: Disillusioned, disaffected, jaded, neo-gothic types, that relish the role of being 'outsiders'. By there [*sic*] own admission, they were influenced by the death-rock of Marilyn Manson and the violence and hype of Hollywood.[7]

In some respects, the indictment of Goth and the band's alleged culpability in fostering the 'nihilistic', 'antisocial', 'anti-Christian' attitudes and behaviour that we are told will inevitably lead young people to unleash an orgy of gunfire against

---

5   Ironically, by the time the shootings occurred in April 1999 Marilyn Manson had long ago abandoned the dark goth image that they so successfully cultivated with the release of their *AntiChrist Superstar* CD in 1996 and the 'Dead to the World' tour in support of it. Though they subsequently readopted that imagery for their 2000 release, *Holy Wood*, at the time of the shooting, and for quite a period beforehand, the band were utilising futuristic, hyper-androgynous imagery (closer to David Bowie's Ziggy Stardust persona than anything 'goth') under the auspices of their 1998 release *Mechanical Animals*.

6   Allegations that Klebold and Harris were Neo-Nazis, Satanists, cultists and members of the 'Trench Coat Mafia' who specifically targeted 'jocks', people of colour, Christians and popular students were not substantiated by forensic reconstructions of the crime scene, nor by any other evidence collected in the almost year-long investigation carried out by the Jefferson County Sheriff's Department and state and federal officials (Jefferson County Sheriff's Department 2000).

7   www.cnn.com/SPECIALS/1998/schools.

unsuspecting teachers and classmates are not at all surprising. Marilyn Manson had been the target of an elaborate moral crusade by the American political and religious Right for much of 1996 and 1997 (Muzzatti 2004). Like Ozzy Osbourne, Judas Priest, the Dead Kennedys, the Beastie Boys, Megadeth, NWA and SnoopDog[8] before them, Marilyn Manson's transgressive style and counter-hegemonic messages served as fodder for all manner of spurious and outlandishly fabricated charges. However, by 1999, Manson's popularity had waned considerably, and moral entrepreneurs had moved on to other targets. While it is true that the band was touring in support of their 1998 CD *Mechanical Animals* at the time of the shooting, they were not nearly as well received by young music fans as they were during the height of 1996's *AntiChrist Superstar*. The band's particular brand of post-industrial gothic punk and roll was largely being displaced by the more commercially viable and easily appropriated white-noise and pop punk of bands such as the Goo Goo Dolls and Blink 182.[9] Perhaps the greatest irony is the fact that interviews with the parents and friends of Klebold and Harris revealed that the two were not Goths and did not even like Marilyn Manson's music. Rather, and contrary to the mediated re-presentations of them as underground, counter culture miscreants, the reality is that both Klebold and Harris were very ordinary young men interested in baseball, sports memorabilia and collectables, video production, A/V technology and computers, and had been choosing a university dormitory for next year (Jefferson County Sheriff's Department 2000).

Figure 12.1 Marilyn Manson: corrupter of youth?

8   The number of musical artists accused of promoting everything from premarital sex and homosexuality to suicide and mass murder is far too long to list, and can in fact traced back to the early days of rock and roll. See Muzzatti 2004.
9   Marilyn Manson had become fodder for satire and ridicule in many circles. In heavy rotation in the spring of 1999, The New Radicals' song 'You Get What You Give' constructed Marilyn Manson as 'has-beens' and 'poseurs' with the lines, '... Courtney Love and Marilyn Manson/ You're all fakes/ Run to your mansions/ Come around/ We'll kick your ass in!'

Flashpoint – Columbine

However spurious the connections between the Columbine shooters and Marilyn Manson/Goth youth culture, the allegations had a deleterious impact on the lives of young people, the ramifications of which were both immediate and concrete, as well as far reaching and removed. Categorical suspicion and indiscriminate hatred were directed at stylistic and ideological dissenters. On the first level of approximation, many young people in the Columbine area, identified correctly or not as being friends and associates of Klebold and Harris, or Goths, were subjected to all manner of humiliation, degradation and dehumanisation at the hands of law enforcement bodies, the media and the community.

In the hours immediately following the shooting, local law enforcement accosted and detained many youths who fit their image of 'Goth'. Local television news broadcast live footage of three young males dressed in black being handcuffed and led away by police in the vicinity of the high school.[10] The national news continued to broadcast the images of the 'apprehension' long after the three were released from police custody.

As part of their investigation into the shootings, the Jefferson County Sheriff's Department formed an 'Associates Team' to question schoolmates and other acquaintances of Klebold and Harris. The team identified 22 youths, searched their computers, had them submit to polygraph tests and subjected them to a combined 71 interviews (Jefferson County Sheriff's Department 2000).

The notoriously conservative Littleton community is well culpable in the marginalisation of stylistic dissenters. Many Goths were further ostracised from the community and prohibited from participating in public grieving ceremonies. Some Columbine students threatened retaliatory violence against Goths if they appeared at the impromptu memorials. Those brave enough to appear were often quite publicly shunned and excluded (Cullen 1999). Once schooling resumed at Columbine, many Goth youths were harassed by other students and as a result, at least half a dozen were effectively prohibited from continuing the academic year at school.[11]

'Justifications' for war

Wars are a very serious business. They disrupt, destroy and end lives, cost a nation a great deal of money, and usually create far more suffering than they cure. Hence, unlike their counterparts in totalitarian regimes who can arbitrarily declare wars and force people to march into them, leaders of democratic societies bear a very heavy burden of proof. In theory at least, with a free press acting as guardians of the public good, the leaders must provide the people with incontrovertible evidence that an 'enemy' exists, poses a real threat to the safety and well-being of the populace, and

---

10 Police soon learned that the three, like hundreds of other people, were only curious onlookers, and released them later that afternoon, but re-interviewed them at length four days later.

11 Approximately a dozen others opted to complete the final few weeks of their school year at Columbine High School, despite the harassment. Similar problems occurred at nearby Chatfield High School (Cullen 1999). While no statistics are available, scattered media reports suggest that this type of harassment of Goths, combined with ineffective responses by school and law enforcement authorities, occurred throughout the US in the months following the shootings.

can only be dealt with by force. In reality, however, this formula is rarely adhered to. Rather, an agenda, which serves elite interests, is in place, actions are planned (and some undertaken) and a media 'event' is manufactured or seized upon and converted to justify the warlike activities that are often already underway. Just as the Bush administration utilised the al-Qaeda terrorist attacks of 11 September 2001 to further its geo-political agenda and plunge America into wars of neo-imperial aggression in the Middle East, neo-conservatives, Christian fundamentalists, corporate interest groups, fear merchants from the crime control and private security industries and other powerful right-wing groups have used the Columbine High School shootings to strengthen and expand upon Zero-Tolerance and other policies and practices designed to control young people in American schools.

Fear, alienation and isolation

Under an increasingly insufferable neo-conservative climate in the US, schools continue to be transmogrified into little more than corporate training farms and adjuncts of the criminal justice system. Long ago stripped of all but the rhetoric of their Jeffersonian/Deweyite mission of providing young people with the skills necessary to be active, thoughtful participants in democracy, schools today seem to be increasingly focused on producing docile, non-resistant creatures unable to question, let alone articulately voice opposition to the 'right' of elites to lie, cheat, steal and suppress dissent in the service of global capitalism and the State. Corporate intrusions in schools train students to be good worker-bees and obedient consumers and repressive policies and practices are in place to punitively address any challenges, real or perceived, to the hegemonic imperatives of those promoting unreflexive hyper-consumption and soft-pedalling fascism under the auspices of 'national security' and economic stimulus packages. Hence, it is little wonder that Marilyn Manson, Goth, or indeed anything associated with oppositional cultural styles and praxis are so vehemently targeted.

Zero tolerance

In the punitive spirit of mandatory sentencing and 'three strikes and you're out' laws used by the criminal justice system to 'deal with' repeat adult offenders, schools across the nation have enthusiastically implemented zero tolerance policies, despite the plethora of evidence that illustrates that, like the federal and state criminal legislation they were modelled after, these policies unfairly target poor and minority youth, and overall are far more detrimental than beneficial. According to the most recent statistics available, approximately 95% of US schools have zero tolerance for guns, slightly over 90% for other weapons and between 79 and 88% for violence, drugs, alcohol and tobacco (National Center for Educational Statistics 2002). In keeping with the requirements for federal funding codified in the 'Gun-Free Schools Act of 1994',[12] zero-tolerance was originally used to suspend any student discovered with a firearm at school, but has broadened considerably, particularly after the Columbine High School shootings, and is now used to 'address' a wide and ambiguously defined gamut of student 'misbehaviour', including such things as board-violations, truancy and defying a teacher's authority. Nationally, well over

---

12 This legislation was a part of the larger Improving America's Schools Act (National Center for Educational Statistics 2002).

60% of student suspensions were a result of non-violent disciplinary infractions (Center on Juvenile and Criminal Justice 2001).

Behaviours that only a few years ago would have resulted in a student being sent to the principal's office for 'a good talking-to' are now resulting in immediate suspension and referral to criminal justice authorities.[13] In Kentucky, between 75 and 80% of school-initiated criminal justice referrals were for just such minor infractions (Richaert *et al* 2003). Across the country young people are being suspended from school for their involvement in minor recess-yard scuffles, or for possessing such 'contraband' as mouthwash, over-the-counter headache medicine, CDs, comic books and squirt-guns. In a comic nightmare of Kafkaesque proportions, zero tolerance policies in Philadelphia public schools resulted in the suspension of some 33 kindergarten children in 2002 (Dale 2002; Richaert *et al* 2003). Under zero tolerance policies, intrusive social controls and punitive sanctions once reserved for despised and marginalised adult populations (such as incarcerated inmates) are now directed against school children. Indeed, as one alternative media columnist put it:

> ... a veritable Kindergulag has been erected around schoolchildren, making them subject to arbitrary curfews, physical searches, arbitrarily applied profiling schemes, and ... random, suspicionless, warrantless drug testing ... If you're a kid in the US today, martial law isn't a civics class lecture unit. It is a fact of life as ... a nearly hysterical emphasis on safety has come to excuse the infliction of every kind of humiliation upon the young. (Cassidy 2002)

Columbine and the repressive state

In the wake of the Columbine tragedy, forces bent on domestic militarisation gained great momentum. Far from following the 'anti-big government stance' that dominated their 2000 election campaign, the Bush machine once in power immediately began to initiate and facilitate highly intrusive government action. In 2001, the United States Supreme Court ruled that an Ohio public high school did not violate a student's right to free speech and due process when it prevented him from attending classes for a week for wearing a tee shirt it deemed 'vulgar, offensive and contrary to the educational message of the school'. The shirt in question, a Marilyn Manson tee, depicted a three-faced Jesus on the front and the word 'Believe' with the letters 'LIE' highlighted on the back. The court said that public schools can prevent students from wearing offensive tee shirts, even if they are not obscene and have not caused a substantial disruption (*Seattle Post Intelligencer* 2001).

Under Bush, mandatory drug testing also gained greater momentum. Far from being reserved for students arbitrarily designated as 'troublesome', intrusive measures such as drug testing cast a net of categorical suspicion over all students. In 2002 the United States Supreme Court ruled that the Pottawatomie County (Oklahoma) School District's policy of mandatory drug testing for student athletes was not a violation of students' constitutional rights.[14] The ruling paved the way for schools to test any student involved in extracurricular activities. Indeed, as evidenced by the Solicitor General's oral arguments, if the Bush administration had

---

13 Michael Moore's *Bowling for Columbine* provides stark images of some ludicrous incidents of young students' suspensions that resulted from broad definitions of violent or threatening behaviour. Among them are reports of a child suspended for pointing a chicken finger as one would a gun, and another for folding a piece of notebook paper into the shape of a handgun.
14 *Board of Education of Independent School District No 92 of Pottawatomie County, petitioners v Lindsay Earls*, United States Supreme Court, 27 June 2002, No 01-332.

its way, all students would be tested, irrespective of their participation in extracurricular activities. Not surprisingly, the ruling elated the Bush administration. The court's decision was also lauded by corporate interests who stand to benefit, not only from the sale of drug testing kits, but perhaps more insidiously from their ability to extend the disciplinary ordinances of an alienating and soul-crushing '"drug-free" workplace' culture into schools.

Across the nation, school 'intervention' (that is, stigmatisation and vilification) strategies are targeted against stylistic dissenters and act as catalysts for increasingly intrusive social control strategies. As a result of juvenile antagonism between Marilyn Manson fans and other students, a Michigan middle school banned 'Goth' clothing, jewellery and hair and make-up styles. Asked by a reporter about the policy as a possible infringement of the students' constitutional rights, an attorney for the school district said, '[The] First Amendment does not protect devil worship in the eighth grade' (Freedom Forum 1998).

Furthermore, in a climate more indicative of a totalitarian state than a democracy, schools in George W Bush's home state of Texas began to closely surveille students who were identified as Marilyn Manson fans or who wore Goth fashions. This included mandatory psychological testing in classrooms, locker searches, scrutiny of their artwork and essays, and monitoring their library withdrawals (American Atheists 2001). Some school systems are investing in new FBI 'student profiling' software to identify potential school shooters. Included among the characteristics the software identifies are 'abusive language' and 'writing reflecting an interest in the "dark side" of life' (Center on Juvenile and Criminal Justice 2001: 20).

In May 2002, the United States Secret Service's National Threat Assessment Center released a study on school shootings and held training sessions based upon it for law enforcement and school personnel throughout the summer. News of the report's release was the lead 'educational news' story for many national news sources. As could be expected, in addition to the 'stock footage' of terrified students and tearful parents, much of the visual storytelling focused on demonised cultural icons such as Marilyn Manson and young people who violate sartorial norms by fusing the transgressive styles of punk, Goth and industrial metal. Perhaps the most egregious offender was CNN's education webpage. Under their standard template, the 'education' banner and the story by-line was a graphic of what appear to be middle school children working at their desks. The photograph had been doctored; superimposed upon it were chunky pixels, borders, a hand gun, target and other graphics designed to make it appear as if it were an image from the a violent 'first-person shooter' video game (CNN 2002).

Militarised schools and waste

We live in a climate of mediated fear (see Furedi 1997; Glassner 1999), rife with intolerance and distrust – a climate where 'education news' consists disproportionately of stories about how to more effectively surveille and control young people – a climate where any sense of perspective is sorely lacking and rights and freedoms are ever eroding.

At a time when educational funding is being cut, misplaced legislative priorities dominate. Instead of investing the increasingly limited funds in educational programmes, schools' infrastructure and teacher education and salaries, school districts across the country pour tax money into the swelling coffers of the 'school security' and 'crime prevention' industries. The state of Texas, home of Enron and

George W Bush, has the ninth highest child poverty rate of all 50 states, and is at the bottom of the rankings for child well-being measures (Center for Policy Priorities 2001), but allocates much needed monies to policing public schools. Likewise, California, with more children in school than many other states combined, spends more than seven times as much on incarcerating people as it does on educating public school children (Moreno 1998). Even with school crime nationally at an 11 year low and juvenile homicides lower than at any time since the FBI began keeping these statistics in 1964, schools continue to spend millions of dollars on metal detectors, emergency communications systems, drug testing, surveillance cameras and ID badge systems (Killingbeck 2001). Police officers, security guards and drug sniffing dogs are almost as commonplace a sight as teachers.

War on crime – war on dissent

Ostensibly part of a war on school crime, zero tolerance policies, urine tests, dress codes and other 'security measures' are part of a war on youth culture and a marginalisation of dissent. Schools in the US offer students little in the way of critical thinking skills, cultural and media literacy, or other requisites for freedom. Instead, mirroring the militarisation and corporatisation of other public spheres, schools repress and control youth, offer them a sanitised, commercialised culture and demand blindly obedient consumerism. In a society that views youth with fear and mistrust, it is little wonder that the social institution in which they spend much of their waking hours constructs them as untrustworthy and amoral, penalises them for wearing the wrong kind of tee shirt, make-up or hairstyle, and generally treats them as violent, drug-crazed superpredators in waiting. Contrary to the discourse of neo-conservatives, the greatest threat to young people in the US does not come from miscreants in Goth make-up and black trench coats who've embarked on a course of emotional and intellectual self-defence by listening to Marilyn Manson CDs, reading *Catcher in the Rye*, watching *The Basketball Diaries*, producing 'dark' art or otherwise accessing and embodying fugitive ontologies and epistemologies. Rather, the threat lies in the concentration of wealth, the hijacking of government by Christian supremacists and the transnational classes, and an adult populace so distracted or paralysed by unwarranted fear that it (sometimes willingly, sometimes unknowingly) acquiesces to policies and practices more indicative of a corporate-fascist state than a modern liberal democracy.

The treatment of young people in America, particularly those who through fugitive styles signal their unwillingness to wholly embrace destructive ultra-right wing corporatised values, is indicative of a wider climate of bigotry, suspicion and fear. In such a climate, state intrusion into the lives of people, the castration of counter hegemonic messages in music and the use of public schools as little more than spaces of containment and control has infringed constitutional freedoms, undermined political agency and had a significant chilling effect on public expressions of dissent, whether overtly political or couched in art and style. The marginalisation of dissent and criminalisation of youth culture are acts of aggression by a range of state agencies and corporations whose repressive functions are becoming increasingly evident. Indeed, American criminologists would do well to be more attentive to these types of state-corporate harms daily inflicted on the domestic population.

References

American Atheists (2001) 'Marilyn Manson Concert Denounced': www.atheists.org/flash.line/manson1.htm

Barak, G (ed) (1991) *Crimes by the Capitalist State*, Albany, NY: SUNY

Benjamin, W (1968) *Illuminations*, Arendt, H (ed), Zohn, H (trans), New York: Harcourt Brace

Boulder News (1999) 'Tragedy and recovery – chronology of events': www.buffzone.com/shooting/22chronology.html

Cassidy, P (2002) 'Last brick in the Kindergulag': www.alternet.org/print.html?StoryId=13616

Center on Juvenile and Criminal Justice (2001) *School House Hype: Two Years Later*

Center for Policy Priorities (2001) 'For kids, everything's bigger in Texas': www.cpp.org/kidscount/press/01natl.html

CNN (2002) 'Study: most school shooting preventable': www.cnn.com/2002/fyi/teachers.ednews/05/16/schoolviolence.ap

Cohen, S and Taylor, L (1978) *Escape Attempts: The Theory and Practice of Resistance to Everyday Life*, New York: Penguin

Cullen, D (1999) 'Inside the Columbine High investigation': www.salon.com/news/feature/1999/09/23/columbine

Dale, MC (2002) 'Zero-tolerance policy puts 5-year-olds out of Philly Classroom', *Associated Press*, 13 December

Ferrell, J (1996) *Crimes of Style: Urban Graffiti and the Politics of Criminality*, Boston: Northeastern University Press

Ferrell, J (1998) 'Criminalising popular culture', in Bailey, F and Hale, D (eds), *Popular Culture, Crime and Justice*, Belmont, CA: West/Wadsworth, pp 71–84

Freedom Forum (1998) 'Parents fearful of Marilyn Manson': www.freedomforum.org/templates/document.asp?documentID=9354

Furedi, F (1997) *Culture of Fear: Risk Taking and the Morality of Low Expectations*, London: Cassell

Glassner, B (1999) *The Culture of Fear: Why are Americans Afraid of the Wrong Things?*, New York: Basic Books

Hebdige, D (1979) *Subculture: The Meaning of Style*, London: Routledge

Jefferson County Sheriff's Department (2000) *Report on the Columbine High School Shooting*, Office of the Jefferson County Sheriff, Golden, Colorado

Killingbeck, D (2001) 'The role of television news in the construction of school violence as a "moral panic"' 8(3) *Journal of Criminal Justice and Popular Culture* 186–202

Moreno, EM (1998) 'Students cut class. Protest spending on prisons', *San Jose Mercury News*, 3 October, p A7

Muzzatti, SL (2000) 'Snake oil and other "cures" for school violence', *McKendree*, Winter, p 24

Muzzatti, SL (2004) *Cultural Criminology, Labeling Theory and Moral Crusades: The Case of Marilyn Manson*, New York: Peter Lang

National Center for Educational Statistics (2002) 'Violence prevention': www.nces.ed.gov.fastfacts/display.asp?id=54

NBC (1999) Breaking News, 20 April

O'Connor, C (1999) 'Manson show called off', *Addicted to Noise*, 23 April

Presdee, M (2000) *Cultural Criminology and the Carnival of Crime*, London: Routledge

Richaert, D, Brooks, K and Soler, M (2003) *Unintended Consequences: The Impact of 'Zero Tolerance' and other Exclusionary Policies on Kentucky Students*, Building Blocks for Youth

Seattle Post Intelligencer (2001) 'School's ban of Marilyn Manson T-shirt OK': http://seattllepi.mwsource.com/national/shirt19ww.shtml, 19 March

Tifft, L and Sullivan, D (1980) *The Struggle to be Human: Crime, Criminology and Anarchism*, Orkney: Cienfuegos

United States Supreme Court (2001) *Boroff v Van Wert City Board of Education*, 00–1020

Part 4

Breaking Open the City

Chapter 13
Space – The Final Frontier: Criminology, the City and the Spatial Dynamics of Exclusion

Keith Hayward

Introduction

The city has always been a flickering presence within criminology, variously the source of immediacy, concern, visibility and inspiration. Yet, despite this interest, the concept of the city has rarely been fully integrated into developed analyses of crime. This tendency is even more pronounced today. The increased prevalence of so-called 'scientific' methodologies within our discipline has ensured that, even though the majority of criminologists tend to study urban crime (in one form or another), seldom does their work overlap with related disciplines such as urban studies, urban geography or indeed even urban sociology. Even within contemporary criminological theory, the city is all too frequently lost in the moment of abstraction, appearing only as an afterthought, a sort of theoretical shadow or 'sideshow'. Urban crime is thus torn free from its physical context – the city. Street crime, for example, exists not as in any way connected to street life (or, for that matter, the life of the street), but as an autonomous, independent act, divested of all the complexities and inequities that are such a feature of the daily urban round. Consequently, what has been lost to criminology is the great potential for understanding the relationship between urban space and urban crime signalled, for example, by Robert Park's (1925) book *The City* – a monument to the city as a living, breathing, socio-cultural entity.

In this chapter, I will argue that cultural criminology can provide a useful corrective – not least because of the way it prioritises questions and debates concerning the thematics of 'postmodern' space in its analysis. The constraints of a short chapter being what they are, I will limit my focus here to one specific example, namely the spatial dynamics associated with 'social exclusion'.[1]

Inside 'outsider spaces': criminology and spatial dynamics of social exclusion

The term 'exclusion' is everywhere so ubiquitous that it seems self-explanatory. For Mike Davis (1990, 1998), the controversial chronicler of post-industrial Los Angeles, it is the death of public space in the dual city; in Jock's Young's *The Exclusive Society* (1999) it is social polarisation; and for Zygmunt Bauman (1987, 1998) it is as much about credit rating as spatial boundaries. This section seeks to stand back from the obviousness of exclusion in an attempt to explore some of its vagaries. My approach here is to pose exclusion in terms of space, specifically the dramas of the unravelling or fragmentation of *modernist space*.

---

1   For a more developed analysis of the notion of urban space within criminological theory see my recent work *City Limits: Crime, Consumer Culture and the Urban Experience* (2004), especially Chapters 3 and 4.

In the work of the French cultural theorist Michel de Certeau (1984), modernist space is identified with the idea of the 'Concept-city', the planner's-eye view, the rational, ordered modelling of the urban environment. Here, modernist space rests on a morphology of form and function ('form dictates function; function follows form'). Modernist space is thus space that is continuous, gapless, and utilitarian; a purposive and semiotically unambiguous grid that maps onto social and economic hierarchies. Nowhere is this better illustrated than in the discourse(s) of crime prevention and administrative criminology, the smooth functionalist flows of modernist space captured in the archetypal crime prevention diagrams and statistical accounts of urban crime. Unfortunately for crime prevention theorists, it is this ordered modernist space that is currently being destabilised by the shifting landscapes associated with post/late modernity. Here the picture is one of discontinuities, flows interrupted, islands and pockets of heterogeneity, spaces that are textured rather than contoured, a realm of 'bricolage', liminality and the semiotics of ambiguity. Exclusion at this level means nothing more or less than this breakdown of modernist space – even, for some (most memorably Mike Davis's high octane account of metropolitan meltdown in Los Angeles), a return from Enlightenment ordering to medieval barbarism and disarray.

It will be argued here that the literature of exclusion (and crime prevention) has failed to recognise that there is more than one dynamic at play in this contemporary spatial transformation. On one hand, there is the classical modernist attempt to *recapture order, re-colonise, re-condition and discipline* these emergent unruly zones – essentially to reintegrate the abandoned post-industrial spaces left in the wake of a superseded Fordism and repair the broken net of the modernist project. On the other hand, the literature points to the appearance of a new and distinctive mode of social control in which overt exclusion is precisely the crucial mechanism, *the 'solution' not the problem*. Under these circumstances, 'social control' is no control except at the boundary (à la Bauman and Mike Davis). Here it is a matter of abandoned zones, guarded perimeters and secure cordons separating this world from the world of the gated community and the heavily surveyed mega mall/entertainment zone (see Hannigan 1998). In these accounts, the only modernist response is to de-exclude, to fill up empty spaces with the useful, functional world of the productive citizen. In this new dynamic, wastelands are left to go to waste, surplus to requirements. This contemporary strategy is a lock-out not lock-in, a world that in some ways evokes John Carpenter's (1981) film *Escape from New York*. I now wish to explore these conceptual conflations through two examples of contemporary social theory.

Discipline denied: modernist recuperation 'versus' exclusionary separation

If it is true that the grid of 'discipline' is everywhere becoming clearer and more extensive, it is all the more urgent to discover how an entire society resists being reduced to it, what popular procedures (also 'minuscule' and quotidian) manipulate the mechanisms of discipline and conform to them only in order to evade them. (de Certeau 1984: xiv)

Over the last two decades, many scholars of urban space have drawn careful attention to the way in which powerful structures of social control have been skilfully and often surreptitiously woven into the fabric of the city (eg CCTV surveillance cameras and street lighting, face recognition software and other digital techniques of control).[2] Stressing the extent to which the 'fear factor' is now a major constitutive element of the contemporary metropolis, these practices are typically described as new and subtle strategies of disciplinary control and surveillance – which, in turn, are often glibly characterised as tools of exclusion and repression.

No doubt such practices are proliferating, but does it make sense to twin security with exclusion in this way? From the above discussion it should now be obvious that disciplinary surveillance is a classic example of the modernist attempt to recapture the dangerous spaces within our midst. The space of surveillance is precisely structured and seamless, the disciplinary grid the perfect match of form and function. In other words, in order for such controlled environments to operate, they must be spaces of *inclusion* not exclusion. For surveillance to manage its wayward subjects, to mould, shape and ultimately ensure conformity of conduct, those subjects must be *inside* the perimeter not *outside*. And, far from being covert, the entire effectiveness of surveillance rests upon its *overtness* (ie on the subject's awareness of being (potentially) ever under scrutiny). Put bluntly, modern space is all about maximum visibility – Haussman's destruction of the old Paris and the demolition of London's infamous rookeries provide two classic examples of the creation of the very conditions for disciplinary hygiene and civic surveillance. Finally, 'disciplinary spaces' classically operate within a marked perimeter. Thus while many commentators see these new exclusionary techniques as further expressions of disciplinary forms, at the same time they fail to recognise that this *conflicts* with the trope of social exclusion. Surely the point is that, in today's world, *both* modernist recuperation *and* late/postmodern separation are occurring *simultaneously* in contemporary developments. Not to recognise this is to conflate their fundamentally distinct dynamics.

While most of mainstream criminology seems oblivious to this point, there is one current analysis within urban sociology that beautifully illustrates this distinction – Nikos Papastergiadis' concept of 'parafunctional' space (Papastergiadis and Rogers 1996; Papastergiadis 2002). The *parafunctional* is an attempt to describe city spaces that are 'abandoned', 'condemned' or 'ruined', 'in-between wastelands' that appear to have 'given up' the struggle of shaping time and space, and where the discarded objects and refuse of an earlier mode of production accumulate. The pararfunctional, Papastergiadis claims, refers to 'all those corners which lurk at the edge of activity, or in the passages where activity occurs but the relationship between use and place remains unnamed. These are places in which names do not matter because the need for communication or the passage of time spent is already deemed to be insignificant, minimal, empty' (Papastergiadis and Rogers 1996: 76) (see Figure 13.1). Here even the most fundamental of modernist linkages is severed – the (functional) link between use and space as operationalised by names.

Or, consider this alternative interpretation of parafunctional space, as glossed by the teaching team at the School of Architecture and Design, University of South Australia:

> Liminal spaces exist in-between – perhaps they've been abandoned or ruined, perhaps they are a set or constellation of surfaces, perhaps they are named 'waste', perhaps they are 'condemned'. These spaces do not 'function' as we might think 'function' functions – as meaning. These spaces do not do as they are told. (This is a sentence to imagine with: place an emphasis on 'do' and 'told', for example.) That is, they do not serve or operate

---

2   Eg Cohen 1979; Shearing and Stenning 1983, 1985; Whyte 1988; Sorkin 1992; Fyfe and Bannister 1996.

'the kind of action or activity proper' to their form, shape, (original) intention. While they function, the functional cannot have an exact relation to design as these spaces are marked by the yet-to-be ...[3]

Figure 13.1 Parafunctional space.

The important thing here is that these functionless, evidently non-modernist, parafunctional spaces also represent *the exact opposite of discipline*. Not only do they lack any formal surveillance mechanisms, they are also typically devoid of any mechanical or human systematised watching. In short, *parafunctional spaces* represent the anonymous, and seemingly meaningless spaces within our midst – the places on the (metaphorical) edge of society.

It is just such paradigmatically criminogenic spaces – the run-down playground, the unsupervised car park, the troublesome block of flats or public house, the abandoned lot or badly lit side street – that are the subject of attention from within the administrative criminology discourse of situational crime prevention (SCP).[4] Under this rubric, the aim is clear: to bring these 'criminogenic' pockets of urban space (or more evocatively 'wild zones', see Stanley 1990) back in line with 'the objective processes of ordered territorialisation'. Indeed, in a statement that, in turn, is highly reminiscent of administrative criminology's various attempts to implement a micro-architecture of 'exclusion', Papastergiadis describes 'how state and council authorities try to keep specific spaces to their specificity: seating is changed in railway waiting rooms and on platforms to discourage sleeping by the homeless, just so they do not "sink" into a parafunctional state of ambiguity and

---

3   http://ensemble.va.com.au/home/prjct_nts.html. I should point out that the School's particular interpretation of parafunctional space is based primarily on Papastergiadis' more recent article 'Traces left in cities' (2002).
4   For a definition of SCP see Hough *et al* 1980: 1; and for a general introduction see Clarke 1997.

contamination' (2002: 45). Yet, once again, the use of the term 'exclusion' is misleading, for administrative criminology/SCP essentially seeks to return space that has lost its function back *within* the ordered planner's fold of the modernist grid. To re-link 'space' and 'use' in one unequivocal functionality is thus a project of semiotic disambiguation – the attempt to close down an object/place's spatial reference so that it has only one unique meaning. Seats are *only* for sitting on – not for sleeping, skateboarding, partying or busking on. Under this rubric, controlling crime becomes as simple as mapping place, function and meaning so that the rational utility-seeking subject no longer has to deal with any form of complexity whatsoever. However, as anyone who takes the time to walk or cycle through the city will surely tell you, city spaces are rarely, if ever, equivocal – or as Papastergiadis comments, spaces tend not to 'do as they are told'.

Equivocal non-functionalities: place, meaning, resistance

> The built environment is seen as literally the terrain upon which ... cultural knowledge is created, transformed, challenged and represented. The landscape is not simply a collection of buildings, streets, parks, fire hydrants, billboards, and other elements, but also a social construction that reflects and refracts both everyday knowledge and macro structures; in other words, it is also a way of seeing ... Cultural activities form an integral component of the socially constructed landscape by acting as channels of discourse, sometimes symbolic and sometimes concrete, that mediate people's relationship with their surroundings and allow opportunities to consider, contest, and come to terms with economic, political and social aspects of place. (Warren 1996: 549)

> Kids don't see the world the same way adults do. They see a beautiful marble ledge as being a great thing to jump off of! (Editor, *Transworld Skateboarding* quoted in Ferrell 2001: 75)

Streets are always complex places, where meaning is contested and forms of cultural resistance occur (Ferrell 1997, 2001: chapter 2; Creswell 1998; Lees 1998; Winchester and Costello 1995). I now want to explore some of the ways in which street scenes challenge the assumed primacy of modernity and its adjuncts – criminology and the market among them. Recent developments in 'the new cultural geography',[5] urban sociology, and certain branches of anthropology have all signposted the often hidden spatial practices and cultural differences that are such a vital component of the urban landscape. In this body of work, urban space is understood almost as if it were a living thing, a multi-layered congress of cultural, political and spatial dynamics.[6]

Such approaches, in turn, implicitly represent a different take on the exclusionary dynamics as analysed so acutely in the work of Zygmunt Bauman (1987). Yet, unlike Bauman (or, for that matter, Jock Young), this growing body of

---

5   See eg Cosgrove 1983, 1989; Cosgrove and Jackson 1987; Massey 1991, 1993; for a brief introduction to the 'new cultural geography' see Warren 1996: 549–53; 1994. See also *Urban Geography* 1996 for geography more generally.

6   See eg Stacy Warren's (1996) interesting article on the underground cultural practices that take place in and around Disney theme parks. Warren charts how, beneath Disney's much vaunted veneer of safety and nostalgia, a catalogue of transgressive and exploitative acts take place, including *inter alia* armed robbery, stabbings, gang fights in the car park, acid trips in Sleeping Beauty's castle, the regular fondling of Minnie Mouse, a violent assault on Alice in Wonderland and the rape of at least two Snow Whites in the parking lot (see Koenig 1994; Schultz 1988).

work urges us toward what one might call an appreciation rather than a denunciation of the dynamics of 'exclusionary space'. This is not to say that they reject Baumanesque concerns but, rather, that they see in these spaces sparks of oppositional practices and the green shoots of future urban possibilities. Two interconnected themes link this otherwise diverse and multidisciplinary raft of work: the distinction between place and space, and the notion of cultural resistance.

As noted above, Papastergiadis implores us to shake off our standard perceptions of outsider spaces as simply abandoned, lost wastelands. For this is merely the 'view from above', from the perspective of de Certau's 'Concept-city'. He asks us instead to consider how such spaces appear when glimpsed from street level; the view one has when walking or cycling through the city, a view cluttered by the sorts of street level interaction and inter-subjectivity that never feature in the plans and maps of the 'official' city. Urban terrain from this perspective is thus to be understood in terms of distinct spatial biographies, relationships (or non-relationships) with surrounding space, intrication with different temporalities, intrinsic social role(s) – both perceived and actual – and networks of feelings and semiotic significance. These are the characteristics that many writers have mobilised in a bid to distinguish place from space.

Buchanan goes some way towards capturing this in his account of de Certeau, when he speaks of 'the life of the city' exceeding the 'concept of the city', the unmappability of urban lives and day-to-day experience, the 'something that always slips away' (2000: 110). This, alas, is merely how it looks 'from above'. More recent writings on place nuance de Certeau's duality in a potentially more sophisticated way, going further than merely filling in more of that elusive street life. Rather, place and space are seen as occupying different registers: they are simply not on the same scale. Consequently, there can be no simple reversal of top down and bottom up. There is literally no space for place in the urban cosmology. Place can only be occupied, not mapped.

Within criminology, there are signs of an emergent engagement with these themes of place and locale. In *A Tale of Two Cities: Global Change, Local Feeling and Everyday Life in the North of England* (1996), Ian Taylor and his colleagues focus on the specific relationship between space and locality – particularly important, they argue, in what are increasingly globalised times – in two industrial cities in the North of England (Manchester and Sheffield). Taking their methodological lead from Raymond Williams (the renowned commentator on culture) and in particular his work on 'local structures of feeling' (Williams 1973),[7] Taylor *et al* utilise personal biographies, focus groups and cultural narrative to produce an undeniably sensitive reading of urban space that considers in great detail place, people, ritual, history, structure, gender, age, not least in relation to strategies of coping and resistance (see also Taylor 1993, 1997). This reinvestment in the elements that constitute the very fabric of towns and cities is thus especially significant for areas described as 'socially excluded'. Ignoring such components of urban locales – what makes them local places and not just segments of grid space – can lead to serious policy errors.

---

7   Drawing on the work of the 'sentiments school' of social history, Williams originally described structures of feeling as 'the particular quality of experience and relationship, historically distinct from other particular qualities, which gives a sense of a generation or period' (Williams 1973: 131 quoted in Taylor *et al* 1996: 312). However, Taylor *et al* extend the concept to include an implicit sense of the local social and class structures. In short they are attempting to understand the 'impact of local place' on 'individual personality formation' and 'orientation to the world'.

Consider, for example, how the policing practices advocated by administrative criminologists and right realists ignore local community particularities in favour of national policies of risk and resource management. Zero tolerance policing might be readily accepted in Teesside, but roundly rejected in Toxteth.

There is one major problem, which, unfortunately, is axiomatic to the way that place has been interpreted by Taylor and others who have adopted a similar approach (see Girling *et al* 1996, 1997, 1998). Essentially, the problem is that place here has become identified with lost tradition, even a thinly veiled nostalgia for some of the forms of 'industrial capitalism', at least as a mark of the city. In *A Tale of Two Cities*, for example, the authors' conception of city life and urban space at times reads like a paean to the demise of the industrial centres of the North of England. Certainly, there is a palpable sense of loss for the shared cultures associated with working-class struggle. The significance of locality (as opposed to the national or the global) is so heavily invested with class-orientation that the very idea of place in this account seems to be defined in terms of the past, of history, of what has gone before – as if place could never have a future or occupy a postmodern present. (It might be an unpalatable thought for some, but the forms of identity and collective practical logics shared by those individuals who spent their lives wedded to the productivist process associated with the classic formulations of industrial capitalism are soon – at the mass level at least – to be lost forever.) This misplaced nostalgia seems rooted in the sociology of tradition, running against the tide of a 'world in transition' and the inevitability feelings of ontological insecurity that late modern society throws up (see Young 1999: 97–104; see also Chris Greer's chapter, this volume). In short, what this body of work presents us with is a vision of city-life that is frozen in time. It tells us much about the past but little of real value about ongoing developments (cf Hall and Winlow, this volume).

If resistance is always resistance to change, there is no way of understanding our urban futures. Once again Papastergiadis is inspiring. For, parafunctional spaces re-approached not as deficient modernist empty spaces but with all the uniqueness and specificity of place can, at the same time, be seen in terms of what de Certeau calls 'minuscule micro-cultural practices' of cultural resistance – 'zones in which creative, informal and unintended uses overtake the officially designated functions. In parafunctional spaces social life is not simply abandoned or wasted; rather it continues in ambiguous and unconventional ways' (Papastergiadis 2002: 45).

Importantly, cultural criminology is already present within these exclusionary/ parafunctional spaces, describing a triumphant resistance through redeployment (eg Ferrell 2001: chapter 2; see, relatedly, Dery 1993):[8]

> Both skaters and [graffiti] writers view the environment different from everyone else. Staircases, handrails, curb cuts, train tunnels, truck yards, and city streets have become the new playground for the next generation. *We find value in what others deem useless.* ('Cycle', quoted in *Thrasher* 209, June 1998, quoted in Ferrell 2001: 75; emphasis added)[9]

> Like the skaters who employ parking garages and [swimming] pools, the 'useless artifacts of the technological burden [are employed] ... in a thousand ways that the original architects could never dream of'. (Ferrell 2001: 81)

---

8 See relatedly, the compelling ethnography of Wacquant (1996, 2001) and Bourgois (1995, 1998).
9 See also the work of nocturnal urban protest artists such as Krzysztof Wodiczko and Zhang Dali.

> When I was younger, I spent many nights grinding curbs, carving banks, shooting hills, and skating my city's streets aimlessly ... This mission has brought me to strange and beautiful places that average citizens will never see. Whether lying in a snowbank watching a maze of monstrous freights crash and roll or taking in the desert sky at an old drainage ditch in the middle of Nevada, I've gained a lot from this quest. I've found parts of who I am in long stretches of train tracks, in abandoned parking lots with makeshift quarterpipes on banks, under bridges, on rooftops ... alone, with the view of the entire city beneath me ... ('Crisis', quoted in *Thrasher* 209, June 1998, quoted in Ferrell 2001: 78)

This is a precursor of a new genre of criminology that approaches so-called 'criminogenic space' in the same way that the new cultural geography approaches 'postmodern space', a criminology that, like cultural geography, is infused with a strong interdisciplinary approach and an ability to think beyond superficial interpretations – whether theoretical, structural or spatial. The era of understanding urban space from a purely rational (as in the discourse of crime prevention) or structural perspective has passed. Our complex, contradictory social world – 'a world in transition' – made more opaque by the muddiness of human action, demands more. It is hoped that a (culturally-inspired) criminology can help focus attention on both sides of the exclusionary coin – those who can afford to protect themselves and those who for whatever reasons are forced onto the margins of society. That this is the current situation is not in question, but what we must now strive for are theoretical analyses that can help us work through (perhaps even with?) such a situation – analyses with the ability to look forward as well as back, while at the same time avoiding broad generalisations that fail to take into consideration the specificities of locality, culture and nation.

Figure 13.2 Sheena Wilson, 'Vandalism and "defensible space" on London housing estates' in *Designing Out Crime* (1980), edited by RVG Clarke and P Mayhew, Home Office Research Unit Publications. Courtesy Home Office/Stationery Office.

Unfortunately for criminology, a countermove has already gathered considerable disciplinary traction. If one pauses to consider some of the various illustrations that frequently accompany the SCP literature, one cannot help but notice that, in these stylised representations, 'criminogenic spaces' typically appear as strangely undangerous, sanitised, even clinical spaces (see Figure 13.2). These diagrammatic representations of 'semi-private through-routes', neighbourhood 'sight lines' or 'points of entrance and egress' are remarkable only in their blandness and homogeneity. To the extent that they are marked out, 'situational spaces' exist only as uncomplicated, unconnected, isolated islands in the sea of the city. Rarely understood as part of a wider social network, the buildings and streets in these diagrams are occupied only by individuals whose spatial and temporal trajectories are assumed and who have the characteristics of 'situational (wo)man' (both victim and offender) projected onto them. Indeed, confirming David Garland's (1997) account of the way the new 'space-target' displaces 'the individual offenders and legal subjects that previously formed the targets for crime control',[10] it is not uncommon for the human actor to be removed from the picture altogether, leaving an image of urban space eerily reminiscent of the opening scene of Robert Wise's film *The Andromeda Strain* (1970) or, more recently, Danny Boyle's *28 Days Later* (2002). In this sense, these illustrations bear a striking resemblance to the architectural plans of the modernist city planners – the lived reality of urban space simply does not feature in the design remit.

In this sense, for all the alleged subtlety of SCP thinking (eg Felson 1988) it is a discourse that operates in much the same way as environmental criminology with its very rigid formalised geography of crime (eg Wikstrom 1991): ie both ultimately translate so-called crime 'hot spots' into the same homogeneous modernist space. Such an approach represents nothing less than the deformation of public space, the *hollowing out* of the urban environment. Complex urban social dynamics are not easily integrated into the type of managerialistic postcode-specific framework that underpins the new space of crime intervention/prevention, and as a result, the various micro processes and cultural specificities that manifest themselves at street level are stripped of their inherent diversity and serendipity.

Conclusion

Let us finish by considering a recent and highly informative example of this pronounced shift in emphasis toward a more sustained focus on highly abstracted ecological and environmental concerns. I refer here to the recent document produced by the US National Institute of Justice entitled *Mapping Crime: Principle and Practice* (Harries 1999). Promoted as an introductory guide to the 'new and

---

10 According to Garland, governments increasingly rely upon 'action at a distance' in evaluating not just the efficacy of localised crime prevention/reduction initiatives (both public and private) but also various other aspects of the criminal justice system. Under such a system, urban space – like the school, the courtroom, and the prison – becomes a focus solely of statistical analysis, at once a place of audit and a testing ground for new initiatives and policy implementation. In other words, so-called 'criminogenic space' simply 'constitutes a new site of intervention for government practices, a new practicable object, quite distinct from the individual offenders and legal subjects that previously formed the targets for crime control. Moreover, the criminogenic situation is like "the economy" or "the population" in being a domain with its own internal dynamics and processes' (Garland 1997: 187; see also Garland 2001 more generally).

innovative' science of crime mapping (using GIS technology) and aimed largely at 'crime analysts and other people interested in visualizing crime data through the medium of maps', *Mapping Crime* offers us a somewhat disconcerting glimpse of the future: a world of 'global satellite orientation', 'scatter diagrams', 'crime moments', 'stick streets', and 'choropleth maps'. This (literally) is criminology's 'out of this world' future: the space satellite as all-seeing eye, the panoptic gaze extended to the nether reaches of space.

Such high abstraction is, of course, acknowledged. Indeed, Harries even poses the question: 'how much abstraction can we tolerate?' The flawed logic of his answer is enlightening. While initially he accepts that 'more abstraction equals less information', he neatly sidesteps this problem by claiming later that one can view this trade-off another way:

> More abstraction equals greater simplicity and legibility (more effective visual communication). Less abstraction equals greater complexity, less legibility (less effective visual communication). (Harries 1999: 10)

The unfortunate thing for Harries and his fellow 'crime analysts' is that crime, incivility and transgressive behaviour are very complex, multi-faceted, ever-changing socio-cultural phenomena. Consequently, while the techniques outlined in *Mapping Crime* might well prove useful in enhancing 'visual communication', they will undoubtedly be of no use whatsoever in helping us understand the complex and diverse social and cultural motivations and individual experiences behind a great many criminal offences.

It is worth considering at this point just how much arch-positivists (and the original precursors of ecological mapping in the mid-19th century) Adolphe de Quételet and André-Michel Guerry would have relished such technology – lest we forget that these early ecologists also looked to the heavens for inspiration about crime and deviance (see Beirne 1993: chapters 3 and 4; Hayward 2004: 88–93). Drawing on a series of early 19th century breakthroughs in statistics, the theory of probability, celestial mechanics – emerging especially in the study of astronomy – de Quételet and Guerry set about mathematising everyday life. Steering a path navigated by 'the starry heavens above', these early mappers transformed observations, 'mere' statistics, dead facts, into *'faits sociaux'* ('social facts', to use de Quételet's term). In today's 'new' discourse of crime mapping the global information satellite is simply the latest (celestial!) calculative instrument for interpreting 'the deviations of the observed'!

In conclusion, this chapter should not be read as an attempt to divorce city-life from essential spatio-environmental questions, or for that matter, those of social structure; rather its aim has been to highlight the need for criminology to develop certain theoretical links between individual experience and the key environmental, structural and (increasingly important) cultural determinants that shape our lives and determine both our place within and our relationship to society. Given the social context in which we now find ourselves – not least what I have described elsewhere as 'the dilemmas of transition' (Hayward 2004) and the notion of the late modern 'subject adrift' – this is a vitally important task. Since its emergence as an academic discipline, criminology has typically fallen some way short of gaining a full and inclusive understanding of urban crime in modernity; the task it now faces is to try to devise new ways of looking at the problem under the even more inchoate conditions of late modernity. Not least it must find answers to a whole new set of questions about the thematics of 'postmodern' space and its effects on the 'subject adrift'. Only when this task has been completed can we begin to understand the processes and motivations that contribute to much contemporary criminality.

References

Bauman, Z (1987) *Legislators and Interpreters: On Modernity, Post-Modernity, and Intellectuals,* Cambridge: Polity

Bauman, Z (1998) *Consumerism, Work and the New Poor,* Buckingham: Open UP

Beirne, P (1993) *Inventing Criminology: Essays on the Rise of 'Homo Criminalis',* Albany: New York UP

Bourgois, P (1995) *In Search of Respect,* Cambridge: CUP

Bourgois, P (1998) 'Just another night in a shooting gallery' 15(2) *Theory, Culture and Society* 37–66

Buchanan, I (2000) *Michel de Certeau: Cultural Theorist,* London: Sage

Clarke, RVG (1997) *Situational Crime Prevention: Successful Case Studies,* Albany, NY: Harrow and Heston

Cohen, S (1979) 'The punitive city: notes on the dispersal of social control' 3 *Contemporary Crises* 339

Cosgrove, D (1983) 'Towards a radical cultural geography' 15 *Antipode* 1–11

Cosgrove, D (1989) 'Geography is everywhere: culture and symbolism in human landscapes', in Gregory, D and Walford, R (eds), *Horizons of Human Geography,* London: Macmillan

Cosgrove, D and Jackson, P (1987) 'New directions in cultural geography' 19 *Area* 95–101

Creswell, T (1998) 'Night discourse: producing/consuming meaning on the street', in Fyfe, N (ed), *Images of the Street: Planning, Identity and Control in Public Space,* London: Routledge

Davis, M (1990) *City of Quartz: Excavating the Future in Los Angeles,* London: Vintage

Davis, M (1998) *The Ecology of Fear: Los Angeles and the Imagination of Disaster,* New York: Metropolitan

de Certeau, M (1984) *The Practice of Everyday Life,* Berkeley, CA: University of California Press

Dery, M (1993) 'Culture jamming: hacking, slashing and sniping in the empire of signs', Open Media Pamphlet Series Vol 25, Westfield, NJ

Felson, M (1998) *Crime and Everyday Life,* Thousand Oaks, CA: Pine Forge

Ferrell, J (1997) 'Youth, crime and cultural space' 24(4) *Social Justice* 21–38

Ferrell, J (2001) *Tearing Down the Streets: Adventures in Urban Anarchy,* New York: St Martins/ Palgrave

Fyfe, N and Bannister, J (1996) 'City watching: CCTV in public spaces' 28(1) *Area* 37–46

Garland, D (1997) '"Governmentality" and the problem of crime: Foucault, criminology and sociology' 1(2) *Theoretical Criminology* 173–214

Garland, D (2001) *The Culture of Control,* Oxford: OUP

Girling, E, Loader, I and Sparks, R (1996) 'Crime reporting and the sense of one's place: press constructions of locality and order in late modernity', paper presented at the American Society of Criminology Conference, Chicago

Girling, E, Loader, I and Sparks, R (1997) 'The trouble with the flats: CCTV and "visions of order" in an English middle town', paper presented at the British Society of Criminology Conference, Belfast

Girling, E, Loader, I and Sparks, R (1998) 'Crime and the sense of one's place: globalization, restructuring and insecurity in an English town', in Ruggiero, V, South, N and Taylor, I (eds), *European Criminology: Crime and Social Order in Europe,* London: Routledge

Hannigan, J (1998) *Fantasy City: Pleasure and Profit in the Postmodern Metropolis,* London: Routledge

Harries, K (1999) *Mapping Crime: Principles & Practice,* Washington, DC: National Institute of Justice

Hayward, KJ (2004) *City Limits: Crime, Consumer Culture and the Urban Experience,* London: GlassHouse Press

Hough, JM, Clarke, RVG and Mayhew, P (1980) 'Introduction', in *Designing Out Crime*, London: HMSO

Koenig, D (1994) *Mouse Tales: A Behind the Ears Look at Disneyland*, Irvine, CA: Bonaventure

Lees, L (1998) 'Urban renaissance and the street: spaces of control and contestation', in Fyfe, NR (ed), *Images of the Street: Planning, Identity and Control in Public Space*, London: Routledge

Massey, D (1991) 'Flexible sexism' 9 *Environment and Planning D: Society and Space* 31–57

Massey, D (1993) 'Power geometry and a progressive sense of place', in Bird, J, Curtis, B, Putnam, T, Robertson, G and Tickner, L (eds), *Mapping the Future*, London: Routledge

Papastergiadis, N (2002) 'Traces left in cities' 156 *Architectural Design, Poetics in Architecture*

Papastergiadis, N and Rogers, H (1996) 'Parafunctional spaces', in Stathatos, J (ed), *Art and the City*, London: Academy Group

Park, RE (1925) 'The city: suggestions for the investigation of human behaviour in the urban environment', in Park, RE, Burgess, EW and McKenzie, RD (eds), *The City*, Chicago: University of Chicago Press

Schultz, J (1988) 'The fabulous presumption of Disney World: Magic Kingdom in the wilderness' 42 *The Georgia Review* 275–312

Shearing, CD and Stenning, PC (1983) 'Private security: implications for social control' 30(5) *Social Problems* 493

Shearing, CD and Stenning, PC (1985) 'From the panopticon to Disneyworld: the development of discipline', in Doob, A and Greenspan, E (eds), *Perspectives in Criminal Law*, Aurora, Ontario: Canada Law Books Inc

Sorkin, M (ed) (1992) *Variations of a Theme Park*, New York: Noonday

Stanley, C (1990) 'Spaces and places of the limit: four strategies in the relationship between law and desire' 25 *Economy and Society* 36–63

Taylor, I (1993) 'Critical criminology and the free market: theoretical and practical issues in everyday social life and everyday crime', paper presented at the British Society of Criminology Conference, University of Wales, Cardiff

Taylor, I (1997) 'Crime, anxiety and locality' 1(1) *Theoretical Criminology* 53–76

Taylor, I, Evans, K and Fraser, P (1996) *A Tale of Two Cities: Global Change, Local Feeling and Everyday Life in the North of England: A Study in Manchester and Sheffield*, London: Routledge

Urban Geography (1996) *Special Issue: Public Space and the City* 17 (2–3): 127–247

Wacquant, L (1996) 'The comparative structure and experience of urban exclusion: "race", class and space in Chicago and Paris', in McFate, K, Lawson, R and Wilson, WJ (eds), *Poverty, Inequality and the Future of Social Policy*, New York: Russell Sage Foundation

Wacquant, L (2001) 'Deadly symbiosis: when ghetto and prison meet and merge' 3(1) *Punishment and Society* 95–133

Warren, S (1994) 'The Disneyfication of the metropolis: popular resistance in Seattle' 16 *Journal of Urban Affairs* 89–107

Warren, S (1996) 'Popular cultural practices in the "postmodern city"' 17 *Urban Geography* 545–67

Whyte, W (1988) *City: Rediscovering the Centre*, New York: Doubleday

Wikstrom, P-O (1991) *Urban Crime, Criminals and Victims*, New York: Springer-Verlag

Williams, R (1973) *The Country and the City*, London: Chatto and Windus

Winchester, H and Costello, L (1995) 'Living on the street: social organization and gender relations of Australian street kids' 13 *Environment and Planning D: Society and Space* 329–48

Young, J (1999) *The Exclusive Society*, London: Sage

Chapter 14
Scrunge City

Jeff Ferrell

Over the years, criminologists have sometimes noted the city's social and cultural ecologies: its close proximities of people and populations, its concentrations of habitation, its zones of revitalisation and decay, its shifting patterns of human movement and symbolic interaction. Criminologists have also posited connections between urban ecologies and particular forms of crime and criminality. Perhaps patterns of criminality reflect the tension between social organisation and disorganisation as the populations of urban areas ebb and flow. Perhaps urban gangs emerge in part out of the cultural proximities and externalised standards of success that the city offers, if not enforces. Perhaps the city surrounds its residents with such sharp contrasts in wealth and status that relative deprivations are experienced as unbearable inequities, to be confronted through violence or other interpersonal violations.

The city's dense human ecology suggests something else as well. It's not just people and populations that exist in intimate proximity, their cultures and experiences crowded close together – it's their possessions that are crowded together, too, in many cases uncomfortably so. Just as the city's residents exist and move about at close quarters, so does the city's everyday material culture, piling up on itself here, circulating there, in networks tightly woven one against the other. Housing, employing, unemploying millions of inhabitants, a large city also houses astounding amounts of personal property, generating countless items of consumption and survival each day. Accumulating in flats, garages, closets, shopping carts, automobiles, storage facilities, rubbish bins, vacant lots and alleyways, this overwhelming material culture gives the city a collective cultural weight, a distinctive urban density and identity, as significant as the shared experiences of its inhabitants.

In the short run, anyway, this urban accumulation can only continue, it seems, and accelerate. Hyperconsumption increasingly drives the contemporary societies of the late capitalist West, along the way constructing a sad sort of store-bought commonality among many of their members. Worse, this hyperconsumptive dynamic appears to be picking up pace across the borders of world culture and economy. The Worldwatch Institute (2004: 4–5, 16) has calculated that, by 2004, the world's 'consumer class' has grown to 1.7 billion people – more than a quarter of the world's population – with almost half of this consumer class now emerging in the 'developing' world. Seeing in these numbers 'a world being transformed by a consumption revolution', the Institute has documented a parallel intensification of general wastefulness, and with it increasing environment degradation in terms of natural resource extraction, waste disposal, and shrinking natural habitats. While 'Americans remain the world's waste champions', their spreading habits of profligate hyperconsumption now seem to herald environmental destruction and material accumulation on a scale as yet unimagined.

Along with the profound environmental harms proffered by a world culture of spiraling hyperconsumption, criminologists and scholars of the city have begun to notice other consequent harms. In fact, as trajectories of increasing urban consumption collide with growing intensities of urban inequality, all manner of deformities emerge in the practice of everyday city life. Elsewhere, for example, I (Ferrell 2001, 2002) have documented the ways in which legal and economic authorities today work not to protect urban public spaces, but to police them – to sanitise city spaces of homeless populations and other urban outsiders who would impinge on the development of a new 'symbolic economy' (Zukin 1997: 240) organised around seductive areas for high-end consumption. Sitting atop heaps of consumer goods so acquired, the privileged urban classes increasingly invest also in surveillance systems, sophisticated locking devices, prickly bordering bushes, guard dogs – invest in anything they imagine might protect their growing accumulation of material wealth – and so find themselves consumers once again, this time shopping the ever-expanding urban market in avarice and fear. Tired of this tension, some of the city's more affluent residents retreat to suburban enclaves and gated communities, abandoning city life altogether. Those left behind worry over rates of automobile theft, identity theft, consumer fraud, burglary, vandalism and shoplifting, cognisant of all the ways in which their mounting material accumulations might be protected or lost.

And yet this particular criminology of urban accumulation hardly exhausts the meaning of the city's growing material density, or its consequences for law and crime. For as much as many city residents face issues of protecting their private property, they face another dynamic, too: finding a place in their lives for all this material accumulation, and finding ways to dispose of that for which there is no place. After all, a society defined by acquisition, a city caught up in the endless manufacture of need and want – a city of consumers – must always follow the next desire as it leads to the next new commodity. But how to make room for the new? And what then to do with vast accumulations of no-longer-new commodities whose value was primarily in their acquisition (Veblen 1953), once the next round of consumption rolls in, as it always will, and soon?

Any answer will, it seems, produce contradictions of one sort or another. Any solution will involve breaching certain cultural and economic barriers, introducing certain sectors of the city uncomfortably and ambiguously one to the other, crossing personal and social margins that some might rather maintain, or imagine not to exist. Especially in the context of the city's ecological and material density, material disposal will offer all the contradictions and inequalities of material acquisition and protection; the flow of material goods out from people's lives will define and complicate city life as much as the flow in. And because of this, the disposal of urban material culture – the ongoing exchange between privately held property and the broader domain of the city and its inhabitants – will by turns reproduce and address urban injustice, offer new dangers and new communities, and become a matter for both morality and law.

All the odds and ends of a great city

The urban spaces and situations in which material possessions are cast out from one life world and collected within another craft the city's human ecology, forming the margins between the city's social, spatial and cultural domains. In a shared apartment house trash bin, the discarded leftovers of private lives coalesce into a dirty public collectivity – and if some of these leftovers are later retrieved, they may become the foundation for someone else's little home, or for another's temporary shelter under bridge or overpass. In the back alley trash bins of commerce, the item that was yesterday a valuable and marketable commodity now transmogrifies into devalued trash, or perhaps a free-for-the-taking treasure; in this commercial alley, the bright front stage of the shop or shopping mall gives way to a backstage of trash piles and broken furniture. At residential curbside trash piles, the homeowner's property line borders and invites the public life of the street, the homeowner's discards transforming from private trash to public disposal problem, or for others public resource. At all of these social and spatial margins legal boundaries are likewise negotiated, with trash piles and trash skips offering situations for deciding between private property and public access, and for distinguishing scavenging from theft. In all of these situations, yours becomes mine and mine yours – but haltingly, imperfectly, ambiguously, as part of the city's complex everyday rhythms. In this cast-off material empire, the immediacy of individual consumption becomes ongoing urban aftermath.

Figure 14.1 Bottle scrounger's cart. Fort Worth, Texas, USA. Photograph by Jeff Ferrell.

Working these material margins, sometimes inhabiting them, is an eclectic, far-flung, and generally illicit urban underground of trash pickers, rubbish scavengers, independent scrap metal haulers, and DIY recyclers. By choice or necessity, their job within the city's larger ecology is to sort among daily accumulations of trash; to imagine ways in which objects discarded as valueless might gain some new value; and always to stay one stealthy step ahead of those official agencies of collection, sanitation and disposal that would haul away such possibilities. By definition, the work of these illicit trash scavengers is and must be marginal. While the director of the city's trash disposal department may earn a handsome living, do-it-yourself urban trash scroungers certainly do not; they operate at the lowest economic margins, finding in the city's trash possibilities of street survival, or other times supplements to minimum wage work. As already seen, the spatial ecology of their work is itself inherently marginal, their labours occurring in back alleys, in and behind trash bins, at the edges of property, at the margins between street and residence. For many, the morality of their work is marginal as well; to pick through the city's trash is to engage all manner of unpleasant questions about cleanliness, propriety, danger, and career.

Because it is marginal, the work of the urban trash scrounger must also be interpretive. One interpretive dynamic occurs as scroungers pick and sort through trash, utilising hard-won knowledge to decide which items of discarded food might offer more nutrition than contamination, and employing elaborate understandings of personal need and market value to determine which material items merit saving, hauling, reusing or selling. Writing of his years as a homeless scrounger, for example, Lars Eighner (1993: 119) recalls not only learning to evaluate the safety of discarded food, but learning to put his background in pharmacology to work in sorting and collecting useful drug discards like antihistamines and antibiotics. Likewise, an urban scrap metal scavenger must learn fine differences between grades of aluminum, copper, brass, lead, tin and iron; must be able to spot these differences as combined within a single material object or buried in a trash bin; and must know something of current prices for scrap metal when deciding what to haul away and what to leave.

Perhaps a more important interpretive dimension, especially with regard to issues of law and crime, emerges around the ambiguous boundaries that separate individual ownership from public resource, and possession from dispossession. In the same way that trash pickers and urban scroungers must analyse the relative value of that which they find, they must analyse the spaces and situations in which they find themselves – and there is little straightforward about it. Full trash skips are widely considered semi-public offerings of discarded materials, and are regularly utilised as such – but they are also regularly decorated with signage warning interlopers away, and protected by city ordinances. Even within a single city, of course, all trash bins are not equal – scavengers' informal access to them, and the likelihood that this informal access will be policed by shop owners or security guards, depend on sight lines, temporal rhythms, traffic density, proximity to buildings, and surrounding neighbourhood dynamics. Open accumulations of used goods near a street or in an alley in turn carry their own ambiguous messages: ongoing remodelling project, temporary storage, house cleaning, eviction, overstock, invitation to take or invitation to trouble. And it is not just urban scroungers who must negotiate these spatial and cultural subtleties – homeowners, shop owners, passers-by and police officers must as well, if they are to decide upon spotting a scrounger to intervene, or encourage, or arrest. The margins that define the exchange between private property and the urban environment, that define the world of the urban scrounger, are themselves not defined; they are malleable, ambiguous, and continually under construction.

An urban trash pile is in this sense less a collection of discarded items than a collection of conflicting symbolic codes, an amalgam of invitations, warnings and seductions to be read, misread and reinvented. The pile itself is a process. Left long enough, some trash piles grow as neighbours or passers-by interpret the existing pile as an invitation to add their own discards; other piles slowly dwindle as scavengers haul away material by foot, bicycle or truck. Occasionally property owners attempt to resolve such ambiguities, or at least to speed the process of pile diminishment, by neatly lining up shoes or small appliances on the curb, or by writing invitations and encouragements – 'Please Take' or 'Everything Here Free' – on the sides of discarded items. But even here new ambiguities emerge. Does an urban scavenger who discovers a big trash pile hold any proprietary rights, develop any ownership stake, as other scroungers arrive? As a property owner continues to haul discards to the curb, and as the pile of discards begins to build back toward the house, does the meaning change? To the scavenger passing by, is the stack of wood up by the house as available as the washing machine on the curb?

Marginality and ambiguity, it appears, are inherent to the informal disposal and repossession of the city's material goods – and these essentially ambiguous characteristics are nothing new. Even the verb 'to scrounge' embodies a long-standing historical uncertainty, evolving as a variant on the dialectal formation 'to scrunge', meaning 'to steal', but more vaguely 'to search stealthily, rummage, pilfer' (*Online Etymological Dictionary*). Interestingly, the term – and the practice – have taken on special currency during the moral and legal disruptions of wartime. In this context the *Oxford English Dictionary* offers a variety of definitions for 'scrounging' – 'To sponge on or live at the expense of others. To seek to obtain by irregular means, as by stealth or begging; to hunt about or rummage ... To appropriate ... To "pinch" or "cadge"' – and includes some equally ambiguous examples of evolving popular usage. 'Scrounging for wire is legitimised by the War Office', reads one missive from World War I – yet a year later another notes 'complaints about "scrounging", which are nothing but outbreaks of loss of moral judgment'. During the next World War a similar report pointedly notes that '"pilfering" by a native is indistinguishable from "scrounging" by an American soldier, and that "chiseling" and resale of Post Exchange supplies is not an act peculiar to Filipinos'.

This long history of legal ambiguity has emerged out of more than wartime necessity or residual etymology. By 1817, for example, New York had enacted a law that forbade junk and scrap dealers from purchasing scrap materials from juveniles. In 1872, Charles Loring Brace (pp 147, 152–54) explained something of such a law's logic, as he included among the 'dangerous classes of New York' those 'exceedingly poor people, who live by gathering rags and bones', their little shanties overburdened with 'all the odds and ends of a great city ... heaped up nearly to the ceiling'. Their sons and daughters, he added ominously, are themselves 'mainly employed in collecting swill and picking coals', a way of life that at least for their daughters 'soon wears off a girl's modesty and prepares her for worse occupation'. During this same period, itinerant peddlers, who had become a 'major institution of nineteenth century economy and ... recycling' in the United States with their bartering of manufactured goods for local rags and scrap metal, nonetheless were 'stereotyped as tricksters and confidence men'. And a half century later, when 'scavenging and junking were nearly universal for working-class children' in the United States, the Chicago Juvenile Protection Association once again argued in its book *Junk Dealing and Juvenile Delinquency* that 'by providing a market, [junk] dealers encouraged children to steal and ... boys went junking mainly to get spending money, not to help their families' (Strasser 1999: 73, 77, 115–16).

In this sense urban scrounging has long existed as a central component of what Stuart Henry (1978: 4, 6, 12) calls 'the hidden economy' – and has long shared with other components of this hidden economy an essential moral and legal ambiguity. Tracing the English hidden economy to the 13th century, Henry characterises it as a place of 'borderline crimes' and 'part-time property crimes' – that is, practices occupying a slippery legal status for participants and authorities alike. Activities like 'pilfering, pinching, poaching, purloining, filching, finagling, flanking, dodging, diddling, dealing, stealing, smuggling, sneaking, gouging, scrounging, and screwing', Henry argues, are 'not the province of "criminals", but an everyday feature of ordinary people's lives' that blur 'the artificial distinction between "honest" and "dishonest"'. As collective urban practices, these activities in turn blur the margins of the city itself. They coalesce into a city of shadows, a subterranean urban empire suffused with shifting boundaries between personal property, discarded trash, and lawful public resource.

Figure 14.2 Save-A-Lot. Ybor City, Tampa, Florida, USA. Photograph by Cécile Van de Voorde.

Standing in the city's shadows

It is in these shadows that I stood for a while. In December 2001 I resigned from a position as a university professor and relocated to my hometown of Fort Worth, Texas. I knew that, at best, this move would leave a gap of eight months or so until I might or might not locate a next academic position. But this gap also meant that I had an eight month period for unfettered field research – if only I could figure out a way to survive economically while doing it. Given my long-standing interest in the often illicit worlds of scrounging, recycling and second-hand culture (Ferrell 1990a, 1990b), the answer seemed obvious, if risky: I'd try to survive as an urban scrounger. I would try to adopt a way of life that was at the same time field research and free-form survival. (See Bartlett 2004 and Ferrell 2005 for more on this undertaking.)

So, early in 2002 I rigged an old bicycle with a second-hand front basket and a back deck, and set out to see what I could find. Daily, I cycled round the neighbourhoods of central Fort Worth, sorting through trash piles, exploring trash skips, scanning the streets and the gutters for items lost or discarded, then returning to my modest home to sort and record my findings. These neighbourhoods in turn provided a nicely varied urban setting for my work; within a bicycle ride of my house were old industrial areas, rail yards, million dollar mansions, working class neighbourhoods, middle class suburbs, little commercial clusters, and the large downtown business district.

The world of the urban scrounger, I found, offered many a spatial permutation. As it turned out, it offered me a remarkably self-sustaining way of life over those eight months. And it offered many an urban margin, many a situation in which I and others negotiated the boundaries between yours and mine, old and new, law and crime:

Just junk, paper junk. Out riding, I roll up on two big cardboard boxes on a homeowner's curb. Stopping, looking through them, I find the cheap horror of the corporate hustle: packets of information for 'sports drink' promotions, including detailed promotional agreements, advertising flyers, posters, and contest forms. While I'm bent over studying these little windows into the service economy's soul, I hear a voice. It's the guy from inside the house, standing in his half-open front door, a grumpy middle-aged scowl on his face, saying something I can't quite make out. Then I pick up a bit of it. '... just junk. There's nothing in those boxes', he yells, 'just junk, paper junk'. I couldn't agree more, but I don't much like his line of work or his tone of voice, so I don't respond. Instead I keep on with my bent-over reading, recalling as I do Lars Eighner's (1993: 121) account of a similar episode: '... I have had only one apartment resident object to my going through the [trash]. In that case it turned out the resident was a university athlete who was taking bets and who was afraid I would turn up his wager slips.'

Now the guy in the doorway adds, tersely, louder, 'I'd appreciate it if you'd get out of there'. I stand up slowly, give him a big smile, a thumbs-up, and a loudly enthusiastic 'OK'. He pauses, then answers with a half-hearted thumbs-up of his own as he turns to retreat into the house, closing the door behind him, apparently no more sure than I whether mine was a gesture of acquiescence or contempt.

Then the guy comes out of the old garage carrying a rifle. Scrounging a curbside garage-cleanout pile, I'm finding some useful items – brass knobs, a coat hook, anchor bolts, aluminum scrap, an (empty) wallet – but I'm wary. The yard sports multiple 'No Trespassing' signs, as well as a hand-lettered sign warning folks away from the leaning, dilapidated garage.

Then the guy comes out of the old garage carrying a rifle.

'How ya doin'?' I ask, turning toward him, throwing him a quick nod. To my relief, he answers with a friendly 'Good'; apparently he's just moving the rifle as part of the garage cleanup. 'Mind if I look through this stuff?' I ask, resuming my work. 'Sure', he says, and then walking toward me, gesturing a closed circle in the air, the rifle tucked under his arm, he adds, 'Just try not to scatter it all around'. 'No problem', I assure him. 'If I'm gonna look through stuff I try to leave it neater than I found it.' This isn't just a line of talk to keep from getting shot, by the way. Over the months of scrounging an assumed social contract seems to have evolved, a negotiated curbside agreement that I try to follow by cleaning up trash piles as I remove items from them, hoping to leave in their place some sense of informal neighbourhood solidarity.

Matching curtains. Riding along, I see ahead of me a big curbside trash pile, and two people already digging in it, their half-filled shopping cart sitting in the middle of the street.

Cycling up, I offer greetings. The man – ruddy, older, heavy, maybe a little drunk – responds with a grunt as he keeps busy ploughing through the pile. But the woman – older, gray hair – strikes up a conversation. She tells me that 'the man said we could look around in here, as long as we put it back and don't leave a mess'. Guessing she means the homeowner, I answer, 'That seems like a fair enough trade', and she says 'Yeah' – but the old guy says, 'Yeah, but who's gonna put it back?'. 'Well, I'll pile it back up before I leave' I tell him – and I do, later on.

Meanwhile, the woman's already pulling clothes out of the pile and handing them to me. She hands me a couple of vintage US Navy wool uniforms, and thanking her I tell her, 'well, sure, I'll take these if you don't want them – but you were here first'. She assures me I should have them, and continues to pull clothes out of the pile for me. 'Is there anything in particular you're looking for that I could help you find?' I ask her, looking to return the courtesy. 'I'm trying to find a curtain to match the first one I found', she tells me. I ask the colour – it's brown stripes – and we look for it without success.

About this time we notice a big tinted-window SUV rolling up on us, a large, middle-aged guy at the wheel, looking us over. 'Honey, you gotta get your cart out of the middle of the street', she tells her partner. 'It's in that guy's way.' But he doesn't, and the SUV eases past.

A few minutes later and the old guy is ready to take off. 'Goddamit, honey, we're gonna be late' he tells her. 'Alright, I'm coming,' she says, but she hangs back, still poking around in the big pile, showing me finds, talking, looking for the lost curtain. This little gendered couple's dance, I think to myself, could just as well be taking place at the shopping mall – except she's shopping curbside, where everything's always on sale.

By now he's reclaimed his cart and headed off down the street, still admonishing her. She gives up her scrounging, begins to walk to catch up to him, and I stand up from my scrounging and tell her, 'Good luck to you'. 'And to you, too,' she says. A minute later, they've disappeared around the corner, though I can still hear him hurrying her.

I'm back to working the pile, and the Yukon rolls up again, the driver easing down the power window. 'Anything good in there?' he asks me, friendly enough. 'Well, I don't know, most of it seems to be broken,' I tell him, looking to put off any well-heeled interlopers – but in fact I sense that he's less interested in checking on the trash than in checking on me.

A while later, finished working the trash pile, I take stock of my finds: the Navy uniforms my friend found for me, and some other old uniforms; a signed silver-plate bowl; a Cadillac insignia; old eight-track tapes and single '45 records; Camus' *The Stranger* and Hesse's *Siddhartha*; Cool Ray Polaroid clip-on sunglasses; a vintage 1970s woman's leather jacket; a Neiman Marcus black and white striped woman's sweater; 14 plastic liquor bottle stoppers; and 32 shiny silver bullets, unspent.

Fuckin' Lan-combe! Out on a ride, I can't resist cruising back over to a curbside trash pile I worked yesterday; I liked the booze and the jewellery I found, and the coffee maker is working great. Besides, a woman at the house was hauling still more big, full trash bags to the curb when I left.

The return trip turns out to be well worth my while. I haven't been there 15 minutes, and I'm already assembling a bikeload of scrounged items: a clock radio; an ornate silver jar; movie videos, some still sealed new in their packages; a glossy *Great American Kitchens* magazine; and a variety of expensive hardcover books including Safire's *Freedom*, Heller's *Good as Gold*, and Beckett's *End-Game*.

Best of all, though, is the company I'm about to keep.

Bending over, sorting through bags with my back to the curb, I'm aware of a car rolling up on me from the north – strange, since this east side of the parkway seems by convention and likely by law to be reserved for travel from the south. As I look up, the car does indeed roll up – and right into the curb, hard, its front left wheel bouncing off as the driver angles it in. Leaning her head out the window is a thin, very tanned, middle aged, working class Texas woman, asking me with a slur and a smile, 'Shit, are they home?'. 'Not that I can tell,' I answer with a smile of my own, having already checked, as usual, for any signs of occupation or annoyance in and around the house. So she gets out, as does her daughter, maybe 20, visibly pregnant in a gauzy white top and shorts, not nearly as tanned or thin or drunk as her mom.

They both jump right in, opening bags, sorting through, talking to each other and to me. Wanting to be friendly, and with the limited space on my bike already full, I start handing them stuff as I pull it out of bags; each time the mom offers an earnest 'thanks'. At one point I dump a bunch of makeup out of a trash bag; her happy response upon seeing this: 'Fuckin' Lan-combe!' I ask if there's anything else in particular they're looking for. 'Just the good stuff,' the mom tells me, though later she asks me if I'm finding any 'kid's stuff', and I do indeed find some children's audiotapes and hand them to her. A little later, the girl picks something up and asks her mom, 'You want this?'. 'Yeah, yeah, anything new' she tells her.

Later the mom asks me, 'Hey, you live around here?'

'Yeah, down across Camp Bowie, where it's not so nice' I tell her, laughing.

'Well, they throw out some good stuff in *this* neighbourhood' she says.

As I'm getting ready to leave, she eases over to me. 'Shit, there's some paper hangin' stuff in there – cheques and stuff', she says, laughing. I laugh too, and I tell her 'Yeah, I found some cheques just the other day, some of 'em signed'. Just a few days earlier I had found two different sets of cheques in two different trash piles, some of them signed and made out to the local Ridglea Country Club. Now that's some *serious* paper hangin' stuff.

Finally, as I'm strapping my scrounging bag onto my bike's rear deck and straightening the pile of books in my front basket, she sees the *Abs of Steel* fitness videotape I've pulled out of a garbage bag and left on the pile.

'How to stay healthy' she says, reading from the tape cover. 'Shit, how to stay high!'

If you just have that look. Once every six weeks or so, when I've scrounged enough scrap metal from trash piles and trash bins, I load up my old pickup truck and haul the metal out to the scrap yard. The scrap yards make up their own urban margin, many of them clustering in one deteriorated section of town, flanked by cheap motels and small auto repair shops, backed by railroad tracks. Ten and a half hours a day, six days a week, the yards buzz and clang with activity as homeless scroungers push in shopping carts full of aluminum cans, independent scrappers arrive with loads of copper and steel piled in dilapidated pickup trucks, and the yards' forklifts push and pile the loads into mountains of sorted scrap metal.

On one trip to the scrap yard, I notice something new above the little pay window: a neatly lettered sign noting that Texas law now requires a photo ID from those cashing in copper or aluminum loads of over 40 pounds. It seems the legal authorities are concerned that copper and aluminum – relatively speaking, two of the most valuable scrap metals – could in fact be of such value that folks might acquire them through theft rather than scrounging. But in a little joke on the authorities, and their new requirement, and the likelihood of its enforcement, the sign carries an additional note, hand-written across the bottom, kidding that the cashiers might also request an ID on a load under forty pounds, 'if you just have that look'.

Salvaging scrunge city

Even these few episodes from those eight months confirm what history and etymology already suggest: that urban scrounging unfolds as a process of inherent marginality and ongoing ambiguity. Moreover, these episodes confirm that these marginalities of meaning are not unfortunate residues of an urban process that might better be systematised and controlled, but rather dimensions of shadow and uncertainty essential to scrounging's viability. Scroungers read trash piles for subtle signs of permission, availability and value, then mine those they consider worthwhile for treasures that others would surely miss. Homeowners and business owners interpret or misinterpret scroungers' intentions, negotiate with them terms of courtesy and community, sometimes re-imagine in the scrounger's presence even the value of their own trash as they decide to forfeit or re-establish control over it. Particularities of legality and illegality are missed or ignored on all sides; specificities of trespass, private property, rightful ownership, public order, state regulation, and proper bullet disposal evaporate as those involved negotiate the informal, situated dynamics of urban reclamation. In this way essential urban borders between private and public are kept open. The margins between disposal and reclamation remain porous, allowing for shifts in meaning, for the fluid transformation of private property into public resource, for the day-to-day leakage of individually accumulated materials out into the broader needs of the city.

The widespread existence of urban scrounging, the marginality and ambiguity of its practice, the porosity of its borders – all of this might be read in any number of ways. From one view this empire of urban scrounging is doubly disgraceful, given that the vast and concentrated economic inequalities of city life not only create these material margins, but push the city's impoverished residents toward them. After all, the same economic order that creates the possibilities of boundless consumption for the privileged relegates others to picking among the discards of this consumption. In this sense the profound economic injustices of late capitalism coalesce, become materially manifest, in every urban trash heap; piled together there are the residues of profligate consumption, the arrogance of ongoing waste, and the pathos of lives consigned to the dirtiest of urban margins. Worse, in a world socialised into consuming always the next new thing, the stigma of yesterday's old trash rubs off on those who pick among it; they are imagined to be filthy, parasitic, out of cultural bounds. If, historically, scrounging has flourished amidst the disruptions of wartime, then perhaps this is the case today as well. In the class war of city capitalism, scrounging proliferates – and the urban trash pile exists as an uneasy demilitarised zone, a marginal place where the privileged can offload some of their material excess into the dislocated lives of the poor.

Yet for all this a second reading is possible – opposite the first, but not unrelated to it. From this view, the porosity of the urban trashpile, the leakage of private goods out into the public realms of the city, constitute a significant economic, political and ecological counter-dynamic within late capitalist society. Amidst the concentrated inequalities of the consumer city, urban scrounging offers a fluid, day-to-day redistribution of wealth – a redistribution neither mandated nor undermined by politicians, but negotiated directly in the streets and alleys of the city. In this sense urban scrounging offers a form of direct social and economic action for consumers and trashpickers alike, an informal, ambiguous second-hand commerce outside the control of charitable organisations, multinational corporations, or governmental bureaucracies.

Figure 14.3 Behind the supermarket. Tampa, Florida, USA. Photograph by Cécile Van de Voorde.

In this second reading the stigma of urban scrounging is trumped by a certain independent dignity – and in fact this street-level dignity emerged regularly and distinctly during my months inside the world of urban scroungers. Down-and-out scrap haulers joked and laughed at the scrap yard, proud of their independence, 'I Love My Boss – Self-Employed' stickers pasted to the bumpers of their beat-up old trucks. Homeless men hauled bottles and aluminium cans in rebuilt shopping carts, explaining to me that if it's this or minimum wage work at WalMart, they'll take the freedom of the shopping cart. As the months rolled by I discovered that I too was becoming something more than a scrounger – an urban prospector, perhaps, a freelancer living off what the city had to offer. Add to this the fact that urban scroungers constitute a vast ragtag ecological army, keeping tons of material from urban landfills every day, and urban scrounging begins to seem, if not an ideal model of social change and economic justice, then at least a viable and valuable enterprise operating within and against consumer society.

But of course a third reading of urban scrounging is also possible – and one that effectively cancels the second. By this reading urban trash piles and urban scrounging constitute accumulating problems of petty crime and public disorder, problems to be contained within legal regulation or controlled by law enforcement. This increasingly common reading references the dual city – the city of official mapping and control on the one hand, and unofficial everyday experience on the other – theorised by de Certeau (1984), Hayward (2004), and others. That is, it reveals an effort to confine scrounging – an everyday urban practice of informality, ambiguity and porosity – within an official urban regime of bureaucratic rationality and legal regulation. Moreover, in attempting to capture within the rigid framework of law an ambiguous urban process, this reading resurrects long-standing critiques of law itself, from Godwin's (1971: 275) 1793 criticism of law as replacing human agency with a 'stagnant condition' and a 'principle of permanence' to Kropotkin's (1975: 30) 1886 claim that law's 'distinctive trait' is 'immobility, a tendency to crystallise what should be modified and developed day by day'.

Whatever its historical antecedents, though, this third reading has taken on special currency today within the emerging urban economy already noted – the 'symbolic economy' of attractively antiseptic consumption spaces and affluent urban lifestyles. Within this economy growing legal constraints on urban scrounging accomplish two purposes: the protection of stylised consumption zones from symbolic intrusion by urban 'undesirables', and the rationalised control of the consumer waste that these zones predictably spawn. While scrounging in Fort Worth, for example – a city intent on 'revitalising' (that is, gentrifying) its downtown and central city neighbourhoods – I've watched the city institute a new residential trash collection system designed to eliminate curbside trash piles, and seen the city organise groups of citizen 'Code Rangers' to report 'outdoor storage of broken and/or discarded items', 'trash and debris accumulation', and the sorts of 'unauthorised garage sales' (Tinsley 2004: 1B) where scrounged items are often sold. Meanwhile, just down the road in Dallas, the mayor admits that she will 'roll down the window and yell and scream' at homeless panhandlers 'to get off the street' (in Grabell 2003: 14A); the city 'makes it illegal to possess a shopping cart off the premises of the business that owns it' (Horner 2004) – and homeless scroungers subsequently resort to hauling scrap metal in hand-built wagons and salvaged baby strollers (Grabell 2004). Elsewhere around the United States, some cities now move to charge fees for a license to scavenge; many other cities large and small push to outlaw outright any scrounging of items from trash piles or trash skips.

These contemporary campaigns to regulate or criminalise urban scrounging operate to erase scrounging's inherent ambiguity, to sanitise and contain a process whose viability resides in its messy uncertainty. To the extent that these campaigns succeed in resolving urban scrounging's legal ambiguities, and so exhausting scrounging's open-ended possibilities, they in turn promise a nasty array of consequent social harms: the reinforcement of hyperconsumption as a monolith of late modern meaning and identity, the clogging of the contemporary city with ever-larger accumulations of material goods, and the destruction of an informal and relatively autonomous economy essential to many at the urban margins. In fact, in the context of global capitalism's destruction of local economies and meaningful work, the outlawing of urban scrounging and the disruption of the economic and ecological alternatives it offers portends a distinctly late modern dystopia, a dystopia defined only by the teeming shopping mall, the towering landfill – and for those at the margins, the poverty of disenfranchisement and dead-end work sans even the dignity of the do-it-yourself scrounge.

This dystopia will be distinctly anti-urban as well. Legally closing down a practice like urban scrounging not only ensures that cities will overflow with consumption and consumer waste; it erodes the sorts of interactive uncertainty that shape the city's very vitality. Even cities of vast economic and political injustice have traditionally offered in counterpoint a relatively porous culture of collective urban citizenship; their scrounged alleyways, their open arcades, their public places have provided engaging if unsteady realms of evocative encounter and interpersonal give-and-take. In combination with other practices of the late capitalist city – the aggressive policing of public space, the promotion of exclusive residential enclaves, the deterioration of neighbourhood economies, the dominance of automotive transit (Ferrell 2002) – the legal containment of urban scrounging threatens to destroy this essential urban dynamic. Given this, residents of the city might well hope that urban scroungers are able to escape increasing legal containment and continue their work along the urban margins, salvaging not just the castoffs of consumer culture but something of the city itself.

References

Bartlett, T (2004) 'The Emperor of Scrounge', *The Chronicle of Higher Education*, L(29), 26 March, pp A10–A12

Brace, CL (1872) *The Dangerous Classes of New York*, New York: Wynkoop and Hallenbeck

de Certeau, M (1984) *The Practice of Everyday Life*, Berkeley, CA: University of California Press

Eighner, L (1993) *Travels With Lizbeth*, New York: St Martin's

Ferrell, J (1990a) 'Dancing backwards: second-hand popular culture and the construction of style', in Guiot, J and Green, J (eds), *From Orchestras to Apartheid*, Ontario: Captus, pp 29–43

Ferrell, J (1990b) 'Degradation and rehabilitation in popular culture' 24(3) *Journal of Popular Culture* 89–100

Ferrell, J (2001) 'Trying to make us a parking lot: petit apartheid, cultural space, and the public negotiation of ethnicity', in Milovanovic, D and Russell, K (eds), *Petit Apartheid in Criminal Justice*, Chapel Hill: Carolina

Ferrell, J (2002) *Tearing Down the Streets*, New York: Palgrave Macmillan

Ferrell, J (2005) *Empire of Scrounge*, New York: New York UP

Godwin, W (1971) [1793] *Enquiry Concerning Political Justice*, Oxford: OUP

Grabell, M (2003) 'Panhandling fines do little to deter long-term homeless', *Dallas Morning News*, 11 November, pp 1A, 14A, 15A: www.wfaa.com

Grabell, M (2004) 'Homeless find ways to roll with shopping cart ban', *Dallas Morning News*, 8 March: www.wfaa.com

Hayward, K (2004) *City Limits: Crime, Consumer Culture and the Urban Experience*, London: GlassHouse Press

Henry, S (1978) *The Hidden Economy*, London: Martin Robertson

Horner, K (2004) 'Losing their carte blanche', *Dallas Morning News*, 14 January: www.wfaa.com

Kropotkin, P (1975) [1886] 'Law and authority', in *The Essential Kropotkin*, New York: Liveright, pp 27–43

Strasser, S (1999) *Waste and Want: A Social History of Trash*, New York: Henry Holt

Tinsley, A (2004) 'City code watchers are hitting the street', *Fort Worth Star-Telegram*, 5 May, pp 1B, 9B

Veblen, T (1953) [1899] *The Theory of the Leisure Class*, New York: Mentor

Worldwatch Institute (2004) *State of the World 2004*, New York: Norton

Zukin, S (1997) 'Cultural strategies of economic development and the hegemony of vision', in Merrifield, A and Swyngedouw, E (eds), *The Urbanization of Injustice*, New York: New York UP, pp 223–43

Chapter 15

The Desert of Imagination in the City of Signs: Cultural Implications of Sponsored Transgression and Branded Graffiti

Heitor Alvelos

In 2002, the cover of lifestyle magazine *Ready Made* spelled it out, loud and clear, in bold, brown and blue type: 'Real is the New Fake'.[1] The article inside proclaimed the exhaustion of gloss culture, the fatigue of perfect looks, and hailed the recruitment of the Average Joe as the next supermodel. It argued that consumers are tired of fabricated, touched-up visuals, too aware of advertising's underlying mechanics, even the most complex ones. Time for advertising that looks like it's not there; time, then, for advertising to jump out of media and become immediate, three-dimensional, *real.*

This study begins by looking into the use of graffiti languages and practices as advertising media in late capitalist culture. It presents a series of case studies undertaken in London between 1997 and 2001. In all of the cases presented, one can recognise the involvement of corporate enterprises in the production of graffiti marks.

The cases studied challenge a prevailing socio-cultural myth – one that regards graffiti's contemporary urban version as a subcultural form of expression, still autonomous, still rebellious, an outlaw enterprise still very much sheltered from outside influence or interference. This scenario is actually increasingly rare.

The cases presented here are time and space specific, as they mostly occurred in connection with the launching of specific goods or services onto the UK market. However, the underlying principles that governed these particular episodes are still in place nowadays, translated into a wide range of 'under-the-radar' advertising tactics. These tactics can further be recognised in other geographical locations around the world, drawing on the blueprints established in the great metropolises and further amplifying their mythologies.

A description of the cases studied, from graffiti to subsequent 'transgressive trends', is followed by an analysis of particular aspects of their social and cultural impact. As will be argued, no subcultural object or practice is appropriated or fabricated without consequences for its original, subcultural referent – and likewise, for the wider cultural landscape.

A conspicuous presence

In retrospect, it was staring me right in the face: at the time, several cases of graffiti in advertising contexts had already been documented. Yet the realisation of this fact took a while to fall into place. It was late 1997, and, lost amidst hundreds of photographs of just as many London walls, the evidence of corporate graffiti hid behind my original ambition to devise an efficient taxonomy of graffiti marks in

1   Issue 5, Winter 2002.

their diversity: hand-scrawled love declarations blended in with stencilled extra-terrestrials, in turn blending in with indecipherable hip-hop tags, *all* in turn partially covered by fly-posters or fresh layers of off-white paint. Yet, just as many graffiti writers' prime ambition consists of scrawling their name on as many public places as possible, so a series of stencilled silhouettes of a man began appearing on numerous walls, in quite distant areas of the city.

These black, red and white silhouettes of a man turned out to be advertising teasers preceding the launch of a CD-single by Robert Miles. Two weeks after the mysterious appearance of the stencilled silhouettes, a fly-poster announced the imminent arrival of the corresponding CD (Figure 15.1).

Figure 15.1 Examples of stencil graffiti promoting a CD by Robert Miles, and corresponding fly-poster, London, 1997.

Once this connection had been established, other cases of advertising graffiti started making themselves recognisable everywhere. The title for Suede's CD *Dog Man Star* had been hand-scrawled a few years earlier. The movie *I Shot Andy Warhol*, from 1996, had seen its title stencilled onto the walls in typewriter-style typography. Bristol music act Massive Attack's 'flame' logo (which appeared on the cover of their first two CD releases) was equally stencilled onto public walls. Daft Punk, a French dance act, first stencilled their logo on London walls in early 1997. One year later, a photograph of one of Daft Punk's promotional graffiti marks was being used as the actual cover for their CD-single *Revolution 909*.

During the early stages of this study, all possibilities were still being considered; in theory at least, these graffiti marks could have been the work of dedicated fans. However, the first case that was followed through in its entirety (Robert Miles, November 1997) made it evident that the graffiti stencil preceded any other visual reference to the artist or product. How could fans possibly emulate a stylistic reference that had not yet reached them? The possibility of an advertising hand at work became more plausible, and a record label's product manager confirmed the graffiti-advertising connection in an interview soon after the first discovery.

This interview, in January 1998, provided a full insight into the mechanics of graffiti campaigns. Graffiti was indeed confirmed as the first stage in the promotional activities that anticipated the product's actual launch. It was to act as a quasi-subliminal teaser that rarely revealed the product in question. Instead, graffiti was meant to instigate a vague awareness of a visual or textual reference, so consumers would later feel that they had 'found' the product by themselves – according to Bond and Kirshenbaum (1998: 112), a process not unlike an Easter Egg hunt.

The use of graffiti as part of a product's campaign is usually a decision made from within its company, more specifically by its marketing department. Occasionally, the product's artists and designers are be involved as well. The actual, physical inscription of these graffiti marks on public walls is made via the subcontracting of a separate company, specialising in advertising and promotion, which in turn generally pays young kids to go out and do the work. Graffiti is generally inscribed on public walls, located in urban areas which themselves possess an underlying urban mythology. Advertising graffiti tends to inhabit the vicinity of nightclubs, street markets, up-and-coming neighbourhoods and trendy hangouts. Additionally, advertising graffiti seems to prefer urban areas that possess a subcultural or counter-cultural history or mystique: Camden Town, Soho and Notting Hill Gate/Westbourne Park, three London neighbourhoods full of historical and current associations with youth culture, are heavily hit by graffiti advertisements on a regular basis.

All parts involved in this process of creating graffiti ads are fully aware that their activities are technically illegal, and do take measures in order to prevent legal problems. The companies involved never include their own name in the product's graffiti advertisement, and neither does a company's name appear on the subsequent (illegal) fly-posters (see Figure 15.1). The cryptic appearance of the actual graffiti marks may further be regarded as a way of safeguarding the companies' public image. In theory, those who recognise the graffiti marks as advertising would be those who enjoy observing graffiti in a bit more depth and generally approve of it; the hostile segment of the larger audience would remain blissfully unaware of the mechanics at work.

The principles of defiance and visibility that characterise hip-hop graffiti do not seem to apply to this context. The advertising graffiti mark does not aspire to be the result of a gravity-defying exercise on the part of its writer.[2] Likewise, graffiti ads do not aspire to compete with billboards, neon signs or bus-shelter ads in their absolute demand for our attention. Instead, they aim for a discreet omnipresence that familiarises us with the product before we have even realised it exists.

The graffiti teaser is not used in every advertising campaign coming from a given company. Its use depends essentially on the product's target audience (young, trendy, urban) and the appropriateness of the product's design. The main objective behind the use of graffiti is not so much to generate sales (as the graffiti marks are generally too cryptic to guarantee an unequivocal product identification), as it is to instil an aura of 'cool', of 'street credibility', on the advertised product.

---

2   The ability to inscribe a graffiti mark in hard-to-access areas is a highly regarded quality in 'hip-hop graffiti' circles. The effect of a writer's mark inscribed on the top of a building, for all to see, is not unlike that of a neon billboard.

The oldest reference to the employment of graffiti as an advertising medium is probably by George Melly in 1976. In the introduction to Roger Perry's photography book *The Writing on the Wall: The Graffiti of London* (1976), Melly laments the use of graffiti ads for the Rolling Stones' 1974 LP *It's Only Rock'n'Roll* (documented in two of the book's photographs). Melly points out that true graffiti needs to be a spontaneous act, not a marketing ploy, but he does not elaborate further.

When contacted in February 2001, in the context of this study, Melly stated that he had no recollection of further examples of advertising graffiti besides the Rolling Stones case. By blurring the boundaries between musician, audience and promoter, the birth of the Punk movement in the mid-1970s would in any case have made it more difficult to understand whether a graffiti mark was advertising in disguise, the work of a dedicated fan, or even the work of the artist him/herself. According to several testimonies, The Clash advertised themselves by scrawling the band's name all over London. And UK band The The would have had their logo stencilled around west London in the early 1980s. Yet in retrospect, how would one be able to fully distinguish these situations from the 'Clapton Is God' graffiti trend in the late 1960s? Time eroded the graffiti marks and the memories of witnesses and those involved, building a resource of counter-cultural mythologies that is now cashed in by corporate interests. A full historical inventory of 'corporate graffiti' remains sketchy, but out of those tentative first steps in viral marketing in the mid-1970s, a true epidemic was in full bloom by the mid-1990s.

Besides the aforementioned examples of Massive Attack, Suede, Daft Punk and Robert Miles, dozens of pop music acts saw their releases promoted via graffiti advertisements in London during the years 1995–2002. A list would include, but would not be restricted to, Tricky, Lauryn Hill, Talvin Singh, Sneakerpimps, Day One, Delakota, The Crocketts, Wu-Tang Clan, Mariah Carey, Destiny's Child, Gorillaz, Eminem, Nine Inch Nails, Nitzer Ebb, Ash, East 17 and The Grid, as well as FSUK, a dance music compilation.

Graffiti adverts did not restrict themselves to pop music either. From 1996 onwards, graffiti advertised a theatre play (*ART*, 1996); television programmes (*The People vs Jerry Sadowitz*, 1998); films (the aforementioned *I Shot Andy Warhol*, 1996, *Goodbye Charlie Bright*, 2001); books (*Class of '88*, 1998); computer games (*Sega Dreamcast*, 1999); websites (*dobedo, playlouder, ammocity, uboot*: 1999–2001); clothing brands (*ECKO* and *Boxfresh*, 2001); magazines (*Wired*, 1996, *Mixmag*, 1997, *Limb By Limb*, 1999); nightclubs (*Fabric* and *G-A-Y*, 2000); and perfume (Calvin Klein's *Crave*, 2001). The list goes on, with advertisements becoming progressively more interwoven with and indistinguishable from 'authentic', spontaneous graffiti.

The death of urban graffiti

Graffiti as an urban practice in Western countries has been rooted in two main historical references. It was widely used in systematic form for the first time during the situationist-inspired Paris riots in May 1968, as the fastest means of communication and propaganda of revolutionary slogans and ideals, a necessary measure in order to keep up with the speed of events. Additionally, it symbolised the bringing down of institutions that housed and represented the 'establishment'.

The second hotbed for contemporary urban graffiti was, unquestionably, *the* American East Coast hip-hop culture that emerged during the mid-1970s. As a cultural phenomenon, hip-hop first surfaced through a convergence of do-it-yourself practices out of American inner-city ghettos. Rap/MCing, DJing and breakdancing provided the immediate socio-cultural context for this form of graffiti. Despite its surface of playfulness, hip-hop graffiti was – and remains – highly competitive and dead serious in its pursuit of artistic status among its practitioners. (For a detailed description of the origins and mechanics of graffiti as a subculture, see Castleman 1982; Ferrell 1996.) Hip-hop also fulfilled the important role of providing urban kids with an alternative to gang membership; as such, it has fulfilled a positive social role that has often been misinterpreted and even turned inside out.[3]

In both of the above cases, graffiti fulfilled its original vocation, that of an *immediate medium*, but, most importantly, it physically supported a desire for social and cultural change. When contrasting these original paradigms with graffiti's contemporary incarnation as an advertising medium, the difference is blatantly evident: graffiti has become one of the most expressive signals of cultural simulation in the late capitalist status quo. This may seem like a particularly heavy claim to be made with regard to a few painted words and images on a few walls in busy Western metropolises. Yet graffiti adverts blatantly speak of complex cultural syndromes, touching on subcultural and counter-cultural issues, historical issues, even ideological issues, and thus constitute one of the most extreme examples of what Jean Baudrillard calls 'the murder of reality'.[4]

Graffiti adverts inhabit the same original, physical space as the historical blueprints described above – public walls in urban areas. However, when created to fulfil a new purpose (advertising), graffiti forsakes its original mythologies in favour of a simulation of those very same mythologies. It ceases to be the evidence of subcultural, counter-cultural or spontaneous activity, rendering 'authentic' graffiti useless. It makes it impossible to observe any piece of graffiti without wondering whether it is an advertisement we are looking at. And it is precisely in this perceptive uncertainty that the problem resides.

This trend of scrawling and stencilling public walls for advertising purposes may be regarded as yet another variation of the appropriation of subcultural and counter-cultural references by mainstream media. Graffiti's aesthetics were, in the past, appropriated and reproduced in magazine advertisements; hip-hop graffiti writers have been commissioned to design soft drink cans and decorate shop windows; and quite a few slogans from the Paris 1968 riots have been used up in TV commercials. However, the actual graffiti mark bearing the (invisible) signature of the brand does inaugurate a relationship of a different kind. It is no longer mainstream culture appropriating signs from fringe culture – it is an omnipresent mainstream culture actively generating a physical manifestation of its own fringes, it is the mainstream *wanting* to be its own fringe.

Graffiti, as an inherently human activity, has historically taken on many guises and served many purposes: political activism, subcultural catalysis, Hobo communication, communal ritual, improvised individual expression and simple vandalism, to name but a few. But rather than adding itself to a possible taxonomy

---

3   According to Phillips (1999: 313), 'kids in lower income neighborhoods with established gang activity recognized hip-hop graffiti crews as an alternative to the gangs they acknowledged as ultimately destructive to themselves and others'. However, and despite the obvious formal and contextual differences between 'gang graffiti' and 'hip-hop graffiti', they are often perceived by the average citizen as one and the same thing.
4   '*Meurtre de la réalité*' in the original. Baudrillard 1995.

of graffiti practices, advertising graffiti insinuates itself into all of those practices, thus blurring the boundaries of perception and purpose. It therefore becomes a prime illustration of Baudrillard's considerations on the subject of hyperreality: 'A hyperreal henceforth sheltered from the imaginary, and from any distinction between the real and the imaginary, leaving room only for the orbital recurrence of models and the simulated generation of difference' (Baudrillard 1983). In fact, the employment of graffiti in advertising contexts comes to cast a shadow of doubt over the origin of *any* graffiti mark, in the process emptying it of *any* purpose.

In its hip-hop incarnation, graffiti has in a sense constituted a form of advertising, as defined and defended by Julian Stallabrass (1996). Graffiti writers generally tag their name everywhere they can, with the purpose of symbolically claiming territory and advertising themselves to their peers, gaining fame and status by the omnipresence of their signature. It can be argued that graffiti adverts follow a similar ambition of 'branding' public space, aspiring to the omnipresence of a graffiti writer's tag. Graffiti adverts have been accumulating in grand palimpsests throughout the years, surviving their referring products and mingling with fly-posters, tags, and political declarations (Figure 15.2). And in a strange role reversal, every 'hip-hop' graffiti tag begins to look like a corporate advertisement. Corporate graffiti no longer reminds us of subculture and rebelliousness; the very opposite occurs: subcultural manifestations may now be perceived as derivative of the corporate universe's visual lexicon.

Figure 15.2 Graffiti palimpsest, including tags, advertisements and political message, London, 1999.

To hyperreality and beyond

As the 'graffiti advert' trend became increasingly common through the late 1990s, so it demanded increasingly more ambitious and creative approaches to its practice. It helped that graffiti writers were developing more daring and diverse creative processes.

Two names in particular stood out amongst graffiti writers in London at the turn of the millennium: Solo One and Banksy. By 2000, Solo One was unanimously considered 'king of stickers' in London's graffiti scene. The pioneer of this graffiti trend in London, in 1999 Solo One began applying pre-tagged stickers onto public walls and lampposts, accomplishing maximum territorial coverage with minimum effort and risk. The stickers used by Solo One were UK Post Office stickers, the ones generally applied to international recorded post (Figure 15.3). By using Post Office stickers, Solo One seemed to be referring to hip-hop graffiti's original travelling mythology, whereby the colourful spray-paint graffiti 'pieces' on New York City trains would carry the artist's name and artwork through places far from the original neighbourhoods. Or it could simply be that it was easy to walk into a London Post Office branch and pick up a handful of free stickers. Whatever the reason, a flood of Post Office stickers carrying Solo One's tag was in full view by late 1999, and by mid-2000 the medium had been widely adopted by countless graffiti writers. Enter Boxfresh, an urbanwear clothing brand.

Recognising the graffiti sticker trend's potential as a marketing medium, Boxfresh launched a series of stickers whose design resembled that of the Post Office stickers used by Solo One. The Post Office logo was replaced by the Boxfresh logo, and the sticker contained a blank area to be used by taggers. By early 2001, Boxfresh had become an unofficial 'sponsor' of the graffiti sticker trend: its freely distributed stickers were used by countless writers around London for 'tagging-and-pasting' (Figure 15.3). This was viral marketing in full effect, further blurring the boundaries of individual expression and mass consumption, of spontaneous and sponsored. But it was about to go one step further. By late 2001, Boxfresh had signed a deal with Solo One, and proceeded to *print* the writer's tag onto their stickers. Boxfresh subsequently distributed the mass-produced Solo One stickers throughout the world, wherever their urbanwear was sold. *Solo One* ceased to be a 'simple' graffiti writer's tag, and became a Boxfresh satellite brand.

Figure 15.3 Solo One's Post Office and Boxfresh stickers, London, 2000/2001.

Boxfresh displayed an insatiable appetite for every available index of *cool* emerging from the streets and beyond. While working on the Solo One sticker front, the clothing brand also appropriated the mythology of the Mexican Zapatista guerrilla movement. The marketing campaign in question used a graffiti stencil representing the iconic masked Zapatista rebel, alongside one of the movement's most celebrated slogans: 'We Are You' (Figure 15.4). As in the case of the Solo One stickers, the Zapatista stencil was distributed around the world as part of a Boxfresh promotional package in late 2001, inviting local distributors to launch their own franchise of the Zapatista graffiti campaign.

Figure 15.4 Boxfresh 'Zapatista' graffiti advertisement, London, 2001.

There was yet another twist to the Boxfresh Zapatista campaign. Visually speaking, it closely resembled the work of Banksy, a graffiti writer from Bristol who moved to London in the late 1990s and is still active to this day. Highly respected in the graffiti community for his original socio-political approach to stencil graffiti, Banksy has never shown signs of restraint on a relentless mission to inscribe his marks in seemingly impossible places. His visually distinctive stencils serve regular doses of a dark humour that revolves around issues of war, authority, politics, history and culture. As Banksy's style began creating a buzz in graffiti circles, Boxfresh readily emulated his style, incorporating it in the Zapatista graffiti campaign.

Banksy has admittedly been contacted by brand giant Nike on several occasions, in order to produce visuals for its campaigns. He has always refused Nike's invitations on ethical grounds; however, his work is not only on display on London's public walls. Banksy's self-published pocket books, documenting his graffiti activities, can be bought in London's Virgin Megastores, and one of his most successful stencil images graces the cover of a CD by pop band Blur: *Think Tank* (2003). Banksy's uncompromising critique of mainstream consumer culture is coupled with an ability to navigate within that very culture, while maintaining the iconic status of an anonymous, independent rebel. But the demand for Banksy's style and mythology, by pop groups and megabrands, further reinforces the disappearance of boundaries of perception and purpose, of creativity and consumption, of authenticity and fabrication.

Pop band Blur's frontman, Damon Albarn, was himself responsible for a classic case of 'hyper-real' graffiti in 2001. Albarn's parallel project, the cartoon pop band Gorillaz, released their eponymous debut album in 2001, while graffiti 'teasers' carrying the band's name/logo preceded the album's launch. A phonetic pun on the words 'guerrillas' and 'gorillas', the band's name hinted at political activism and rebelliousness (the Zapatistas again?), while possibly paying tribute to a cartoon pop band from the 1960s, The Monkees. Gorillaz were one of the biggest sellers of 2001, owing much of their success to good pop craftsmanship, yet cleverly playing the novelty card of a fictitious band made up of cartoon characters. The ultimate paradox came in the shape of the band's graffiti advertisements. These constituted the single physical evidence of the fictitious band in the real world.

Law, crime and transgression rebranded

The above examples constitute but a fraction of the contemporary phenomenon of graffiti being produced for marketing and advertising purposes. In all of the above cases, the aura of 'cool' is pervasive: graffiti is used in conjunction with pop products to self-construct a 'streetwise' status, or to reinforce an already existing, consensual status. These actions have made it increasingly difficult to ascertain the purpose of any and all graffiti marks, all lost in a hall of mirrors paved with ambiguities of meaning and engaged in circular processes of self-digestion. The arrival of media giants and high-profile brands in graffiti territory clearly registers on the barometer of marketing opportunism. But it also signals the corporation's desire to re-conquer an experiential connection with the world, a fatigue of detached models of knowledge, a longing for a form of non-mediated/immediate perception that could never occur in hyper-real mode, soulless, ironic, devoid of value.

Another conundrum, of a very pragmatic nature, emerges from the scenarios described above. If police authorities are so actively involved in the crackdown on graffiti activity, even creating special task forces that read graffiti, investigate its patterns and follow the actions of graffiti writers, why does graffiti advertising seem immune to legal intervention and punishment?

A high-profile incident with the law involving advertising graffiti occurred in April 2001, in the United States. Computer giant IBM spraypainted the sidewalks of major American cities with a series of logos advertising their Linux operating system. The spraypaint used was allegedly non-permanent, and it would allegedly wash away with the first rainfall. However, IBM was reprimanded by San Francisco authorities, and was fined in Chicago for defacement of public property. One of the kids who had been paid to stencil the logos on the pavement was prosecuted after being caught in the act. As a result, IBM halted the campaign and vowed not to repeat the graffiti marketing strategy.

The logos used in IBM's campaign were variations of the 'love' and 'peace' signs from 1960s counterculture. There was a fair amount of public outcry regarding the corporate appropriation of these 'free symbols', and a fair amount of public outrage at the fact that the corporation was defacing public space. IBM actually spray-painted the sidewalks in San Francisco's Haight-Ashbury area, a neighbourhood particularly rich in historical associations with Hippie counter-culture. However, the larger audience seemed to remain unaware of the fact that many other corporations were engaging in the same marketing strategies. It all seems to boil down to the 'buzz' generated around the phenomenon: it is non-existent until the media spotlight is cast upon it.

Police authorities, on the other hand, are clearly aware of the phenomenon of advertising graffiti on a larger scale, and, apart from the IBM incident, they seem to choose to ignore it. While hunting down, arresting and prosecuting graffiti writers and taggers, police authorities tend to leave the companies behind advertising graffiti untouched. One reason for this may be the fact that graffiti adverts do tend to inhabit areas that are already 'bombed' – that is, saturated with graffiti interventions – and thus tend to blend in with the environment rather than openly defying legal authority over these areas. But the reasons for advertising graffiti's apparent immunity run deeper than circumstance. In reality, despite breaking the law, graffiti as an advertising medium is primarily *advertising*, and thus reinforces the late capitalist status quo. The essence of its discourse is precisely the enactment of transgression, rather than actual transgression. Ephraim Webber (editor of *Graphotism*, an internationally renowned magazine on graffiti) pointed this out in an interview in August 2001. Webber also emphasised that an eventual fine would not necessarily cause the company any significant financial damage. The apparent freedom of action that companies enjoy in their graffiti ventures is probably less to do with immunity and more to do with impunity.

This corporate impunity does not express itself solely in the graffiti territory. Product sales for clothing brand French Connection UK rose exponentially at the turn of the millennium when the brand was re-launched as a variation of a slang word: FCUK.[5] In 1999, UK internet café chain EasyEverything used Che Guevara's famous portrait on their billboards advertising the 'digital revolution'. The same Che Guevara portrait was printed on t-shirts worn by waitresses serving drinks at the opening of the Saatchi Gallery's 'New Labour' exhibition on 1 May 2001. The 2001 MOBO awards ceremony, sponsored by Mastercard and Channel 4 TV, was advertised through a series of fake fly-posters that were, in fact, a single billboard also containing the words 'bill posters will be prosecuted' (was Mastercard proposing to self-prosecute? ...). In early 2002, clothing brand Diesel claimed sponsorship of human emotions. The following season, it mocked socio-political activism in a series of web and magazine advertisements, capitalising on the anti-capitalism movements sprawling around the globe. It eerily precluded the anti-Iraq war demonstrations of early 2003 by a few months.

In early 2004, giant soft drink firm Pepsi and Apple music software iTunes joined forces and launched the online music download service to end all download music services: one hundred million songs for free. The corresponding advertisement (available at www.apple.com) featured a series of American teenagers who had been officially prosecuted for illegally downloading music files using file-sharing software. The advertisement hung some heavy words over the enhanced portraits of these pubescent kids: 'charged', 'prosecuted', 'incriminated'. Meanwhile, the kids carried on downloading music and happily drinking Pepsi Cola.

The ad's strange pun contrasts the keywords 'free' and 'legal' as if they were somehow mutually exclusive, if not for Pepsi's intervention. It appropriates the mythology of the kids' transgressive actions and glorifies them, not without

---

5   Incidentally, and according to Abel and Buckley (1977), the word 'Fuck' is by far the most common word in male toilet graffiti.

reassuring all involved that the process looks and *feels* transgressive but is, in fact, perfectly legal. Pepsi and Apple do not want it all to be illegal – they just want it to look and feel *as if* it were illegal, to be as much fun as if it was forbidden. And so we go back to the corporation's construction of the fake authentic, of its own permanent search for the thrill of the illicit. But we go forward as well, as we witness the redemption of the wrongdoers, who raise their big plastic bottles in a toast to Pepsi and Apple for their gift of freedom. In the meantime, any sense of value that could be restored to the actual *music* is nowhere to be seen – apart from the ad's generic 'testosterone-rock' soundtrack, there is no reference whatsoever to the musical contents of this download service. Who cares? It's all free, it's all for free, it's all about freedom.

All these scenarios merge reality and fiction, actual transgression and fabricated transgression, the desire for resistance and the impossibility of resistance. Baudrillard argues that we have witnessed the 'murder of reality', and increasingly we witness the death of imagination as well, as the history of transgression is re-enacted in its entirety, in real time and real space, while the next chapter is being pre-emptively rehearsed. Accordingly, the individual must become a hybrid, a hyper-conformist, if he or she is to traverse this ocean of fake authenticity. For the time being at least, the word 'against' has simply lost its cultural meaning, for any bail will automatically be paid by the soft drink of the day. The sooner one realises the current inefficacy of confrontational models, the sooner the work may begin elsewhere, namely in the process of recognising the areas of human knowledge and experience that remain immune to the hyper-real. But those shall remain unnamed for the time being – so that they may remain unbranded.

References

Abel, EL and Buckley, BE (1977) *The Handwriting on the Wall: Toward a Sociology and Psychology of Graffiti*, Connecticut: Greenwood

Baudrillard, J (1983) *Simulations*, New York: Semiotext(e)

Baudrillard, J (1995) *Le Crime Parfait*, Paris: Galilée

Bond, J and Kirshenbaum, R (1998) *Under the Radar: Talking to Today's Cynical Consumer*, New York: John Wiley & Sons

Castleman, C (1982) *Getting Up: Subway Graffiti in New York*, Cambridge, MA: MIT Press

Ferrell, J (1996) *Crimes of Style: Urban Graffiti and the Politics of Criminality*, Boston: Northeastern University Press

Phillips, A (1999) *Wallbangin': Graffiti and Gangs in LA*, Chicago: University of Chicago Press

Stallabrass, J (1996) *Gargantua: Manufactured Mass Culture*, London: Verso

Chapter 16
'Crime Talk' and Crime Control in Contemporary Urban Japan

Mark Fenwick

Introduction: Japan as a 'low crime culture'

Although English language criminology has tended to neglect Asia, Japan has proved to be the focal point for a significant body of comparative criminological research. The main impetus for this research has been the perceived uniqueness of Japan. Japan achieved the transition from the feudal dictatorship of the Tokugawa family to a highly affluent, secularised, post-industrial society in a little over a century without the kind of rapid increase in crime rates found in other countries. As such, Japan is one of the rare examples (often mentioned alongside Switzerland) of a society that has avoided the modernisation-crime nexus that has often been identified by criminologists (Shelly 1981). Accounting for this 'anomaly' (Archer and Gartner 1981) – examining the reasons *why* Japan has enjoyed such low levels of officially recorded crime in spite of undergoing a period of profound and rapid social change – has interested criminologists in search of a better understanding of the causes of crime and more effective forms of crime control.

In accounting for low crime rates, most criminologists have focused on Japanese culture. The findings of an earlier generation of social anthropological writings on Japan have been utilised to explain the crime rates by referring to certain features of Japanese culture.[1] Although economic and demographic factors have received some attention (for example, Evans 1977; Merriman 1991), the abiding concern of the English language literature has been with the claim that Japanese culture is particularly effective at socialising individuals into law-abiding subjects. Heavily influenced by Ruth Benedict's (1946) *The Chrysanthemum and the Sword*, criminologists have argued that Japanese cultural values have created an environment in which informal social controls exert a tremendously powerful pressure to conform. As such, this framework owes much to the insights of Travis Hirschi's (1969) control theory.[2]

The broad pattern of this argument is well documented.[3] It is suggested that Japanese culture ascribes a special value on the group as the source of personal identity. Self-control is strongly encouraged in the context of a social order where failure to live up to the expectations of others has profound social and psychological consequences (Doi 1977: chapter 1). Everyone develops a deep stake in conformity and a desire to preserve the harmony of the 'in-group' (Komiya 1999: 372–74). A consequence of this emphasis on the group is that individualism is equated with selfishness and is hence discouraged. Those crimes that do occur tend to be group

---

1   For an authoritative version of this argument see Komiya 1999; see also Clifford 1976; Adler 1983; Westerman and Burfeind 1991. Fujimoto 1978 offers an illuminating discussion of this issue in the context of Japanese Americans.
2   For a cultural criminological perspective on the Japan and control theory argument, see Morrison 1995: 277–81.
3   See eg Benedict 1946; Nakane 1970; Reischauer 1978; Magasatsu 1982; Hendry 1987.

based (most obviously, organised or politically motivated crime), where individuals in fact 'conform to the non-conformity' (Clifford 1976: 31; see also Raz 1993). The low crime statistics simply reflect the social reality: a culture in which informal social controls exert a tremendously powerful pressure to conform.

Although this literature contains many insights into Japanese culture, the emphasis on explaining the *absence* of crime has meant that other features of Japanese society have been neglected, most obviously the *presence* of images and narratives of crime in everyday life, as well the relationship between these images and patterns of crime control. To use the concept developed by Theodore Sasson (1995), 'crime talk' is as pervasive in Japan as in countries with much higher rates of crime. The idea that Japan is a 'nation not obsessed with crime' (Adler 1983) in some sense misses this crucial point. The unspoken assumption in the English language literature seems to be that since crime rates are *comparatively* low then so must be the degree of 'talk' about crime. From a Japanese point of view, however, the situation can appear very different. Comparative criminologists interested in Japan could, therefore, adopt a method that is sensitive to social representations of crime rather than assume that relatively low crime rates reflect the absence of crime from ordinary social experience. A more pluralistic conception of a crime problem and the concept of crime talk can highlight what is rarely commented upon in the English language literature, namely the constant proximity and pervasiveness of images, representations, and fictions of crime in social life. In this chapter, therefore, the question of explaining Japanese crime rates will not be considered directly. Rather, the next section will introduce Japanese crime talk, and the role that this kind of discourse plays within the Japanese system of crime control. It will be suggested that with its particular emphasis on private ordering through community action, penal modernity in Japan has taken a distinctive form and that 'crime talk' has been central in manufacturing a sense of insecurity that is necessary in mobilising communities, particularly urban communities, to actively participate in the co-production of public safety. The final section will then suggest that this type of crime control has come under pressure in recent years and that as a result of this crisis a new kind of emotionally charged, 'populist' crime talk is increasingly prevalent. The argument will be illustrated through a discussion of images of the foreigner-as-criminal in the speeches and writings of Tokyo Governor Shintaro Ishihara.

'Crime talk' and crime control in Japan

There are various ways that crime is present in everyday life in Japan. Firstly, there is the presence of crime in popular entertainment. As in the United States and Europe, crime forms a staple component of many TV dramas, films and print-based media. This category includes film directors who are well known in the West for their violent thrillers such as 'Beat' Takeshi (*Sonatine* (1993), *Fireworks* (1997), *Brother* (2000)), Miike Takashi (*Audition* (1999), *Ichi the Killer* (2001)) and Kinji Fukasaku (*Battles with Honor and Humanity* (1973), *Battle Royale* (2000)), but also a whole series of crime B-movies and TV shows that are rarely shown abroad, but which continue to be immensely popular domestically (for an incisive account of this genre see Buruma 1984: chapter 10). Crime and violence are also central to the world of the *manga* comic books, as well as in the fiction of contemporary novelists such as Haruki Murakami (*Hard-Boiled Wonderland*) and Natsuo Kirino (*Out*). In this respect, Japanese literary and popular culture is as fascinated with acts of transgression and their consequences as elsewhere.

Of more importance to this chapter, however, are non-fictional forms of crime talk. Crime receives extensive coverage in the Japanese news media due, in part, to the introspective nature of a news media whose primary concern is with domestic, rather than international, affairs. However, the extent of the coverage given to crime is startling to anyone who comes to Japan expecting the low crime rates to be reflected in the daily news. Moreover, it can appear that there are few restrictions on journalistic reporting of crime. In a particularly striking instance of this kind of press 'freedom', journalists jostled to conduct interviews with primary school children after a man had broken into their school in Ikeda City, Osaka and killed several of their classmates and a teacher on 8 June 2001. The so-called 'wide shows' – daily, tabloid-style magazine programmes – feature extensive coverage of crime-related issues. Seemingly unlimited restrictions on what can be reported and the close links between journalists and the police mean that a large amount of officially sanctioned information is leaked to the press. Moreover, the journalists often conduct their own investigations in the shadow of the police, with victims and witnesses being interviewed on camera, and former police and prosecutors being called upon to comment on every aspect of a case.

Finally, there is also a proliferation of information about crime and crime prevention in everyday life. Again this is a topic that has received very little attention in the English language literature. Of particular importance are local crime prevention activities. Most households in Japan belong to a network of local committees, comprising members of the immediate neighbourhood, who on a rotation basis take it in turns to manage various local affairs. These activities involve information distribution, organising waste disposal, local festivals and street cleaning, as well as mediating any low-level disputes that may arise. However, some of the most important tasks are directly related to crime. Local crime prevention committees co-ordinate with local police and government officials to provide regular circulars on crimes that have occurred in the area or to report on the suspicious activities of strangers. They also produce posters that contain crime warnings as well as street patrols that police areas around local schools. Moreover, they provide extensive information and advice on crime prevention and security. In this way, a direct and very tangible conception of the pressing crime problems in each neighbourhood is communicated to all residents.

What, then, are we to make of the prevalence of this kind of crime talk in a low crime society like Japan? In answering this question, it is important to situate crime talk in the Japanese system of crime control. An instructive contrast can be made with David Garland's (2001) characterisation of crime control in Europe and North America. According to Garland, penal modernity gradually emerged from around the late 18th century when the task of enforcing the criminal law was increasingly removed from non-state actors and monopolised by public authorities. For Garland, penal modernity within the United States and Europe is synonymous with the emergence of a strong and centralised criminal justice state:

> The modern system for apprehending, prosecuting and punishing violators of the criminal law thus came to be a specialized, differentiated one, forming an integral part of the modern state apparatus. Over time it has come to be administered by professional bureaucrats, utilizing institutions, laws, and sanctions specially designed for that purpose. These historical processes of differentiation, statization, bureaucratization, and professionalization are the key characteristics of what we might term the 'modernization' of crime control and criminal justice. (Garland 2001: 30)

The corollary of this process of 'modernisation' was the marginalisation of community action. Vigilante justice against criminals was increasingly excluded from law enforcement and criminal acts were seen as 'public matters to be tried in the criminal courts' (*ibid*: 29). As such, there was '[n]o need for a policy to encourage private action. No need to involve the public or individual victims. No need for an emphasis upon social or situational prevention. All that was required was a framework of legal threats and reactive response' (*ibid*: 34). Of course, Garland goes on to argue that with spiralling crime rates and rising middle-class anxieties about crime, there has been a crisis in this form of penal modernity, and that one response to this crisis has been the re-emergence of community-based crime prevention (*ibid*: 123–31). However, for the purpose of this discussion, it is the specific form of penal modernity in Europe and North America that is worthy of mention, namely the combination of strong criminal justice state and the marginalisation of private, community-based responses to criminal activity.

In Japan, however, penal modernity took an altogether different form, particularly with regard to the role of non-state actors in crime control. Unlike in Europe and North America, enlisting various forms of community support and manufacturing co-operation between state and non-state actors remained central to Japanese crime control even after the reception of Western forms of criminal justice in the period after the Meiji restoration of 1868. Crime was addressed not only in a direct fashion via agents of the criminal justice system but also through indirect action achieved by non-state actors, notably local communities, who were activated by government authority. The connection that Garland identifies between the 'modernisation' of penality and the marginalisation of community action never occurred in Japan.[4] Rather, penal modernity in Japan established a loosely directed and quasi-informal style of crime control that not only complemented but in many cases extended well beyond the formal criminal justice system. Sovereign power in Japan never disregarded informal patterns of social control, as Garland suggests occurred elsewhere from around the early 19th century, but rather preserved a dispersed and pluralistic system of social control that co-existed with a Western-style criminal justice system.

Penal modernity in Japan thus developed a different distribution of responsibility for crime control. Not simply a task of the state nor left entirely to the community, it was conceptualised as the joint responsibility of local communities working in collaboration with state actors. Crime control was not restricted to *ex post facto* detection and prosecution, but included a diverse range of community-based activities. Of particular importance to this system has been the interface between the police and the national network of crime prevention committees that can be found throughout Japan (see Kusuda-Smick 1990; Bayley 1991: chapter 5; Thornton and Endo 1992). As mentioned above, these crime prevention committees constantly distribute information and offer advice on local crime prevention matters and much crime talk originates from the interaction between police and community associations of this kind.

Obviously, this system of community participation in crime control depends on a significant degree of public co-operation as well as trust between state and non-

---

4   This chapter will remain neutral on the veracity of Garland's claim regarding penality in the US and Europe, as well as the question of the form taken by the criminal justice state in Japan. On this latter issue, see Miyazawa 1991; Foote 1992.

state actors. Certainly the community-based style of policing associated with local police boxes (*koban*) has facilitated relationships between the police and crime prevention associations (for more on *koban* and the manufacturing of public trust in law enforcement, see Bayley 1991: chapter 2). By maintaining an active and visible presence in every community and by extending the scope of police activities beyond responding to crime to include a wide range of social services, the Japanese police have for much of the post-war period been very successful in fostering public confidence.

The community presence of the Japanese police ensures that space – particularly urban space – is divided up and organised in such a way that it is rendered transparent to state actors. The Japanese literary critic Ai Maeda suggests that the principle of 'seeing everything at a glance' was the 'organising principle' for all the institutions of Japanese modernity (Maeda 2004: 36). Maeda illustrates this claim with several fascinating examples, including the reform of prisons. The emergence of Japanese-style policing would be a further illustration. In his account, Maeda emphasises urban planning, in particular the reorganisation of Tokyo in the post-Meiji period. Maeda describes how Haussmann's reconstruction of Paris was appropriated by Japanese urban planners and used to transform Tokyo in such a way that the 'shady underworld of the slums' (*ibid*: 44) was rendered transparent to state agencies keen to construct state-community partnerships for ensuring social order. As such, Maeda highlights that the Japanese community is not a naturally existing phenomenon but rather the result of a very deliberate political strategy adopted in the unsettled period immediately after the collapse of the Tokugawa regime. Although Japanese crime control has preserved a central role for community action, it should be not regarded as informal social control independent of state action.

Ensuring public trust in the police remains a high priority and rendering urban space visible to state agencies was crucial in the emergence of the Japanese version of penal modernity. Equally important, however, has been the proliferation of crime talk. Crime talk plays a key role in manufacturing a sense of insecurity and anxiety that is necessary to mobilise communities into actively participating in the co-production of public safety. By raising awareness, and possibly fear, of crime to artificially high levels, this style of crime control fosters a sense of danger that motivates a psychological investment in co-operative crime prevention activities and ensures that non-state actors play their part. Crime talk – particularly locally situated crime talk – is crucial to the construction of the sense of responsibility that this kind of strategy requires if it is to be successful. Crime talk persuades communities to exercise their informal powers of social control, and modify their practices in order to reduce criminal opportunities and engage in the self-policing of communities, and thus enhance the effectiveness of crime control.

In the absence of such crime talk, any sense of urgency would be diminished and quasi-informal patterns of control might lose any systematic quality. No doubt communal action would occur (as no doubt it continued to do in North America and Europe), but only spontaneously and on an *ad hoc* basis in response to specific incidents. A high degree of state authorised crime talk thus ensures that individuals retain a sense of urgency regarding crime and do not disinvest from communal life. Crime talk ensures that individuals retain a psychological stake in the production of security and a motive for engaging in crime prevention. If this system of crime control has played a part in the low rates of crime in Japan, alluded to above, then it highlights a connection between high levels of community-based crime talk and the successful operation of community-based crime prevention strategies. The apparent anomaly of high levels of crime talk in a low crime culture begins to make sense when the crime talk is located in the specific context of Japanese penal modernity.

Crises of penal modernity and the emergence of populist crime talk

The Japanese system of crime control described in the previous section has come under increased strain in recent years. Rising crime rates combined with a clearance rate that has fallen dramatically to a little over 20% in the past decade appear to have damaged public confidence in police-community partnership as the most effective strategy for responding to crime. This confidence has been further damaged by a string of corruption scandals involving the police that have severely damaged their legitimacy. A survey conducted by the *Yomiuri* newspaper in March 2001 reported that 60% of those surveyed said their trust in the police had 'declined in recent years' and that 40% of those surveyed said they 'did not trust the police at all'.

Other developments have compounded public concerns about criminal justice more generally and prompted reforms that have resulted in a more punitive, expressive system of criminal justice. Putting the point slightly differently, declining public confidence in quasi-informal control has been paralleled by calls for a strengthening of the criminal justice state. For example, the lack of disclosure of information to victims in criminal proceedings, as well as public perceptions of inadequate sentencing by the judiciary, have led to the emergence of a vocal victims' rights movement that elicits extensive public support and has prompted the government to consider enacting a new victims' rights law. A series of high profile murders by juvenile offenders and mentally ill offenders has led to reforms in how the criminal justice system deals with these two classes of defendant that shift the balance away from the 'psy'-professions towards a more punitive approach.

Of course, the economic and social background to these crime control developments is a decade-long recession and a process of 'de-subordination' that has increasingly undermined the respect for authority and hierarchy that has been a legacy of Japan's Confucian history. Urbanisation and, in particular, the rapid expansion of the Tokyo metropolitan area has meant that community-based measures described above have lost their effectiveness as a result of more anonymous and individualistic patterns of social life. An increasingly large percentage of the Japanese population live their lives in mega-cities where the patterns and experiences of social life are quite detached from the pre-war period.

A detailed analysis of this crisis in crime control and its social causes is beyond the scope of this chapter. However, what is interesting is how this crisis seems to have been driven, in large part, by the emergence of a new and emotionally charged *political* discourse on crime. In this sense, the kind of politicisation of crime that has occurred in the US and UK has also occurred, albeit in a nascent way, in Japan. To illustrate this new populist, political discourse on crime, this section will consider the statements of one of the most popular and high profile politicians in Japan, the Governor of Tokyo, Shintaro Ishihara. First elected Governor in 1999 and re-elected by a landslide in April 2003, Ishihara became famous as a university student when his book, *Taiyo no Kisetsu* ('Seasons of the Sun'), won the prestigious Akutagawa Award in 1955. Shintaro and his younger brother Yujiro became national celebrities when they starred in a film based on the book. While Yujiro concentrated on his career as an entertainer (he went on to become one of the most popular actors in post-war Japan before his death in 1987), Shintaro focused on writing novels and a burgeoning political career, becoming a government minister in the 1980s before quitting national politics in 1995 in protest at the 'lack of vision' of his fellow legislators.

Ishihara is well known for being outspoken. With Sony's Akio Morita he co-wrote in 1989 *The Japan That Can Say No*, a book widely interpreted as anti-American. He has also claimed that the 'Rape' of Nanking was a 'fabrication' and suggested that Japan's occupation of Korea was a 'merger' initiated at the request of the Korean authorities. Less controversially, he has called on the US to give up its air base at Yokota, believes that poor people 'should eat barley instead of rice', and has spoken openly about the ineptitude and corruption of the national government.

In spite of these opinions, and perhaps even because of them, Ishihara has proved to be extremely popular with a wide cross-section of the electorate. Most political analysts agree that his electoral success is partly a vote against the traditional style of Japanese politicians in favour of blunt talking and clear expression. In a culture that places an overwhelming emphasis on indirectness and subtlety of expression, Ishihara's personal style may appeal simply because it marks a refreshing break from the norm. It may also be that he has been very successful in articulating popular discontent during a period of economic contraction and social uncertainty. Many of his more xenophobic statements may resonate with ideas that many individuals have some sympathy for but are unwilling to articulate in public. Ishihara's style has been adopted by a number of other 'celebrity' politicians who have managed to succeed in gubernatorial elections across the country. Ishihara has let it be known that he would like to be Prime Minister at some point, and has plans to launch a new political party to achieve this goal. These plans have been put on hold due to Prime Minister Koizumi's continuing popularity, but given that nearly a third of Japan's population reside in the Tokyo area, Ishihara's ambitions should not be dismissed lightly.

In this context, however, what is important is the centrality of crime to Ishihara's political rhetoric, and in particular the theme of crime committed by foreigners. To illustrate the kind of position he takes, I will consider one representative example, an article, 'Nihon yo: uchinaru bouei wo' ('Japan: defend the home front') published in *Sankei Shimbun* on 8 May 2001. Ishihara begins the article with a nostalgic longing for a lost past:

> When I look at the country that Japan has become, it seems obvious to me that the forces binding us together as a nation have become weakened. As a result, we have lost many of our irreplaceable virtues and beautiful traditions. Some of the factors causing this loss come from within, while others come from without. One of our vanishing virtues is the blessing of public safety that has been admired by people of other lands, but today seems well on its way to becoming a rapidly-disappearing legend. Factors leading to the breakdown of public safety also come from both within and without, but in this modern era of internationalization, the nature of crime in this country is undergoing major changes. (Ishihara 2001)

This theme of the decay of traditional virtues is a familiar one in nationalist discourse, and it provides the basis for the identification of the cause of this decline as something external and alien. Ishihara develops his argument by describing how during a visit he made to the National Police Agency Headquarters in Tokyo, officers described a case in which a murder victim had the skin stripped from his face so as to conceal his identity. According to Ishihara, the police were convinced that the killer was Chinese:

> This conjecture was based on the fact that this type of modus operandi is simply not used by Japanese people. In due course, the perpetrators were captured, and, just as had been suspected, the crime was one of revenge among Chinese criminals. There is fear – and not without cause – that it will not be long before the entire nature of Japanese society itself will be altered by the spread of this type of crime that is indicative of the ethnic DNA of the Chinese. (Ishihara 2001)

The jump from what may well have been a reasonable conjecture on the part of the police based on the circumstances of the particular case to the assertion that this type of crime will soon become commonplace as a result of the 'ethnic DNA' of Chinese is particularly striking. It brings us to Ishihara's main claim, namely that as a result of increased internationalisation Japanese cities are likely to be overrun by illegal Chinese migrants who are genetically predisposed to criminal activity:

> Let me also note that in the Tokyo areas of Shinjuku, Ikebukuro, and Roppongi you wouldn't even think you were in Japan during the hours from after midnight until early dawn. It may seem ironic or even comical, but the truth is that even the Japanese gangsters hesitate to enter these outrageous areas. Probably most of the foreigners gathering there have illegally entered the country or are illegally overstaying their visas. (Ishihara 2001)[5]

To be sure, Ishihara is not alone in adopting this kind rhetoric about foreign crime. In fact, it has become almost routine to find articles or speeches by politicians that are either explicitly or implicitly predicated on the assumption that crime rates amongst the foreign population are disproportionately high. In another high profile incident, Kanagawa Governor Shigefumi Matsuzawa was recently forced to apologise after he described foreigners as 'a bunch of sneaky thieves', when discussing the growing Chinese population in his prefecture.

Whether these claims about foreign crime rates have any statistical basis is unclear, as the official crime statistics make meaningful comparisons extremely difficult. To give just one example, the crime statistics have included visa violations in the category of 'heinous crimes', meaning that overstaying one's visa (a crime that can only be committed by a foreigner) will be classified along with much more serious offences. And even if there was some basis for the suggestion that foreigners commit a disproportionate amount of crime, one would have to note that the majority of foreigners in Japan are young people brought by the government to work in so-called '3k' jobs, that is *kitanai, kiken, kitsui* (dirty, dangerous and difficult). That is to say, foreigners in Japan are disproportionately likely to be young, as well as economically and socially marginalised, so any comparison with rates of crime amongst the Japanese population *in general* is likely to be an unfavourable one.

Of course the question of whether Ishihara's fears have any basis in reality is perhaps of less significance than the social and political effects of this kind of rhetoric. It is certainly the case that this populist crime talk has changed the political context within which crime as well as immigration policy is being formulated in Japan. Undoubtedly, this has implications for the formal criminal justice system, but what may be of more importance is how this new form of crime talk plays out in the kind of community-based crime prevention context that the previous section identified as the distinctive feature of penal modernity in Japan. It seems clear that the police seem

---

5 See Hayward 2004 for an alternative interpretation of Roppongi as a 'fusion' of East and West: 'Roppongi is an extraordinary fusion of rampant Japanese consumerism, technological innovation, Western youth cultures and hedonist expression. Consequently, it has become a late modern playground – not just for the Japanese, but for "ex-pats" and tourists from Europe, Asia, North America and Australia' (Hayward 2004: 193).

to be stressing the threat posed by foreign crime in the kind of crime prevention materials discussed in the previous section. The *Mainichi* newspaper reported on 22 February 2001 that Nagano banks and government offices displayed prefectural police notices about foreign money-snatchers. The article also mentioned December 2000 Tokyo Metropolitan Police flyers that suggested citizens call the police 'if you hear someone speaking Chinese'. In February 2000, the Shizuoka Police Department distributed to shopkeepers a handbook entitled *Characteristic Crimes by Foreigners Coming to Japan*. It offers hints on dealing with local Brazilian and Peruvian customers: if a 'group' of 'two to four' foreigners park outside your store, 'write down their license plate and report it to the police'. More far-fetched was the recent revelation that the Police Research Agency had received a 175 million yen ($1.6 million) research grant to establish an index of 'foreignness'. According to their website, police would be able to test minute samples of blood or other evidence from crime scenes to determine whether the suspect is foreign or not. Predicated on the spurious notion that Japanese DNA is somehow biologically different from that of foreigners, this kind of policy resonates with the kind of thinking associated with Ishihara.

Japanese politicians seem increasingly willing to resort to populist rhetoric when discussing crime and it seems likely that this will result in a trend towards more emotionally charged criminal justice policies. However, as has been intimated, the emergence of this kind of populist discourse on crime takes place against the backdrop of a very different experience of penal modernity. Although there have been some reforms of the criminal justice system that have introduced a more punitive edge, notably changes in the juvenile justice system and new measures for dealing with mentally ill offenders, these are relatively limited in comparison to other jurisdictions. Certainly, there has not been the systematic crisis of the rehabilitative ideal and explosion in incarceration found in the US or UK. In large part this reflects the fact that crime rates have not risen as rapidly or to such levels as has occurred elsewhere. High levels of crime are not yet a routinised feature of the everyday urban experience in Japan.

This is not to suggest, however, that the effects of the kind of populist discourse on crime are limited, but rather to suggest that the principal site for the emergence of populist punitiveness in a Japanese context may well be community-based crime prevention practices. The recent proliferation of police-sanctioned images of the foreigner-as-criminal as disseminated by local crime prevention committees seems to support this view. As such, this serves to emphasise a further point regarding Garland's account, namely that crises of penal modernity are likely to take a distinctive form in an Asian context. Specifically, the kind of opposition that Garland makes in his account of recent developments in the US and UK between 'adaptation' (in the form of the emergence of crime prevention and the criminologies of everyday life) and 'denial' (in the form of the re-emergence of punitive sanctions and expressive justice in criminal justice) may not be applicable in a Japanese context where populism has informed crime prevention, as well as reforms of criminal justice.

Conclusion

In an economically and socially uncertain world, the kinds of fears associated with foreign crime, youth crime and crimes of the mentally ill – to take the three dominant themes in the populist discourse on crime in Japan – may provide an emotionally powerful mechanism for mobilising urban communities to take continued responsibility for community safety. This may have particular resonance amongst the rapidly increasing number of people who reside in Japanese cities. Unlike crime prevention in its earlier form, however, this will be a mobilisation of populations that is detached from the reality of the local crime problem, and influenced by an image of the threat of crime that is based on the demonisation of socially marginalised others. Although such a trend may foster some sense of ontological security or belonging for those who reside in the anonymous mega-cities of contemporary Japan, the kind of communities that will be fostered by such a discourse will be discriminatory and exclusive rather than cosmopolitan and open. Moreover, the effectiveness of these closed communities of fear in responding to what appears to be a genuine increase in crime rates over recent years seems to be highly doubtful, not least because the perception of risk is dominated by images of dangerous groups, such as foreigners, that represent a statistically insignificant section of the population.

References

Adler, F (1983) *Nations Not Obsessed with Crime*, Littleton, CO: Fred Rothman

Archer, D and Gartner, R (1981) 'Homicide in 110 nations: the development of the comparative crime data file', in Shelley, LI (ed), *Readings in Comparative Criminology*, Carbondale: Southern Illinois University Press

Bayley, D (1991) *Forces of Order: Policing Modern Japan*, Berkeley, CA: University of California Press

Benedict, R (1946) *The Chrysanthemum and the Sword*, Tokyo: Tuttle

Buruma, I (1984) *A Japanese Mirror: Heroes and Villains in Japanese Culture*, London: Phoenix

Clifford, W (1976) *Crime Control in Japan*, Lexington, MA: Lexington Books

Doi, T (1977) *The Anatomy of Dependence*, Tokyo: Tuttle

Evans, R (1977) 'Changing labor markets and criminal behavior in Japan' 16 *Journal of Asian Studies* 477–89

Foote, DH (1992) 'The benevolent paternalism of Japanese criminal justice' 80 *California Law Review* 317

Fujimoto, T (1978) *Crime and Delinquency Among the Japanese Americans*, Tokyo: Institute of Comparative Law

Garland, D (2001) *The Culture of Control*, Chicago: University of Chicago Press

Hayward, KJ (2004) *City Limits: Crime, Consumer Culture and the Urban Experience*, London: GlassHouse Press

Hendry, J (1987) *Understanding Japanese Society*, London: Routledge

Hirschi, T (1969) *Causes of Delinquency*, Berkeley, CA: University of California Press

Ishihara, S (2001) 'Nihon yo: uchinaru bouei wo', *Sankei Shimbun*, 8 May

Komiya, N (1999) 'A cultural study of the low crime rate in Japan' 39 *British Journal of Criminology* 369–90

Kusuda-Smick, V (ed) (1990) *Crime Prevention and Control in the United States and Japan*, Tokyo: Transnational Juris

Maeda, A (2004) 'Utopia of the prison house', in Fuji, JA (ed), *Text and the City: Essays on Japanese Modernity*, Durham, NC: Duke UP

Magasatsu, M (1982) *The Modern Samurai Society: Duty and Dependence in Contemporary Japan*, New York: AMA

Merriman, D (1991) 'An economic analysis of the post-World War II decline in the Japanese Crime Rate' 7 *Journal of Quantitative Criminology* 19–39

Miyazawa, S (1991) 'The private sector and law enforcement in Japan', in WT Gormley (ed), *Privatization and its Alternatives*, Madison: University of Wisconsin Press

Morrison, W (1995) *Theoretical Criminology: From Modernity to Post-Modernism*, London: Cavendish Publishing

Nakane, C (1970) *Japanese Society*, Tokyo: Tuttle

Raz, J (1993) *Aspects of Otherness in Japanese Culture*, Tokyo: ISL

Reischauer, EO (1978) *The Japanese*, Tokyo: Tuttle

Sasson, T (1995) *Crime Talk: How Citizens Construct a Social Problem*, New York: Aldine de Gruyter

Sato, I (1996) *Kamikaze Biker*, Chicago: University of Chicago Press

Shelly, L (1981) *Crime and Modernization: The Impact of Industrialization and Urbanization on Crime*, Carbondale: University of Southern Illinois Press

Thornton, RY and Endo, K (1992) *Preventing Crime in America and Japan: A Comparative Study*, London: ME Sharp

Westerman, TD and Burfeind, JW (1991) *Crime and Justice in Two Societies: Japan and the United States*, Pacific Grove: Brookes Cole

Part 5

Terms of Engagement

Chapter 17
Drug and Alcohol Research: The Case for Cultural Criminology

Fiona Measham[1]

Introduction

> It will only be the re-emergence of humanity, meaning that due acknowledgement is given to the properties and powers of real people forged in the real world, which overcomes the present poverty of social theory.
>
> *(Archer 2000: 306)*

This chapter considers recent developments in legal and illicit drug use, paying particular regard to the last 20 years in the UK. With an escalation and diversification in the consumption of legal and illicit drugs by contemporary youth and young adults, there has been a renewed focus of attention by academics, policy makers and practitioners in this area. Much of the research has, of necessity, involved charting overall trends in usage, alongside the medical, legal and policy implications of this consumption. For example, in the UK there are a substantial number of studies charting changes in illicit drug use, including longitudinal studies of young people (eg Aldridge *et al* 1999), annual national schools surveys of pupils (eg Balding 2001), and annual national household surveys of adults (eg Ramsay *et al* 2001). It is timely now to move beyond such 'mapping' exercises to reflect on the broader conceptual issues regarding these changing patterns of consumption.

One such attempt to move from mapping to explaining changing patterns of drug use is the normalisation thesis advocated in the UK in the 1990s and outlined in more detail below. The normalisation thesis is an explanatory framework that attempts to account for the drug-related attitudinal and behavioural change by both users and non-users through a consideration of the socio-economic and cultural context for such change. It is suggested that factors such as the extension of adolescence, a changing labour market, and the globalisation of goods and services might all play a part in changing patterns of consumption. A central component of the normalisation thesis relates to the rationality of consumption practices; it suggests that young people utilise a cost-benefit analysis in which they assess both the positive and negative aspects of drug use in their drug taking decisions.

After discussing the normalisation thesis, this chapter considers the possible benefits of cultural criminology for the drug and alcohol field, making the case to modify the normalisation thesis by a consideration of not only the rationality but also the emotionality inherent in the pursuit of pharmacological pleasure and the desire for altered states of intoxication. Drawing on recent developments in cultural criminology and their reconsideration of the agency-structure debate, I suggest that drug and alcohol research can benefit from the emergent criminology of transgression and its reconsideration of agency.

1 With thanks to Eddie Scouller, Maria Measham and the editors. For Rob McCracken – original junglist, Manchester crew – 1972–2004.

The normalisation debate

In the mid-1980s there were early indications of changing patterns of consumption of illicit drugs in the UK, and more recently across mainland Europe, North America and elsewhere (EMCDDA 2000). From the early 1990s onwards, increased lifetime prevalence of drug use was evident in a range of studies of young people including national schools surveys (eg Miller and Plant 1996), local longitudinal studies (eg Measham et al 1994; Aldridge et al 1999), and other local surveys of young people (eg Meikle et al 1996). In the British Crime Survey, for example, an annual national household survey of adults that provides the most robust British data on prevalence of drug use, lifetime prevalence of drug use by 16–29 year olds increased from 28% in 1992 to 50% in 2000 (Ramsay et al 2001).

'Normalisation' refers to the accommodation, acknowledgment or recognition of a minority group or minority behaviour within a larger group or society. In relation to drugs, this accommodation is accomplished by non-users as well as users, and is thus reflected not only in youth culture but also in wider society. A growing body of UK research across the 1990s indicated considerable changes in the drug-related attitudes and behaviours of drug users and non-users, which thus demanded an examination of the broader socio-economic and cultural context for such change. Significant changes underway in relation to drug users, for example, included increased availability, experimentation and use by young people from across the social spectrum, suggesting that previously central structural determinants such as socio-economic class, poverty and unemployment, along with gender and ethnicity and even age to some extent, could no longer be clear predictors of (or protectors from) experimentation with illicit drugs (Parker et al 1995). Previous sociological and psychological theories of drug use – which had drawn upon subcultural theory (eg Hall and Jefferson 1976), individual pathology (eg Hawkins et al 1992), peer pressure (eg Dielman et al 1987) and structural determinants (eg Coffield et al 1986) – could not adequately or entirely explain this process of change in relation to recreational drug use during the 1990s.

Alongside the undoubtedly large quantitative upsurge in young people's recreational drug use over the last 15 years or so in the UK, proponents of normalisation have argued that there has been an equally significant cultural and attitudinal shift in wider society. The concept of normalisation was adopted to help explain an ongoing process of change with indications that young people's recreational, non-problematic drug use was starting to move from its previously marginal, deviant and subcultural status towards inclusion within mainstream popular culture and weekend leisure-time celebrations. Thus South considers that 'it cannot be denied that drug use is of enormous contemporary importance – whether as symbol, social problem or fashion accessory ... the whole issue and persistence of drugs as a feature of everyday life has become and will remain "normalised"' (1999: 6–7).

Two caveats to the normalisation debate have relevance to the discussion in this chapter. Firstly, whilst some consensus has been reached regarding a process of normalisation of cannabis and a lack of normalisation of heroin and crack cocaine in the UK (eg Shiner and Newburn 1999; South 1999), the debate continues in relation to so-called recreational and dance drugs such as ecstasy, cocaine and amphetamines (eg Measham et al 2001; Shiner 2003). Secondly, this ongoing process of recognition and accommodation does not necessarily extend to moral acceptance or approval of illicit drug use.

The normalisation thesis adopted six key indicators of change: drug availability or offers; drug trying or lifetime prevalence of use; current or regular drug use; future intentions in use; being 'drugwise'; and the cultural accommodation of the illicit (Parker *et al* 1998). The eroding of significant differences in overall drug offers and drug trying by gender, ethnicity and socio-economic class led to a need for a conceptualisation of recreational drug use that went well beyond structural determinants to consider the role of young people's own decision-making processes in experimentation and use. Moving beyond statistics, the normalisation thesis attempted to initiate a conceptual reconsideration of motivations and meanings of drug use in recent years. In particular, a new emphasis on adolescent agency was recognised in the cost-benefit decision-making processes young people discussed when interviewed about drugs (eg Coffield and Gofton 1994; Hirst and McCameley-Finney 1994; Perri 6 *et al* 1997). This cost-benefit analysis emphasised the potential rationality of psychoactive consumption in the functional pursuit of leisure-time pleasures, drawing on rational choice theory in criminology (Cornish and Clarke 1986).

There have been two limitations to the subsequent normalisation debate. Firstly, although the normalisation thesis has resulted in some welcome debate regarding the broader significance of drug trends, both the critique of normalisation (eg Shiner and Newburn 1997, 1999) and overviews of normalisation (eg Taylor 1999; Henderson 1999) have concentrated on the quantitative component in their characterisation of the normalisation thesis and in the ensuing debate on young people's drug use in the UK. Whilst the normalisation thesis kick-started a conceptual debate and recognised the importance of cultural change in relation to recreational drug use, the concentration on lifetime prevalence largely excluded the five other indicators of normalisation outlined by Parker *et al* (1998) and arguably excluded the most important one, which was the wider cultural accommodation of drug related attitudes and behaviours amongst drug-using and non drug-using groups of young people and in society more generally (*ibid*: 156–57). The notable exception has been South (1999), who has noted the cultural shift from deviant to everyday in relation to British recreational drug use when arguing that 'something profound has happened in relation to the place of drugs in everyday life since the mid-1980s' (*ibid*: 6).

Secondly, whilst research on cost-benefit decision-making processes by young people has been a valuable antidote to peer pressure explanations that denied the individual agency of youthful recreational drug use, there has been an over-emphasis on rationality in drug decision-making. It is necessary, therefore, both to reassert the relevance of culture and to reintroduce emotionality to a conceptualisation of agency in contemporary consumption.

Given the enormous changes in drug-related attitudes and behaviours and the wider socio-economic context of consumption in the last 20 years, and given that drug use can no longer be considered a result merely of individual pathology, peer pressure, subcultural rebellion or structural determinants, a new explanatory framework has become necessary. Cultural aspects of drug use then take centre stage. However, whilst there has been some recognition of the importance of the broader socio-cultural context of drug and alcohol use in relation to gender (eg Measham 2002; Ettorre 2004), and in relation to the 1990s dance drug and dance club scene (eg Redhead 1993; Thornton 1995), by and large little consideration has been given to the broader setting for consumption since Zinberg's classic study (1984).

Thus changing patterns of consumption demand further inquiry, in relation to both the cultural context of drug use and a reconsideration of agency and structure. In this enterprise cultural criminology – a criminological perspective that focuses on the convergence of the cultural and the criminal worlds – may be of use.

The contribution of cultural criminology

In relation to the drug and alcohol field, cultural criminology is relevant both to explorations of the ways in which crime and deviance can be conceptualised as culture – in terms of cultural meanings, styles and representations of drug-related attitudes, behaviours and social groups – and also to the ways in which popular and subcultural worlds come to be problematised and criminalised (Ferrell and Sanders 1995). The latter is particularly pertinent to youth culture and young adults when considering contemporary political and media concerns about recreational drug use, such as the 'rave' and dance club scene and 'binge' drinking in the UK (Brain and Parker 1999; Murji 1998; Shapiro 1999; Forsyth 2001). The relevance of cultural criminology to the cultural context of young people's recreational drug use is apparent in both the historical grounding of cultural criminology in cultural studies and the influential work on youth subcultures by the Birmingham Centre for Contemporary Cultural Studies in the 1970s, and the contemporary focus on the ways in which criminal and deviant behaviours are located in everyday cultural practices.

'Carnival' and the crime-leisure continuum

The core relationship between culture and crime in cultural criminology leads to the identification of a crime-leisure continuum. In the UK there are historical continuities in the characterisation of the 'problem of leisure' as the 'problem of youth' with decades-old concerns about young people's drinking, drug use, disorder and presence on the streets (Pearson 1983; Kohn 1997). Historical and socio-cultural analysis suggests that drug and alcohol consumption can be contextualised in the central role of licensed leisure locations to young people, with the pub or bar remaining the primary leisure location. The British distinctions of a 'binge and brawl' culture include the juxtaposition of weekday sobriety and restraint with weekend drunkenness and disorder and consequent public anxiety about youth and young adults at play (Tuck 1989; Gofton 1990; Marsh and Fox Kibby 1992; Tomsen 1997; Engineer et al 2003). Official responses, however, have resulted in a gradual and ongoing liberalisation of licensing restrictions on licensed leisure venues in the UK which has facilitated the development of a thriving city centre night-time economy and the pre-eminence of alcohol-fuelled leisure (Hobbs et al 2000). Thus popular cultural worlds may be sanctioned and regulated whilst concurrently being problematised and criminalised.

With increased working hours, increased work-related stress and the packaging of the weekend as 'time out' from weekday pressures, the notion of 'carnival' is as pertinent to contemporary leisure as it was in the Middle Ages (Presdee 2000). The relevance to drug and alcohol studies is that the concept of carnival recognises the *bounding* of consumption evident in contemporary recreational drug and alcohol use. The carnival is a period of pleasure and excess that sanctions and elevates temporary transgression from everyday life, bounded by time, space, participants and behaviour. Thus the notion of carnival recognises both the everyday and the fantastical in night-time leisure. The significance for drug and alcohol studies, and in particular the normalisation debate, is that, whilst proponents of normalisation argue that illicit recreational drug use is moving from subcultural to mainstream popular culture, and whilst critics of normalisation maintain the transgressive nature of drug use, the notion of carnival can facilitate an accommodation of both in contemporary performative society.

Furthermore, whilst there has been an emphasis on the dichotomous relationship between the culture of control and surveillance at work on the one hand, and the desire for freedom from such constraints in weekend 'time out' on the other, a more useful avenue of exploration is the relationship between cultural and criminal practices evident in the notion of a crime-leisure continuum. The dynamic and dialectical rather than dichotomous relationship between constraint and creativity in the commodification and performance of leisure can be explored in the meanings and motivations for the consumption of illicit drugs as a leisure-time pursuit, which can be seen as both conforming to and challenging consumption-based leisure. By locating the consumption of drugs and alcohol in their cultural context on a crime-leisure continuum, rather than as necessarily problematic, addictive or dependent behaviour, such consumption can be seen as one aspect of the 'controlled loss of control' in late modern consumer society (Hayward 2002; Measham 2002). Drugs potentially serve therefore as both escape from regulatory consumer-oriented society through self expression and liberation, and yet as the logical consequence or extension of consumer society, with one's body/mind potentially the ultimate leisure machine, in the psychoactive facilitation of 'head space' as leisure space (Measham 2004).

Young people show a willingness to experiment with and enjoy a range of risk taking, exhilarating and aspirational activities and sensations, which includes the experience of intoxication. Both increased sessional consumption of alcohol and increased recreational drug use by young people through the 1990s and into the 21st century are indications of an increased desire for altered states of intoxication or determined drunkenness, with the packaging and prioritising of the pursuit of physical and pharmacological pleasure (Measham 1996, 2005). In relation to alcohol, studies have shown that young people across the social spectrum prioritise 'having fun', and increasingly having fun is associated with enjoying the physical as well as social effects of drinking alcohol and in particular getting drunk. A sizeable minority of young drinkers (for example, 28% of 16 year olds in Parker *et al* 1998) report that they enjoy drinking alcohol precisely because they like the experience of being drunk. This pursuit of pleasure is seen as both an expression of and reaction against the experience of growing up in late modern consumer society, with increased stress and debt, longer working hours, less job security and delayed full adult independence, linked to 'the discontent arising out of material and ontological uncertainties which globalization engenders' (Young 2003: 402).

An important issue that crosses the boundaries of cultural criminology, cultural geography and sociology relates to the night-time economy, the contemporary crime-leisure continuum and the emergent criminology of transgression. Within the crime-leisure continuum, the responses and responsibilities of national government, local authorities and the alcoholic beverage industry in the regulation, containment and criminalisation of leisure become a cause for concern. Local councils and licensing authorities are aware of tensions in policing and regulating the night-time economy alongside the promotion of the commercially profitable, corporate leisure sector. Changing notions of leisure and pleasure in late modern consumer society relate to the growth of a pick 'n' mix culture of chemical consumption (Parker and Measham 1994) and can be seen as part of a far broader shift in late modern times towards a commercial exploitation of the pursuit of pleasure and a commodification of transgression across a spectrum of illicit and exceptional activities in Western performative culture (eg Rojek 2000). Furthermore, the revival of the body as a site of study has led to a consideration of issues relating to the gendering and sexing of the body as a site of criminalisation and medicalisation, and to issues of materiality and subjectivity, evident not only in illicit drug use but also body piercing, cosmetic surgery, tattoos and body art (eg Featherstone 2000). At the heart of the crime-leisure continuum is the city itself, physically, socially and symbolically the 'wild zone' (Stanley 1997) at the centre of urban life, of leisure and of humanity, embodying pleasure, excess and gratification. This results in, as Hobbs *et al* note, 'the establishment of the commercial exploitation of traditional forms of liminal expression into part of the bedrock of the local political economy' (2000: 712).

Even more than with alcohol, however, this has been the case with drugs. The repertoire of illicit psychoactive drugs which may be consumed during leisure time before, during or after attending pubs, clubs or bars, and which vary by region and demographic base, now includes cannabis, ecstasy, cocaine, amphetamines, methamphetamine, ketamine, magic mushrooms, GHB, poppers and Viagra (Measham *et al* 2001; Deehan and Saville 2003). Moreover, the marginalisation and criminalisation of (some) leisure is evident in official responses to the dance drug and dance club scene that developed in the UK from the late 1980s onwards (Measham *et al* 1998; Shapiro 1999).

The bounding of consumption relates not only to temporality but also spatiality. The casualties of the prioritisation of pleasure are, inevitably, those excluded from the new leisure society and those most vulnerable to exploitation and abuse within it. Changes in licensed leisure locations, licensing legislation and police targeting and enforcement have resulted in the mushrooming of urban café bars facilitating *al fresco* alcohol consumption (at a price) whilst local by-laws in the UK outlaw drinking on streets and park benches, resulting in the marginalisation and criminalisation of street drinkers economically excluded from the new licensed leisure venues (Brain and Parker 1997; Chatterton and Hollands 2003). This is part of a wider process of regulation and surveillance of urban space with the expansion of CCTV and private security firms, and with increasing restrictions on young people's use of public space, producing a 'culture of control' (Garland 2001) which perversely results in heightened rather than reduced anxieties of crime and disorder (Ditton 2000; Hayward 2002). With the commercial development of clubs and café bars, the contemporary commodification of pleasure, with CCTV surveillance on the streets and in the clubs and pubs of cities across the UK, there is evidence that the 'wild zone' is now being pushed to the perimeters of the city, to out-of-town leisure centres, to virtual space, to wastelands, and to the subversion of urban space (Measham 2004).

And what of the employees in the crime-leisure 'wild zone'? The apparent increase in the international smuggling and trafficking of human beings (as well as drugs) has fed into the sex and drugs industries and led to an upsurge in related violence, assault, rape and murder (Vocks and Nijboer 2000; Aronowitz 2001). For those at the front line and lowest levels of the illegal economy (drug 'mules', street-level dealers, sex workers, illegal workers), working within a limited range of life choices, the minimal rewards are offset by high risks such as assault, imprisonment or deportation. For the consumers of the sex, drugs and leisure industries, however, the politics of pleasure may be of less concern.

Emotionality and agency

Cultural criminologists such as those writing in this volume are engaged in the conceptual development of the agency-structure debate and a reconsideration of the role of emotionality in criminality, both of which can potentially enrich drug and alcohol studies and allow the field to move beyond the current plethora of mapping and prevalence work. Crucial to cultural criminology is the role of both collective experience and individual agency in criminality and the resulting recognition of the performance of pleasure in crime. Petty and persistent crime by young people – for example joyriding, gang membership, computer hacking, cyber crime, 'binge drinking' and shoplifting – may have little to do with rational decision-making or material gain. In relation to shoplifting and joyriding Katz has noted that 'getting away with something in celebratory style is more important than keeping anything or getting anywhere in particular' (1988: 52).

As discussed above, whilst the normalisation debate has assisted a deeper understanding of the motivations for consumption and a recognition of the positive perceptions of users, the emphasis has been on the rationality of the cost-benefit decision-making process. Cultural criminology stresses the pleasures as well as problems in criminological enterprise and allows both a reassertion of the role of emotionality in drug use and a reconsideration of agency. As Young (2003: 408) highlights, 'for the transgressors ... the utilitarian core is often there, but around it is constructed a frequent delight in excess, a glee in breaking the rules, a reassertion of dignity and identity'. However, although Young suggests that 'Katz throws the baby out with the bath water, simply to invert the conventional wisdom by highlighting agency and rejecting structure' (2003: 408), Hayward has noted that, in order to attempt to understand the complexities of agency and structure in relation to criminological motivations, it is first necessary to reassert the significance of agency in a debate embedded in liberal criminological structural determinism. Thus as Hayward points out (2004: 152–57), simply to state, as Young does, that we must embrace 'Merton with energy, Katz with structure' is to miss the point; Katz was reasserting agency when already working within a climate of structural determinism.

Clearly, in relation to the recreational use of legal and illicit drugs, decision-making processes involve a consideration of aspects of price, access, availability and cultural desirability of specific drugs. Not simply a lifestyle choice, however, the changing nature of drug use must be located within the broader context of socio-economic and cultural change in the last 20 years. The differential impact of socio-economic change on different sections of society means that choice – including choice in relation to drug use – is not something shared equally by all those within and on the margins of consumer society. This is illustrated in the national figures on self-reported cocaine and heroin use in the *British Crime Survey* (Ramsay *et al* 2001). Self-reported cocaine use is higher amongst those who are economically active and in higher household income, higher educational attainment, and higher social class categories living in affluent urban areas; whilst self-reported heroin use continues to be more likely to be reported by those who are economically inactive and in lower household income, lower educational attainment, and lower social class categories living in mature home-owning and council estates/low income areas. Self-report studies, however, have identified increased cocaine usage by women, lower income groups and younger adults than previously (eg Parker *et al* 2002).

Drugs, then, represent both the escape from contemporary capitalist consumer society and are themselves the object of consumption; demonstrating a combined emotionality and rationality in motivations for drug use. However, whilst there has been a recognition of the pleasures of consumption in relation to gender and drug use (Ettorre 1992; Henderson 1999), the complexities of the elements of both emotionality and rationality in the leisure-time pursuit of pharmacological pleasure have yet to be fully explored in the drug and alcohol field. Katz's point relates to drug and alcohol research, as much as to criminology in general, when he states that 'the study of crime has been preoccupied with a search for background forces, usually defects in the offenders' psychological backgrounds or social environments, to the neglect of the positive, often wonderful attractions within the lived experience of criminality' (Katz 1988: 3).

Within criminology, the agency-structure debate has been developed in the work of Messerschmidt. Messerschmidt's theory of structured action and the concept of 'doing gender' through 'doing crime', which itself builds on earlier work on the relationship between agency and structure by Giddens, West, Zimmerman and Fenstermaker (eg West and Zimmerman 1987), suggests that it is through social action that specific social structures are constructed. Indeed Messerschmidt notes that 'social action is creative, inventive, and novel, but it never occurs separately from, or external to, social structures' (1993: 77).

The decision-making processes and pathways through drug offers, abstinence, experimentation, use and cessation can be likened to the realist social theorist Archer's concept of 'internal conversations'. These internal conversations are directed both inwards towards our own personal concerns and outwards as reflections on the external world and our social roles in it, resulting in an internal dialogue of 'ethical, creative and personalised reflection about how far should we go, and what do we judge to be the best way to do it' (2000: 299). Allowing a move beyond the rational cost-benefit equation, Archer suggests that 'the "inner conversation" is how our personal emergent powers are exercised on and in the world ... it is what determines our being-in-the-world'; indeed 'it is we human beings who determine our priorities and define our personal identities in terms of what we care about. Therefore we are quintessentially evaluative beings' (*ibid*: 318). In Archer's attempt at 'revindicating human powers' she suggests that 'the story to tell is about the confluence of causal powers – those of external reality, and our own which emerge from our relations with it: the two ultimately being mediated through the "internal conversation". It is the only story really worth telling, for it is about the transcendental power of human beings to transform the social world and themselves' (*ibid*: 315).

Archer's body of work developing the agency-structure debate has two elements of particular significance to the cultural criminology enterprise. First, she attempts to disentangle the interplay between culture, structure and agency in order to understand the specifics of the relationship between the three. Secondly, Archer reasserts the emotionality of agency. These ongoing debates within and alongside cultural criminology on agency-structure, structured action and the emotionality of agency can potentially both inform and invigorate the field of drug and alcohol research.

Conclusion

For drug and alcohol abuse, then, there has been the need for a new conceptual understanding of contemporary consumption that can account for significant changes in drug-related attitudes and behaviour experienced within the broader context of socio-economic and cultural change. Thus the work of Parker *et al* (1998) (see also Coffield and Gofton 1994; Coggans and McKellar 1994; South 1999) has explored the ways in which motivations for drug use might not be adequately explained by peer pressure, psychological dysfunction, subcultural style, or by structural determinants alone, but may be understood as rational, cost-benefit decision-making processes young people undertake when accepting and rejecting the drug offers which undoubtedly mark contemporary adolescence. A consideration of contemporary cultural criminology, however, encourages us to push beyond these rational cost-benefit decisions when exploring motivations for drug and alcohol use by recognising too the emotional aspects of psychoactive consumption (see relatedly Hayward 2004: 101–04).

Cultural criminology can enhance drug and alcohol research in a number of ways. Firstly, it encourages a consideration of the broader historical and socio-cultural context for consumption by locating individual behaviours on a crime-leisure continuum, thereby facilitating an understanding of the complexities of behaviours which may or may not be illegal in certain countries at certain times but nevertheless involve an element of state regulation or social control. Moving forward from normalisation, the notion of the performance of carnival allows an incorporation of elements of both transgression and accommodation in weekend leisure-time excess and facilitates progress beyond the *impasse* of normalisation. Secondly, a reassertion of agency and a deeper understanding of the emotionality as well as rationality of consumption is one of the most stimulating areas for future research in drug and alcohol studies. Indeed, as Archer has noted, the causal powers of agency 'enable people to reflect upon their social context, and to act reflexively towards it, either individually or collectively. Only by virtue of such powers can human beings be the active shapers of their socio-cultural context, rather than the passive recipients of it' (2000: 308). Finally, and in general terms, cultural criminology locates the changing nature of drug and alcohol use within the broader socio-cultural dynamics of consumption, control and leisure time/space, and thus aids in the development of a broader criminology of transgression.

References

Aldridge, J, Parker, H and Measham, F (1999) *Drug Trying and Drug Use Across Adolescence: A Longitudinal Study of Young People's Drug Taking in Two Regions of Northern England*, DPAS Paper No 1, London: Home Office

Archer, M (2000) *Being Human: The Problem of Agency*, Cambridge: CUP

Aronowitz, A (2001) 'Smuggling and trafficking in human beings: the phenomenon, the markets that drive it and the organisations that promote it' 9 *European Journal on Criminal Policy and Research* 163–95

Balding, J (2001) *Young People in 2000*, Exeter: Schools Health Education Unit

Brain, K and Parker, H (1999) *Drinking With Design: Alcopops, Desginer Drinks and Youth Culture*, London: Portman

Chatterton, P and Hollands, R (2003) *Urban Nightscapes: Youth Cultures, Pleasure Spaces and Corporate Power*, London: Routledge

Coffield, F and Gofton, L (1994) *Drugs and Young People*, London: Institute for Public Policy Research

Coffield, F, Borril, C and Marshall, S (1986) *Growing Up at the Margins*, Milton Keynes: Open UP

Coggans, N and McKellar, S (1994) 'Drug use amongst peers: peer pressure or peer preference?' 1(1) *Drugs: Education, Prevention and Policy* 15–26

Cornish, D and Clarke, R (eds) (1986) *The Reasoning Criminal: Rational Choice Perspectives on Offending*, New York: Springer-Verlag

Deehan, A and Saville, E (2003) *Calculating the Risk: Recreational Drug Use Among Clubbers in the South East of England*, Home Office Online Report 43/03, London: Home Office

Dielman, T, Campanelli, P, Shope, J and Butchart, A (1987) 'Susceptibility of peer pressure, self esteem and health locus of control as correlates of adolescent substance abuse' 14 *Health Education Quarterly* 207–21

Ditton, J (2000) 'Crime and the city: public attitudes towards open-street CCTV in Glasgow' 40 *British Journal of Criminology* 692–709

EMCDDA (2000) *Annual Report on the State of the Drugs Problem in the European Union – 2000*, Luxembourg: Office for Official Publications of the European Communities

Engineer, R, Phillips, A, Thompson, J and Nicholls, J (2003) *Drunk and Disorderly: A Qualitative Study of Binge Drinking Among 18 to 24 Year Olds*, Home Office Research Study No 262, London: Home Office

Ettore, E (1992) *Women and Substance Use*, Basingstoke: Macmillan

Ettorre, E (2004) 'Revisioning women and drug use: gender sensitivity, embodiment and reducing harm', *International Journal of Drug Policy*, Special Edition: Social theory in drug research and harm reduction, forthcoming

Featherstone, M (ed) (2000) *Body Modification*, London: Sage

Ferrell, J and Sanders, C (eds) (1995) *Cultural Criminology*, Boston: Northeastern University Press

Forsyth, A (2001) 'Distorted? A quantitative exploration of drug fatality reports in the popular press' 12 *International Journal of Drug Policy* 435–53

Garland, D (2001) *The Culture of Control: Crime and Social Order in Contemporary Society*, Oxford: OUP

Gofton, L (1990) 'On the town: drink and the "new lawlessness"' 29 *Youth and Society*, April, 33–39

Hall, S and Jefferson, T (eds) (1976) *Resistance through Rituals: Youth Subcultures in Post-war Britain*, London: HarperCollins

Hawkins, J, Catalare, R and Miller, J (1992) 'Risk and protective factors for alcohol and other drugs problems in adolescence and early adulthood' 112(1) *Psychological Bulletin* 64–105

Hayward, K (2002) 'The vilification and pleasures of youthful transgression', in Muncie, J, Hughes, G and McLaughlin, E (eds), *Youth Justice: Critical Readings*, London: Sage

Hayward, K (2004) *City Limits: Crime, Consumer Culture and the Urban Experience*, London: GlassHouse Press

Henderson, S (1999) 'Drugs and culture: the question of gender', in South, N (ed), *Drugs: Cultures, Controls and Everyday Life*, London: Sage, pp 36–48

Hirst, J and McCameley-Finney, A (1994) *The Place and Meaning of Drugs in the Lives of Young People*, Sheffield: Sheffield Hallam University

Hobbs, D, Lister, S, Hadfield, P, Winlow, S and Hall, S (2000) 'Receiving shadows: governance and liminality in the night-time economy' 51(4) *British Journal of Sociology* 701–18

Katz J (1988) *Seductions of Crime: Moral and Sensual Attractions in Doing Evil*, New York: Basic Books

Kohn, M (1997) 'The chemical generation and its ancestors: dance crazes and drug panics across eight decades' 8(3) *International Journal of Drug Policy* 137–42

Marsh, P and Fox Kibby, K (1992) *Drinking and Public Disorder: A Report of Research Conducted for the Portman Group by MCM Research*, London: Portman Group

Measham, F (1996) 'The "Big Bang" approach to sessional drinking: changing patterns of alcohol consumption amongst young people in north west England' 4(3) *Addiction Research* 283–99

Measham, F (2002) '"Doing gender" – "Doing drugs": conceptualising the gendering of drugs cultures' 29(2) *Contemporary Drug Problems* 335–73

Measham, F (2004) 'Play space: historical and socio-cultural reflections on drugs, licensed leisure locations, commercialisation and control', *International Journal of Drug Policy*, Special Edition: Social theory in drug research and harm reduction, forthcoming

Measham, F (2005) 'The decline of ecstasy, the rise of "binge drinking" and the persistence of pleasure', *Probation Journal*, Special Edition: Rethinking drugs and crime

Measham, F, Aldridge, J and Parker, H (2001) *Dancing on Drugs: Risk, Health and Hedonism in the British Club Scene*, London: Free Association

Measham, F, Newcombe, R and Parker, H (1994) 'The normalization of recreational drug use amongst young people in North-West England' 45(2) *British Journal of Sociology* 287–312

Measham, F, Parker, H and Aldridge, J (1998) 'The teenage transition: from adolescent recreational drug use to the young adult dance culture in Britain in the mid-1990s', in Power, R (ed), *Journal of Drug Issues* 28(1) Special Edition: *Contemporary Issues Concerning Illicit Drug Use in the British Isles* 9–32

Meikle, A, McCallum, C, Marshall, A and Coster, G (1996) *Drugs Survey on a Selection of Secondary School Pupils in the Glasgow Area Aged 13–16*, Glasgow: Glasgow Drugs Prevention Team

Messerschmidt, J (1993) *Masculinities and Crime: Critique and Reconceptualisation of Theory*, Lanham: Rowman and Littlefield

Miller, P and Plant, M (1996) 'Drinking, smoking and illicit drug use among 15 and 16 year-olds in the United Kingdom' 313 *British Medical Journal* 394–97

Murji, K (1998, 2000) 'The agony and the ecstasy: drugs, media and morality', in Coomber, R (ed), *The Control of Drugs and Drug Users: Reason or Reaction?*, Amsterdam: Harwood Academic

Parker, H and Measham, F (1994) 'Pick 'n' mix: changing patterns of illicit drug use amongst 1990s adolescents' 1(1) *Drugs: Education, Prevention and Policy* 5–13

Parker, H, Aldridge, J and Measham, F (1998) *Illegal Leisure: The Normalization of Adolescent Recreational Drug Use*, London: Routledge

Parker, H, Measham, F and Aldridge, J (1995) *Drugs Futures: Changing Patterns of Drug Use Amongst English Youth*, ISDD Research Monograph No 7, London: ISDD

Parker, H, Williams, L and Aldridge, J (2002) 'The normalisation of "sensible" recreational drug use: further evidence from the north west England longitudinal study' 36(4) *Sociology* 941–64

Pearson, G (1983) *Hooligan: A History of Respectable Fears*, Basingstoke: Macmillan

Perri 6, Jupp, B, Perry, H and Laskey, K (1997) *The Substance of Youth*, York: Joseph Rowntree Foundation

Presdee, M (2000) *Cultural Criminology and the Carnival of Crime*, London: Routledge

Ramsay, M, Baker, P, Goulden, C, Sharp, C and Sondhi, A (2001) *Drug Misuse Declared in 2000: Results from the British Crime Survey*, Home Office Research Study No 224, London: Home Office Research, Development and Statistics Directorate

Redhead, S (ed) (1993) *Rave Off: Politics and Deviance in Contemporary Youth Culture*, Aldershot: Avebury

Rojek, C (2000) *Leisure and Culture*, Basingstoke: Macmillan

Shapiro, H (1999) 'Dances with drugs: pop music, drugs and youth culture', in South, N (ed), *Drugs: Cultures, Controls and Everyday Life*, London: Sage

Shiner, M (2003) 'Out of harm's way? Illicit drug use, medicalization and the law' 43 *British Journal of Criminology* 772–96

Shiner, M and Newburn, T (1997) 'Definitely, maybe not? The normalisation of recreational drug use amongst young people' 31(3) *Sociology* 511–29

Shiner, M and Newburn, T (1999) 'Taking tea with Noel: the place & meaning of drug use in everyday life', in South, N (ed), *Drugs: Cultures, Controls and Everyday Life*, London: Sage, pp 139–59

South, N (1999) 'Debating drugs & everyday life: normalisation, prohibition & "otherness"', in *Drugs: Cultures, Controls and Everyday Life*, London: Sage, pp 1–15

Stanley, C (1997) 'Not drowning but waving: urban narratives of dissent in the wild zone', in Redhead, S (ed) with Wynne, D and O'Connor, J, *The Clubcultures Reader: Readings in Popular Cultural Studies*, Oxford: Blackwell

Taylor, I (1999) *Crime in Context: A Critical Criminology of Market Societies*, Cambridge: Polity

Thornton, S (1995) *Club Cultures: Music, Media and Subcultural Capital*, Cambridge: Polity

Tomsen, S (1997) 'A top night: social protest, masculinity and the culture of drinking violence' 37(1) *British Journal of Criminology* 90–102

Tuck, M (1989) *Drinking and Disorder: A Study of Non-metropolitan Violence*, Home Office Research Study No 108, London: HMSO

Vocks, J and Nijboer, J (2000) 'The promised land: a study of trafficking in women from Central and Eastern Europe to the Netherlands' 8(3) *European Journal on Criminal Policy and Research* 379–88

West, C and Zimmerman, D (1987) 'Doing gender' 1(2) *Gender and Society* 125–51

Young, J (2003) 'Merton with energy, Katz with structure: the sociology of vindictiveness and the criminology of transgression' 7(3) *Theoretical Criminology* 389–414

Zinberg, N (1984) *Drug, Set and Setting: The Basis for Controlled Intoxicant Use*, New Haven: Yale UP

Chapter 18

Crime, Culture and Visual Methodologies: Ethno-mimesis as Performative Praxis

Maggie O'Neill

Introduction

This chapter will discuss the importance of visual and performative methodologies to cultural criminology in helping to facilitate a better understanding of social issues and problems – such as sex work and anti asylum feeling. Society, as Presdee argues (2000), is saturated by images of crime. The combination of social research and cultural analysis of fictive texts can give us a richer understanding of crime and deviance. We can also approach a more sensuous understanding of society and lived experience through an examination of fictive texts that emerge from social processes and practices. For example, in my second level sociology module we look at the detective novel to explain transgressive imaginations. Discussing the crime novel, Clarke asserts that 'rather than crime being an object of "repulsion" detective stories suggest that crime is simultaneously an object of fascination and attraction – an issue from which we gain pleasure' (2001: 101). Detective fiction therefore provides alternative 'ways of seeing' crime that can add to the ways we understand and imagine relationships between order and disorder.

My own socio-cultural research (with sex workers, communities affected by prostitution and 'new arrivals') is situated at the intersection of critical theory, ethnography and experimental/alternative forms of re-presenting the lived experience of those on the borders, at the margins, and in the liminal spaces.

Using participatory action research (PAR), and what I call renewed methodologies for working and writing in contemporary society marked by post-emotionalism, consumerism and commodification (indicative of Bauman's (1995) liquid modernity) the lived experience of marginalised communities is presented artistically through performative praxis. Re-presenting ethnographic work in art forms can help audiences to gain a rich understanding of the complexity of lived experience, that may throw light on broader structures, processes and practices. Moreover, in re-presenting ethnographic work visually, artistically, poetically, we may reach a wider audience, beyond academic communities, and inspire interventions that produce action/praxis/change. I have argued elsewhere that the university has an important civic role to get involved in such work and promote praxis. Bauman (1995: 235–43) talks about the role of intellectuals as interpreters as against legitimators of social knowledge. Drawing upon Lyotard, the plight of the intellectual in the post legitimation era is to simply 'advance without authority' through the duty 'to express what otherwise would remain silent … taking risks – taking *responsibility* for the audibility of the dumb' (*ibid*: 241–42). This interpretive role is crucial in the development and impact of cultural criminology.

Finding alternative, creative ways of re-presenting ethnographic research is part of the duty we have as interpreters and producers of social knowledge. What follows in this chapter is an account and discussion of my attempt to work with marginalised groups who are situated on the borders, in the liminal spaces of our social worlds, in order to interpret and understand their lived experiences with a view to producing social change or transformation. The potential for social change is ever-present. Our task as critical theorists is to take responsibility for catalysing 'dialogic understanding in the general public, to opening up and keeping open spaces for what has been called "critical discourse"' (Bauman 1995: 242).

Methodology: ethno-mimesis as performative praxis

One potential catalyst for generating dialogue is to develop renewed methodologies that speak to a broader audience, beyond academic communities. What follows explores this possibility.

In earlier work I argued that renewed methodologies for social research could explore and represent the complexity of lived reality, transgressing conventional or traditional ways of presenting research data. I developed the concept of ethno-mimesis to provide a conceptual basis for renewed methodologies that incorporate photography, film, performance, theatre and provide multi-vocal and dialogic texts that can make visible 'emotional structures and inner experiences' (Kuzmics 1997: 9) that may move the audience through 'sensuous knowing ' (Taussig 1993) to develop action or praxis (purposeful knowledge).

Until quite recently the visual in ethnographic research was used to illustrate rather than interpret and critique lived experience and cultures. Emmison and Smith argue that 'we live in a massively visual society, and researchers should be more reflexive about the visual; more methodologically skilled within it; and indeed this would enhance the quality of their research' (2000: ix).

I was personally interested in developing an approach to socio-cultural research that incorporated the transformative possibilities for representing social research in artistic form (through photography, performance art, poetic work) within the context of participatory action research (working with communities to create change). Ethno-mimesis is a phenomenological, hermeneutic way of exploring, analysing and seeking to transform social and sexual inequalities through artistic re-presentation of ethnographic research. Ethno-mimesis as performative praxis is reflexive and phenomenological and shows that there is no single overriding vision of the world, but multiple realities, multiple meanings. It helps to deconstruct and show the truth in life's fictions. Ethno-mimesis transgresses the traditional boundaries for ethnographic research, taking research outside of the usual binaries in order to challenge identitarian thinking. The mimetic re-telling of lived experience in artistic form can focus upon the transformative, change-causing gesture involved in PAR.

For example, in work with a Bosnian community in the Midlands over a period of four years we developed intertextual research with 'refugees' and 'asylum seekers', using PAR. This work as a work in progress, as 'micrology', sought to create intertextual social knowledge as ethno-mimesis to help us avoid accepting reified versions of 'reality' and re-present the complexity of lived experience and lived relations in postmodern times. The research also aided the community development process for the community (social regeneration and renewal) and made important interventions in relation to cultural citizenship for individuals and the community.[1]

---

1 Cultural citizenship is understood – drawing upon Jan Pakulski's work (1977) – as the right to presence and visibility; the right to dignifying representation; and the right to identity and maintenance of lifestyle.

The participants were the co-creators of the research. Their life history narratives were re-presented in visual forms through photography and digital media.

The life story narratives re-presented three key themes that emerged in the interviews. First, the participants' experiences before the war that included dislocation marked by post-communist citizenship. Second, experiences during the war, that included being displaced and abstracted from history citizenship and the law and for some living in concentration camps. And finally, participants' experiences of living in the UK, re-locating, re-building communities and lives.

Our research proved to be transgressive across three levels of praxis. First, *textual,* via the documenting of their life stories as testimony to the loss, pain and suffering they encountered at the hands of friends, neighbours, family members, public services and government – army, police. Second, *visually,* performed through the production of art forms to re-present life stories and say the unsayable with the help of community artists. Finally, *the performative level of praxis* combined the textual and visual through exhibiting the work in galleries and community venues. The gallery and community spaces as public spaces provided safe spaces for re-presentation and dialogue that ultimately was cathartic and also fostered understanding and awareness in those who visited as well as processes of community development for the Bosnians.

Figure 18.1 Fahira Hacedic created a digitally photographed installation on the theme of 'good neighbour'. This installation was developed with the support of artist Karen Fraser as part of the 'Global Refugees: exile, displacement and belonging project' (funded by the AHRB, based at Staffordshire University).

At every phase of the PAR research there is the possibility for change:

(1) The process of interviews can validate the experience of the participant.

(2) Involving 'participants' as co-researchers democratises and transforms their role from passive subject to active participant.

(3) Outcomes of the research can inform, educate, remind, challenge and empower those involved and the audiences.

(4) Outcomes can reach a wider audience beyond academia, and be print based, visual, or performance based.

Ethno-mimetic work can speak in empathic ways with participants marginalised in society. Moreover, such work can re-present their lives through the performance text and serve to counter post emotionalism, valorising discourses and the reduction of the Other, to a cipher of the oppressed/marginalised.

As Hillis-Millar has argued, the concept of the 'performative' is intrinsically political, for it both describes and celebrates, preserves and enfranchises cultural studies – *and in this case, cultural criminology*. Drawing upon Walter Benjamin, Millar tells us that

> works of art bring something new into the world rather than reflecting something already there. This something new is constitutive rather than being merely representational ... Works of art make culture. Each work makes different the culture it enters. (Hillis-Millar 1992: 151)

For Adorno (1984), it is by trying to say the unsayable, the sensual, the non conceptual that we can approach a 'politics' that undercuts identity thinking and criss-crosses binary thinking and remains un-appropriated. Works of art are ciphers of our social worlds. Moreover, the art critics Susan Sontag, Victor Burgin and Douglas Crimp show that photography can subvert dominant ideologies by critiquing notions of authorship, and also emphasise photography's emancipatory potential (see O'Neill *et al* 2002). Through art works we are able to get in touch with our social worlds (our 'realities') in ways that demand critical reflection. For Shierry Weber-Nicholsen (1993) it is photography's potential to pierce us, so we can grasp 'reality in its otherness' (within the context of an image based society that attempts to tame and inhibit critical reflection) that creates the potential to help us develop a broader, more compassionate and more accurate consciousness.

Ethno-mimesis is the interrelation, inter-textuality between art forms and ethnography. Using Adorno and Benjamin – especially the dialectic of mimesis and constructive rationality – captures, for me, the relationship or mediation between emotion, sensuousness, feeling, on the one hand, and the constructed materiality of life on the other. Immersed in critical theory and with a commitment to changing – not simply describing – the social world, I looked for a method (PAR) that would include the stereotypical subjects of research in the entire research process, thus developing praxis as purposeful knowledge.

Adorno's work on coming to know the work of art was for me constitutive of the research process. This process includes a number of stages that are not linear but overlap. First, immersion in and identification with the art work (or social group/community/social issue). Second, objectification-critical distancing (being present and immersed but retaining an objective stance, a distance that enables or allows reflexive analysis and critique – akin to Bourdieu's 'Understanding').[2] The final stage is that of commentary and criticism.

The above account describes the methodological approach embedded in constructing 'feeling forms' through ethnographic life story work. Adorno is very useful for this work in contemporary times as he emphasises the utter complexity of the lifeworld and the need for non-identical thinking. His work focuses on micrology – the minutiae of lived experience, and upon living a damaged life through the ambiguity and ambivalence of hyper-modern times (1978).

Ethnographic research and artistic re-presentations can inform each other, developing greater knowledge and understanding by producing texts and discourse that contain 'truths' in life's fictions. Such texts can help us to acquire a more complex and nuanced understanding of our social worlds – including similarities and differences – and give us a glimpse of the sedimented stuff of society – what Presdee (2000) calls the 'second life of the people'.

After a brief discussion contextualising sex work through concepts of 'liminal spaces and places' and 'psychic and social alienation', I will proceed by focusing on two recent examples of PAR. Both were conducted with sex workers and/or communities affected by prostitution. They are illustrative of the usefulness of ethno-mimesis as performative praxis for cultural criminology.

Sex work and liminal spaces and places

Sex work is located on borders of 'decent' society in the liminal spaces and places. Prostitution takes places in the margins of law and order between the illegal and legal. Prostitution is not illegal but associated activities are – procuring, living off immoral earnings, operating a brothel. Red Light Areas involve spatial organisation that exclude 'disorderly' 'polluting' prostitution from 'orderly' 'purified' sites of sexual morality. Those on the borders and margins of 'mainstream' society experience pyschic and social alienation. Consider, for example, the following quote:

> Prostitutes are as inevitable in a metropolis as sewers, cesspits and rubbish tips; the civil authority should treat the one as it does the other – its duty is to supervise them, to reduce the dangers inherent in them as far as possible, and to this end to hide them and relegate them to the darkest corners; in short, render their presence as inconspicuous as possible. (John 1994: 44–48)

Psychic and social alienation

Alain Corbin's (1987) analysis of commercial sex in 19th century France describes how the interrelated discourses of municipal authorities, hygienists, the police and judiciary combined to organise the regulation of prostitution around three major

---

2   'Understanding' for Bourdieu is: 'Attempting to situate oneself in the place the interviewee occupies in the social space in order to understand them as *necessarily what they are* ... [T]o *take their part* ... is not to effect that "projection of oneself into the other" of which the phenomenologists speak. It is to give oneself a *general and genetic comprehension* of who the person is, based on the (theoretical or practical) command of the social conditions of which she is the product: a command of the conditions of existence and the social mechanisms which exert their effects on the whole ensemble of the category to which the person belongs ... and a command of the psychological and social, both associated with a particular position and a particular trajectory in social space. Against the old Diltheyan distinction, it must be accepted that *understanding and explaining are one'* (Bourdieu 1996: 22–23; emphasis in original).

issues: the need to protect public morality; the need to protect male prosperity; and the need to protect the nation's health. The prostitute was perceived as an active agent for the transmission of disease. For Corbin, these three major issues are rooted in five key images of the prostitute: the prostitute as the *putain* 'whose body smells bad' (1987: 210); the prostitute as the safety valve which 'enables the social body to excrete the excess of seminal fluid that causes her stench and rots her' (p 211); the prostitute as decaying and symbolically associated with the corpse, with death; the prostitute as diseased symbolically associated with syphilis; and finally, the prostitute as submissive female body 'bound to the instinctive physical needs of upper class males' (p 213).

For Corbin, these key images reinforce the ambiguous status of the female body, specifically the lower class, submissive body of the prostitute that is 'at once menace and remedy, agent of purification and drain ... at the beck and call of the bourgeois body' (pp 212–13). Corbin goes on to illustrate how these discourses led to a series of principles which structured the regulation of prostitution: the principle of tolerance, the principle of containment, and the principle of surveillance.

Through social stigma, marginalisation, criminalisation, and the effects of disempowering sexual relations with both paying and non-paying partners, women and young people experience psychic alienation.

To 'be denied an autonomous choice of self, forbidden cultural expression, and condemned to the immanence of mere bodily being is to be cut off from the sorts of activities that define what it is to be human' (Bartky 1990: 31). This constitutes alienation, 'an estrangement from self, a splintering of human nature into a number of misbegotten parts' (*ibid*), or, using Fanon's term, this constitutes 'psychic alienation'. Black women, working as prostitutes, experience a further 'splintering'.

The problem of prostitution (usually understood by the state and the public imagination as the problem of women) is often dealt with by regulating women working as prostitutes and controlling women's sexuality, with particular regard to the sexual health of their bodies (Smart 1992). Confined in certain spaces/places/locations, sex workers utilise various tactics and strategies to resist and transgress the exclusionary geographies of prostitution:

- Cards advertising sexual services are left in telephone boxes by 'maids' and 'sticker boys' who work for sex workers. The stickers/cards are regularly removed by police/clean-up operations and the sticker boys continually replace them.
- CCTV cameras and other techniques of surveillance are used creatively. For example, some sex workers use CCTV cameras as a safety device – ensuring clients/cars are caught on film before the woman and client leave for the space/place to do 'business'. Sleeping policemen are very helpful at slowing down the traffic so sex workers can make eye contact with potential clients. The obverse of this is that it unsettles men who are not looking to buy. Mark Webster in O'Neill *et al* (2004) writes: 'At night the Green takes on an altogether different character. Fast food eateries and Balti restaurants stretch up Caldmore Road. Groups of men hurry home from the mosque. Women standing on corners peer questioningly into the windows of cars cruising through or ask male pedestrians if they want "Business". The speed bumps – *Sleeping policemen* – ensure that essentially all drivers become kerb crawlers, and the humps raise the eye line of inadvertent drivers so that they have to meet the gaze of the women eye to eye. Police vans patrol ominously whilst hurried transactions take place in shadowy doorways and back alleys.'

- Women resist attempts at control through the use of time and space; making use of back alleys, pubs and cafés; working after hours on street. Women may work from about 2–3 am until 8/9 am to avoid policing practices; and/or move temporarily to other towns/zones.
- Solidarity and networking are important aspects of managing and subverting control, containment and surveillance and sustaining a degree of tolerance in an area (see Hubbard 1999: 181). Sex workers will share information about dodgy punters as well as tips of the trade and informal rules and codes as well as legal rights.

Moreover, transgression from the margins into the ordered spaces of policy/media/ academy serves to undermine the 'regulatory fiction of heterosexual coherence' (Hubbard 1999: 209). Prostitutes' rights, politicisation and unionisation are important strategies to resist marginalisation and liminality (see O'Neill et al 2000).

Hubbard, drawing upon de Certeau, writes about everyday resistances. 'Resistances are assembled from the materials and practices of everyday life ... the very act of walking is resistive', describing it as a 'process of appropriation of the topographical system on the part of the pedestrian' (Hubbard 1999: 182). And, whilst the strong/powerful may classify, survey and order space, those on the borders – the marginal and marginalised – can divert, manipulate and subvert order; and act 'out of place'. 'While it would be foolish to romanticize the liberatory potential of sex work, its sites may sometimes act as the locus of new forms of moral and sexual order' (ibid: 181).

Thus, confinement in spaces and places can be resisted and re-territorialised. Alternative discourses can be created that challenge and re-imagine the social order/ organisation of prostitution; and in turn foster responses to policy and practice that are woman-centred and transformative. These processes can be supported by cultural criminologists working through PAR methodology as interpreters (Bauman), and with sex workers, communities, and the relevant statutory and voluntary agencies (see O'Neill and Campbell 2001).

The 'prostitute' is marked out as 'other', as separate from ordinary women, a body-object of fascination and desire, an 'aestheticised' body. Our gendered bodies are heavily symbolised in the social construction of everyday life. The body and our embodiment is a cultural process whereby the body 'becomes a site of culturally ascribed and disputed meanings, experiences, feelings' (Stanley and Wise 1993: 196). Bodies are not simply cultural, linguistic creations but physical, material, experiential realities (ibid: 197).

As such we need to theorise the aestheticised body of the 'prostitute' alongside the interrelationship between bodies, space and place – the (liminal) geographies of prostitution – as well as broader social and psychic structures and processes including regulatory mechanisms, the law, resident action etc that facilitate the social organisation of prostitution. We can do this through visual and participatory methodologies and hopefully challenge the 'whore stigma' that has so far operated for centuries.

The next section documents and discusses two PAR projects: 'Not all the time ... but mostly ...' and 'Safety Soapbox'. The first is an account of research with performance artists that led to the production of a trilogy of artforms based on life history interviews with sex workers. A community deeply affected by street prostitution commissioned the second project. Both projects provide exemplars of ethno-mimesis and transgressive imaginations.

Not all the time ... but mostly ...

Sara Giddens, a lecturer in performance art, was given transcripts from life story interviews I had conducted with sex workers (rigorously anonymised). The collaboration includes Sara working with performance artist Patricia and sound artist Darren to develop alternative representation of the data. The group worked with me to finalise a live 'performance' that led to a trilogy of works performed at a range of venues across the Midlands and the South West. The finished work went out to consultation with sex workers before being shown in public.

The live art performance as ethno-mimetic text engages people as human beings not 'stand-in political subjects' and in so doing represents the ambivalence of prostitution, and the situation of the women involved located as they are between discourses of good and bad women. The inter-textual relation between the ethnographic life story and the dance/performance as live art represents a re-covering and re-telling of lived experience as embodied performance. It recovers the stories of the oppressed on the borders and liminal spaces as well as telling of the resistances to disempowering sexual and social structures. The performance focuses our attention on the performing body, the fetishised and fragmented body, the unfinished and commodified body.

In the live performance an evocative tension is created between the performance on stage and on screen (a nine-minute video runs alongside the live performance), and the relationship the viewer has with the performance. One is left feeling 'stunned' yet also able to feel the traces of the prostitute's work within the context of a life – albeit for some a damaged life – that both humanises the woman and allows the engaged viewer to approach a genuinely felt involvement – an involvement that demands critical reflection and de-constructs stereotypes and 'otherness'.

Safety Soapbox

Rosie Campbell and I were successful in our tender to Walsall South Health Action Zone to develop consultation research on prostitution in Walsall. Walsall South Health Action Zone commissioned research having identified street prostitution as a significant issue for residents in terms of well-being and community safety. The challenge to the research team was to consult with residents, sex workers, and statutory and voluntary agencies over a period of 10 months to get as clear a picture as possible of the major issues, concerns, experiences and ideas for change.[3]

---

3   Using PAR methods we worked with a number of groups and agencies and representatives of Caldmore and Palfrey local committees; Walsall Community Arts team and Walsall Youth Arts; the SAFE project; and Streeteams who delivered outreach and targeted support to sex workers (see www.safetysoapbox.com). Baseline data was collected and analysed through a sex worker survey, client survey and short questionnaire on pimps and pimping that some probation officers completed. Residents were interviewed through focus groups, at home and also in local businesses. Representatives from the major statutory and voluntary agencies were contacted and interviewed. In addition, we accompanied the SAFE project outreach service, Streeteams outreach service, Addaction and SAFE drop-in. We also conducted our own independent outreach. We commissioned Walsall Youth Arts via Walsall Community Arts Team to conduct creative consultation with young people at risk of involvement in prostitution, sex workers and residents to produce visual re-presentations of their lived experiences, concerns and hopes for change in visual form using photography and computer arts.

Three groups were involved in the Safety Soapbox consultation working with Kate Green, community artist: sex workers, residents and young residents. Visual re-presentations can often have a much more powerful effect than words alone, and feed into local and national social and cultural policy. In re-presenting social research in visual/artistic form we hoped to reach as wide an audience as possible, facilitating better understanding of the experiences of the local community (including residents and sex workers) and ideas for change or managing the current situation.

One aim of the creative consultation was to make visible people's experiences and ideas for change and show that collaboration (with local committees, agencies, residents, women and young people involved in prostitution) produces rich understanding and social texts (report, strategic action plan, exhibition) that can be useful to the wider community, including local and national policy makers. Furthermore, in this collaboration ethno-mimetic texts can enhance our understanding of prostitution by the production of visual texts that mimetically show the experiences and ways of seeing of all those involved – residents, statutory and voluntary agencies, women and young people involved in prostitution.

As our various projects suggest, the arts have a vital role in the processes of regeneration, communication and building communities (O'Neill et al 2002, 2003, 2004; Hussain et al 2003). To participate in cultural life is a key aspect to our health and well-being. Participation in arts and culture enriches our life but also promotes balance in life. In 'Towards a cultural strategy for working with refugees and asylum seekers', I and Tobolewska (2002) point to the role of the arts in sharing experiences and enabling recovery, healing and inclusion for displaced and often traumatised communities. 'Challenging and resisting dominant images and stereotypes of "refugees" and "asylum seekers" and making this work available to as wide an audience as possible can serve to raise awareness, educate and empower individuals and groups' (ibid: 3).[4]

Outcomes of the overall research included a report (Working Together to Create Change); an art exhibition ('Safety Soapbox'); and a pamphlet (What you told us about prostitution), published by the community 18 months after the research ended. This publication was for the community, ensuring that the outcomes of the research were not shut away in a drawer, but kept alive and on the local agenda.

In previous work the research team argued that using arts-based consultation (creative consultation),[5] PAR provides the opportunity for reflection and transformation; it adds value and can produce sustainable interventions.

Through 'reflection', PAR provides opportunities for people to work through issues through dialogue and create a piece of art that makes visible their concerns/ ideas/responses. Firstly, this process is 'transformative'. In creating a piece of work that makes visible concerns, ideas, future possibilities, art works bring something new and tangible into the world that contributes to a better understanding of an issue. Secondly, the arts process 'adds value' at lots of levels. At the level of the participant (community member/citizen), the arts are a way of engaging, consulting and involving people in decisions and planning for the future of their community.

---

4   For more on the role that participation in arts and cultural activities has in raising self-esteem, self-confidence and well-being (both for individuals and communities) see Webster 1998.
5   The National Institute for Access to Continuing Education (NIACE) toolkit was commissioned by GOEM to highlight the benefits of working with communitites using participatory methods.

And finally, such work can be *'sustainable'*. The arts support innovation and experimentation in local communities and have a vital role to play in processes of community development, social inclusion and creative regeneration (see O'Neill *et al* 2004).

Our collaboration was based upon principles of participatory action research and participatory arts. PAR and PA is a process and a practice directed towards social change with the participants. It is interventionist, action oriented, and interpretative. The local community were instrumental in commissioning the research, feeling that they were already living in a zone of toleration. They wanted as clear a picture of prostitution as possible with a view to addressing the emerging issues and developing change.

Conclusion

PAR develops partnership responses to social issues and problems and seeks to include all those involved, thus facilitating shared ownership of the development and outcomes of the research. PAR uses innovative ways of consulting local people, for example through community arts workshops, and has processes of monitoring and evaluation built in to the research outcomes. It is action oriented and interventionist. The use of visual methodologies and ethno-mimesis can produce knowledge that provides a sensuous understanding of lived experience and of our social world's structures, practices and processes. Such knowledge can help us to avoid identitarian thinking and feeling and enable us to engage in a rich and diverse cultural criminology that involves re-thinking and re-imagining the relationships between lived experience, crime, order, control and social policy/practice.

Ethno-mimesis as performative praxis produces purposeful knowledge and enables or facilitates the transformative impact of cultural criminology. The production of knowledge uncovers the 'truths' in life's fictions and helps us to acquire a more complex and nuanced understanding of our social worlds. Through renewed methodologies our task as intellectuals, academics, *cultural criminologists* is to brush against the grain of the social fabric, to understand and to produce change/praxis, to produce critical theory in practice.

Drawing upon Bauman and Lyotard, the task of writing cultural criminology is a duty; 'the duty to express what otherwise would remain silent' (Bauman 1995: 241). Moreover, this

> does not bring strategic certainty nor guarantee success, nor any assurance of support from history, to those who would wish to follow it. It demands courage and perhaps sacrifice without promising reward other than the feeling that the duty has been done. (*ibid*: 243)

References

Adorno, TW (1978) *Minima Moralia: Reflections from a Damaged Life*, Jephcott, EFN (trans), London and New York: Verso

Adorno, TW (1984) *Aesthetic Theory*, Lendhart, C (trans), London: Routledge

Bartky, SL (1990) *Femininity and Domination: Studies in the Phenomenology of Oppression*, London: Routledge

Bauman, Z (1995) *Life in Fragment: Essays on Postmodern Morality*, London: Sage

Bordieu, P (1996) 'Understanding' 13(2) *Theory, Culture & Society* 17–39

Clarke, J (2001) 'The pleasures of crime: interrogating the detective story', in Muncie, J and McLaughlin, E (eds), *The Problem of Crime*, London: Sage

Corbin, A (1987) 'Commercial sexuality in nineteenth century France: a system of images and representations', in Gallagher, C and Laquer, T (eds), *The Making of the Modern Body: Sexuality and Society in the Nineteenth Century*, Berkeley, CA: University of California Press

Emmison, M and Smith, P (2000) *Researching the Visual*, London: Sage

Hillis-Millar, J (1992) *Illustration*, London: Reaktion

Hubbard, P (1999) *Sex and the City*, London: Ashgate

Hussain, A *et al* (2003) *Integrated Cities: Exploring the Cultural Development of Leicester*, University of Leicester

John, N (ed) (1994) *Violetta and Her Sisters: The Lady of the Camellias – Responses to the Myth*, London: Faber and Faber

Kuzmics, H (1997) 'State formation, economic development and civilisation in North Western and Central Europe' 16(2) *Geschichte und Gegenwart* 80–91

O'Neill, M (2001) *Prostitution and Feminism: Towards a Politics of Feeling*, Cambridge: Polity

O'Neill, M and Campbell, R (2001) *Working Together to Create Change: Walsall Prostitution Consultation Research: A Participatory Action Research Project*, Staffordshire University and Liverpool Hope University College

O'Neill, M, Galli, F *et al* (2004) 'New arrivals: research report on access to training, employment and social enterprise', paper commissioned by GOEM, Staffordshire University

O'Neill, M and Tobolewska, B (2002) 'Towards a cultural strategy for working with refugees and asylum seekers', paper funded by AHRB, Staffordshire University

O'Neill, M, Webster, M and Woods, PA (2003) 'New arrivals: report of research on the inclusion of pupils and families to Leicester City Education', paper commissioned by GOEM and Leicester LEA, Staffordshire University

O'Neill, M *et al* (2000) 'Love for sale: the politics of prostitution in Stoke on Trent', in Edensor, T (ed), *Reclaiming Stoke on Trent: Leisure, Space and Identity in the Potteries*, Staffordshire University Press

O'Neill, M *et al* (2002) 'Renewed methodologies for social research: ethno-mimesis as performative praxis' 50(1) *Sociological Review*, February

O'Neill, M *et al* (2004) 'Red lights and safety zones', in Bell, D and Jayne, M (eds), *City Cultures*, London: Ashgate

Pakulski, J (1977) 'Cultural citizenship' 1 *Citizenship Studies* 73–86

Presdee, M (2000) *Cultural Criminology and the Carnival of Crime*, London: Routledge

Presdee, M (2004) 'Cultural criminology: the long and winding road' 8(3) *Theoretical Criminology* 275–85

Smart, C (1992) *Regulating Womanhood*, London: Routledge

Stanley, L and Wise, S (1993) *Breaking out Again*, London: Routledge

Taussig, M (1993) *Mimesis and Alterity*, London: Routledge

Weber-Nicholsen, S (1993) 'Walter Benjamin and the aftermath of the aura: an aesthetics for photography', in O'Neill, M (ed), *Adorno, Culture and Feminism*, London: Sage

Webster, M (1998) *Finding Voices, Making Choices*, London: Educational Heretics Press

Chapter 19
Taking a Beating: The Narrative Gratifications of Fighting as an Underdog

Curtis Jackson-Jacobs

Introduction: culture, criminology, and brawling in Tucson

'How much can you know about yourself if you've never been in a fight?', Tyler Durden ponders in the movie *Fight Club*. Persistent, real life fighters also ask themselves this question. From their perspective fights are contexts for deep self-revelation. Two complementary thrills of revelation reward a successful fighter. The first thrill is to discover a charismatic primal self through physical and emotional urgency: fundamentally acute, courageous, and of 'strong character' (Goffman 1967). The second thrill is to realise a storied self: a self that will become publicly and enduringly admired, immortalised in epic fight stories told for years to come. In fact, fighters fantasise as much about telling stories as actually fighting. For example, one of my research subjects, Rick, once told me about a new post in the military: 'Sometimes I want to get in a fight on my new ship ... Like, I think about how it would be cool if I got in a fight with some really big guy and I won. So that people would like talk about me and stuff.'

Goffman noted that fateful forms of action have 'reputational consequences'. For fighting and some other kinds of risk-taking, however, the statement could be made more forcibly. The consequentiality for one's reputation is no accident. In fact, the prospects of narrative risks and appeals – the prospects of generating stories that reflect negatively or positively – powerfully motivate violent conduct at each moment, often more so than the physical risks and appeals. Indeed, narrative consequences are often the *raison d'être* of risk.

Brawls are the most common type of fight enacted by the group of young men from Tucson, Arizona, reported on below. They are typically performed by groups of strangers in front of audiences, arising from verbal character contests, opening and closing in the same scene. The prospect of 'getting stomped' is made palatable to fighters by how they understand fighting. Most importantly, physical risks (which are almost always non-lethal, non-disabling and non-disfiguring) and appeals are used as resources for constructing narrative ones. A fighter's true self, as they see it, can only be apprehended through trial by ordeal. Until a fight happens, fighters cannot be sure if they will be heroes or cowards 'when it comes down to it'. Thus, they measure the value of the violent test as proportionate to its physical fatefulness and urgency. Only by performing with immediate action and composure can they cast the self as brave, loyal and heroic. Recalling Goffman (1967: 216) again: 'the sudden high cost of correct behavior may serve only to confirm his principledness.'

Western scholarly theories treat violence as repellent and horrifying, despite the enormous attractive potential it holds for violent actors themselves, not to mention the broader cultures they live in. Major theories of violence almost always rely on one or more of a very few basic ideas. One holds that violent actors lack psychic 'self-control' (Gottfredson and Hirschi 1990). Another sees violence as simply a way of managing conflicts that exist independently of their climactic end results and could be counselled away with more civil ways (Black 1983). Yet others maintain that violent people are so frustrated with one thing or another that eruption is all but inevitable (Freud 1930). All patently fail to account for violence looked at in the context of spectatorship, performance, and participatory attractions.

As foreign as brawling as an underdog is to many non-fighters, appreciating the activity is not. In popular narratives – historical and contemporary – numerous glorious underdog characters abound, from the biblical story of David slaying Goliath, to Sylvester Stallone's *Rocky*. Fighters appreciate their own violence in much the same way that witnesses do, appreciating their self-as-object, admiring themselves as if observing from a distance. Fighters intend their brawls to make good stories that reveal themselves as charismatic. And so they enact storylines that they expect will both test their character and be applauded by audiences.

From the field to a theory of brawling

As Morrison and others note, much criminology lacks sensitivity to motivation, desire, and actors' own understandings of what they are doing (1995; Hayward 2004). In my research I drew from symbolic interactionist and phenomenological sociologies – descriptive approaches that, along with a comparative perspective, lend themselves to situated explanations of why people do crime, act violently, or take risks (eg Katz 1988, 2002; Luckenbill 1977; Lyng 1990; Marsh *et al* 1978).

In December 1999 I returned to my home city of Tucson in the southwestern United States. I rekindled old friendships with young men from one of its more affluent neighbourhoods who I knew 'liked to party' and who would sometimes get into fights; they had other friends with tough reputations. Tape-recorder in hand, I constructed my sample by following the lines of acquaintanceship in the network of friends, interviewing whoever was regularly hanging out in the group. The sample includes 85 members. They are mostly white, though a few define themselves as Latino, Mexican, Native American, or Indian. The majority grew up in economically comfortable families. Some lead criminal lifestyles, others are college students, and still others are skilled labourers or unskilled office workers.

The network is organised primarily around male friendships. The women who regularly hang out are current and former girlfriends and their friends. Most of the women in the network have been in one or more physical fights, including one brawl involving six women and two men that I observed to be as violent as many all-male brawls. Unlike the men, however, the women invest much less of their sense of self in their fighting histories. The men's fighting histories are often central to how they define each other and their peer group. Performing well in a brawl is a sure way to construct themselves as 'men of action' in each other's minds. The rare male members of the network without fighting histories are considered either partially deficient or untested.

In this chapter, I focus mainly on one character, Rick (all names fictional), in order to trace the experience of participation in a brawl as it progresses. Rick, 20 years old at the time, is tall and athletically built – six-foot-three, 200 pounds. He competed in martial arts tournaments regularly as a youth. Waist-high trophies and a black belt adorn his bedroom. He is well liked for his frequent and hearty laughter, quick sense of humour, and knack for putting anyone at ease. Though he joined the military and moved to California at the age of 18, he returned to Tucson at least once a month. Brian was one of several military buddies that would listen with envy as Rick related fight stories from Tucson. He was less experienced than the Tucsonans but visited partly to gain experience. TJ grew up in the same neighbourhood as most of the friendship network, but attended a private school rather than the public high school. Of above-average height and lanky, he looks somewhat athletic, neatly dressing in fashionable, youthful styles. TJ is strikingly intelligent and good humoured. Although less outgoing than Rick, TJ wins acquaintances over with a cheerful openness. Socially skilful young men, they can also be equally offensive when motivated.

The description of the brawl below is based on interviews with TJ and Rick, a written account by James – all shortly after the fight – and brief conversations with Joe, Brian, Bob, and Aaron. To corroborate some details and fine-tune the description I took Rick back to the location of the brawl in March 2004, tape-recording as we walked through the scene. Credibility is a concern worth comment; the potential for embellishment or misremembering cannot be totally eliminated. Though I did not experience the fight firsthand, the process described seems strikingly similar to many other incidents I have witnessed whilst undertaking my research. Both the fight and this writing are public, discouraging the respondents from explicit deception. The accounts are similar enough on all important details that intentional or inadvertent misrepresentation is minimal.

The March 2000 brawl

All brawls done by the Tucson friends proceed through four stages. First, the key actors set the scene by going out into a public leisure place occupied by diverse strangers. Second, at least two strangers use situational resources to construct a character contest. Third, one or (usually) both sides violently attack the other. Fourth, each side re-groups and talks about the fight. What distinguished this as a specifically 'underdog brawl' was that Rick's group knew they would be beaten yet committed to testing their character through violence anyway.

Setting the scene: 'going out'

By far the modal setting for a brawl is the nighttime, weekend, drinking outing with a group of friends. Weekends are reserved for large outings of up to a dozen or more friends to a bar or to a house where someone is throwing a large party. The more people present, the better the chance that one or more of them will get into a fight with some stranger. Group outings of any size often begin with unspoken agreements that, as Leigh, a young woman put it, 'we were gonna go out and get in a fight'. What kind of fight they will get into and what kind of story the fight may tell about the self (and about the group) remain unclear in important ways until the violence has been done. Those uncertainties, though, represent pervasive thrills in their leisure outings and during their attempts to stir up trouble.

The night in March 2000 started in the usual way. James, a friend from high school, had 'heard about a party' from 'some girls' he knew that lived near the university campus in Tucson. The announcement that 'there's a party' usually comes only that evening. These young Tucsonans, and the local party culture at large, take this announcement as implicit permission to then invite anyone they know, in turn giving them the same permission. By 9 or 10 pm a hundred or more people, many of them complete strangers to each other, arrive at the house of someone they don't know, not quite sure what the party will be like, but hoping for excitement and action.

'James called us and told us there was a bunch of hot chicks ... So we were real happy about that,' Rick recalled. James didn't tell anyone much more than that, though. TJ remembered feeling 'unsure what it was going to be like ... The possibilities are that it could be just a few people hanging out, or it could be a huge party. Hopefully as many girls as possible'. Unlike many outings, Rick and TJ claimed that at first they weren't hoping for a fight, but for another type of action – casual sex. Brian, though, had violent trouble at the front of his mind, as soon became clear.

It was the kind of place where 'parties' used to go on every weekend when I was in my late teens and early twenties. Indeed, I had been to parties at that exact house before. Interestingly, it was not the kind of setting for violence usually written about in American studies. This was not 'The Ghetto' – there were no outward signs of social deprivation and certainly no apparent 'broken windows'! Instead, this was a well-kept college student neighbourhood, filled with the kind of one-storey, single-family brick homes, surrounded by front and back yards, typical of Tucson.

Rick recounted that, upon arrival:

> I saw a bunch of people in the courtyard right there of that house ... It was just like, there was – they were playing music and stuff. And dude, there was like girls everywhere ... We paid for our cups. We were hittin' the keg ... And most of the time we were just out here at the courtyard just like drinking and stuff ... It was a great time. We were talking to girls and stuff. Just like shooting the shit with everybody.

TJ added that he and Rick soon started to hope for trouble (by Rick's account about an hour into the party): 'And – I'm not sure at what point – Brian said he wanted to get into a fight. He just said, "I want to get into a fight". And Rick was like, "Yeah, I kinda want to get in a fight too" ... So I was like, "Yeah I want to get in a fight too".'

Why the shift in sentiment? What about the party makes it seem like a viable place to pick a fight? What about it entices violent intentions?

The social organisational conditions are ripe for public troublemaking. Parties are understood to be moments of freedom from usual constraint, encouraging revelry, presenting a landscape of free-moving bodies and the pursuit of action. Parties provide a prospective audience and numerous strangers as potential opponents. In this culture at least, the brawl is intended to be a one-time affair, settled 'then and there' in a single course of (inter)action. By contrast, fights with friends and intimates often result in prolonged conflicts that damage relationships, or end in a series of apologies. Strangers entice by promising a non-committal relationship.

Invitations to action: situational disputes, rumblings of trouble

Once in the mindset to 'get in a fight', the would-be brawler must still find a willing opponent and initiate a dispute. But how does one go about finding an opponent amongst strangers? And, having picked one out, how does one go about getting into some kind of dispute, especially the kind that would lead to violence?

I asked TJ, 'What were you thinking about your prospects?':

> Probably pretty likely given the attitude of Brian. I figured he'd probably start something. And he was making a good effort. He made some good tries. A couple times some people would be leaving, and so he'd just go stand in front of them and just stare at them. And they would just have to squeeze by him. That was the most subtle thing he did.

Hopeful brawlers tend also to wait for opportunities to present themselves. They hope someone will bump into them or insult them, meaning that fights happen much less frequently than they would like. TJ reported that 'these other guys were leaving. And as they were leaving, Brian just started throwing rocks at them … But they just ignored him'. The success rate is low. If like-minded people happen to receive the invitation, then a brawl is a strong possibility, and this does work on occasion. But most people, themselves not so interested in fighting, simply dismiss these tactics.

As TJ went on to describe, certain people seem to almost call out to be challenged to a fight. People who would make good characters in a fight story especially attract attention. He recalled that 'a group of enormous people showed up. I don't think they were the group we got in a fight with. Maybe they were. They said they were University of Arizona football players. And Joe said he was trying to start a fight with them'.

Their attempts to start a fight – to put on a show for the party and create a narratively rich event to remember – were going nowhere. A couple of hours later TJ was feeling let down as the party dwindled. 'I was starting to think, you know, nothing's going to happen. It was past one [after which commercial sales of alcohol become illegal] … And all the girls were leaving. It was mostly just guys. It was a lot of people. But there was no beer.' There would be no show, no self-revelations, and no fight story through which to proclaim spectacular identities.

Rick, though, saw the dwindling party in a different light. Just as two sources of action vanished another appeared:

> And the keg was running out. And the girls started leaving. And I remember saying, 'Oh man, it's just us and those really big dudes!' I remember thinking that ... cause you know how like that's when always the trouble starts. Like I know there's gonna be trouble when the hot girls are leaving … and all the beer's gone … You know? And these guys looked like a bunch of steroid monsters anyway, though, so I knew it was only a matter of time before they started to get angry.

Then a sudden clamour came, the rumblings of a fight. TJ realised, 'suddenly there was this commotion outside the house down by the corner. So everyone runs out there. A bunch of random people. Like 20 or something'. He is drawn along with the other bodies in motion, intent on getting a glimpse of or getting involved in violence. For most of TJ's group it was pure spectatorship – for the moment at least. Rick, however, was keen to participate. As audience members vie for position, prospective fighters recognise without pause that if they 'jump in' there will be an attentive crowd watching. Rick gave me a 'show and tell' demonstration:

> Well, we were out here in the courtyard, and Dukey [a former high school classmate] like ran back here or something. And then a whole bunch of people were talking like, 'Oh, there's gonna be a fight! They're gonna kick his ass! They're gonna kick his ass! Blah blah blah'. You know? So we we're like, 'Oh, sweet!' [With enthusiasm.] 'They're gonna beat up that guy!' Or we thought – I thought possibly, maybe, I'll try and like jump in since I know him, you know, and maybe defend him.

Note the indeterminacy in what exactly Rick expects to happen. From his account, Rick was excited that either Dukey will get beat up and he can watch, or, preferably, Dukey will get beat up and he can try to 'maybe defend him'.

Most explanations of violence and conflict in the social sciences presume that a much different causal model is universal. Regardless of the specific theory, they assume that people would fight only in order to resolve an independently existing conflict, either as a practical means of managing conflict or because of unmanageable rage. For brawling, though, this explanation does not work. Rick was not enraged but, instead, enthused. Nor did he have any deep relationship to whatever conflict Dukey was embroiled in – not even by association. In fact, he hardly knew the man. 'How well do you even know this guy?', I asked. Rick explained, 'I had a couple classes with him when I was like 14 or 15 [six years earlier] ... So for, basically, I don't know, no real reason'.

Just as things started to 'get interesting', though, the trouble with Dukey fizzled out. He escaped the crowd of men pursuing him and sped away in his car. By that time, though, everyone was primed for a fight. TJ, Joe and Brian expected at a minimum to see some action. Rick was hoping to get in on some. Their heart rates and blood pressure still elevated from the excited sprint to the rear of the house, everyone lingered around the front yard and the street.

By then it seemed to TJ and his friends that everyone was 'set on' violence in some form. Their definition of the situation, including their perception of everyone present, had changed profoundly. 'The steroid monsters' were now proven violent in the eyes of Rick's crowd. Looking through brawlers' lenses, the big guys were starting to appear more and more like appealing characters to cast in a scene of dramatic violence.

The kind of fight Rick, TJ, Joe and their group could get into had remained unclear through most of the night: Would someone do something to morally outrage a member of the group, leading them to perform a righteous beating? Would one of them casually strike up a dispute during the night with an opponent, leading to a brawl experienced through the metaphor of a sexual 'pick up'? The range of possibilities had narrowed. James noted early on that the opponents were 'about 15–20 guys all over six feet and 200 pounds'. If a fight were to happen with those men, they would fight as underdogs. The only questions would be: how well would they take their beatings, what kind of character would they be able to claim for themselves, and what kind of story would they be able to tell in the future?

In this culture the disputes that constitute what Goffman called 'character contests' (Goffman 1967; Luckenbill 1977) are categorised as 'talking shit'. Such disputes tell a story about two voluntary combatants, each willing to stand up for themselves and brave unpredictable action. The disputes themselves unfold over a number of turns of insult and counter-insult, challenge and counter-challenge. To the extent possible, the actor tries to construct his own participation as either that of someone unjustly affronted, or as an equal participant in a process of escalation. The identity developed is that of an aggrieved party, who is either the victim of unfair persecution or, at worst, no more than an equal participant in a two-way dispute (see also Gulliver 1973).

Playing up to the audience, skilful disputants find opportunities to develop novel variants on the standard script. Proper shit talking gives the fight memorable, 'quotable' narrative elements, allowing the fighter to both feel like and present himself as the kind of dramatic character who makes apt or cool remarks under pressure. In every case the fighter knows well that future stories about his fight will focus in detail on how and how well he 'talked shit'.

Who, exactly, would start talking shit was not yet clear. TJ explained:

... by the time I got out there, there was a crowd of about 20 or 25 people watching ... And all these big guys were angry because they wanted to beat someone up ... They were standing around their car, saying stuff like, 'That guy better get out of here'. And then they were looking around ...

Enter Brian. I had the chance to speak with him for only a few moments after the fight, but Rick, TJ and James reported that he took the initiative to stand in the street staring back at the 'big guys', one typical way of provoking a bout of shit talking.

> TJ: they look over at Brian. And Brian's just standing there staring at them. And this big black guy starts walking toward him and said, 'What's your problem, dude?' And Brian takes a look at him, and takes a drag off his cigarette and flicks it at him ... 'I don't know, man. It looks like you're the one that's trippin'.

Though he had come off as rather juvenile and clearly ineffective in his rock-throwing stunt earlier that night, everyone was struck by his composed bravado in the face of numerous antagonists, many of whom probably outweighed him by close to 100 pounds. Brian's friends were especially impressed by his striking use of the cigarette. Rick made sure to act the scene out for me. Holding back a grin, Rick narrowed his eyes toward an imaginary person and flamboyantly extended his elbow to the side, bringing the cigarette to his lips. He took a drag ceremoniously, drawing hard and loud. 'Took a drag off his cigarette and went – [dramatic pause] – *ffffffffff!*' Rick exhaled long and slow, as if savouring what would possibly be his last puff of tobacco, extending his hand a foot in front of his face. As the forceful exhale began to wind down, Rick flicked the burning butt several yards at head-level in a straight line. He concluded the demonstration: 'And then like a whole bunch of them started swarming around Brian.'

Talking shit is an important moment in the process of brawling for several reasons. First, it restructures the public nature of the event. To begin with, it draws attention. Talking loudly, making threats and issuing challenges, the disputants make an irresistible public display of themselves. Witnesses feel compelled to focus on the argument, lest they miss the action or even receive unwelcome attention themselves. If no one tries to break up the fight, then typically the audience forms a circle or semi-circle, placing the fighters centre stage.

Second, talking shit is a commitment to a fateful gamble. By publicly taking the 'line' (Goffman 1967) of violently arguing, each disputant claims a steadfast character and commits himself to a course of action that will lead to violence. While still talking shit the actor maintains the ability to act reflectively, make decisions, and self-consciously manage his identity. Yet he is at the same time committing to a violent course of action in which he will sacrifice these capacities. The actor is claiming that he can perform not only with verbal composure and speed but also that he will be able to demonstrate strength of character by fighting with honour. The gamble is all the bolder due to the risk that once an opponent actually starts violently attacking he may show himself to be 'all talk' if he does not fight until he either wins or is totally incapacitated.

Strangely enough, although the shit-talker is deeply attentive to and concerned with how present and future audiences will interpret his action, the action itself demands that he become oblivious to the audience and future considerations. Much of the reason to talk shit, especially to add creative details like punctuating a quip by flicking a cigarette, is to impress the audience and to construct a self that will reflect positively in future stories. By making this verbal commitment, though, the shit-talker places himself in a relationship with his audience that becomes increasingly asymmetrical. The more involved one becomes in talking shit the more one must attend specifically to the risk posed by the opponent rather than the gratifications of audience appreciation.

Third, talking shit is social-psychologically essential to consummating violent conflict. To do violence, most people, including people who fight routinely, must undergo what they experience as 'authentic' transformations to violent emotion. Often the actor 'wants to' get into a fight, but does not have the proper bodily disposition or emotional energy to summon a violent outburst. Gesturing wildly, flicking cigarettes, and often shoving, fighters begin to work their bodies up, feeling increasingly imposing. Simply reciting a script of fighting words often helps to conjure the necessary emotions. By going through the motions of saying 'What the fuck are you looking at?' or 'What's your problem?', fighters can summon a certain amount of rage, even if there is no 'objective', independently existing conflict to get angry about. Furthermore, for the fighter, delivering an insult has the effect of inspiring a self-defensive fear: by provoking the opponent's rage, one provokes in oneself a violent readiness to defend against that rage.

Fourth, talking shit to an opponent may be, counter-intuitively, a way of constructing the self as the victim. One way this can happen is by inspiring the opponent to retaliate with massive verbal escalation. Another is by encouraging the opponent to throw the first punch, thus creating a sense that one is only 'fighting back', potentially absolving one of the moral culpability of an 'attack'. In fact, many fighters prefer to be struck first, for just that reason.

The climax: transforming the event to violent chaos

This was almost certainly going to be a 'losing battle' in the purely physical sense. Yet there was still the potential for a narrative victory.

Rick had borrowed a small knife from Aaron a few minutes earlier when Dukey was being chased, and now was fingering it in his pocket with anticipation. TJ was watching in admiring disbelief as Brian actually stood up to opponents that were 'like three times his size'. For a brief few seconds Brian had become a spectacle, centring attention around himself in the service of his group's project to 'get into a fight' and his project to cast himself as a courageous character. Almost always one member of the group gets himself overwhelmed, sacrificing his body on the faith that the others will also sacrifice themselves attempting to 'save' him. Rick continued, 'they just like rushed at him ... A guy punched him and he went down instantly. Like, he didn't even get one good punch in'.

One of the most pressing narrative risks in this scenario is failing to act quickly, that is, being too cautious of the physical dangers, thus risking cowardice. An intimidating opponent stopped Rick in his tracks for a brief moment before he made it to the crowd piling on Brian. He was confronted with both a physical and a narrative threat. The latter became especially troublesome when he hesitated. After holding his hands up to suggest, 'I come in peace', he strategically was able to rush past the first opponent toward Brian, though someone soon struck him on the head knocking him to the ground. Suddenly he had to worry about himself – abandoning his demonstration of loyalty.

The first few moments of a brawl take on disproportionate magnitude, since the fighters know they may have only seconds to define their own participation. Joe managed the risks well, immediately charging into the midst of the crowd surrounding Brian. For a moment Rick caught a glimpse of him throwing punches wildly at everyone he could. Almost as quickly as Brian, though, Joe was also pounded to the ground and kicked and punched repeatedly as he lay bleeding on the pavement.

Rick regained his footing, but remained in a precarious position. Brian and Joe had committed themselves to violent entanglements with much larger opponents.

Rick, however, was still on the periphery of the brawl. He found a moment, though, to gather his composure when the attention shifted away from him:

> And there was like four or five guys behind me. More guys coming out of the house. And probably like ten guys over here [beating up Brian] – ... I pulled out the knife, and I just started *talking shit*, dude, as loud as I could. And screaming and telling them to get off Brian or else I was gonna stab them, you know? ... And they all just started running at me ... And I remember thinking, 'Oh shit, there's no way that I can take on like fifteen guys'.

TJ saw this as reminiscent of another frequently recounted underdog brawl: 'Then Rick ran over and pulled out this knife and started talking shit, just like the time he saved Chad's life.' Though Rick had paused at first, he redeemed himself at least for that moment, leaping into a familiar and deeply storied identity as 'saviour'. If one fails to make the important commitments during a moment of panic, then redemption is possible by re-committing oneself to violence in a later moment of reflective planning.

TJ began running to Rick's aid when the crowd 'readjusted their focus on him instead of Brian'. Whereas Rick felt reluctant at first, TJ felt drawn in by the enormity of the situation. Years of talking and symbolically imbuing brawls with an enticing aura paid off. Rather than experience the flock of violent men as dangerous and repellent, TJ felt their threat and Rick's vulnerability as a siren call to action:

> It wasn't that I was afraid ... I think I was actually kind of excited. Like, 'Okay, it's really gonna happen!' I didn't think about the fact that we were probably going to get annihilated. So I started going over. I thought we weren't going to have any chance if we were all split up, so I started going over by Rick.

Indeed, TJ seems to have been so excited that he did not recognise this brawl as an underdog one at that point. The underdog side depends on having at least one or two members who react like TJ did, overjoyed to finally get the opportunity they've been waiting for throughout that night and many others. Before he made it to Rick, though, TJ was also struck from behind. He was stormed over by the mob of pursuing attackers, soon unable to stand up. Even in the midst of the furor, though, he attended to narrative qualities of what was happening. From a purely practical standpoint, it would probably be most wise to simply assume the fetal position from the moment he was knocked down. Yet one risk is to fail to put up some form of violent resistance, or in the extreme, to construct oneself simply as a masochist in it only for the beating. Instead, TJ kicked out wildly for several seconds landing several blows, no doubt with little effect besides furthering his opponents' fury. TJ continued to be kicked in the head and the rest of his body. Having made a respectable effort and beginning to fear for his life he then elected to take the practical course of action: curl up defensively. Preferring not to come off as sadistic, those who share this culture of party fighting tend to stop their beatings soon after establishing clear physical domination (except in cases of deep moral outrage). Having reduced TJ to the fetal position, it would have been sheer perversion to beat him further.

During this Rick was running across the park ahead of TJ, and then down the street 'at a full sprint':

> thinking they're right on my heels, you know? And I got to right about here, up here in the middle of the street, past the car. And that's when I noticed that no one was following me anymore. And I turned around and that's when I saw TJ ... Getting kicked. I realised that no one was following me anymore.

Again, Rick found himself in a more threatening position than TJ, Brian or Joe. They had all by that time been overwhelmed and kicked into the fetal position. The possibility was growing that the 'steroid monsters' would begin to feel satisfied with their victory. If he suffered no injury or saw no real action the shame and disappointment would surely be preserved in his own and the group's memory. His options were narrowing. He would have to get beat up – badly.

Rick made a dash back toward the park where TJ was being stomped, 'screaming and waving my arms' again:

> And then probably like four or five guys saw me and turned around and started bolting at me. And then I started running again this way ... There was one who was catching up to me. And he picked up one of these fucking boulders right here [a softball-sized river rock] ... and said he was gonna smash me with it.

Too 'scared' to fight the opponent who was larger than he was and armed with a rock, Rick continued a narratively risky course of action. Sooner or later he was going to have to turn around and take a beating. Finally crouching behind a ten-foot-tall juniper tree, he demonstrated to me what he did when his opponent rounded the corner:

> And then he comes running dude, like full force ... I jumped out and I went, 'Ahraaa!' And then I went like this [showing me a continuous series of kicks and punches, the knife protruding from the bottom of one fist, used to slash his opponent's forearms] ... And he goes, 'Naa-raa-na'. [In a whimpering tone, as he crumples submissively toward the ground.]

Rick had, in that moment, drastically transformed his role in the event. Whether he had run away out of cowardice or to strategise became unimportant. It worked. He had won the only victory in the fight, beating and slashing one opponent to the ground. The fight was about to continue: 'I hear, "*Pat-pt-pt-pt-pt*" [patting his palms in the air like running feet] ... And coming down the street are all his buddies. So I go, "Oh shit!" And I turn around and I kept on running.'

Rick's luck soon ran out. The rest of his adversaries gained ground. Finally he found a wall and backed up against it to make his 'last stand'. Rick at last made a commitment that ensured his risky moments of running away would be out-weighed by a final beating. They knocked him to the ground, where they kicked him until he was covered in blood, leaving him to crawl along the sidewalk in search of help.

He had encouraged Brian – promising, in effect, to back him up – and drawn TJ in. Yet he had 'run away' several times. Complicating things further, Rick was the largest of the group and a trained fighter. In fact, he was the only one who was even close to the same height and weight as their opponents. The risk had become massive, especially since Rick spent much of the fight running around 'strategising'. Had the strategy failed completely, he would have come out of the fight looking much different. But his strategy seemed up to that point to have worked. Of course, for the final rewards he would have to wait until the chaotic scene was reordered.

The denouement: reordering the chaotic scene

What happens during the fight does not automatically dictate what sense will be made of that fight – what kinds of selves they will be able to construct. The first moments after a fight are always uncertain ones. Would anyone, for example, think Rick acted bravely? Would they chastise him for running away? Given that four members of the group ended up on the ground being kicked repeatedly by groups of much larger men, that each had experienced the violence from a different perspective, and that they did not completely 'stick together', how would they find gratification in this defeat? How would they reorder the scene?

After a group brawl the participants on each side almost invariably regroup as soon as possible to talk excitedly about what has just happened. Whereas the fighters blur each other's perception of group boundaries and blur the details of the narrative sequence in the swirl of running and punching, they re-establish them in talk, re-grouping in a different sense. Once the dust has settled they are able to reflect on what has just happened. If everything has gone well, the fighters begin to realise that the selves they have fantasised about have become a reality. They thrill at what the fight has revealed: that individually and collectively they have acted with courage, daring, and loyalty; and that these characteristics of the self and the group will be public and enduring. If the fight went well, each recognises that all made a personal sacrifice. They quickly become aware that 'this is one for the books'.

After this fight, though, the reordering first meant picking up the wounded, in particular Rick. 'By this time,' James explained, 'all the guys had run away and Rick was missing in action.' Once the remainder of the group had picked themselves up off the ground, they drove around calling out Rick's name. In the meantime he had crawled along a sidewalk about two blocks north of where they had first parked, until he recovered enough to stand. He walked to a house where a 'get-together' was in progress and politely asked to use the telephone.

TJ received the phone call. They drove two blocks to pick up Rick, who was painted in the evidence of a proper performance: 'just covered in blood', TJ described it. 'From his head – Just the whole side of his head, his shirt, the side of his pants. He was just soaked in blood.'

How was everyone reacting, I asked TJ, especially Rick:

> He was like euphoric it seemed like. Like silly kind of. Like happy silly ... We get out of the car when we get back to my apartment, and Rick walks up to this car and starts humping it. He just starts grinding his pelvis into it ... He was just like 'Ooh, yeah!' Like that's an expression of how he felt.

By the end of the night they had achieved the final product, the major incentive to fight: a dramatic fight story that will endure for years, retold to impress others of their daring selves, and to conjure both individual accomplishments and a sense of deep solidarity. The fighters walk away with battered bodies. But injuries heal and disputes are forgotten. The stories are not: they will be retold, remembered and cherished for years. The narrative becomes a permanent fixture of the fighter's biography.

Their enthusiasm continued through the next day, as TJ explained. 'The next day was kind of celebratory. We all got together pretty early and had some beers at my apartment in the afternoon ... It wasn't like celebration. But we basically talked about the fight for the next 36 hours.'

Aaron and Bob had failed to participate. They had some excuses: Aaron didn't see it because he was too drunk and Bob was talking to a girl inside. The others griped once or twice but let it go. James was absolved of any moral failure, simply because he 'does not fight', and also because he did help TJ get off the ground at one point. In any case, TJ, Rick, Joe and Brian spent little time focusing on who failed to participate. From the fighters' perspective it was their loss. Indeed it was: Aaron and Bob missed out on the thrill of having revealed the self as steadfast and heroic, and they were left out of the story that has been told countless times since.

Rick felt that the fight was a victory of sorts.

I figure we kind of won, in a way. Because I fucked one of them up real bad. And I'm pretty sure I broke that other guy's nose. And Joe broke his hand on the big black guy's face. He said he hit him in the mouth, so he probably hurt that guy. We got hurt worse than them, but none of us even had to go to the hospital. And TJ only got black eyes. If our friends had beat people up with those odds they would have been hurt a lot worse. So I figure we won that fight.

TJ provided the moral of the story, in terms of what it revealed about himself in relation to other, imaginary, future brawling scenarios: 'I think it was good that we fought those guys, though. Because now I'm not afraid to fight really big guys anymore, because they didn't really hurt me.'

Conclusion: where to go next?

One of cultural criminology's aims is to understand similarities and differences across motivations to do various kinds of troublemaking, risk-taking, and thrill seeking. So far the field has paid special attention to a few close studies, including Lyng's (1990) research on the thrills of 'edgework' among skydivers and Katz's (1988) descriptions of interaction, emotion and bodily experience in several varieties of crime. Citing those studies, later writing has focused mostly on similarities common to almost all crime: it is organised in interaction; it is marked by intense emotional and bodily sensuality; and it presents fateful threats to the self. It is important, though, also to attend to differences in criminal motivations. Those general findings can also be understood to point out dimensions along which all crime varies, and where to look in order to document varieties of criminal experience (see also Katz 2002). Because the interactional, sensual and fateful dimensions of crime apply so generally, cultural understandings could benefit from using them to guide investigation, document variety, and analyse comparatively. From Lyng we learn that 'edgework' involves tempting fate, defying nature's power, and situating skill in moments of extreme risk; from Katz we see that crime is diversely motivated by 'righteous', 'sneaky' and 'bad' sensualities. The particular social organisation, sensuality, and thrill of brawling are further variations.

Brawls are initiated by a loosely structured *pick-up*. Other common forms of interpersonal violence are specific to domestic settings, involve intimates or acquaintances, and are designedly coercive. In many ways brawls resemble casual sex more than enraged assaults. Brawlers go out and mix in with an anonymous swarm of urban or suburban partygoers, looking hopefully for receptive partners, teasing each other by talking shit, embracing in brawl, and finally separating, never to see each other again. Indeed 'getting in a fight' and 'getting laid' are the reasons these men give for what they hope to get from going to bars and parties.

The sensuality of the event is *ritualised urgency*. Although the pick-up follows certain ritual sequences, the chances of moving from each step to the next are low. Each time the brawler gets a step closer to physical blows his anticipation heightens until his emotion transforms to an authentically violent one. When a crisis point arrives and the brawlers attack each other, the situation begins to resemble non-planned emergencies. The brawler must suddenly deploy his body at pace and with an intensity exceeding anything experienced in ordinary daily routines. Reflective thought becomes difficult or impossible. There are no timeouts, as in 'sneaky thrills' like shoplifting (Katz 1988). Unlike people racing cars or motorcycles, brawlers expect some degree of non-lethal physical damage in every event – indeed, they often relish it.

Brawlers pursue thrills by managing competing *narrative gratifications and narrative threats*. Physical sensation may be the ultimate aim for skydivers and the like (as Lyng (1990) notes, such protagonists very often actually prefer *not* to describe the feeling), but brawlers use bodily appeals and risks – compelling as they are during battle – as resources for a more enduring project (see Ferrell, Milovanovic and Lyng 2001). Sensual urgency in the moment allows the brawler to look back, after the fact, into regions of the self that are ordinarily invisible. Until the fight happens he does not know if he has what it takes to do the right thing. He thrills at having revealed deep strength of character, seeing it in himself and presenting it to others through the narrative structure of a brawl.

Several tentative hypotheses relevant to cultural criminology are worth considering. First, brawls like the one described may happen only in affluent leisure cultures, where population is concentrated enough but also mobile enough to continually bring new batches of strangers together. Second, brawling may depend on notions of masculinity that encourage fleeting, emotionally distant relationships. The pursuit of urgency in leisure may be a way to negate stifling restrictions on bodily conduct and emotionality in contemporary suburban American culture, or perhaps a way to salvage a sense of personal control in a life that makes the individual feel insignificant. Third, brawling as storied action may be explained partly in relation to mass-mediated entertainment. Television and cinema demonstrate generally how to achieve a charismatic self through publicly witnessed narrative events. Further, they provide specific frames of reference to explain and construct behaviour, showing ways to be the kind of character who achieves notoriety and celebrity.

A central argument in cultural criminology's programme is that crime, violence and risk are organised and experienced differently in late-modern consumer cultures than they were before the mid-20th century and in other cultural milieus (see Hayward 2004). Although some of cultural criminology's texts are historically attentive, developing more detailed comparisons of criminality across historical epochs is critical. Ways of fighting certainly vary over time; some kinds of fighting are now lost to history, including, mercifully, the Appalachian-style gouging matches of the 19th century (Gorn 1985). Perhaps the sort of brawling described here retains something of past violence; perhaps it reflects something of consumer culture's odd permutations; and perhaps it too will one day be lost to history. Through further comparative and historical analyses it may be possible to decide exactly what about contemporary crime is new and what is enduring.

References

Black, D (1983) 'Crime as social control' 48(1) *American Sociological Review* 34–45

Ferrell, J, Milovanovic, D and Lyng, S (2001) 'Edgework, media practices, and the elongation of meaning' 5(2) *Theoretical Criminology* 177–202

Freud, S (1930) *Civilization and its Discontents*, New York: Jonathan Cape and Harrison Smith

Goffman, E (1967) *Interaction Ritual: Essays on Face-to-Face Interaction*, New York: Pantheon

Gorn, E (1985) '"Gouge and bite, pull hair and scratch": the social significance of fighting in the southern backcountry' 90(1) *American Historical Review* 18–43

Gottfredson, M and Hirschi, T (1990) *A General Theory of Crime*, Stanford: Stanford UP

Gulliver, P (1973) 'Negotiations as a mode of dispute settlement: towards a general model' 7(4) *Law and Society Review* 667–91

Hayward, K (2004) *City Limits: Crime, Consumer Culture and the Urban Experience*, London: GlassHouse Press

Katz, J (1988) *Seductions of Crime*, New York: Basic Books

Katz, J (2002) 'Start here' 6(3) *Theoretical Criminology* 255–78

Luckenbill, D (1977) 'Homicide as a situated transaction' 25(2) *Social Problems* 76–86

Lyng, S (1990) 'Edgework: a social psychological analysis of voluntary risk taking' 95(4) *American Journal of Sociology* 851–86

Marsh, P, Rosser, E and Harré, R (1978) *The Rules of Disorder*, London: Routledge and Kegan Paul

Morrison, W (1995) *Theoretical Criminology: From Modernity to Post-Modernism*, London: Cavendish Publishing

Chapter 20
Stories from the Streets: Some Fieldwork Notes on the Seduction of Speed

Heli Vaaranen

with an introduction by Mike Presdee

Introduction: telling stories about night-time car racing in Helsinki

In Chapter 3 of this book I talked of the ways in which we might excavate transgression through working closely, in a qualitative way, with those who create criminalised cultures through their everyday lives. Both our words and our subjects' words, I suggested, become the raw material within which lie both the meaning of social life and the ways in which that meaning was made. When we do social excavation we can reveal the way social sediments have been laid down and solidified through the pressure of pre-determined social structures. Here, then, is our raw material, waiting for us to historicise and analyse it in an effort to attain a more creative understanding of the social intentions buried in everyday life experiences.

We do not have, and cannot have, a handy template that describes this or that behaviour as criminal, anti-social, transgressive. These labels incorporate meanings defined and imposed by those with power and authority; meanings where social life is made to fit pre-existing ideological and theoretical propositions that describe certain groups and individuals as anti-social, or criminal, or evil. In qualitative excavation we reject that approach and privilege our 'subjects' as creative social beings living life within pre-ordained social structures as best they can – at times with great desperation and at times with a great love of life.

This short chapter offers us some of that raw material: notes from the field produced by Heli Vaaranen, a research fellow at the University of Helsinki who spent the years 1997 to 2001 talking with and interviewing young street racers on the streets of Helsinki. She has been back many times since, updating and excavating further this criminalised and dangerous culture. She has talked over the years to many 'players' within this social milieu, and in particular depth to six young men (some of whom feature in the following ethnographic vignettes).[1]

Many of her field notes revolve around the relationship between masculinity and the automobile. When we transposed the ancient male domain of 'horse power' to the modern combustion engine and the motorcar, we transferred the domain of masculinity with it. The image of men grappling with the pure muscle power of the horse, harnessing its power for their own needs and pleasure, was designed into the new petrol engine from its beginning, when we equated the power of the engine with 'horse power'. Mechanised horse power is today often admired by some men as if they still have hold of the reigns. Indeed car cultures involve the forming of public identities where social and sexual tensions are played out in an arena of 'homosociality', creating a public hierarchy of skill that contributes to the making of 'winners' and 'losers' in both social and sexual categories. The aesthetics of illegal night racing appear at first sight to amount simply to fun, noise and destruction; in

---

1 All names have been changed.

reality it is the setting for the expressing of emotion, sexuality and desire, driven by the seductions of speed, immortality and danger.[2] Heli Vaaranen's notes from the field contain within them this dynamic aesthetic of transgression, excavated and ready for analysis and interpretation.

Voices from the streets of Helsinki

At the edge of immortality

Romeo (a 24-year-old, self-taught car mechanic and stylish street racing-enthusiast):

> When you've been at the edge, and you're hanging onto life by a thread, you get the best feeling. When you're driving a motorcycle down south without a helmet, with shorts and a t-shirt on, and in turns the asphalt is just inches from your head and your bare knee, or when you drive in the mountains with a two hundred metre fall on the other side of the path and rocks on the other, and you drive as fast as you can, then when you get to your destination like to a party you feel so great that you can talk anyone into anything. When you're feeling that great you have so much to give that people just gather around you. Especially the girls.

Mr D (a 26-year-old construction worker with a taste for fast motorcycles) interrupts:

> When you're driving you feel immortal. I don't take it all the way to the edge anymore. I used to do it a lot with a motorcycle. A friend of mine drove twice into the woods when we were racing bikes together. He's had two car accidents and two motorbike accidents. He's been to hospital a lot. He's fucking crazy.

The dream of freedom

Henry (a 26-year-old stagehand and a committed lone rider of Harley Davidsons):

> When I'm out there riding my bike...that's freedom.

Heli:

> But what's freedom?

Henry:

> Freedom is like ... a dream. It doesn't need any clichés. You enjoy your freedom when your bike works and the motor runs. It's freedom bought with money. Expensive freedom. That's why it feels better than anything else. Freedom means you can come and go as you wish. Every Finn knows what freedom is. Finns are free. Part of your freedom is where you're going. It's good to go off when you leave nothing bad behind you, nothing unclear. When you've taken care of things so that things are all right behind you and in front of you. And where you're driving there is a place that welcomes you. Life works like saloon doors: they swing both ways. You get and you give. That's freedom.

---

2   The full extent of illegal street racing (both cars and motorcycles) in Finland is difficult to estimate with any real accuracy. Not only does the majority of the racing take place at night but it also typically occurs in remote areas, such as industrial sectors of the city or on the highways and dirt roads of the countryside. In large part this increasing fascination with speed and dangerous driving can be attributed to the Finnish nation's love of motor sport – in all its many variants. Certainly, an analysis of the country's accident statistics is revealing: a brief review of the *Central Organization of Traffic Safety in Finland* report (August 2003) indicates that young males dominate the accident statistics, with 40% of all automobile accidents involving the young taking place while driving 'off road'. Of all drivers receiving fatal injuries, 75% were young men.

The seduction of speed

Jake and *Juri* are two brewery workers in their 20s. Although they are best friends, they fiercely disagree about cars: Jake is fond of driving new cars, while Juri advocates re-modifying and driving aged BMWs. One Friday night they came to pick me up. We were going to watch some illegal Bombers – motorbike racers – behind the airport. The lads called me up and I went down to the street to meet them. Another old wreck of a car, I thought: a black BMW from the early 1980s. No airbags, torn seat belts, the car thick with cigarette smoke. Juri drove and Jake sat behind me looking sour. Juri sped down the street away from the city. No one wore seat belts. There were heavy tools and toolboxes scattered on the back seat.

We arrived at the scene. The long, wide street was blocked off from traffic. Gangs of lads were arriving on motorbikes and in cars. School-kids came through the woods on their bicycles. The show would start soon.

We drove on through a side street to meet some of Jake's pals. We turned into a dirt road and Juri sped along. Jake's friends were waiting for him at a crossing behind a small hill, drinking, but we didn't know which hill and which crossing. Juri decided to do some rally racing. There was no time to look at the speedometer. I glanced at the ditch and the thick trees on the other side of it. Juri was soon out of control. He did not know the road or the frequency of traffic there. At times, he drove on the wrong side of the road. There were small hills and crossings everywhere but Juri would not stop or slow down. Jake spoke on the cell phone trying to find out where his pals were. He kept calling and I overheard him, 'cancelled … cops'. There wouldn't be any Bombers racing tonight, at least not here.

The night wasn't going well. Juri threw the car into reverse and floored the gas. The car sped backwards. He stopped the car, sped forward, pulled the handbrake and the car span around fast. There was a sensation of flying, of being taken over by the rotating mass, of being dominated by the laws of physics.

Driving back to the city Juri dropped Jake off at a gas station. The mood changed. Juri took hold of himself and cruised slowly towards the centre of Helsinki.

Notes on the spectacle of a show strip party

It was a light night. I was out walking at a Cruising Night for American Cars with *Mika*, a 24-year-old electrician and American cars aficionado. We were waiting for the show to begin. People were amassing on the parking lot already: viewers, car fanatics, drunkards … Some American cars came into view. The drivers started roaring their engines and burning tyres. There was a calmness in the air. Mika pushed his head into a white cloud of smoke that emerged from the burning tyres. 'Fuck,' he said, 'Fuck this smells good.' He started talking with some people and I moved away. I went for a walk behind the scenes. I went for the camera in my purse but my hands shook and I didn't take it out. The atmosphere was turning bad. People were frustrated. The tricks displayed out there – speeding, burning tyres and jumping in and out of moving cars – didn't please the crowd. The crowd wanted more – faster cars, more roaring engines and more exploding tyres. More noise, more danger.

Figure 20.1 Street car rally, Helsinki, 2000.

Figure 20.1 Street car rally, Helsinki, 2000.

The carnival of danger

'Why don't you sit in the front seat,' *Miro*, a 26-year-old factory worker said. He was wearing a BMW cap. I want to go home soon, I thought. This is too much: me in a BMW on icy streets. *Nipe* (a 24 year old technician), Miro's childhood friend and fellow BMW devotee, drove out from the parking space and steered down the waterfront. He drove too fast. The car would never stop if something happened. The frozen street turned slightly to the left. The car slipped out of control for a moment, skidding and sliding to the side. I screamed. The lads laughed. Miro sang in the back seat, 'too much wine, too much song'. Nipe accelerated and the engine roared. The car started to skid and slide again. I felt the fear sink down to my stomach. The car slid on four wheels to the side, not much but enough that the car was now out of control. The rear end slid to the left and then to the right again and back to the left. My legs, I thought – I won't have legs after this ride. I pulled my knees up as high as I could, picturing the front of the car crashed into a lamppost. The lads laughed, shouted, sang. The car kept sliding to the side. 'This is Fucked!', Miro shouted. I screamed as the car slid towards oncoming traffic. Nipe steered the car back. His conduct spoke of routine, practice, and control of nerves.

Again Nipe accelerated and the car skidded and slid around a bend and I screamed as loudly as I could. 'Fuck this street is all frozen, frozen like a mirror,' Nipe shouted. I held my breath as we drove over the icy train tracks. We turned away from the waterfront and the street was easier to drive on. We had just driven through what was called 'stage race thirteen'. A stretch of road the lads had practiced thousands of times. They knew every stone, every angle, every turn. They knew the rhythm of oncoming traffic and they knew there would be no trains tonight. They knew exactly how far to push the speed. The route was named 'stage race thirteen' after six boys had collided their cars right there, with one of them driving straight at a wall.

Part 6

Questions of Agency and Control

Chapter 21
Speed Kills[1]

Jeff Ferrell

> Maybe you got a kid
> maybe you got a pretty wife,
> the only thing that I got's been botherin' me my whole life.
> Mister state trooper please don't stop me.
>
> *(Bruce Springsteen, 'State Trooper', 1982)*

By all accounts Lloyd Aragon was a good highway patrolman, a sharp-eyed, tough-minded state trooper who knew his way up and down his highway. Working the wide-open stretches of Interstate 40 that wind through northern New Mexico, Aragon and his police dog Barry tracked down speeders and, in keeping with the United States drug wars of the last two decades, focused especially on intercepting the shipments of marijuana and methamphetamine that flowed out of the southwest along I-40. Patrolling those long open stretches, Aragon knew what other cops and criminologists know: When it comes to drug shipments and drug busts, I-40 is a mainline vein that's been opened up more than once in the past 20 years.

In the autumn of 1999, Aragon opened it up again. Near Grants, New Mexico, Aragon pulled over Adrian Valdez-Rocha on suspicion of speeding, and wound up administering a field-sobriety test that Valdez-Rocha promptly failed. Meanwhile, Barry the police dog was letting Aragon know that Valdez-Rocha's car was failing a similar test, this one canine-administered. A search warrant and a careful car inspection later, and Aragon and other patrol officers found what Barry had sensed: a pound and a half of methamphetamine, neatly divided and plastic-wrapped into six bundles. Speeding, as it turned out, was the least of Valdez-Rocha's problems; there was also ... well, the speed.

Nearly two years later – 1 August 2001 – and Aragon was still on Valdez-Rocha's case, as Aragon and Officer William Cunningham rolled down that same stretch of I-40, heading east toward Albuquerque to testify at Valdez-Rocha's federal drug-trafficking trial. Zacharia Craig was also heading east toward Albuquerque that summer morning, just a few miles behind Aragon and Cunningham, and closing fast. Blowing down the interstate in a stolen Toyota Tacoma pickup, Craig was trying to outrun a chase team made up of state troopers and local police. Craig, it seems, had started his day early, at the Grants' Wal-Mart, trying to shoplift Sudafed – the over-the-counter nasal decongestant used in cooking methamphetamine.

When Officers Aragon and Cunningham caught word of the chase on their police radio, they decided to put their participation in Valdez-Rocha's trial on hold for a while, and to give their full attention to stopping Craig. Parking their cruiser in the highway median near the Los Lunas exit, they hurried to deploy a portable tyre-flattening device, a 'stop stick', in the interstate's eastbound lanes. They did their job well, and quickly; by the time Craig got there, the stop stick was in place.

---

1   Reprinted from (2003) 11 *Critical Criminology* 185–98 by kind permission of Kluwer Law International, The Netherlands.

Craig gunned the pickup for the highway median. Maybe he thought he could out-manoeuvre the stop stick, outflank the cops, and outrun the shoplifting charges. Or like Springsteen (1982) said, maybe he was running from something bigger than just the shoplifting, from something that'd been bothering him his whole life. Maybe it was the earlier charges against him for receiving and transferring a stolen vehicle. Maybe it was the SWAT team that had showed up the time he barricaded himself in his house or the tear gas they'd used to subdue him when he was wanted for stealing cable company vehicles. Maybe it was those charges back in May for possessing drug paraphernalia, for reckless driving, or for resisting arrest – and the arrest warrant they took out on him after he skipped his court appearance. Who knows, maybe for a minute, he thought he was some invincible automotive action figure.

Whatever it was, whoever Zacharia Craig was at that moment, his high-speed manoeuvre into the median cost Lloyd Aragon his life. Craig ran Aragon down – and he did so, it seemed, with a sense of purpose. 'It does not appear the vehicle was out of control,' reported the state police; Craig would've 'had plenty of room to escape' the stop sticks without hitting Aragon (Jones 2001a: A1)

Later that year, early December 2001, I'm rolling down I-40 myself, heading west. But I'm not chasing shoplifting suspects; I'm chasing shrines. For several years now, in fact, I've been investigating the roadside shrines and crosses that friends and family members construct in memory of those killed in automobile accidents. Developing in many cases out of the Latina/Latino and Native American tradition of *descansos* (resting places) in the southwestern United States, such shrines are increasingly found throughout the United States, and in various other forms throughout the world. My interest in the shrines is both cultural and criminological (Ferrell and Sanders 1995; Ferrell 1999). Each shrine creates a new sort of cultural space (Ferrell 1997b, 2001a), remaking the roadside as a memorial to a life lost, salvaging something of the sacred from the profanity of noise and litter. As friends and family members affix toys, photographs, key chains, compact discs, work tools, and other personal memorabilia, each shrine also takes shape as a public display, a symbolic life history of each individual victimised by automotive violence. And discovered day after day, mile after mile, these shrines have coalesced for me into something more: a roadmap of sorrow and loss, a vast graveyard splayed out along the open road, a suggestion of something more insidious than individual tragedy.

Cruising along today as slowly as the fast I-40 traffic will allow, I spot yet another shrine, this one in the highway median. It's Lloyd Aragon's shrine, the one that friends and family have built for him in the months since Craig killed him. The cross is built from 4x4 lumber, set in cement; it suggests its own serious sense of purpose. It also suggests something about the layers of Aragon's identity. His name is written on the cross arm, his dates of birth and death below; but above, at the top of the cross: 'NMSP' – New Mexico State Police. Two eagle heads and an angel rest at the cross's base. Little angel stickers decorate it. Plastic flowers and an American flag adorn the top.

A second, more intimate shrine sits just beside the cross, a circle of sorrow and remembrance carefully arranged on the median's rough ground. Here are more angels, doves, plastic flowers, and American flags – but also a little metal tubular cross with a single red rose, a Harley-Davidson doll, a Skoal chewing tobacco can, rosary beads, and feathers. Here are elaborations on Lloyd Aragon's NMSP identity: uniform patches that read, 'Patrolman, Laguna Police, New Mexico', and 'Seventy Fifth Anniversary InterAgency Law Enforcement Route 66'. And here, sad and lonely, is Lloyd Aragon's family. Sealed inside a plastic bag, a little framed picture, 'To Uncle Lloyd'. Wrapped also in plastic, a photo of an older boy and a younger girl sitting in front of a freshly filled grave, 'Lloyd Aragon' just visible on the new headstone in the photo. That would be his 11-year-old son, Lloyd Jr, and his four-year-old daughter, Audrianna. I can almost hear Springsteen again: Maybe you got a kid. Maybe you got a pretty wife. Maybe you can only take so much.

It gets worse when I stand back up and remember where I am. In the median of this northern New Mexico interstate, amidst the beer cans and broken mirrors, there's no refuge, no place to hide, only the sharp south wind whipping across the highway. And out here at Lloyd Aragon's shrine there's no heavenly choir, no towering gilded pipe organ echoing assurances against that wind. There's only the usual road shrine soundtrack: the blasting concussive roar of 18-wheelers booming by on both sides of me. And so, if on this December day I find the sadness and the vulnerability too much, I wonder how immeasurably worse it must have been for Lloyd Aragon's wife, Monica, for his friends and family and kids, building the shrine out here in the middle of all this thundering noise and deadly speed. And how unthinkably worse for Lloyd Aragon himself, for a veteran of so many big highway trucks and bad highway accidents, seeing Zacharia Craig and that Toyota pickup bearing down.

Chasing justice

But in fact, by this day in early December, much more than a roadside shrine had already been built out of the sadness of Aragon's death. To begin with, Valdez-Rocha's lawyers had built a plea bargain. Without Aragon to testify in court later that August day, prosecutors were forced to cut a deal – a five year prison term for Valdez-Rocha on 're-entry of a deported alien previously convicted of an aggravated felony', in exchange for the 20 years he would likely have received on the methamphetamine charges (Contreras 2001). A week later, Aragon's police dog Barry had already built a new drug case, and evened the score a bit. Out on patrol with a new officer, Barry helped bust two Michigan women driving down I-40 – just about five miles east of the spot where Aragon was killed – on charges of hauling 165 pounds of marijuana in their luggage (Jones 2001b).

Even by the time of that dope bust, only a week or so after Aragon's death, some deeper after-effects were also beginning to build. Noting both Aragon's death and another high-speed police chase through northern New Mexico on the same day, recalling also the death of a bystander in an earlier police chase, the *Albuquerque Journal* newspaper (2001) had editorialised that 'police could do a much better job of balancing the potential risk of high-speed chases to police as well as innocent bystanders with the severity of the suspect's crime. Shoplifting, the crime that cost state police officer Lloyd Aragon his life Wednesday, does not merit such risk'. A month later, a University of New Mexico professor and others had begun a campaign to change police policy regarding high-speed chases. Professor Ted Jojola, whose only son Manoa was killed by a vehicle fleeing a police chase, argued that such a chase 'sets off a chain of events that is really irreversible', threatening public safety far more than protecting it. By that autumn, New Mexico legislators were hearing testimony from Jojola and others, and were proposing legislation to regulate such chases more carefully (Linthicum 2001; Miles 2001).

For Jojola, Aragon, and others victimised by high-speed police pursuits, the life-and-death consequences of these pursuits make an obscenity of the usual police-chase image offered up for entertainment by television cop dramas, news programmes, action movies, and reality television shows. For fathers like Jojola, for wives like Monica Aragon, the chases are heart-breakingly real – real death races co-produced by fleeing suspects and pursuing police officers, real roadside shrines in the making. In fact, hoping to jar the public from the mediated fantasy of police chases as choreographed action entertainment, Jojola talked directly of dispelling the mediated 'folk hero' mythology of the pursuing police officer, and added, 'We're thinking the only way to change this is for the victims to tell our stories and to show what can happen. The danger is to any of us' (Miles 2001: E3; Linthicum 2001: A1).

Figure 21.1 Roadside shrine, northern New Mexico, USA. Photograph by Jeff Ferrell.

Back out on I-40, Aragon's shrine does indeed continue to show what can happen, to tell its own victim's story about a police chase gone bad, as it stands in that median day after day. Other shrines do also, and in their accumulation begin to document the degree to which 'the danger is to any of us', if not from high speed police chases then from other high-speed dangers. Some 10 miles west of Lloyd Aragon's shrine, out past Mesita, a still-functioning stretch of old Route 66 curves around a big hill as it parallels I-40. An even older, long-abandoned alignment of Route 66 – the 'Mother Road' of the US, the way west for 1930s Dust Bowl refugees and post-World War II auto tourists – angles off it into the red rocks above I-40. Along the southern edge of this lost alignment stands an old handmade roadside cross that predates Aragon's by who knows how many decades, a shrine I've visited more than once over the years.

Charred by brush fire, weathered by years of high country wind and sun, left to decay, it's lost the precision of personal remembrance that Lloyd Aragon's shrine embodies. But it stands as an equally sad story, an equally powerful reminder – a reminder that the danger was to any of us then as well as now, that there were worse things than kicks on Route 66, that not every Dust Bowl traveller or 1960s tourist made it to the promised land.[1]

More shrines are scattered and clustered all along this stretch of I-40. In fact, the day I discovered Lloyd Aragon's shrine I came upon another shrine, not 1,000 yards away down that same highway median. Unremarkable in most ways – no identification attached to the shrine, just the usual bunches of plastic flowers – it was remarkable in its configuration. Welded to the primary white metal cross, suspended from the end of it, was a smaller blue metal cross, and attached to this cross a cherub, violin in hand, playing against the wind and the big trucks. Kneeling to photograph this odd double cross, imagining that it signified a parent and child or some other tragic partnership, still thinking about Lloyd Aragon and his family, I noticed just beyond it a road mileage sign: 'Grants 44, Gallup 104, Flagstaff 288'. I wondered how many more shrines stood between me and Grants or Gallup or Flagstaff, how many life stories come and gone, how many crosses fallen to ruin, hidden away in the weeds along lost Route 66 alignments.

Shaken awake by Lloyd Aragon's death, Ted Jojola's testimony, *Albuquerque Journal* editorials, and other public pressures, the New Mexico legislature did in fact pass that proposed legislation to rein in high-speed police chases in early 2002 – and so in its own way began to acknowledge the collective tragedy of these countless shrines strung out along the state's highways. As it turned out, New Mexico Governor Gary Johnson vetoed the legislature's 'Law Enforcement Safe Pursuit Act' in March 2002, citing its potentially negative 'fiscal impact' on state budgets (Pawloski 2002: 1). But while Gary Johnson and the legislature may have missed connections on this one, they in other ways began to put into perspective the relative consequences of various public policies and public crimes.

By the end of his gubernatorial term in 2002, Johnson had emerged as one of the few public officials in the United States to challenge the last two decades' war on drugs, arguing that 'the current war on drugs is draining the nation and state of vital resources that could be spent more wisely and effectively', and proposing instead a 'harm reduction' drug policy founded on 'a medical model rather than a criminal justice model' (New Mexico 2002: 1; Johnson 2001: 1). In this light Johnson and his allies in the New Mexico legislature sponsored a variety of drug reform bills, including bills aimed at creating a Compassionate Use Medical Marijuana Act, decriminalising possession of small amounts of marijuana, reforming civil asset forfeiture policies, and reinstating judges' discretion in sentencing.

As with the Law Enforcement Safe Pursuit Act, Johnson and the New Mexico legislature missed some connections on this package of drug reform bills during the legislative session, but still managed to push through some significant changes. While bills on medical marijuana, marijuana decriminalisation and drug treatment programmes were voted down, the measures reforming asset forfeiture policies and reinstating judicial discretion were passed into law. These legislative wins and losses in New Mexico and elsewhere certainly constitute important early moments,

---

1   A (mislabelled) photograph of this shrine can be found in Ferrell 2001a: 249; see also the shrine photograph on p 250, and the shrine photograph in Ferrell 2001b: 102.

perhaps historic moments, in what I hope will become a burgeoning national movement for a peaceful resolution to the war on drugs. Yet of equal importance, it seems to me, is another historic moment – a moment in which various New Mexico citizens and New Mexico legislators began to reconsider two fundamental understandings: the presumed safety and normalcy of the automobile, and the presumed danger and deviance of drugs. This momentary juxtaposition – in which automotive pursuits were re-imagined in terms of their inherent damage and violence while illegal drugs were being re-imagined in terms of decriminalisation and non-violent medical treatment – offered New Mexicans, and all of us, something significant. It offered a crack in the social order, a breach of taken-for-granted assumptions. It suggested some new sense of balance and imbalance.

On balance, speed kills

About this imbalance allow me to be blunt, morbid and statistical. The interstate drug interdiction work of Lloyd Aragon and other New Mexico state troopers notwithstanding, Barry the police dog's big marijuana bust notwithstanding, police chases killed more people than did marijuana in the year Lloyd Aragon died – and police chases kill more people every year, in every state, by a magnitude of preposterous proportions. Despite Adrian Valdez-Rocha's meth case and thousands like it over the course of the war on drugs, automobiles cause the violent demise of more people than does methamphetamine – and in fact New Mexico road accidents generate more deaths, year after year, than all the state's illegal drugs combined. The war on drugs notwithstanding, the ongoing wartime construction of drugs as enemy and threat notwithstanding, there's a far more deadly adversary out there.

During 2000, for example, New Mexico recorded 435 traffic fatalities. That same year the Office of Medical Investigator reported 261 'drug caused deaths', including 228 in which narcotics were present, and seven involving methamphetamine; other sources listed 167 illicit drug overdose deaths for the year (Division of Governmental Research 2001; ONDCP 2001; Smith 2002). The next year, the year Zacharia Craig killed Lloyd Aragon, New Mexico traffic fatalities were up to 478; but illicit drug overdose deaths, those from heroin, cocaine and methamphetamine combined, were down to 139 (Westphal 2002; Smith 2002). Even the numbers of automotive pedestrian deaths alone, of those run down like Lloyd Aragon, are revealing in contrast to drug deaths. In 2000, the year in which New Mexico recorded seven methamphetamine deaths, the state recorded 48 pedestrian fatalities; by 2001 pedestrian deaths had jumped to 77 (Westphal 2002: 1).[2]

And all of these numbers must in turn be understood within a larger number, and a larger context: some 40,000 highway fatalities in the United States every year: 41,730 during 2001, 42,815 during 2002.

Like all published data, these numbers are of course more suggestive than definitive. To begin with, state and federal drug-fatality statistics generated during a high-profile and politically charged war on drugs may well tend toward intentional or unintentional inflation, and so in fact *underplay* the extent of the imbalance between car deaths and drug deaths (see Sanders and Lyon 1995: 35). On the other hand, it could be argued that such fatality numbers are not comparable, since not

---

2   The Environmental Working Group (2002) actually gives even higher numbers: 85 pedestrians killed and 1,740 injured each year in New Mexico.

everyone uses illegal drugs, while almost everyone drives – but the fact that almost everyone drives is in large part the problem, and the foundation for the thousands of fatalities that follow. Further, cases of convergence between the two categories are certainly possible – for example, cases of automobile drivers killing others while under the influence of drugs. Yet other sorts of convergence, ironic and unintended, seem more likely. It seems likely that some significant portion of illicit drug overdose deaths are more products of the drugs' illegality – that is, of the historical and ongoing criminalisation of drugs – than of the drugs themselves, given the dynamics of impurity and misinformation that necessarily accompany illegal drug distribution, use and control (see Young 1971; Kappeler *et al* 2000). More to the point, it seems likely that police chases of 'dangerous' drug suspects – 'dangerous' in part because they are defined as such by those commanding the war on drugs – cause more danger and death than do the drugs themselves. In medicine this is called iatrogenesis – doctor-induced illness, a cure worse than the disease. In criminal justice, it should be called bad policy and bad politics.

All of which raises some other troubling questions of statistics, and politics, and imbalance, among them: How is it that a social problem that kills 40,000 people a year, at a cost of $140 billion (Burns 1998: 9), remains largely excluded from public discussion in the United States? How is it that the pervasively violent consequences of some social arrangements are ignored while the depravity and violence of others are so readily imagined? How is it that stories about crack babies and crack attacks, about eight-year-old heroin addicts and superhuman meth junkies (Reinarman and Levine 1997; Reinarman and Duskin 1999; Jenkins 1999) are so readily believed, yet the stories written by countless roadside shrines so seldom read? Regarding the imbalance between deaths from speeding and deaths from speed, who are the real pushers, and who's pushing what?

Most readers know the first part of the answer: The war on drugs has from the first been fought not just against meth mules running open stretches of I-40, but more so against the possibilities of open debate and open minds; it has been a war waged primarily in the realms of image and ideology. As in earlier wars on one drug or another (Becker 1963: 135), political and media machines have operated in tandem to construct self-confirming moral panics around particular drugs and drug communities, to push the agendas of the powerful in the guise of public awareness, and 'thereby ... to forge a public prepared to swallow the next junkie stereotype and to enlist in the next drug war' (Reinarman and Duskin 1999: 85).

The answer's second part parallels the first, and reverses it: An ongoing automotive war on people and the environment has for decades been masked by the same machineries of media and politics that promote the contemporary war on drugs; carefully constructed universes of image and ideology minimise the dangers of the automobile in the same way that they inflate the dangers of drugs. Governmental transportation policy not only underwrites the economics of the automotive industry, offering up the infrastructure on which it continues to ride, but intertwines with an endless campaign of car commercials and automotive sponsorship that infiltrates everyday life to a degree war-on-drugs campaigners can only envy. In this world, 40,000 deaths a year somehow serve not to create moral panic, but to deflate it. Inside the culture of the car – inside the world of cigarette-sponsored Sunday afternoon automotive racing, 'Carmageddon' video games, and car customising magazines from *Car and Diver* to *Custom Rodder* and *Lowrider* –

elevated social status and reclaimed individual autonomy seem to accompany every ride.[3]

This second part of the answer in turn suggests one more set of questions, perhaps the most troubling: Why have critical criminologists, so adept at seeing through conventional ideologies of crime and justice, at exposing the arrangements of power that hide some crimes while inventing others, devoted so little time to exposing the everyday crimes of the automobile? Why have critical criminologists who have so courageously confronted the traditional (and political) exclusion of certain social harms from the domains of crime and justice – domestic violence, political criminality, hate crime – so seldom noticed this pervasive social harm? Why does the day-to-day criminology of the automobile remain an all but abandoned outpost in the already lonely 'Siberia of corporate criminology' (Mokhiber and Weissman 1999: 25)? In more personal terms, in Springsteen's terms: Why have all sorts of social injustice been botherin' me my whole life, but until recently, not this sort?

The injustice of the automobile is certainly rooted in the history and economy of the United States. Arguing that the peripatetic movement of workers around a factory constituted 'wasted motion and misspent energy' – or more bluntly, that 'walking is not a remunerative activity' – Henry Ford (in Braverman 1974: 310n; in Robbins 1999: 19) first introduced the fixed-station, endless-conveyer assembly line into the cultural economy of the United States workplace. With it, he ushered in a dynamic that has now a century later become the model for making hamburgers, managing *maquiladoras* and creating 'the electronic sweatshop' as well (Garson 1988). This innovation served to promote both the mass production and the mass consumption of the automobile; but soon enough an even larger mass market was needed. And so, beginning in 1932, the US auto industry and its allies worked to ensure that if walking was not a remunerative activity, neither was operating or riding an electric mass transit system. Partnering with Standard Oil, Firestone Tires, and Mack Truck, General Motors bought out and destroyed electric rail systems in New York, Philadelphia and Los Angeles – eventually eliminating more than 100 such systems in some 45 US cities.

The immediate result of this co-ordinated campaign was the conviction of General Motors, Standard Oil of California, and Firestone in 1949 on charges of criminal conspiracy – though no individual ever served prison time for the crime (Mokhiber 1988; Kay 1998). The long-term consequences of such activities, on the other hand, have locked us all in a prison of profound ecological destruction and social harm. In Paris, Rome, Bogota, Tehran, and other world cities, residents wear air masks as they move about in suffocating automotive pollution, and officials institute car-free days in an attempt to reduce it. Meanwhile, the ongoing, frenetic construction of roads and freeways continues, cutting urban neighbourhoods down the middle, carving the city into atomised isolation, and 'colonizing ever more spaces that were once devoted to human exchange and transforming them into systems of parking lots connected by highways' (Korton 1995: 283). Such spaces isolate people from each other and create lost ecologies left 'inaccessible to everyday experience' (Brissette 1999); they in addition underwrite the city's sprawl into a countryside itself caught in a tightening web of roads and highways. Of course, even where no road

---

3   Unsurprisingly, the culture of the car even spills out into the intersections of necrophilia and auto-erotica; see for example Ballard 2001 and Rupp 2001.

runs, the ruinous effects of endless oil exploration, of snaking oil pipelines and leaking oil tankers, of global warming, add to the car's awful consequences.[4]

And if all this is not enough, cases of egregious corporate malfeasance regularly punctuate this ongoing historical pattern of environmental degradation, community dissolution, and social atomisation. When General Motors introduced its new Corvair model to the United States in 1959, for example, engineers and executives at GM already knew of the deadly defects inherent in the car's rear-engine, swing-axle suspension design. The company's response to the injuries, deaths and lawsuits that followed was to buy up evidence and to settle the lawsuits surreptitiously. When Ford Motor Company rolled out its Pinto in 1971, the Pinto likewise sported a gas tank that the company's own safety tests had shown to be dangerously defective. But rather than fitting the Pinto with a safer fuel tank – at a cost of just under 10 dollars per car – Ford quite literally calculated that burn deaths and injuries from fuel tank explosions would cost the company less in the long run than the safer fuel tanks, and so released the car as originally designed. When the combined design and manufacturing defects of Firestone tyres and Ford Explorer SUVs orchestrated yet another rolling tragedy at century's end, the 271 deaths recalled not only Firestone's role in ripping up electric rail systems, but Firestone's premeditated marketing of defective steel-belted radial tyres in the mid-1970s (Nadar 1965; Mokhiber 1988; Cullen *et al* 1987; Skrzycki 2000, 2003).

To this can be added the paroxysms of state criminality and state-sponsored terrorism that have long defined the role of the United States and other Western countries in the oil politics of the Middle East – and all of this now fuelling an emerging global economy and sustaining the existence of automotive and energy corporations that rank among the most ruthless and powerful in the world.[5]

Yet for all this, criminology's blind spot seems to be not so much the scandal of automotive industry misbehaviour or the politics of oil imperialism, but the everyday criminality of the automobile – the daily automotive degradation of community life, the daily victimisation of passengers, pedestrians and cyclists by the thousands. After all, as day-to-day collective behaviour – that is, as the dominant form of human transport in the United States, as a 'vast spontaneous conspiracy' (Ballard 1973: 19) saturating the situations of everyday life – even cars with safe fuel tanks and sound tyres still kill quite efficiently; even automobiles offering better fuel economy still exhaust and pollute earth and community alike; and even the most honest of auto executives still manufactures fast-moving machineries of death (Burns 1998).

Since the day in December 2001 that I visited Lloyd Aragon's shrine, I've visited many more around the western United States, continuing to record and photograph their tragic beauty, trying to understand the communities of life and death they commemorate. I've discovered that it's here at these small sacred places amidst the expanse of weeds and roadside debris that I'm best able to think through the dynamics of this blind spot. Sometimes, lost within the process of framing and focusing on a photograph, I find myself back-pedalling to the very edge of the highway just as an SUV or 18-wheeler thunders past, the concussion of its air

---

4   Schlosser (2001) in addition links the cultural and structural dominance of the automobile to the modern degradation of food sources and diet.

5   As Clinard (1990: 39) makes clear, 'No US corporate industry has abused the American public more or had as bad a record of unethical and illegal behavior for a longer period of time than the oil industry'.

displacement knocking me off balance, the danger of its passing speed sending me scurrying back off the shoulder. At these moments, with the visceral proximity of automotive death still fresh in my gut, I think that perhaps the amount of time we spend inside the insulated comfort of our automobiles renders us unable to appreciate fully the discomforts, not to mention the dangers, faced by all those who confront automobiles from the outside (Ferrell 1997a).

Other times, overwhelmed by a shrine of especially heartbreaking tragedy – like Lloyd Aragon's with the photo of his kids posing in front of his headstone, or the shrine along a lonely stretch of New Mexico's Highway 6, where the children have put up crosses for 'Mom' and 'Dad' and written 'we-love-you-forever' on the blades of a little pinwheel – I think about the notion of hegemony, of domination so thoroughgoing as to become taken for granted. I wonder if maybe the culture of the car is so interwoven with contemporary life in the United States – so tightly intertwined with patterns of housing, work, pleasure and consumption – that critiques have been rendered unimaginable and alternatives unthinkable, even for those accustomed to critique, even in the face of 40,000 fluttering pinwheels a year.

Mostly, though, I've found in Lloyd Aragon's shrine and all the others the beauty of hand-made human remembrance, and with it the possibilities of new perspective. In their loving commemoration of so many lives lost, the shrines challenge us to confront the circumstances of this ongoing collective tragedy. They push us to look past the lies – past the ideological alchemy of war-on-drugs advertising campaigns, the slick unreality of television police chases, the commodified self-aggrandisement of corporate car commercials – and to notice instead the absurd imbalance of contemporary arrangements. Encoding the life-and-death consequences of such arrangements in the texture of the human landscape, they help us understand that today, and every day, the greatest danger to human life comes not from the traffic in marijuana and methamphetamine, but from the steady flow of high-speed automotive traffic, the rolling big rig truck parade, and the cops in hot pursuit.

After all, what's true for the occasional methamphetamine overdose is true for the everyday dose of highway death.

Speed kills.

References

Albuquerque Journal (2001) 'Police should balance risks', 5 August, p O4

Ballard, JG (1973) *Concrete Island*, New York: Picador

Ballard, JG (2001) *Crash*, London: Picador

Becker, HS (1963) *Outsiders: Studies in the Sociology of Deviance*, New York: Free Press

Braverman, H (1974) *Labor and Monopoly Capital: The Degradation of Work in the Twentieth Century*, New York: Monthly Review

Brissette, P (1999) 'Save the city!', *Bike Summer*, San Francisco: Bikesummer Ad Hoc Organizing Committee, p 3

Burns, R (1998) 'Non-crimes in the automobile industry' 9(1) *The Critical Criminologist* 7–10

Clinard, M (1990) *Corporate Corruption: The Abuse of Power*, New York: Praeger

Contreras, G (2001) 'Drug trial ends with plea agreement', *Albuquerque Journal*, 2 August, p A2

Cullen, FT, Maakestad, WJ, and Cavender, G (1987) *Corporate Crime Under Attack: The Ford Pinto Case and Beyond*, Cincinnati: Anderson

Division of Governmental Research, University of New Mexico (2001) *Draft Report for New Mexico Traffic Safety Bureau*, Albuquerque: Division of Governmental Research

Environmental Working Group (2002) *Mean Streets: Pedestrian Safety and Reform of the Nation's Transportation Law*, Washington, DC: Environmental Working Group

Ferrell, J (1997a) 'Criminological *verstehen*: inside the immediacy of crime' 14 *Justice Quarterly* 3–23

Ferrell, J (1997b) 'Youth, crime, and cultural space' 24 *Social Justice* 21–38

Ferrell, J (1999) 'Cultural criminology' 25 *Annual Review of Sociology* 395–418

Ferrell, J (2001a) 'Eleven dead caddies and one dead punk', in Brottman, M (ed), *Car Crash Culture*, New York: Palgrave, pp 247–57

Ferrell, J (2001b) *Tearing Down the Streets: Adventures in Urban Anarchy*, New York: Palgrave/Macmillan/St Martin's

Ferrell, J and Sanders, CR (eds) (1995) *Cultural Criminology*, Boston: Northeastern University Press

Garson, B (1988) *The Electronic Sweatshop: How Computers are Transforming the Office of the Future into the Factory of the Past*, New York: Penguin

Jenkins, P (1999) *Synthetic Panics: The Symbolic Politics of Designer Drugs*, New York: NYU Press

Johnson, GE (2001) 'Bad investment' at MotherJones.com (10 July 2004)

Jones, J (2001a) 'Officer trying to stop I-40 chase hit, killed', *Albuquerque Journal*, 2 August, p A1

Jones, J (2001b) 'Slain officer's dog aids in drug bust', *Albuquerque Journal*, 9 August, p D1

Kappeler, V, Blumberg, M and Potter, G (2000) *The Mythology of Crime and Criminal Justice*, 3rd edn, Prospect Heights, IL: Waveland

Kay, JH (1998) *Asphalt Nation*, Berkeley: University of California Press

Korten, D (1995) *When Corporations Rule the World*, West Hartford: Kumarian and San Francisco: Berrett-Koehler (co-publication)

Linthicum, L (2001) 'Wrong place, wrong time', *Albuquerque Journal*, 9 September, p A1

Miles, D (2001) 'Police pursuits contested', *Albuquerque Journal*, 17 November, p E3

Mokhiber, R (1988) *Corporate Crime and Violence: Big Business Power and the Abuse of the Public Trust*, San Francisco: Sierra Club Books

Mokhiber, R and Weissman, R (1999) *Corporate Predators: The Hunt for Mega-Profits and the Attack on Democracy*, Boston: Common Courage

Nadar, R (1965) *Unsafe at Any Speed: The Designed-In Dangers of the American Automobile*, New York: Grossman

New Mexico Legislators' Drug Reform Bill to Improve Public Health and Improve Fiscal Responsibility Receive Governor's Support (2002) News Release at http://governor.state.nm.us (8 January 2004)

ONDCP Drug Policy Information Clearinghouse (2001) *State Profile* (New Mexico), Rockville, MD: Drug Policy Information Clearinghouse

Pawloski, J (2002) 'To chase or not to chase', *Albuquerque Journal*, 1 September, Journal North section, p 1

Reinarman, C and Duskin, C (1999) 'Dominant ideology and drugs in the media', in Ferrell, J and Websdale, N (eds), *Making Trouble: Cultural Constructions of Crime, Deviance, and Control*, New York: Aldine de Gruyter, pp 73–87

Reinarman, C and Levine, HG (1997) *Crack in America: Demon Drugs and Social Justice*, Berkeley: University of California Press

Robbins, RH (1999) *Global Problems and the Culture of Capitalism*, Boston: Allyn and Bacon

Rupp, JC (2001) 'The love bug', in Brottman, M (ed), *Car Crash Culture*, New York: Palgrave, pp 77–81

Sanders, CR and Lyon, E (1995) 'Repetitive retribution: media images and the cultural construction of criminal justice', in Ferrell, J and Sanders, CR (eds), *Cultural Criminology*, Boston: Northeastern University Press, pp 25–44

Schlosser, E (2001) *Fast Food Nation*, New York: Houghton and Mifflin

Smith, B (2002) 'Fatal overdoses decline in NM', *Albuquerque Journal*, 21 May, Journal North section, p 1

Skrzycki, C (2000) 'The regulators: "Firestonewalling" again? Two decades later, echoes of earlier testimony', *Washington Post*, 12 September, p E01

Skrzycki, C (2003) 'Quality data is for US eyes only, auto industry says', *Washington Post*, 14 January, p E01

Springsteen, B (1982) 'State Trooper' on the album *Nebraska*, New York: Columbia/CBS

Westphal, D (2002) 'Statistics show New Mexico traffic fatalities were up in 2001', *Albuquerque Journal*, 19 February, p D1

Young, J (1971) 'The role of the police as amplifiers of deviancy, negotiators of reality, and translators of fantasy', in Cohen, S (ed), *Images of Deviance*, Harmondsworth: Penguin, pp 27–61

Chapter 22
What Happened to the Pathological Gang? Notes from a Case Study of the Latin Kings and Queens in New York

David C Brotherton

Between the years 1996 and 1999, my colleagues and I at the Street Organization Project at John Jay College of Criminal Justice spent many of our waking hours doing field work with one of the most notorious street gangs in the United States, the Almighty Latin King and Queen Nation (see Brotherton and Barrios 2004 and Kontos, Brotherton and Barrios 2003). The group had gained its infamy firstly through the reputation of its parent organisation in Chicago during the 1980s and secondly through its own actions in New York during years of internal blood letting in the early 1990s. The eight homicides that resulted in the most recent period were the occasion for one of the biggest gang trials in recent memory and led to the severest federal sentence (excluding capital punishment) since World War Two for the group's leader, King Blood: 250 years in a supermax facility, the first 45 to be spent in solitary confinement.

In this brief essay, I want to elaborate on two key analytical foci that helped us to make sense of the data: (1) the twin notions of agency and resistance, and (2) the alternative definition a politicised street gang, or what we have termed a street organisation. While cultural criminology as a self-described approach has seldom been applied to the ethnographic study of *bona fide* street gangs, there are many similarities in the works of Vigil (1988), with for example his emic evaluation of barrio gangs; Conquergood's (1997, 1993, 1992) discourse on street performances and communicative systems; and my/our own studies (2004, 2003, 1999, for example) on the notion of historicity. Certainly the major concerns of cultural criminology – ie, the quest for a fuller treatment of crime as sensual and psychological experience (as well as the incorporation of experience into methodology); the relationship between background and foreground factors in crime as action; and the production of a deviant/subversive aesthetic (Katz 1988; Ferrell 1996; Lyng 1990) – are extremely relevant and applicable to the life-worlds of gangs. Consequently, the research world would gain immeasurably if more studies were carried out in this vein.

In the following essay I begin with a brief survey of the changing history of societal responses to gangs in the US and their reflection of larger ideological impulses. This discussion will segue into a critical re-engagement with a selection of findings from our study in an effort to relate them to the project of cultural criminology.

Social control and the changing responses to US gangs

As youth street gangs throughout this century have ebbed and flowed, largely organised around class, racial, ethnic and gender configurations, their relationship to the problems of society has been consistently framed by society's most powerful interests. Today, it is as if the key holders to our moral economy have given the gang an unassailable status among the panoply of domestic demons, as evidenced by the recent apocalyptical utterings of Los Angeles' Police Commissioner, William Bratton:

> There is a giant need for Congress and [the] president to recognize that gangs are the emerging monster of crime in America. The war on terrorism now needs to focus on domestic terrorism. People in America's biggest cities aren't concerned about a hijacked plane hitting their neighborhood as much as they are on edge about drive-by shootings and stabbings on their front lawns. (Wood 2004)

Thus, from Los Angeles to New York and from Chicago to Miami, the street gang is commonly conceived and perceived as one of the most intractable problems of delinquency and crime. Not only are gangs said to be more numerous and violent than at any time since the Second World War, but it is also said that the age at which youth are joining gangs is younger, the length of time members stay in the gang is longer, and that gangs themselves have moved beyond their big city confines to small towns in the suburbs and even to unsuspecting rural communities (Office of Juvenile Justice and Delinquency Prevention 1998). As these qualitative and quantitative changes in gangs are said to have occurred so US society has changed the way it has responded both conceptually and practically (Spergel 1995).

In contrast, for most of the 20th century, the street gang was primarily considered a lower class social and economic issue, best dealt with by Durkheimian-inspired interventions designed to bring youth and adults back from the periphery and into society's conformist centre. These models of delinquency and adult crime prevention were reflective of 'good society' values and varied according to the progressive, 'pastoral' and/or welfare state strategies that were in vogue at time. From urban experiments such as the 1930s Chicago Project, to the 1950s New York and Chicago street outreach workers, to the 1960s policies of expanded opportunities provision, a long line of pragmatic prescriptions for social control were tried with varying levels of success. Ultimately, however, the so-called 'gang problem' continued, undergoing public scrutiny every few years in what Gilbert (1986) has called 'cycles of outrage', much like Cohen (1972) has described the role of 'moral panics' in Britain during the 1960s and Hall, Jefferson *et al* (1978) have analysed the period just prior to Thatcherism.

Nowadays, recoiling from any inclusive, liberal treatments of yore, the growing repertoire of praxes that fall under the social control umbrella terms 'gang preventions and interventions' bespeaks a criminology and criminal justice of a previous century (the 1800s), when deviant individuals were endowed with pathological properties and the citizenry was neatly divided into 'good' and 'bad' elements (Spergel 1995: 173). Indeed, a brief glance at the mass of gang seminars and 'trainings' found on the (US) internet reveals an extraordinary range of ways to depict 'The Other', all with the singular aim of suppression and/or purgation (see *inter alia* www.knowgangs.com, www.gangwise.com, www.gangwar.com, www.talkjustice.com, and www.streetgangs.com). But perhaps the highest point of this Darwinian/Baccarian trajectory has yet to be reached as we await the debate and possible passage of a bipartisan proposal in the Congressional Senate that, if adopted, will: (1) make gang-recruitment a federal crime, and (2) flush $700 million to local police jurisdictions to continue their hard-pressed, underappreciated war against our domestic non-white street subversives (note few resources are planned for curtailment efforts against the self-described paramilitaries of the extreme right or against the white supremacists of the Ayrian Brotherhood (Hamm 1993, 2004)). Certainly, Young (1999) is correct to assert that in late capitalist modernity, exclusion has become par for the course *vis à vis* processes of social ordering and containment, especially with such quintessentially hyper-real 'deviants' as gang members.

Figure 22.1 A monthly meeting of the Almighty Latin King and Queen Nation (courtesy of Steve Hart).

From the repressive state to the case of resistance

The street gang, therefore, despite the absence of a universal definition (see Katz and Jackson-Jacobs 2004) is a subject/object about which the government and the state have reached a consensus: first, it is above all a crime problem; and second, the solution to this problem lies in its organisational destruction and symbolic erasure. Consequently, when one of the most 'threatening' and criminally pursued gangs in the US, the Almighty Latin King and Queen Nation, declared that it was a social movement acting on behalf of the dispossessed, it was time to take a closer look at the gang phenomenon.

Focusing primarily on its social, cultural, spiritual and political characteristics, I (with my colleague Luis Barrios) carried out a case study of the Almighty Latin King and Queen Nation in New York City during 1996–99. In contrast to the media-criminology-criminal justice hyperbole surrounding the group, we found that its members were not the predictable results of discrete processes of social (mal)adaptation or, worse still, of social and individual pathologies, but instead reflected the contradictory, misunderstood and often ignored outcomes of socio-historical agency, cultural resistance and political struggle. I have likened this phenomenon to that of collective behaviour found in the international social movements literature (Castells 1997; McAdam 1982; Melucci 1989, 1996; Morris 1984; Touraine 1988) and to the various modernist and postmodernist interpretations of lower class contestation developed in (sub)cultural studies in Britain and elsewhere (Hebdige 1979; Hall and Jefferson 1975; Kincheloe and McLaren 1994; McLaren 1993; McRobbie 1994; Willis 1977). In the following I discuss two of the major findings of the study and draw linkages between them and the larger theoretical ambitions of this volume.

(1) Changing the form and the content of a gang through agency

The ALKQN came to New York State in 1986, founded in Collins Correctional Facility by (among others) Luis Felipe, better known as King Blood. What began as a small Latino inmate self-defence organisation, based on a strict hierarchical command structure, with organisational principles and rituals drawn from the Latin Kings in Chicago, by the early 1990s had become an extensive 'street gang' in New York City, with perhaps a thousand male members and a hundred female members spread throughout all five boroughs. It was during this period that the organisation was labelled by law enforcement as one of the most dangerous and disciplined gangs in the city. In 1994 almost the entire leadership was indicted by a grand jury for multiple counts of murder and assault against other members of the group, the result of an extraordinary bout of internecine warfare and powerplay that had few parallels in other US street gangs (see Brotherton and Barrios 2004).

Thus, by 1996, the organisation was in dire need of reform, not to reorganise its depleted ranks and restore its badly bruised reputation but to save it from itself. Some of the most important changes made by the ALKQN were to: (1) develop a politically progressive agenda which allowed it to recast its image as a pro-social, pro-community grassroots organisation – see below; (2) end the many punitive disciplinary procedures that were formerly used to bind members obsessively to the organisation; (3) pay closer attention to the social, psychological, economic and emotional needs of its membership; (4) embrace a non-denominational spirituality, drawing on both established and popular religious practices and beliefs; and (5) channel its abundant social resources into self-organised programmes such as literacy, cultural history and school tutorial classes, AIDS outreach, Alcoholics Anonymous and Narcotics Anonymous meetings, counselling on domestic violence, and trainings in conflict resolution. All of these changes were brought about by the group's unique interpretation of agency that saw it develop not only patterns of social and cultural resistance, for example by filling voids in the social safety net through strategies of self-reliance, but also acts of political contestation and social transformation that directly challenged the status quo. In other words, the group went beyond what Ferrell (in reference to Katz's seminal contribution to the phenomenology of deviance) calls the 'consciousness of contradictions in which they (deviants) are caught' (1991: 120), and analysed, planned and carried out actions that sought the resolution of these contradictions (and not just magically).

These major shifts in the civilian group's practical and philosophical orientation influenced the workings of the organisation in prison and, importantly, helped to interrupt the processes of recidivism for members re-entering society. But such changes also raised two major questions: (1) What were the deeper social and phenomenological forces behind these changes? (2) How might we explain this sophisticated type of street agency or historicity (Touraine 1988), particularly the group's struggle to understand and respond to the interpenetration of background and foreground factors that if left unchecked could tear the group apart? Below, I discuss four themes that bring together community-related issues of space, identity, colonisation and empowerment with both the predictable and unpredictable processes of domination.

Anti-colonial consciousness versus the continued marginalisation of barrio youth

Based on interviews with the group's members and observations of its activities I found that both in the prison and on the street, the inter-generational cultural, social, educational and economic marginalisation of barrio and ghetto youth was fostering an anti-colonial consciousness that found expression in the group's myriad forms of interactional rituals, texts and aspirations. For example, the group's manifesto and prayers were filled with exhortations to: overcome psychological states of subordination; develop high levels of unity; challenge domination and exclusion; build levels of self-esteem; and reclaim dignity and respect. Similarly, the organised acts of self-proclamation, the chants of 'Amor de Rey' (King Love), the physical gestures of the group's signing processes, are all forms of a group aesthetic and performance that consciously rupture the silence of the hegemonic culture. These acts of social celebration and shared emotional highs also tear to shreds the curtains of invisibility and in so doing reverse the processes of stigma that class society uses so effectively when dealing with social dynamite (Spitzer 1975).

In the case of the ALKQN in the prison system, these overt and latent sentiments of self-transcendence were laced with a Puerto Rican nationalism that bolstered the group's internal discipline and secured its cohesiveness against other groups. These same sentiments were translated by the reformist street leadership into an ideology and identity of individual renewal and collective empowerment. However, instead of the focus of the solidarity being the prison administration or other prison gangs, it was encouraged to find an external real and/or symbolic target, eg the city's right-wing Republican Mayor, the prison-industrial complex, the corporate dominated media, the sell-out local politicians, or the substandard public school system. At the same time, in a bid to aid this transitional phase, the reformist leadership sought alliances with a range of radical constituencies in the community, including churches. Therefore it warmed to those who could lend it material and cultural support in its efforts to penetrate the barrio's social closure (Wacquant 2002) and to reach beyond its parochial and outlaw-based isolation. Despite some resistance from the more apolitical elements, the group managed its changes quite fluently, causing great consternation among the leaders and foot soldiers of the state. Hence, there was a sustained and concerted campaign by the establishment to undo this experiment and thereby thwart what appeared to be a potentially dangerous example for the city's and nation's subaltern populations, much like the thinking that governs US foreign policy in Haiti, Venezuela and elsewhere. While there have been other historical moments where street gangs have sought to politicise their oppositional (sub)cultures (see Dawley 1992) it has been rare to see them form such powerful alliances with civic groups or allow themselves to be so radicalised out of this encounter.

The non-violent evolution of street youth

A strong argument can be made that the generation of youth that joined the ALKQN during the late 1990s learned that violence is not the only way to resolve conflicts. In New York, as in many other inner cities, youth experienced a critical mass of suffering brought about by the incessant social and economic assaults on barrio and ghetto communities during the Reagan and Bush years combined with the introduction of 'crack' as a new means to escape the indignities of everyday life. In contrast to the dire predictions of youth crime burgeoning throughout the 1990s (Fox 1998; Bennett *et al* 1996) and of a more remorseless type of street youth, the opposite was the case. In New York City, rates of serious youth crime fell, in line with the decline in serious adult crime (Correctional Association 2000), and reflected what Males (1996) pointed to as the modelling effect in the longitudinal trends of youth behaviour throughout the 20th century. Currently, another so-called remarkable turnaround is also happening among barrio and ghetto youth: they are getting pregnant less often as teenagers (*New York Times*, 8 March 2004). These examples of contestation and purposive lifestyles among ghetto/barrio youth and adults run counter to the images of fatalistic, unmediating and wooden parodies that flow from the pens of both liberal and conservative opinion-makers and alert us to the existence of an enormous constituency that is ripe for subversive, counter-hegemonic, political development.

The influence and changing role of women

Figure 22.2 A Latin Queen 'representing' during a monthly meeting (photo courtesy of Steve Hart).

During the late 1980s when the ALKQN was still in its gang phase, there were few roles for women. By the early 1990s, however, females were entering the organisation in increasing numbers and over time began to articulate a set of concerns specific to their own gendered interests. These early steps toward semi-autonomy gained widespread support almost immediately after the reformist phase was initiated. These new look Latin Queens, in which self-respect, independence, family support, ethnic identity and self-empowerment were the main items on their agenda, attracted a wide variety of barrio females who had been drug addicted, victimised and/or neglected by families, spouses and partners through much of their lives.

The involvement of such females searching for a new life (along with those without such pasts but who simply saw the group as a means to greater barrio solidarity) encouraged both leaders and the rank-and-file to become more nurturing, more cognisant of family matters, more inclusive in the sharing of power and less coercive in the group's use of discipline and rhetoric.

This shift among the women was not unlike that of the young males, in that they were both looking for ways to reclaim their lives and regulate their environments. In the case of the men, their major concerns were the loss of access to public spaces in their neighbourhoods whereas the females were more concerned with private spheres, such as the home and their own bodies. In both cases, however, the yen for agency is what brought them together and the fact that the vehicle for this transformative trajectory was the ALKQN reflects how opportunity structures have been reconfigured from above and below during the most recent period. It should be mentioned that as these female-based influences took hold, they inevitably strengthened the reform process and brought to the group a much greater range of cross-class supporters than would have been possible had its hyper-masculine image remained intact.

Prison-to-street gang origins and the effects of increased punishment

As is well known, the federal and state 'war on drugs' dramatically increased the rate of incarceration for Black and Hispanic males during the 1990s, with the vast majority of those convicted in New York City coming from just seven zip codes. As Latino inmates were released they took their gang identities with them. During the early 1990s, this caused the civilian membership of the Latin Kings to grow significantly, with ex-inmates disseminating their prison-based ideologies to a growing stratum of street youth looking to: (1) develop and ground their ethnic identity against the meaningless multiculturalism that masked their colonised and dehumanised state, and (2) build disciplined and high functioning organisations that could challenge the drug posses. Fortunately, this interpenetration of the codes, rituals and norms of the prison subculture and the life-worlds of street youth never hinged on or stimulated territorial sensibilities, as was the case with New York's 'jacket gangs' of the 1970s or its ethnic 'fighting gangs' of the 1950s.[1] This social fact about the group was also present in other gangs around the city, ensuring that the gang landscape was largely devoid of the internecine street conflicts of Chicago and Los Angeles. This key characteristic of the New York street scene allowed the ALKQN to concentrate its resources on its political agenda rather than on maintaining and defending territorial claims, and provided its members with an assortment of external societal enemies against which they could build their cohesion and their identities.

---

1   New York gangs in the 1950s and 1970s were strongly wedded to local neighbourhoods often bound by ethnic identities. Much of the gang fighting during these periods was caused by territorial disputes, the quest for respect and the need to defend personal and collective honour. The term 'jacket gangs' refers to the attire worn by members of the subculture. Hence, they would wear Levi jackets with the sleeves cut off and a highly stylised moniker of the gang or club sewn on the back. Another local New York term used to describe the street youth groups of this period was 'flying cut sleeves', which is also the title of an excellent documentary made by Henry Chalfant and Rita Fecher (1989) on the subcultures of this era.

In addition, by the mid-1990s, many ex-inmates were facing increasingly severe mandatory sentences and consequently were not willing to go back 'inside'. Neither, for that matter, were they willing to leave the organisation to which they had been affiliated while 'doing time'. As a result, a critical mass of non-recidivists emerged who understood that these new functions of the group would increase their chances of living with their stigma, finding entrée into the job market and eventually becoming legitimate members of civil society. It is important to note that during this period the New York region was an integral part of the longest boom in US history and a range of legitimate opportunities in both skilled and unskilled sectors of the labour market was available (see also Bourgois 2003). Consequently, what set the ALKQN apart from many other groups was that its agenda was not sufficiently compromised either by territorial gang feuds or by ex-inmates who felt unable to function outside of institutionalised, criminalised or violent street worlds.

(2) The difference between a gang and a street organisation

It should be clear by now that both the content and form of the ALKQN did not fit either the stereotype of the US street gang or its range of academic definitions. This 'finding' is consonant with a central concern of cultural criminology which is to challenge paradigms and truths of the dominant discourse and to promote explorations of social life that reveal unseen, overlooked and misread processes of creative resistance (see a range of contributions with this orientation in two edited volumes by Ferrell and Websdale (1999) and Ferrell and Sanders (1995)). In keeping with this perspective, therefore, an alternative descriptive and theoretical term, the street organisation, was developed in the course of the field work. Below, I compare some of the primary characteristics of the Latin Kings during the period that most of its members would have self-identified as gang members and the period during which it was fostering a new image and praxis.

A comparison of street organisations and gangs

While limitations on space do not permit me to deal specifically with each of the comparative characteristics listed opposite (see Brotherton and Barrios 2004), suffice it to say that the nature and breadth of the group's transformation played havoc with many of the stated and unstated assumptions that shape current and future debates on gangs. Consider, for example, two of the most popular definitions of the gang that appear in the literature. The first is by Klein (1971: 13) and the second is by Thrasher (1927: 46):

> any identifiable group of youngsters who (a) are generally perceived as a distinct aggregation by others in their neighborhood, (b) recognize themselves as a denotable group (almost invariably with a group name), and (c) have been involved in a sufficient number of delinquent incidents to call forth a consistent negative response from neighborhood residents and/or law enforcement agencies.

> (ii) an interstitial group originally formed spontaneously and then integrated through conflict ... The result of this collective behavior is the development of tradition, unreflective internal structure, esprit de corps, solidarity, morale, group awareness, and attachment to a local territory.

Comparative characteristics of street organisations and gangs

	Street organisations	Gangs
Period	1996–99	1985–95
Structure	vertical with increasing level of decentralisation	vertical with limited level of local autonomy
Territory	extra-territorial	situationally territorial
Ideology	communitarian/ utopian/spiritual	street survivalism/ entrepreneurial/cultish
Education	pro-school rhetorically and in practice	anti-school in practice but rhetorically pro-school
Delinquency	although some individuals do engage in delinquency this is not sanctioned by the group	rhetorically anti-delinquent but high tolerance in practice
Conflict management	mostly negotiation & mediation in inter- and intra-group conflicts with physical solutions as a last resort	negotiation & mediation used but confrontational & retributional solutions to inter- and intra-group conflict are common
Attire	beads & colours often situationally displayed	colours universally displayed & also artefacts of conspicuous consumption
Integration	high solidarity maintained through moral and political group pressure	loyalty maintained through physical threats and group pressure
Duration	long term commitment; exiting and entering the group through signed mutual consent	long term commitment; entering through mutual consent, exiting more difficult and may include physical penalties
Communication	local & general meetings; newsletters; face-to-face meetings	local, general & face-to-face meetings but many decisions made through secret missives

In the case of the former, the group characteristics are so broad that even with the pro-social changes taking place this delinquent definition could still be applied. The problem, of course, is that its use would necessarily omit practically all the qualitative transformations that were making the group so worthy of study. As for the second definition, many of its properties are simply not part of the group's history, although its emphasis on process and collective behaviour at least makes it possible to consider developments in the group's agency and its different forms of plasticity. Ultimately, we found that both the above definitions and every other that was being applied in the fields of criminology and criminal justice failed to advance either the empirical or theoretical scope of our study. Further, it showed how important it was to maintain a critical distance from many of the discursive and epistemological claims that effectively build hidden assumptions into the subject while conditioning the contours of inquiry. Finally, after much debate within the research team the following notion of a street organisation emerged. It is my/our assertion that such a concept, though not particularly criminological, encompasses many of the practices and states of consciousness in the group as we found them:

> a group formed largely by youth and adults of a marginalized social class which aims to provide its members with a resistant identity, an opportunity to be individually and collectively empowered, a voice to speak back to and challenge the dominant culture, a refuge from the stresses and strains of barrio or ghetto life and a spiritual enclave within which its own sacred rituals can be generated and practiced.

Conclusion

I have drawn on a number of themes from our long term study of the ALKQN in New York that appear to resonate with a range of concerns characteristic of the insurgent field of cultural criminology. I would argue that chief among these themes, at least from the perspective of an ongoing, progressive and innovative research agenda on US gangs, are agency, resistance, historicity and definitional privilege. The latter is particularly highlighted in our refusal to endorse hackneyed categories of deviance that long ago lost their meanings to the techno-linguists of state repression or to practice methodologies of urban discovery that legitimise the art of bean-counting pleasure and of reifying difference while managing to suppress all thoughts of shared humanity.

Unfortunately, given the predicaments and career trajectories of those caught in the academy, trapped between the research foci of the dominant criminal justice and health funding agencies and the heavily patrolled borders of orthodox criminology, it is doubtful that my/our critical assessments of the field will find too many adherents. Still, this is no cause for dismay, for hanging out in the margins, with the marginalised, if done ethically and reflexively, yields a lot more insights and is a lot more principled than swimming in the stagnant waters of the mainstream. Almost half a century since C Wright Mills implored us to use our sociological imagination, it is hard to see much of this sound advice being taken seriously in the study of gangs. It is therefore at this juncture where theoretical poverty meets methodological rigidity that cultural criminology as an alternative way of thinking, doing and imagining deviance will find its mark and continue to guide students of the street toward the unexpected, the non-rational, the resistant and the playful – even if such data cannot be easily quantified or turned into predictable models of social behaviour.

References

Bennett, WJ, Diliulio, JJ, Jr and Walters, JP (1996) *Body Count – Moral Poverty ... and How to Win America's War Against Crime and Drugs*, New York: Simon and Schuster

Bernstein, N (2004) 'Behind fall in pregnancy, a new teenage culture of restraint', *New York Times*, 7 March, p A1

Bourgois, P (2003) *In Search of Respect: Selling Crack in El Barrio*, 2nd edn, New York: CUP

Brotherton, DC (1999) 'The old heads tell their stories' 2(1) *Free Inquiry in Creative Sociology* 1–15

Brotherton, DC and Barrios, L (2004) *The Almighty Latin King and Queen Nation: Street Politics and the Transformation of a New York Gang*, New York: Columbia UP

Castells, M (1997) *The Power of Identity*, New York: Blackwell

Chalfant, H and Fecher, R (1989) 'Flying cut sleeves', New York: Cinema Guild

Cohen, S (1972) *Folk Devils and Moral Panics: The Creation of Mods and Rockers*, London: McGibbon and Kee

Conquergood, D (1992) 'On reppin' and rhetoric: gang representations', paper presented at the Philosophy and Rhetoric of Inquiry Seminar, University of Iowa

Conquergood, D (1993) 'Homeboys and hoods: gang communication and cultural space', in Frey, L (ed), *Group Communication in Context: Studies of Natural Groups*, Hillsdale, NJ: Lawrence Erlbaum, pp 23–55

Conquergood, D (1997) 'Street literacy', in Floord, J, Brice Heath, S and Lapp, D (eds), *Handbook of Research on Teaching Literacy Through the Communicative and Visual Arts*, New York: Simon and Schuster, pp 354–75

Correctional Association Bulletin (2000) *New York: The Correctional Association of New York*, Vol 1(1)

Dawley, D (1992) *A Nation of Lords: The Autobiography of the Vice Lords*, 2nd edn, Prospect Heights, IL: Waveland

Ferrell, J (1991) 'Making sense of crime: a review essay on Jack Katz's *Seductions of Crime*' 19(3) *Social Justice* 110–23

Ferrell, J (1996) *Crimes of Style: Urban Graffiti and the Politics of Criminality*, Boston: Northeastern University Press

Ferrell, J and Sanders, CR (eds) (1995) *Cultural Criminology*, Boston: Northeastern University Press

Ferrell, J and Websdale, N (eds) (1999) *Making Trouble: Cultural Constructions of Crime, Deviance and Control*, New York: Aldine de Gruyter

Fox, JA (1998) *Homicide Trends in the United States*, Washington, DC: US Department of Justice Programs

Gilbert, J (1986) *A Cycle of Outrage: America's Reaction to the Juvenile Delinquent in the 1950s*, New York: OUP

Hall, S and Jefferson, T (eds) (1982) *Resistance through Rituals*, London: Hutchinson

Hall, S, Jefferson, T, Crichter, C, Clarke, J and Roberts, B (1975) *Policing the Crisis: Mugging, the State and Law and Order*, New York: Holmes and Meier

Hamm, M (1993) *American Skinheads: The Criminology of Hate Crime*, Westport: Conn Praeger

Hamm, M (2004) 'Apocalyptic violence: the seduction of terrorist subcultures' 8(3) *Theoretical Criminology* 323–39

Hebdige, D (1979) *Subculture: The Meaning of Style*, London: Methuen

Katz, J (1988) *Seductions of Crime: Moral and Sensual Attractions in Doing Evil*, New York: Basic Books

Katz, J and Jackson-Jacobs, C (2004) 'The criminologists' gang', in Sumner, C (ed), *The Blackwell Companion to Criminology*, Oxford: Blackwell

Kincheloe, JL and McLaren, PL (1994) 'Rethinking critical theory and qualitative research', in *Handbook of Qualitative Research*, Thousand Oaks, CA: Sage, pp 138–57

Klein, M (1971) *Street Gangs and Street Workers*, Englewood Cliffs, NJ: Prentice Hall

Kontos, L, Brotherton, D and Barrios, L (eds) (2003) *Gangs and Society: Alternative Perspectives*, New York: Columbia UP

Lyng, S (1990) 'Edgework: a social psychological analysis of voluntary risk taking' 95 *American Journal of Sociology* 851–86

McAdam, D (1982) *Political Process and the Development of Black Insurgency 1930–1970*, Chicago: University of Chicago Press

McLaren, P (1993) *Schooling as a Ritual Performance: Towards a Political Economy of Educational Symbols and Gestures*, 2nd edn, New York: Routledge

McRobbie, A (1994) *Post Modernism and Popular Culture*, New York: Routledge

Males, M (1996) *The Scapegoat Generation: America's War on Adolescents*, Monroe, Maine: Common Courage Press

Melucci, A (1989) *Nomads of the Present*, Philadelphia: Temple UP

Melucci, A (1996) *Challenging Codes: Collective Action in the Information Age*, New York: CUP

Morris, AD (1984) *The Origins of the Civil Rights Movement*, New York: Free Press

Office of Juvenile Justice and Delinquency Prevention (1998) *1998 National Youth Gang Survey*, Washington, DC: US Department of Justice, Office of Justice Programs

Spergel, I (1995) *The Youth Gang Problem: A Community Approach*, New York: OUP

Spitzer, S (1975) 'Toward a Marxian theory of deviance' 22 *Social Problems* (June) 641–51

Thrasher, F (1927) *The Gang: A Study of 1,313 Gangs in Chicago*, Chicago: University of Chicago Press

Touraine, A (1981) *The Voice and the Eye: An Analysis of Social Movements*, New York: CUP

Touraine, A (1988) *Return of the Actor*, Minnesota: University of Minnesota Press

Vigil, JD (1988) *Barrio Gangs: Street Life and Identity in Southern California*, Austin: University of Texas Press

Wacquant, L (2002) 'Deadly symbiosis', *Boston Review*, 1 May, pp 1–25

Willis, P (1977) *Learning to Labour: How Working-Class Kids Get Working Class Jobs*, Westmead: Saxon House

Wood, DB (2004) 'As gangs rise, so do calls for a US-dragnet', *Christian Science Monitor*, 4 February, p 1

Young, J (1999) *The Exclusive Society: Social Exclusion, Crime and Difference in Late Modernity*, London: Sage

Chapter 23
Barbarians at the Gate: Crime and Violence in the Breakdown of the Pseudo-pacification Process

Steve Hall and Simon Winlow

> The predatory actions of capitalism breed, by way of defensive reaction, a multitude of closed cultures, which the pluralist ideology of capitalism can then celebrate as a rich diversity of life-forms.
>
> *Terry Eagleton,* The Idea of Culture *(2000)*

Introduction: criminology, economism and culturalism

Gregg Barak (2000) recently made the observation that neither the global system nor local culture can be allowed to eclipse each other if sophisticated criminological analyses are to be made. Although he could be insisting on compulsory balance in an extremely variable relation where balance is not always to be found, his comment certainly does describe the intellectual spectrum that has come to be defined at its extremes by economism/structuralism and culturalism. Economism, the notion that most of what we think, feel or do is determined in the last instance by the prevailing economic system, has along with biologism and conservatism been the principal target of critique in post-war liberal criminology. However, although much of that critique is deserved, we think it's also fair to say that the alternative possibility of criminology becoming too heavily influenced by culturalism has received far less critical attention. Culturalism is of course an extreme variant of cultural theory, a sort of inverted base/superstructure model that posits culture's diverse sets of meanings and values as the essentially pluralist bedrock of human existence, in which everything else – nature, economy, social relations, identity, politics and of course crime and violence – becomes a malleable, contested product of inter-subjective interpretations and discursive power-struggles rather than a feature of the mutating realities produced by historical processes (Hall 1997; Eagleton 2000).

An unbridled culturalist approach is always in danger of becoming one of global capitalism's principal apologists by helping to propagate the popular notion championed by neo-liberal thinkers such as Fukuyama (1999) that this particular economic system can allow more freedom of cultural form and personal identity than any other. The degree of faith placed in the consumer market system since World War Two has been immense, and the collapse of communism in Eastern Europe seemed to testify to it. Not only did the market promise freedom in the traditional American conception of the word, but also prosperity, stability, progress and the avoidance of the ugly imperialist political forms that had blighted the modernist project. It was tacitly accepted that in an era of increased peace and prosperity the social stability of the 1950s would continue. Things could only get better.

However, when it came down to crime and violence, they didn't. Despite rising affluence and the expansion of abstract rights and freedoms, things started getting worse. By the mid-1990s many American criminologists admitted that crime and violence rates in the USA were 'staggering' (Hagan 1994), Currie (1997) reminded us of the steeply escalating rates in the former command economies of Eastern Europe, Russia and China as they shifted rapidly to the market-capitalist economic model, and Reiner (2000) more recently pointed out that British crime and violence rates had throughout the 1980s and 1990s been undergoing *real* rises that were not simply the result of changes in recording practices. Although some parts of Britain and the USA enjoyed increasing prosperity and reductions in crime, the rates of murder and serious violence amongst young adults inhabiting areas of permanent localised recession remained unacceptably high (Zimring and Hawkins 1997; Taylor 1999). These rather gloomy criminological observations were made during a time of unprecedented free-market expansion that produced significant increases in the wealth of the world's billionaires alongside the persistence of near-absolute poverty for over a billion of its inhabitants (Ellwood 2001) and intensified feelings of relative deprivation amongst the increasingly insecure lower classes in the West (Lea 2002). The notion that things were getting better had to be qualified, as Hutton (1995) reminded us, by the fact that they were getting a lot better for the upper strata, fluctuating a bit for the middle strata and getting a lot worse for most of those who seemed to be permanently stuck in the lower strata.

The pervasive acceptance that the capitalist system might not be superseded or even brought under democratic political control in the foreseeable future has, with a few notable exceptions (see for instance Taylor 1999; Ruggerio 2000; Lea 2002; Wacquant 2002), created something of a hiatus in which thought has been largely distracted from critical investigations into ways in which human beings are interfacing in more *direct* ways with the demands of consumerism and global market capitalism. Without paying a huge amount of attention to the epochal reconfiguration of class relations going on in the background (Marshall 1997), the new liberal multi-culturalist model of governance, attempting to build on the successes of, amongst others, the post-colonial, black civil rights, feminist and gay movements, looked to the conferment of abstract legal rights on diverse cultural groups struggling in a fundamentally unchanged and minimally regulated economic system in order to create a 'level playing field' of equal opportunity. The key to justice and civility was the encouragement of tolerance and the celebration of difference as a means of cultivating convivial relations in the trying circumstances brought about by the inevitable disruption and reconfiguration of traditional industrial or agrarian ways of life (Hall 1997; Eagleton 2000).

This intellectual trend encouraged the return in the 1980s of administrative-reformist criminology, with its traditional focus on the criminal justice system augmented by the inclusion of cultural relations. However, the persistence of high crime and violence rates in specific locales and regions, together with the increase in prison populations across the industrialised West, tend to suggest that the multi-cultural liberal-reformist approach to the social management of capitalism is achieving even less success than the traditional state-welfare and socialist models (Taylor 1999; Wacquant 2002; Hall and Winlow 2003). In broad terms, we want to argue that the current difficulties experienced by the Western social administrative apparatus are tightly bound up with the virtual abandonment of any attempt to exert democratic political control on global market forces in favour a galaxy of brightly shining but rather distant and ineffective cultural gesture politics (Zizek 2000; Eagleton 2000). Our general contention is that cultural criminology, rather than becoming absorbed too deeply in this ideological principle that posits the emancipation of culture and identity as the key to a civilised life, should continue to consolidate the tendency shown by many of its practitioners (see Presdee 2000; Winlow 2001; Wacquant 2002) to place culture and identity firmly in their politico-economic and historical contexts.

Instrumentalism, economic exclusion and the 'new barbarism'

Here we present a synopsis of a body of work we have carried out on the future of social cohesion and the emergence of instrumentalism and barbarism in a period when historical capitalism's core cultural practice of competitive individualism has completed the colonisation of virtually every aspect of Western life. In this process have emerged codes of meaning and practice that combine the barbarism of the past and the predatory relations at the heart of today's market capitalism to produce cultural forms and identities that are closed, intolerant and violent, and, as such, constitute a threat to civilised life. Although we could have approached our investigation of advanced capitalism's 'new barbarians' (Angell 2000) by highlighting spectacular, exotic and successful manifestations, such as the Carlyle Group or the Russian Mafia, we selected something much more common and closer to home. Since 1995, our research has focused upon forms of criminality and violence emerging in micro-communities within locales that were first established and exploited only to be recently discarded by the economic processes and cultural currents of historical capitalism. A large number of working-class communities established during the industrial heyday of the capitalist project have now been left in a very precarious position as the functional economic point of their existence has evaporated in the globalisation process. Throughout the project our research data suggested a novel and quite disturbing type of despair emerging in specific locales within these areas, whose inhabitants have experienced the greatest difficulties in adapting in legitimate ways to the demands of the new consumer/service economy (Horne and Hall 1995; Hall 1997; Winlow 2001).

The term *anelpis* was used to describe this despair and its frequent visceral manifestations. This concept posited an historically unique section of humanity, which cannot be described as an 'underclass' in the structural sense because their wage needs have priced them out of the global labour market. They now inhabit locations of *permanent recession* (Taylor 1999; Lea 2002) in the old industrial West that are not only disconnected from capitalism's productive supply requirements but also have little chance of being reconnected in the future (Crowther 2000; Winlow 2001). However, despite this economic severance, our research data indicates that most of this group's members (especially the younger generations) have become ever more tightly connected to the demand side as a cultural group under the spell of consumerism, suffering the same status-anxiety and insecurity as others, only to a much more intense degree (Winlow and Hall forthcoming). Central to the original concept of *anelpis* was the presence of virtually total cynicism and nihilism: virtually no opinions, no realistic expectations, no hope and no fear of authority (Horne and Hall 1995), although we did find 'fear' in the form of susceptibility to the vague, nagging status-anxiety and insecurity mentioned above.

This condition described many men and a smaller number of women living in economically abandoned zones, and it is an outcome of the historical trajectory of the *visceral cultures* that were cultivated as functional units in the productive/military phase of capital (Hall 1997; Taylor 1999). Physical hardness, fortitude, persistence, endurance, mental sclerosis and a general 'hardening' of the psychosomatic nature were at the core of this being. These skills and qualities were encouraged and cultivated by high-capitalism's hegemony as vital functions in that phase of economic development, and they were reproduced internally in working-class culture by generations of practical enaction as *habitus*, a suite of deeply internalised dispositions that together constituted something much more impenetrable and durable than mere 'identity' (Bourdieu 1990) and are still reproduced with great fervour across the generations in these micro-communities. Ironically, it seems that the masculine cultural form that enjoyed almost iconic status in that past world – physically durable, macho, resistant to education and all things designated feminine (Faludi 1999; Beynon 2002), outspoken and sometimes driven by a crude but very penetrative political consciousness (Hall 1997) – is, if it continues to be faithfully reproduced, the one now suffering the most complete excision from the legitimate commodity cycle and the mainstream cultural hierarchy (Horne and Hall 1995; Winlow 2001). As our research moved temporarily into the areas of violent crime, drug markets and the expanding occupation of 'minding' in the criminal economy and the semi-legitimate nocturnal economies that continue to expand across the world (Winlow 2001), we found that this form's generative roots are not exclusively or even primarily cultural, but economic and practical, shaped by local opportunities and restraints, driven by the primal insecurity that capitalism has learnt to harness and use as its most powerful motivation for human activities. Rather than prompting progressive cultural change and new 'identities', these local economic conditions tended to intensify the visceral habitus that now is of relatively little value to the mainstream economy (Hall 1997, 2002; Taylor 1999).

Further work explored the link between the anelpic condition, crime and violence, highlighting the bleak reality of urban 'undersharks' and their victims. Deep in the heart of locales in permanent recession we found the last decaying vestiges of a mutuality that had, in the space of one or two generations, been virtually forgotten in language and practice. Here, our research continued to reveal 'hardened' micro-communities of predatory criminality and intimidated victims. We have been at pains to point out that predatory criminality is not simply 'caused' by relative deprivation or lack of education and jobs, and that it does not prevail amongst the majority of people inhabiting Britain's poor areas. However, persistently high rates of intra-class crime, violence, low educational achievement, family breakdown and recidivism appearing against a backdrop of hostility revealed to us what some who are hamstrung by liberal-capitalism's edict of compulsory optimism might prefer to remain hidden: micro-communities impervious to the effects of piecemeal legislation, social policy and inclusionary development programmes (Horne and Hall 1995). Extreme forms of economic exclusion are indeed emerging in and beyond the margins of advanced capitalism's old industrial societies (Byrne 1995), and a growing number of individuals who inhabit the communities that throughout the 20th century were serviced by unstable but usually available low-grade or casual occupations are now engaging routinely in crime and violence (Winlow 2001; Wacquant 2002).

Our research moved on to the analysis of what appeared to be a ubiquitous culture of hyper-individualism and instrumentalism emerging from the ruins of the social capital that had developed as a fragile bulwark against the barbarism of capitalism's military/industrial phase (Winlow and Hall forthcoming). Struck by the ubiquity of these enacted values and the virtual absence of substantive differences across the shifting strata of the new 'working' class (Marshall 1997), we rejected the excesses of existentialism and purist forms of sub-cultural theory that stressed the relative autonomy and free negotiation of meaning and became much more attracted to earlier forms. Some of these schools of thought, stretching from classical Marxism and Freudianism through the Chicago School to Mertonian strain and anomie theories, furnished us with valuable ideas, but, with the exception of Freudianism, tended to gloss over the essential insecurity at the heart of the human psyche (Lasch 1979; Hall and Winlow 2005) and the restraints imposed upon culture by the logical demands and imperatives of the social and economic systems (Eagleton 2000). Even the Birmingham School's attempt to ground culture and biography in society's socio-economic structure (see Hall and Jefferson 1975) was underpinned by the romantic and naturalistic notion of cultural resistance to authority (Sumner 1994; Hall 1997).

We were also struck by our respondents' determination to acquire the status symbols of manufactured culture at virtually any cost, which attracted us to older forms of cultural theory that stressed the mass media's persuasive power rather than individual choice and 'resistance'. What Giddens (1994) claimed to be a balance between cultural/agentic enablement and structural restraint seemed to us to be in reality heavily skewed towards the latter, and it became apparent that a significant number of individuals who were deeply absorbed in consumerism's object-sign-value system (see Baudrillard 1983) and simultaneously devoted to visceral cultures in danger of extinction were trying to engage with the stringent demands of global capitalism in their own inimitable way (Hall 1997; Winlow 2001). We were observing a different and manifestly impolite way of practising the powerful and ubiquitous cultural current of instrumentalism that grew in the transition from the relative stability of productivism to the unprecedented insecurity of global neocapitalism.

Moving to a more mid-range analysis, the insecurity that – although sometimes hidden by overstated bravado and steely instrumentalism – haunted so many of our respondents seemed to be based *experientially* on the fragmentation of communal ways of life, shared meanings, values and practices, and, above all, traditional and readily available ways of earning a living (Winlow 2001). The new occupational opportunities presented to our younger respondents by the retail/service industry were usually regarded as drudgery in the same way that previous generations regarded the ones they replaced, but they lacked the compensations of status, communality, collective resistance and stability. The main division we found between our economically excluded and included young respondents was not in basic values or individual attitudes to work and consumption but in their degree of deference towards legal and informal authority and, in the classic Mertonian (1957) sense, their willingness to use illegal means to satisfy ubiquitous ambitions. We quite simply did not find sufficient substantive differences in fundamental cultural values to support the concept of an 'underclass' in the cultural sense (Crowther 2000; Lea 2002; MacDonald and Marsh 2004), but we certainly did find sufficient differences in attitudes to criminality to support our own claim that a growing number of micro-communities experiencing virtually complete excision from the legitimate circuits of commodity circulation are conforming to mainstream culturo-economic values in notably visceral and occasionally violent ways.

As the Left Realists have been at pains to point out, there is nothing romantic or politically rebellious about these micro-communities or their inhabitants (Lea and Young 1993). Standard indicators of social problems, associated cultural phenomena and a cluster of well-known and extensively researched socio-economic processes were consistent with the cultural make-up of these micro-climates, what we might call a generalised anatomy of the anelpic zones (Horne and Hall 1995). Since the late 1970s, permanent localised recessions, widening income polarity, the current inflation of the housing market, the emerging fortress mentality of the new 'respectable classes', the intensification of educational selection and occupational accreditation, the tendency of better-educated working people to move out of troubled areas, the failures of social integrationism in the 70s and 80s, the expansion of drug markets and a host of accompanying factors contributed to the gradual ghettoisation of problem families and petty criminals in Britain and America (Wilson 1987; Taylor 1999; Wacquant 2002). A disproportionate number of downwardly mobile female-headed one-parent families and unstable, violent patriarchal families were strongly linked to the appearance of extreme examples of the now problematic 'visceral' masculine habitus at early ages (Beynon 2002). Mocking work and education, becoming involved with petty crime, adopting an attitude of extreme cynicism and instrumentalism towards most aspects of life and in a minority of extreme cases leading a virtually feral existence, this form became one of the accepted norms in these micro-communities. Further research revealed the erosion of traditional long-term friendships amongst young people *in general*, replaced by temporary instrumental alliances based on meanings and values manufactured by the fashion and leisure industries. Although practices, demeanours and attitudes to legal authority were entirely different, status-anxiety, competitive individualism and instrumentalism were common amongst both criminal and non-criminal young people (Winlow and Hall forthcoming).

Traditional values were not simply abandoned en masse, rather those useful to immediate survival were retained to be reworked in the new context and combined with the pseudo-libertarian values of post-war consumer culture in ways that most liberals either didn't expect, denied or didn't care about as the delicious prospects of personal freedom and satisfaction of desire captured their attention. For instance, the tradition of recognising mutual interests and organising collective responses to problems in the political or economic spheres virtually disappeared whilst the equally traditional tendency to establish closed micro-communities and become absorbed in the art of personal survival and prosperity on the basis of competition, suspicion, hostility and fear flourished (Taylor 1999). Instrumentalism quite simply began proving itself to be useful in everyday existence under the demands of the new global market economy and consumer culture. The anthropomorphic and often indiscriminate Kierkegaardian fear of the shadowy, threatening other replaced the traditional collective fears of hard times and oppressive rulers as the very concepts of politico-economic class and geographical community evaporated. This fear became a primary reason for entering into temporary, hostile and defensive alliances in a tense, paradoxical relationship with individualised instrumentalism (Davis 1990; Taylor 1999). As the global system goes through a phase of 'neo-feudalization' (Fletcher 1997), powerful feelings of fear, hostility and contempt in an uneasy alliance with envy and star-struck admiration permeate the relations that constitute the rapidly mutating and polarising structures of advanced capitalism, a matrix of emotions that once characterised the barbarian past (Veblen 1967; Diggins 1978; Mestrovic 1993). Ehrenreich (1997) warned of the return of the archaic connection between the joy of violence and the removal of threat, where relief is obtained by the destruction of the object that has been made to symbolise the cause of tension and also the primary obstacle to its resolution; a powerful and ubiquitous drive that has the potential to operate in all dimensions from the micro to the macro. Today, tension is generated as the primeval insecurity lying at the base of each human psyche approaches a condition of over-stimulation in consumer culture (Lasch 1979), a tension that is ironically individualised, confused and deflected by the quite deliberate under-representation of the collective danger posed by the 'new barbarian' business classes' global escapades (Taylor 1999; Eagleton 2000; Hall and Winlow 2003). Despite the nagging anxiety, so many have so little idea of what – beyond unemployment, looking unfashionable, terrorist bombs, immigration and petty crime – they should be really anxious about.

However, in a sterling effort to avoid becoming too broad or even apocalyptic in the midst of what we regard as powerful psycho-cultural currents flowing through the Western way of life, for the moment we have restricted our research to the ways in which two groups of young people – low-grade service industry workers and persistent criminals – are enacting in very different ways the instrumental relations and vague but powerful feelings of status-anxiety and insecurity that are common to both. Very early in this long-term research project we felt that these young people were entering adulthood to experience economic conditions, social relations and personal micro-interactions that, despite the alleged expansion of personal freedoms, rights and opportunities, were significantly less secure, convivial and emotionally fulfilling than those experienced by previous generations (Winlow and Hall forthcoming). Although we do not expect the evidenced claim that instrumentalism is eroding traditional communality and often being worked out in criminal and violent ways in economically abandoned zones to be regarded as too controversial, the accompanying claim that this possibly indicates a move towards a significantly more divided, hostile and barbaric future that cannot be prevented by cultural gesture politics and piecemeal socio-economic engineering (Hall and Winlow 2003) requires more substantial argumentation.

The breakdown of the pseudo-pacification process

As an icon and role-model, the rugged, ruthless and instrumental individual, rather than the cultured *flaneur*, the educated functionary or the mutualist member of the politically constituted community, occupied the high-ground in the eyes of many of the young people we interviewed, but especially those persistently involved in criminality (Hall *et al* forthcoming). They displayed a growing admiration for and affinity to the general barbarism that the Enlightenment and capitalism's unique civilising project had palpably failed to leave behind, and which seems to be making a comeback in both the top and bottom strata of neocapitalist societies (Horne and Hall 1995; Mestrovic 1993). This puts into question the purposes behind this so-called civilising process, purposes other than the pursuit of the Platonic or Hegelian ideal of civilisation itself or the classical liberal ideals of civility, progress, freedom and democracy. Surely, if civilisation, in the sense of the incremental and cumulative movement towards more humane, convivial and intelligent ways of interacting accompanied by a preoccupation with higher forms of cultural expression, had itself been the primary purpose of the Western 'civilising process', after 600 years its foundations would be strong enough not to be shaken so profoundly by such apparently innocuous phenomena as the partial slackening of sexual repression, the invention of some better machines and the further expansion of a global trading system that, as Braudel (1985) notes, has existed for a very long time.

However, examining the way in which the market-capitalist system has stimulated and harnessed the human propensity for insecurity can help us to understand the system's tendency to social instability, even in the face of rising affluence and expanding freedoms. The central role of insecurity in human history is revealed very clearly in the writings of Thomas Hobbes (Tuck 1989), for whom the social contract was a way of formalising the makeshift order imposed on society by the state and church as the preferred alternative to the climate of fear and barbaric violence that characterised earlier forms of socio-economic organisation. It seems that nascent elements of governmental pragmatism and rational consequentialism were complementing the super-ego controls and state controls that Elias (1994) saw emerging in Early Modern Europe's 'civilising process' as ways of controlling human anxiety, volatility and violence. However, missing from both Hobbes' and Elias' formulations was the standard Marxist/Weberian account of how market-capitalism and its developing socio-legal system emphasised the acquisition and protection of private property, its promises of safety, freedom and prosperity offering a seductive alternative to bonded serfdom or the vilification suffered by the merchant classes at the hands of the feudal aristocracy and the medieval Catholic Church. In the midst of all these economic demands and pragmatic, relativistic preferences it is very difficult to present the Western civilising process as a 'blind' evolutionary form (Elias 1994), a cultural ideal or even a practical end in itself (Hall and Winlow 2003).

There is little doubt that the civilising process did have some success in reducing rates of murder and serious violence in the internal territories throughout the modern era, although organised state violence remained high, which again indicates that primary value was placed on economic growth and military power (Hall and Winlow 2003). Our view, which in some qualified ways supports the classical Marxist account, is that the prime purpose of the internal civilising process, operating with the safety-net of a potentially if not always manifestly punitive criminal justice system, was to create conditions conducive to the development of the market-capitalist economy and the success of its principal bourgeois actors. The whole project was dependent on the ability of as many actors as possible to indulge in brutally competitive, instrumental, acquisitive and exploitative practices in economic and social life without resorting too easily to those bouts of internecine privatised violence that threatened the property rights and social stability required for the expanding production and circulation of commodities. Thus the development of internalised emotional repugnance towards violence and bloodshed and the reduction of general interpersonal hostility were primarily historical by-products of the logical need to reduce privatised violence in everyday life (without reducing the state's monopolised military and internal policing powers) to secure property rights and create a brutally competitive yet more cohesive, deferent, pacified and productive population. This was not a process that balanced relations of abstract socio-cultural power to 'civilise' and 'stabilise' for their own sakes, but one that for primarily politico-economic ends attempted with some success to temporarily pacify the everyday lives of most sections of the population: a *pseudo-pacification process* (Hall 2000; Hall and Winlow 2003).

The first step was to disarm the violent and politically dominant aristocracy, then to tame the banditry that emerged as sweeping dispossession and disruption of customary rights and lifestyles in the early stages of the process produced the countervailing phenomena of marginalisation, insecurity, hostility and rebelliousness. Under these circumstances internal violence was slow to fall, and the class and gender distribution of pacification was uneven. However, by the 19th century most women, who had been much more active in criminality and political protests up to the late 18th century, had been functionally pacified (Heidensohn 2002; Chesney-Lind and Pasko 2004). So to a lesser extent had most men who were directly involved in the circulation of commodities and professional occupations. The old aristocracy were still loosely connected to the organised violence of the military, but it was the displaced proletarian men working in the most brutal forms of heavy industry and militarism or sub-proletarians involved in the criminality that shadowed the capitalist project who were less pacified in terms of the internalisation of anti-violent sensibilities and deference to the state's monopolisation of violence (Winlow 2001; Hall 1997, 2002). This uneven distribution was chiefly a result of the fundamental paradox between the simultaneous need for pacification and deference on the one hand and serviceable forms of physical toughness and violence on the other, a paradox that is at the heart of industrial-capitalist forms of working-class masculinity that have always experienced various functional turnovers and identity crises as the 'pseudo' aspect of the pseudo-pacification process figured very highly in their lives (Hall 2002).

However, what concerns us here is the connection between instrumentalism, criminality and the *breakdown* of the pseudo-pacification process. The stimulation, subsequent sublimation and economic harnessing of insecurity were at the root of the social relations and cultural hegemony of early capitalist development (Hall and Winlow 2005). Although until very recently a high degree of *social stability* was vital, any political counter-movement that threatened to provide too much *economic security* for the mass of the population was fundamentally counter-productive to the capitalist project (Hall 1997). Striking a balance between social stability and economic insecurity was the main difficulty, but it is quite suggestive that the process achieved some relative success under the exploitative yet inclusive and relatively stable period of heavy industrial production, and even more under wartime conditions, where external threats produced the required fear and insecurity at the same time as the need for internal cohesion exceeded the level of social organisation and concerted effort required to be highly innovative and productive. Oddly, the monolithic economic engine of high capitalism, although far from perfect in its magnanimity, tolerance of difference and distribution of wealth and power, seemed to cope rather better – in the sense of being less polarised – with a fairly wide diversity of function and cultural form across the class and gender axes than today's self-proclaimed society of freedom and opportunity.

The major problem facing the pseudo-pacification process is that today's atomised, culturally-driven consumer society requires a high level of competition and instrumentalism in its *personal* relationships as well as its *business* relationships (Beck and Beck-Gernsheim 2002). This has led to the socially uneven breakdown of many of the more stable forms of culture and communality that, despite their repressive insularity and interpersonal tensions, for most individuals acted as refuges from the market's brutal competition and the major bulwarks to the destabilisation of industrial-capitalist societies beyond a critical point. There are now fewer refuges as even family relations, work relations and personal friendships become competitive and instrumental (Lasch 1979; Winlow and Hall forthcoming) and political collectives are gradually dissolved by the shifting demands of the economy and the systematic assaults of neo-liberal politicians, cultural leaders and media producers. At the same time as the dissolution of the communal refuges and hope-enhancing political collectives, the functional value of fortitude and physical endurance virtually disappeared as militarism became technologised and production became out-sourced and fully automated. Caught in a severe historical irony, the survival capabilities of the visceral form are now working against themselves in a consumer/service economy where the primary economic function of competitive instrumentalism has been fully sublimated, accredited and pacified in a rule-bound game that pervades not just economy and society but also cultural and personal identities (Hall 2002; Winlow and Hall forthcoming). Our research indicated that most young people are adopting quite ruthless instrumental attitudes in general, but whereas those with reasonable family support and education are finding places in the mainstream economy where the practising of these attitudes can remain relatively sublimated and pacified, many of the least supported, educated and adaptable individuals inhabiting closed cultural forms beyond the margins are now becoming visibly more hostile and destructive in their practices and prone to violent criminality (Winlow 2001; Taylor 1999).

Although Veblen (1967) saw the survival of the barbarian mentality in the generous predators that were the nations of the monopoly capital era as an historical continuity, our feeling – backed up by the absence of the everyday generosity that characterised the noble dimension of the old barbarian and the palpable presence of cold, utilitarian calculation in the nations of the corporate overshark and the criminal undershark – is that this is the path to a hitherto unknown zone where the nascent 'new barbarism' of the present bears no real resemblance to that of the past other than its potential for privatised violence. The breakdown of the pseudo-pacification process is the product of the failure of neocapitalism to find status and functions for visceral cultures that performed vital services in the nation-bound productive economies of high capitalism at the same time as its neo-liberal political classes presided over the wholesale dissolution of the traditional occupations, ethico-cultural codes, communities and political collectives that might have acted as secure platforms for adaptive change (Hall and Winlow 2003). Many of those who are wholly unable to adapt to the ever more stringently enforced rules of sanitised and pacified participation in the global consumer economy will inevitably form or join one of capitalism's quintessential 'closed cultures'. Here, they can practice the ubiquitous values of instrumentalism and competition in their own inimitably impolite and often quite vicious ways.

Conclusion

The emergent field of cultural criminology holds much promise for the analysis of crime and social disorder in the coming years. However, in one very important way it has emerged at a rather hazardous time in the general current of Western intellectualism, born at a crossroads where one major road leads in the direction of socially and economically transcendent culturalism and the other in the direction of cultural analysis grounded firmly in the economic logic of advanced capitalism. So far it shows a healthy tendency to channel much of its energy along the latter route. This article, in placing rising rates of crime and violence in the context of increasing instrumentalism in consumer culture and the breakdown of the pseudo-pacification process, warns of the danger of losing sight of the underlying politico-economic and processual contexts and drifting into extreme culturalism, and tentatively postulates the beginnings of a means of conceiving the historical macro-process that connects capital's economic logic with its criminal cultures.

References

Angell, I (2000) *The New Barbarian Manifesto,* London: Kogan Page

Barak, G (ed) (2000) *Crime and Crime Control: A Global View,* London: Greenwood

Baudrillard, J (1983) *In the Shadow of the Silent Majorities,* New York: Semiotext(e)

Beck, U and Beck-Gernsheim, E (2002) *Individualization,* London: Sage

Beynon, J (2002) *Masculinities and Culture,* Buckingham: Open OUP

Bourdieu, P (1990) *The Logic of Practice,* Cambridge: Polity

Braudel, F (1985) *Civilization and Capitalism, Volume 3: The Perspective of the World,* London: Fontana

Byrne, D (1995) 'Deindustrialization and dispossession' 29 *Sociology* 95–116

Chesney-Lind, M and Pasko, L (2004) *The Female Offender,* London: Sage

Crowther, C (2000) 'Thinking about the underclass: towards a political economy of policing' 4(2) *Theoretical Criminology* 149–67

Currie, E (1997) 'Market, crime and community: towards a mid-range theory of post-industrial violence' 1(2) *Theoretical Criminology* 147–72

Davis, M (1990) *City of Quartz: Excavating the Future in Los Angeles,* London: Verso

Diggins, J (1978) *The Bard of Savagery: Thorstein Veblen and Modern Social Theory,* Hassocks: Harvester

Eagleton, T (2000) *The Idea of Culture,* Oxford: Blackwell

Ehrenreich, B (1997) *Blood Rites: Origins and History of the Passions of War,* London: Virago

Elias, N (1994) *The Civilizing Process,* Oxford: Blackwell

Ellwood, W (2000) *The No-Nonsense Guide to Globalisation,* London: Verso

Faludi, S (1999) *Stiffed: The Betrayal of the Modern Man,* London: Chatto and Windus

Fletcher, J (1997) *Violence and Civilization,* Cambridge: Polity

Fukuyama, F (1999) *The Great Disruption,* London: Profile

Giddens, A (1994) 'Elements of a theory of structuration', in *The Polity Reader in Social Theory,* Cambridge: Polity

Hagan, J (1994) *Crime and Disrepute,* Thousand Oaks, CA: Pine Forge

Hall, Steve (1997) 'Visceral cultures and criminal practices' 1(4) *Theoretical Criminology* 453–78

Hall, Steve (2000) 'Paths to Anelpis, 1: dimorphic violence and the pseudo-pacification process' 6(2) *Parallax* 36–53

Hall, Steve (2002) 'Daubing the drudges of fury: the piety of the hegemonic masculinity thesis' 6(1) *Theoretical Criminology* 35–61

Hall, Steve and Winlow, S (2003) 'Rehabilitating Leviathan: reflections on the state, economic management and violence reduction' 7(2) *Theoretical Criminology* 139–62

Hall, Steve and Winlow, S (2005) 'Anti-nirvana: insecurity and instrumentalism in the twilight of the pseudo-pacification process', *Crime, Media, Culture*

Hall, Steve, Winlow, S and Ancrum, C (forthcoming) 'Radgies, gangstas and mugs: imaginary masculine identities and the culture industry in the twilight of the pseudo-pacification process', *Social Justice*

Hall, Stuart and Jefferson, T (1975) *Resistance through Rituals,* London: Hutchinson

Heidensohn, F (2002) 'Gender and crime', in Maguire, M, Morgan, R and Reiner, R (eds), *The Oxford Handbook of Criminology,* 3rd edn, Oxford: OUP

Horne, R and Hall, Steve (1995) 'Anelpis: a preliminary expedition into a world without hope or potential' 1(1) *Parallax* 81–91

Hutton, W (1995) *The State We're In,* London: Jonathan Cape

Lasch, C (1979) *The Culture of Narcissism,* New York: Norton

Lea, J (2002) *Crime and Modernity,* London: Sage

Lea, J and Young, J (1993) *What is to be Done about Law and Order?,* London: Pluto

MacDonald, R and Marsh, J (2004) *Disconnected Youth? Growing Up in Poor Britain,* Basingstoke: Palgrave

Marshall, G (1997) *Repositioning Class*, London: Sage

Merton, R (1957) *Social Theory and Social Structure*, New York: Free Press

Mestrovic, SJ (1993) *The Barbarian Temperament: Towards a Postmodern Critical Theory*, London: Routledge

Presdee, M (2000) *Cultural Criminology and the Carnival of Crime*, London: Routledge

Reiner, R (2000) 'Crime control in modern Britain' 34(1) *Sociology* 71–94

Ruggerio, V (2000) *Crime and Markets*, Oxford: OUP

Sumner, C (1994) *The Sociology of Deviance: An Obituary*, Buckingham: Open UP

Taylor, I (1999) *Crime in Context*, Cambridge: Polity

Tuck, R (1989) *Hobbes*, Oxford: OUP

Veblen, T (1967) [1899] *The Theory of the Leisure Class*, London: Penguin

Wacquant, L (2002) 'Scrutinizing the street: poverty, morality and the pitfalls of urban ethnography' 107(6) *American Journal of Sociology* 1468–532

Wilson, WJ (1987) *The Truly Disadvantaged*, Chicago: University of Chicago Press

Winlow, S (2001) *Badfellas: Crime, Tradition and New Masculinities*, Oxford: Berg

Winlow, S and Hall, S (forthcoming) 'Living for the weekend: instrumentality, consumption and "individualism" in youth identities', *Journal of Youth Studies*

Zimring, FE and Hawkins, G (1997) *Crime is Not the Problem: Lethal Violence in America*, Oxford: OUP

Zizek, S (2000) *The Ticklish Subject*, London: Verso

Chapter 24
The USA Patriot Act and the Politics of Fear

Mark S Hamm

The terrorist attacks of 11 September 2001 left Americans with a myriad of powerful emotions – anxiety, fear, sorrow, despair, and incandescent rage. Among these emotions, scholars argue that *fear* represents the common baseline for comprehending the complex aftermath of 9/11 (Barkun 2003; Berry 2001; Louis 2002). That fear was caused by extraordinary images of indiscriminate violence – planes crashing into buildings, skyscrapers in flames, men and women leaping to their deaths, and landmark structures collapsing to the ground as panicked crowds ran for safety amid a whirlwind of dust and debris. This vivid imagery demonstrated that the point of terrorism is fear. And fear, in turn, would define the very fabric of subsequent responses.

Apocalypse and public policy

'The shocking imagery of 9/11 redefined the scope of events,' argues Michael Barkun, 'transforming spectators into survivors.' We all became survivors on 9/11, writes Barkun, survivors of nothing less than 'a world-destroying power' (2003: 17). Indeed, the very name given to the World Trade Center site – Ground Zero – came from the lexicon of nuclear weapons, themselves associated with the capacity to destroy civilisation. The emotional aspects of September 11 were therefore directly associated with its political aspects via a long-standing American fascination with Christian apocalyptic speculation. The 9/11 attacks led to a marked increase in church attendance and a spectacular rise in sales for books with apocalyptic themes published in the United States (Benjamin and Simon 2002). According to a 2001 Time/CNN poll, roughly 30% of Americans believed that the attacks were predicted in the Bible. Another 35% thought about the implications of the daily news for the end of the world and 60% believed that the future will unfold in accordance with the Book of Revelation (*ibid*).

These visions were reinforced by the 19 hijackers, and their leader – Osama bin Laden – whose messianic pronouncements claimed that the attacks were prophesied in Muslim apocalyptic literature which predicts a disintegration of Islam followed by epic events that will lead to a worldwide resurgence of the Islamic faith (B Lewis 2003). The US response to 9/11 was also specifically apocalyptic in belief and intent. From his very first speeches following the attacks, President George W Bush nationalised our fear by launching America on a 'crusade' of 'infinite justice' against 'evil-doers' who had committed 'barbarism'. To fight this evil, Bush was willing to take on extremist elements of the Muslim world, in almost a Biblical sense. 'We will rid the world of evil-doers,' he said on 14 September 2001. 'Either you are with us or against us. You're either evil or you're good' (Bush 2001). The war on terrorism was therefore presented to the world as a mandate from God. 'I know many Americans feel fear today,' the President acknowledged when he began the war on 7 October (quoted in Woodward 2002: 209). 'To answer these attacks and rid the world of evil,' he said, 'we will export death and violence to the four corners of the earth in defense of this great nation' (*ibid*: 49).

Anthrax and the USA Patriot Act

While 9/11 was known for its agonising imagery, the anthrax attacks were marked by silence. Beginning on 4 October 2001, 23 cases of cutaneous anthrax were reported in the United States, resulting in five deaths. It hardly mattered that there was no evidence linking al-Qaeda to the attacks, for in terms of popular opinion the anthrax outbreak become part of the 9/11 narrative, thus amplifying the nation's fear. Nowhere was this more evident than on Capitol Hill.

On 15 October, an intern in South Dakota Senator Tom Daschle's office cut open a taped business envelope, letting out a puff of airy white powder that entered the ventilation system of the Hart Senate Office Building. As the airborne anthrax wafted through the building, chaos erupted in government buildings across Washington. Mail deliveries were suspended, bundles of mail and packages were quarantined, meetings were postponed, tours were cancelled, and military specialists were dispatched to search for biological and chemical agents. Soon anthrax spores were turning up in other Capitol office buildings, prompting discussions about shutting down the government (Thompson 2003). Against this turbulent backdrop Congress enacted one of the most sweeping criminal justice reforms in American history.

On 26 October 2001, President Bush signed the USA Patriot Act into law. The short-term objective of the Act was to enhance the authority of the Federal Bureau of Investigation's (FBI's) 'PENTBOMB' case. PENTBOMB focused on identifying the terrorists who hijacked the planes on 9/11 and anyone who aided them. The Act's long-term objective was to avert subsequent terrorist attacks in the United States and against US interests abroad (US Department of Justice 2003, hereafter referred to as DoJ).

But much had already been accomplished prior to passage of the Act. The day after 9/11, President Bush had directed the FBI to develop a 'scorecard' on the investigation as a way to measure its progress (Woodward 2002). In response, PENTBOMB investigators began compiling a watch list of potential hijackers and other individuals who might be planning future attacks. By 22 September, the watch list had grown to a staggering 331 names. That meant that there were 331 suspected al-Qaeda operatives in the United States – 15 times the number of terrorists who had hijacked the planes on 9/11. 'I was floored,' Bush later recalled to Bob Woodward. 'And [given the trauma of 9/11] the idea of saying, there's 331 al-Qaeda-type killers lurking, to the point where they made a list ... just wasn't necessary' (*ibid*: 117). This executive decision, meant to shield Americans from the fear of terrorism, created a model of intense secrecy that would characterise the Patriot Act. Ironically, while the Act was intended to curb the fears of 9/11, it would actually reproduce those fears in its own execution.

The USA Patriot Act – an acronym for Uniting and Strengthening America by Providing Appropriate Tools Required to Intercept and Obstruct Terrorism – gives far-reaching new powers to both the FBI and international intelligence agencies, based on revisions of 15 different statutes. It also eliminates the checks and balances that previously gave courts the opportunity to ensure that these powers were not abused.

Among its provisions, the 342-page Act grants the Justice Department the authority to: (1) share foreign intelligence surveillance information, (2) increase penalties for money laundering, (3) seize foreign assets in US-based accounts of foreign banks if there is probable cause that the funds were obtained illegally, and (4) place stricter controls on immigration, including the authority to detain non-citizens without a hearing, and to deport immigrants without any evidence that they have committed a crime. For US citizens and non-citizens alike, the Act also grants Justice the authority to: (5) tap telephones, email messages and personal computer hard drives (including roving wiretaps) without a legal probable cause, (6) request private and personal business and bank records without a court hearing, and (7) solicit a patron's list of library books. The Act also allows the Justice Department to: (8) investigate a person who is not suspected of a crime and/or is not the target of a terrorist investigation, (9) secretly conduct 'sneak-and-peek' searches without a warrant, (10) withhold names and other information about individuals arrested and detained, (11) hold closed hearings, and (12) monitor jailhouse conversations between attorneys and clients. Finally, the Act (13) creates a new definition of domestic terrorism, (14) gives government the power to designate domestic groups, including religious and political groups, as 'terrorist organizations', and (15) expands the authority of the President to designate individuals as 'enemy combatants'.

According to the Justice Department, these expanded powers are necessary because 'the threat presented by terrorists who carried out the September 11 attacks required a different kind of law enforcement approach ... The Department needed to disrupt such persons from carrying out further attacks by turning its focus to *prevention*, rather than investigation and prosecution' (DoJ: 13).

The controversy

Controversy surrounding the Patriot Act began almost immediately and it centred on three issues, all of which turned on the matter of government secrecy. First, the media started to report allegations of mistreatment among the terrorist suspects who had been rounded up and detained because their names had appeared on the FBI watch list. (Once the number of detainees reached 1,200, officials stopped keeping statistics.) Through their attorneys, these 'special interest' detainees, as they were known (nearly all Muslim or Arab men who were not US citizens), alleged that they were not informed of the charges against them for extended periods of time; were frequently denied contact with attorneys; remained in detention even though they had no involvement in terrorism; or were physically abused and mistreated in other ways while incarcerated (DoJ). Attorneys also argued that the Justice Department subjected detainees to arbitrary detention; violated due process by holding closed proceedings against them; trampled basic free speech rights – including the public's right to know 'what their government is up to' – by refusing to release the names of detainees; and ran roughshod over the presumption of innocence by presuming that the detainees were guilty of terrorist activities. The attorneys concluded that the Justice Department shielded itself from scrutiny by keeping from the public information that is crucial to understanding the extent to which the Patriot Act had been enacted in accordance with US law and international human rights law (Human Rights Watch 2002).

Many of these charges were confirmed in June 2003 when the Justice Department's inspector general released a blistering report that found 'significant problems' in the post-9/11 detention of suspected terrorists. Many detainees were classified as terrorism suspects on scant evidence, or no evidence at all. Others were detained for months without charge. There was a 'pattern of physical and verbal abuse' and detainees were routinely denied bail and access to lawyers. The report said that the Justice Department had 'poorly handled' its policies and practices. Although the report generated headlines around the world that spoke of 'unduly harsh conditions' imposed by American officials, Attorney General John Ashcroft dismissed these charges by saying that the Justice Department made 'no apologies' for how it went about protecting the American public from further acts of terrorism (Lichtblau 2003a).

Such hubris hardly ever goes unnoticed, and Ashcroft's pugnacity created a unique opportunity for lawmakers and government officials to reflect candidly on what took place behind the scenes during passage of the Patriot Act, leading to the second major controversy. Although the Patriot Act passed 357:66 in the House of Representatives and 98:1 in the Senate, these figures belie the politics of fear that gripped Congress during the anthrax attacks. Conservative Representative Don Young (R-Alaska), a member of the Homeland Security Committee, admitted to reporters that the Patriot Act was 'the worst act we ever passed. Everybody voted for it, but it was stupid, it was what you call "emotional voting"' (quoted in Tapper 2003). Then Representative Bob Barr (R-Georgia) declared it the 'most massive violation of civil liberties in our history' (quoted in Hentoff 2003a). A Congressional observer estimated that 'fewer than five percent of the people who voted for the bill ever read it' (quoted in Tapper 2003). Representative Ron Paul (R-Texas) explained why. 'The bill was not made available to members of Congress,' he said, '[it] wasn't even printed before the vote' (quoted in O'Meara 2001). Even Rand Beers, the Bush administration's senior counter-terrorism policy advisor, weighed in with a criticism. The Patriot Act, he said, was 'making us less secure, not more secure. As an insider, I saw the things that weren't being done' (quoted in Krugman 2003).

Resistance

The third issue also generated wide interest, though it received only marginal attention from the media. This issue, too, arose from fear – a fear that the Patriot Act threatened fundamental civil liberties. The most dramatic response to this was a collective resistance of local governments to the federal law. As of this writing (July 2004), 133 communities in 25 states have passed resolutions condemning the Act (Clymer 2003). These have included big cities like Philadelphia, Detroit, Baltimore, and San Francisco, and small towns like Dillon, Montana, Reading, Pennsylvania, Takoma Park, Maryland, and Ithaca, New York. Statewide resolutions have been passed in Alaska, Hawaii and Vermont. In all, nearly 12 million Americans live in communities that have passed anti-Patriot Act resolutions (Wenzel 2003).

These resolutions assert that the Act contradicts and undermines constitutionally protected rights without making the United States more secure from terrorism. Although these resolutions are largely symbolic, since federal law trumps any local ordinance, they nevertheless speak volumes about the extent to which the extended law enforcement powers have undercut public support for the war on terrorism. In Carrboro, North Carolina, city police are required to stand in the way of any unreasonable searches and seizures conducted by the FBI under authority of the Patriot Act. Police in Detroit are authorised to decline federal requests that are considered 'fishing expeditions', such as compiling a list of mosque attendees. And in the tiny town of Arcata, California, enforcing the Patriot Act is actually a crime punishable by a fine.

Other opponents have made the more serious charge that the anti-terrorism laws are being misapplied to advance agendas that have nothing to do with preventing another attack on America. Of primary concern are the revised intelligence-gathering powers of the FBI. Since 9/11, the agency has reportedly collected intelligence on environmental and anti-globalisation groups in the US, even though these groups have not engaged in terrorism (Dreyfuss 2003). The greatest threat to freedom in the United States, then, is posed not by terrorists themselves but by the government's own response. No less a publication than the *New York Times* reported that one of the nation's leading scholars of international law suggested at a meeting of diplomats that President Bush's advisors were planning to use the authority of the Patriot Act to suspend the elections of 2004 (Traub 2003). In other words, the erosion of civil liberties under the Bush administration constitutes an early stage of the kind of fascism that Hitler brought to Germany. In this nightmare, John Ashcroft is the reincarnation of Hermann Goering.

Cultural conflict

These denunciations served to legitimise the belief that people can and should organise themselves politically to repeal the new anti-terrorism initiative. Many of these local efforts combined politics with culture to produce a colourful collective resistance. Here in Bloomington, Indiana, for instance, the anti-Patriot Act resolution was presented to the City Council in a four-hour meeting that included speeches from scholars, human rights activists, Vietnam veterans, artists, and common citizens. These presentations ranged from legal and sociological analyses of the Patriot Act to poems, songs, and personal testimonies of fear. The name John Ashcroft was mentioned pejoratively in nearly every presentation – sometimes accompanied by tambourines, guitars, burning incense and sage. The emotional highpoint came with the testimony of a librarian – known to all as a peaceful young woman – who had recently been approached by two severe FBI agents and told to turn over the borrowing records of several Muslim students from Indiana University. She did not comply and was threatened with arrest.

Such local efforts were part of a wider cultural resistance that occurred as more and more Americans became aware of the Patriot Act's implications for civil liberties. Rocker John Mellencamp released a remake of the traditional American ballad, 'To Washington', with references to the president who 'had made things worse'. Mellencamp then issued a highly controversial open letter to America, declaring, 'We have been lied to and terrorised by our own government and it is time to take action'. Neil Young released a song critical of the Patriot Act while such divergent rock, punk, country, and hip hop artists as Merle Haggard, Eddie Vedder, Green Day, Willie Nelson, Jay-Z, Steve Earle, and the Dixie Chicks used their voices to take aim at the Patriot Act, US policy on Iraq, and the Bush administration's assault on the environment. The crowning moment of this artistic tirade occurred at New York's Shea Stadium on 4 October 2003 when America's working-class poet laureate, Bruce Springsteen, was joined by legendary troubadour Bob Dylan for a glorious romp of 'Highway 61 Revisited'. Springsteen then told the crowd of 50,000 adoring fans, 'Shout a little louder if you want the president impeached!' (Cave 2003).

The response

This assault forced the government to launch its own lobbying efforts to calm the public's fear of the Patriot Act. First, the White House assured Americans that any encroachments on civil liberties would affect only foreign nationals (Hentoff 2003b). Then President Bush enthusiastically praised Attorney General Ashcroft for doing a 'fabulous job' in the war on terrorism (*ibid*). Ashcroft addressed his critics with these words:

> For those who scare peace-loving people with phantoms of lost liberty, my message is this: your tactics only aid terrorists, for they erode our national unity and diminish our resolve. They give ammunition to America's enemies, and pause to America's friends. They encourage people of goodwill to remain silent in the face of evil. (Ashcroft 2001)

In subsequent Congressional testimony, Ashcroft claimed that the Patriot Act had made it possible to increase surveillance powers, thereby uncovering the status of al-Qaeda cells in the United States and abroad. According to the Attorney General, this led to critical intelligence about al-Qaeda safe houses, financing, recruitment, training camps, weapons caches, and locations in the US being scouted for potential attacks by al-Qaeda. In summarising these successes, Ashcroft declared that '*more than 3,000* foot soldiers of terror have been incapacitated ... and *hundreds* of suspected terrorists have been identified and tracked throughout the US' (Ashcroft 2003; emphasis added).

As for the anti-Patriot Act resolutions, the Attorney General proclaimed: 'We do not stand for abuse' (*ibid*). 'The guarding of freedom that God grants is the noble charge of the Department of Justice,' he told reporters, adding: 'The terrorists who attacked the United States have exploited God's gift.' And the Patriot Act, he said, would be used 'to guarantee God's gift' (FOX News 2002).

Far from being an impediment to freedom, then, the Bush administration considers the Patriot Act a valuable tool. Indeed, it is considered a *God-given* tool that has enhanced the ability to investigate and thwart terrorist attacks. 'Let me state this as clearly as possible,' said the Attorney General. 'Our ability to prevent another catastrophic attack on American soil would be more difficult, if not impossible, without the Patriot Act. It has been the key weapon used across America in successful counter-terrorist operations to protect innocent Americans from the deadly plans of terrorists' (Ashcroft 2003).

Terrorism research in a time of war

Strangely silent in this controversy has been a group whose professional training most prepares them to comment on the ramifications of criminal justice policy: academic criminologists. Such an analysis would consider two essential questions: (1) To what extent are the policy outputs of the Justice Department consistent with the original objectives of the Patriot Act? (2) What effects, in turn, do these outcomes have on subsequent legislative decisions (Mazmanian and Sabatier 1983)? What follows is a brief attempt to address these problems, along with several challenges facing scholars during a time of war.

The USA Patriot Act has one, and only one, clearly stated output. 'Our *single* objective', said the Attorney General, 'is to *prevent* terrorist attacks by taking suspected terrorists off the street' (Ashcroft 2001). The objective of the Act is not to investigate or prosecute terrorist acts, but to prevent them by bringing suspected terrorists under state control.

To the extent that this objective is achieved, it has important implications for subsequent legislative actions. The Patriot Act carries a 'sunset' provision to expire on 31 December 2005. (Some surveillance provisions do not expire.) Should the Act achieve its stated objective, then Congress will presumably renew it. Should it fail, then presumably the Act will be either revised or terminated. There is presumably only one failure scenario: the FBI fails to prevent another terrorist attack on America.

At least four methodological issues obtain from this sum-zero game, each with its own set of implications for criminological research. First and foremost is an issue of logic: Any evaluation of the Patriot Act requires disproof of a negative, which is notoriously difficult. If there are no future attacks on the United States by al-Qaeda or other terrorist groups, then it may be assumed that the Act has achieved its objective. But if there are no attacks, how do we know that they were actually 'prevented' by the Patriot Act? How do we know whether the absence of terrorism was related in part to the Act (and if so, what parts worked?), or whether the Act was unrelated to the absence of terrorism? And, at what point can we be assured that terrorism does not *in fact* exist?

Implications for research

The objective of the Patriot Act reflects a particularly Western slant on a problem framed by the legal institution responsible for its prevention. Yet terrorism is a dynamic phenomenon that is increasingly framed by non-Western sensibilities – most notably, the idea of *jihad*, or international holy war. Certainty about this worldwide *jihad* may not come for a long time. A major lesson of 9/11 is that al-Qaeda works on its own time line, often coming back to targets it might not have destroyed the first time around. The 9/11 attacks were the result of eight years of elaborate planning, religious indoctrination, and paramilitary training that began after the 1993 attack on the World Trade Center (Benjamin and Simon 2002).

Because terrorism occurs within a distinctive context of social, political and cultural factors, changes in any one these factors (eg increased public awareness) can explain an absence of terrorism. By ignoring these possible changes, the Patriot Act suffers from its own parochialism and isolation. Consistent with the Bush administration's global war on terrorism, the Patriot Act deals with the symptoms rather than the root causes of terror and extremism. As Turk notes, terrorism cannot be stopped solely by a public policy. It can only be ended by 'removing the deprivations ... that create the environment in which people's fears and hopelessness make terrorism appear to be their only option' (Turk 2002: 349). In this case, those fears are lodged in Muslim grievances. Moreover, there is no way to develop a comparative understanding of the *granularity* of the Justice Department's institutional performance – whether through aggregate quantitative analysis or through ethnographic and historical work – with other nation-states whose post-9/11 counter-terrorism achievements (eg Pakistan) have taught us that complex problems require nuanced solutions. These solutions involve not only law enforcement and intelligence capabilities, but also cross-cultural fluency and diplomatic skill.

The second methodological problem involves the Bush administration's doctrine of secrecy. President Bush has taken the firm position that the government's actions in the war on terrorism will remain 'secret even in success' (quoted in Woodward 2002: 108). Indeed, FBI Director Robert Mueller is on record as saying that 'terrorist attacks have been prevented' since 9/11 but these successes 'don't become public' (Mueller 2003). Yet Attorney General Ashcroft *has* released aggregate numbers on the war's success by stating that more than 3,000 'foot soldiers of terror' have been incapacitated, 'hundreds' more have been identified and tracked, thereby interrupting their 'deadly plans' of terror. But how can these figures be verified when the press, legislators, advocacy groups, social scientists, and law academics are denied independent access to basic information about these terrorists or their plots? Even the names of terrorist suspects are withheld from the public.

These conditions fail to meet even the most rudimentary standard for policy-oriented research on terrorism. Analysts therefore have little hope of assessing whether the administration's actions under the Patriot Act are actually preventing terrorism. They also have no way of evaluating whether the provisions of the Act are being applied in accordance with the law, nor do they have a way of evaluating whether the fundamental values and principles of America's constitutional republic are being compromised in the process.

The third problem relates to the credibility of official statements about the Patriot Act's effectiveness. Take, for example, the Attorney General's claim that hundreds of terrorists have been identified and tracked across the United States via the Patriot Act, leading to the successful disruption of numerous plots. Publicly available information paints a very different picture:

- The Justice Department's own inspector general examined the files of 762 of the 1,200 'special interest' detainees arrested following September 11. None of them was ever linked to 9/11 or any other terrorist plot (DoJ).
- Under the Patriot Act, the Justice Department has conducted a massive counter-terrorism sweep to deport some 13,000 Muslim men. Of that group, more than 3,000 have been arrested under the premise that they pose a 'security threat' to the United States. Yet the Justice Department has acknowledged that the majority of these men were involved in offences such as violating immigration rules, using fake identity documents, and various civic infractions (Dreyfuss 2003). There is no evidence that any of them were involved in plotting terrorist attacks against the United States.
- Since 9/11, approximately 680 men from more than 40 countries have been detained indefinitely at the US naval base at Guantanamo Bay, Cuba. The vast majority of these 'enemy combatants' are suspected al-Qaeda fighters who were captured on the battlefields of Afghanistan; thus the actions leading to their incapacitation are unrelated to the Patriot Act (N Lewis 2003). And while the FBI has used the Act's provisions to interrogate some of these enemy combatants, to date terrorism charges have been brought against only one of them.
- The Patriot Act has contributed little to what the administration considers its most important successes in the war on terrorism. These include the arrests of Abu Zubaydah, an al-Qaeda planner and recruiter; Khalid Sheikh Mohammed, the al-Qaeda chief of operations; José Padilla, the former Chicago gang member turned al-Qaeda operative who allegedly planned to attack a US city with a crude radioactive bomb; Zacarias Moussaoui, reportedly the 20th hijacker of 9/11; Richard Reid, who tried to set off a shoe bomb on a trans-Atlantic flight; and John Walker Lindh, the so-called 'American Taliban'. None of these suspects was incapacitated under the Patriot Act.
- There has been only one major terrorism trial since 9/11. This case involved two Arab immigrants from Dearborn, Michigan, convicted in June 2003 for plotting

to attack US airports, military bases, and landmarks. Yet these immigrants were arrested on 17 September 2001 – before the Patriot Act was implemented (Hakim 2003).

- There *are* cases in which the Patriot Act has been used to arrest suspected terrorists in the United States. In each case, though, suspects have been arrested for conspiring to provide 'material support and resources' to al-Qaeda. None has been accused of preparing, planning or committing acts of terrorism. These cases include Minnesota resident Illyas Ali and two Pakistani accomplices, currently incarcerated in a Hong Kong prison for trying to sell drugs to raise money for al-Qaeda; James Ujama, convicted of running an al-Qaeda training camp in Bly, Oregon; six young Yemeni men from Lackawanna, New York, convicted of training at an al-Qaeda camp in Afghanistan; and five residents of Portland, Oregon, convicted of making an unsuccessful attempt to visit a bin Laden camp (Arena 2002; *Associated Press* 2002).
- Under the Patriot Act, only one known al-Qaeda member has been charged with plotting a terrorist attack against America. Iyman Faris – a 34-year-old Kashmiri resident of Columbus, Ohio, who suffers from mental illness – was taken into custody by the FBI in 2003 for planning to destroy the Brooklyn Bridge in New York City shortly after 9/11. Accounts vary as to why his plan was aborted, yet the plot was not prevented by the Patriot Act (Lichtblau 2003b).

The disjunction between official claims-making and publicly available information creates a reliability problem. Because the problem of reliability is a basic one in social science – especially in criminology – researchers have developed a number of techniques for dealing with it. Yet each technique requires a baseline accounting of fact (eg police records) which is prohibited under the Patriot Act. This problem is exacerbated by the numerous classifications used to define individuals affected by US counter-terrorism policy in the post 9/11 era. What terrorism researcher can keep track of so many disembodied 'special interest' detainees, 'security threats', 'enemy combatants', 'terrorist suspects', and 'American Taliban' catalogued in US military stockades, jails, prisons, and foreign lock-ups?

Finally, any analysis of the Patriot Act will face a serious time-series problem. Earlier I listed 15 provisions of the Act as it was originally implemented in October 2001. (Again, this is only a partial listing.) Since then, the Attorney General has instituted more than a dozen Executive Orders changing various rules of the Act. These have dealt mainly with surveillance and matters relating to the interrogation of material witnesses. Justice Department attorneys have drafted a blueprint for the Domestic Enhancement Security Act (Patriot Act II), which contains additional provisions for expanding arrest and deportation authority.

Although there is a time-series design for examining such a fluid implementation problem (Campbell and Stanley 1966), the solution requires data. And, once again, there is little reliable data afforded under the Patriot Act. As such, any systematic analysis of the Act must be viewed as the social scientific equivalent of nailing jelly to a wall.

Conclusions

Using selected statistics for a political purpose is one of the oldest tricks in the book. A classic example occurred in the mid-1960s when the Federal Bureau of Narcotics (FBN) reported a 66% drop in federal prosecutions for drug offences from 1925 to

1966. The FBN concluded, therefore, that narcotics prohibition was a successful policy, thereby guaranteeing increased budgets and the development of new technologies of power targeted on vulnerable populations of urban blacks and foreign nationals. Against the FBN figures, criminologist Alfred Lindesmith contrasted non-federal prosecutions (state and municipal), showing that prosecutions had actually *increased* by more than 500% for the period in question, thereby raising doubts about the nation's drug policy. Lindesmith concluded that the official data were 'worthless ... they are nevertheless popularly accepted because the Bureau is in a position to repeat them endlessly in the mass media' (Lindesmith 1965: 119).

The same can be said of the Patriot Act. Not only are official claims about the Act uncritically reported in the media, oftentimes the media function as a public relations organ for the Justice Department. In its coverage of the Attorney General's 2003 Congressional testimony, for example, the *Associated Press* reported: 'The USA Patriot Act has stopped more than 3,000 "foot soldiers" of terror, Ashcroft said' (Holland 2003). Ashcroft did not say that. Publicly-available information indicates that some 3,000 al-Qaeda fighters have been incapacitated in the *global war* on terrorism, largely through the efforts of intelligence agencies in Pakistan, Jordan, Spain, Germany and France. The Patriot Act played no role whatsoever in this effort.

Nevertheless, the Justice Department has used the Act to justify substantial spending increases. For 2003, the Department's budget request was $30.2 billion, representing a 13% increase over its 2002 request (Ashcroft 2002). Even though counter-terrorism is the Department's top priority, its post 9/11 requests have included increases in more than 60 programmes that do not directly involve that priority (eg cybercrime, prisons, drug enforcement). As it turns out, the Attorney General has failed to endorse FBI requests for counter-terrorism field agents, intelligence analysts, Arabic translators, and domestic preparedness (Clymer 2003; White House Press Release 2003).

The Justice Department's budget increases are therefore based less on the pragmatics of combating terrorism than they are on institutionalising the politics of fear. In dozens of press conferences, the Attorney General and the FBI Director have failed to comment on the details of the Patriot Act and how the law will affect ordinary Americans. Instead, they have repeatedly played on the fears of Americans and their inability to assess terrorism threats. Return to the case of José Padilla for a moment.

On 8 June 2002, Ashcroft revealed in a dramatic announcement via satellite from Moscow, 'We have disrupted an unfolding terrorist plot to attack the United States by exploding a radioactive dirty bomb' (quoted in Lee 2003). President Bush deemed Padilla so grave a threat to national security that he ordered that he be held incommunicado until the war on terrorism was over. A day later, the administration began to backpedal. Assistant Secretary of Defense Paul Wolfowitz told reporters that there was not an actual plot 'beyond some fairly loose talk' (quoted on CBS News, 9 June 2002) while other sources reported that Ashcroft had been chastised by the White House for overplaying the Padilla arrest. But the damage had already been done. By exaggerating the 'dirty bomb' threat, Ashcroft ignited public anxiety and ill reasoning, setting off a buying frenzy for duct tape and survival supplies. This is not an isolated incident, but part of a pattern of Justice Department warnings about impending doom. Director Mueller has repeatedly proclaimed on national television, 'We can *expect* more terrorist acts in the United States' (eg Mueller 2003).

The Justice Department asserts that critics fail to understand the seriousness of the terrorism threat, and misconstrue how the Patriot Act is used to prevent another attack. But given the administration's doctrine of secrecy, it is effectively asking the public to take things on faith. Add to this the results of emerging research showing that Justice Department prosecutions of terrorism-related cases since 9/11 have produced few significant results (Burnham and Long 2003),[1] plus the methodological problems presented in this essay, and we arrive at a situation where there is virtually no way for researchers to verify Ashcroft's contention that progress is being made in the war on terrorism. This situation has occurred not through oversight but by design. That is, the Patriot Act carries no requirement for the Justice Department to report to Congress about how the policy has been employed and no requirement for reporting to the federal courts. The veil of secrecy, invoked in the name of national security, has effectively prevented public scrutiny of the government's 'key weapon' in the fight against terrorism.

Yet Congress has the responsibility to do *precisely* that as it goes about the business of deciding whether the sun should set on the Patriot Act at the end of 2005. So, in this vein, I will end with a modest proposal.

A test

The most contentious part of the Patriot Act is the increased ability of the federal government to conduct surveillance on anyone without a search warrant. This provision is contained in section 213 of the Act (Authority for Delaying Notice of the Execution of a Warrant). Also known as the 'sneak-and-peek' provision, section 213 allows law enforcement to avoid giving prior warning when searches of personal property are conducted. Before the Patriot Act, the government was required to obtain a warrant and give notice to the person whose property was to be searched. The Patriot Act took away the right of every American to be protected under the Fourth Amendment against unreasonable searches and seizures.

Congress can examine the extent to which this provision has *in fact* prevented acts of terrorism against the United States. If the provision has failed to achieve the Patriot Act's primary objective – or worse, it has been misused to round up and incarcerate innocent people – then Congress faces a different kind of problem, namely: How can the abrogation of freedoms be justified when there is no proof that security is enhanced in the trade-off?

There is, however, an even more important test for the provision: Would it have made any difference in stopping the September 11 attacks? The starting point for this test is the widely cited fact that 9/11 was the result of a massive intelligence failure caused by a legal wall prohibiting the sharing of information between law enforcement and intelligence communities. The Act was designed to tear down the wall and there is little public anguish over this section of the policy. Yet when combined with new surveillance provisions, it increases the likelihood of creating an intelligence overload.

For instance, the FBI now has the authority to investigate religious and political groups to determine their possible ties to terrorist organisations, leading to the

---

1   Since 11 September 2001, about 6,400 people have been referred by investigators for criminal charges involving terrorism, but fewer than one-third actually were charged and only 879 were convicted. The median prison sentence was only 14 days.

surveillance of mosques and the Muslims who attend them. The FBI is now allowed to tap their telephones, monitor their emails, confiscate their business records, and secretly search their homes and businesses without having to show evidence of a crime. The FBI can then share that information with the CIA, and the CIA can share it with foreign intelligence agencies. Used often enough, this strategy can create more data than intelligence systems can effectively manage. And to what end?

In general, terrorists keep a low profile and do not advocate publicly for social change. The 9/11 hijackers evidenced no public or religious activism during their time in the United States. Instead, they were busy penetrating airline security. In July 2001, a Phoenix FBI agent sent a memo to Washington headquarters recommending that the Bureau investigate the possibility that Islamic radicals were receiving training at US flight schools. The agent determined that several Middle Eastern flight students were linked to bin Laden's terrorist network. Yet counter-terrorism specialists did not discover the Phoenix memo until after September 11. It had been buried in an intelligence overload (Benjamin and Simon 2002).

In the final analysis, popular support for the war on terrorism will turn on evidence made available to the public. That evidence will be based on intelligence. To the extent that Congress is able to extract this intelligence from its administrative sources, it will be able to open up a national debate that may inspire confidence in the government's approach to counter-terrorism. Such a strategy may brake the currents and crosscurrents of fear caused by 9/11. In so doing, the government might well avoid Samuel Taylor Coleridge's dire warning, 'In politics, what begins in fear usually ends up in folly' (quoted in Glassner 1999: xxviii).

References

Arena, K (2002) 'Seattle man indicted on terror charges', CNN, 3 September

Ashcroft, J (2001) Address before the US conference of mayors, 25 October

Ashcroft, J (2002) Prepared remarks of Attorney General John Ashcroft, Senate Committee on Appropriations, Subcommittee on Commerce, 26 February

Ashcroft, J (2003) Testimony of Attorney General Ashcroft, US House of Representatives, Committee of the Judiciary, 5 June

Associated Press (2002) 'Drugs-for-arms al Qaeda plot uncovered', 6 November

Barkun, M (2003) 'Defending against the apocalypse: the limits of homeland security' 3 Governance and Public Security 17–28

Benjamin, D and Simon, S (2002) The Age of Sacred Terror, New York: Random House

Berry, W (2001) 'In the presence of fear': oriononline.org

Burnham, D and Long, S (2003) 'Few prison terms in terror trials', Associated Press, 8 December

Bush, G (2001) White House press conference, 14 September

Campbell, D and Stanley, J (1966) Experimental and Quasi-Experimental Designs for Research, Chicago: Rand McNally

Cave, D (2003) 'Rockers unite to oust Bush', Rolling Stone, 11 December

Clymer, A (2003) 'In the fight for privacy, states set off sparks', New York Times, 6 July

Dreyfuss, R (2003) 'The watchful and the wary', Mother Jones, July/August

FOX News (2002) 'Ashcroft says justice department guarantees God's gift of freedom', 21 February

Glassner, B (1999) The Culture of Fear: Why Americans Are Afraid of the Wrong Things, New York: Basic Books

Hakim, D (2003) '2 Arabs convicted and 2 cleared of terrorist plot against the US', New York Times, 4 June

Hentoff, N (2003a) 'Conservatives rise for the bill of rights!', *Village Voice*, 25 April

Hentoff, N (2003b) '100th civil liberties safe zone!', *Village Voice*, 30 May

Holland, J (2003) 'Ashcroft seeks sharper teeth for USA Patriot Act', *Associated Press*, 6 June

Human Rights Watch (2002) *Presumption of Guilt: Human Rights Abuses of Post-September 11 Detainees*, Washington, DC: Human Rights Watch

Krugman, P (2003) 'Dereliction of duty', *New York Times*, 14 June

Lee, C (2003) 'A lifetime in limbo', *Village Voice*, 4 June

Lewis, B (2003) *The Crisis of Islam: Holy War and Unholy Terror*, New York: Modern Library

Lewis, N (2003) 'Secrecy is backed on 9/11 detainees', *New York Times*, 18 June

Lichtblau, E (2003a) 'Ashcroft defends detentions as immigrants recount toll', *New York Times*, 5 June

Lichtblau, E (2003b) 'US cites al Qaeda in plot to destroy Brooklyn Bridge', *New York Times*, 20 June

Lindesmith, A (1965) *The Addict and the Law*, Bloomington: Indiana University Press

Louis, D (2002) 'In the presence of fear: brief comment and syllabus': Stopviolence.com

Mazmanian, D and Sabatier, P (1983) *Implementation and Public Policy*, Glenview, IL: Scott, Foresman and Co

Mueller, R (2003) Interview, *Larry King Live*, CNN, 8 July

O'Meara, K (2001) 'Police state', *Insight*, 9 November

Tapper, J (2003) 'Conservative constitutional catfight', *Salon*, 11 April

Thompson, M (2003) *The Killer Strain: Anthrax and a Government Exposed*, New York: HarperCollins

Traub, J (2003) 'The Weimar whiners', *New York Times Magazine*, 1 June

Turk, A (2002) 'Confronting enemies foreign and domestic: an American dilemma?' 3 *Criminology & Public Policy* 345–50

US Department of Justice (2003) *The September 11 Detainees*, Washington, DC: Department of Justice, Office of the Inspector General

Wenzel, E (2003) 'Who's afraid of the Patriot Act?', www.pcworld.com, 3 May

White House Press Release (2003) Department of Justice: Highlights of 2003 funding

Woodward, B (2002) *Bush at War*, New York: Simon and Schuster

Printed in the United Kingdom
by Lightning Source UK Ltd.
102385UKS00001BA/46-609